NO MAN IS ALIEN

ESSAYS
ON THE UNITY OF MANKIND

NO MAN IS ALIEN

ESSAYS
ON THE UNITY OF MANKIND

EDITED BY

J. ROBERT NELSON

LEIDEN
E. J. BRILL
1971

In Honor

of

WILLEM ADOLPH VISSER 'T HOOFT

whose life

of

constant witness to the

Unity of the Church

and

significant service to the

Unity of Mankind

inspires the preparation

of this book

CONTENTS

THE AUTHORS

J. G. ARAPURA, Indian scholar, is professor in the Department of Religion, McMaster University, Hamilton, Ontario, Canada.

W. BARNETT BLAKEMORE is Dean of the Disciples Divinity House of the University of Chicago, Illinois, U.S.A.

ERNEST J. BURRUS, S. J., is director of the American division of the Jesuit Historical Society, residing in Rome, Italy.

MOSHE GREENBERG, until recently the Ellis Professor of Hebrew and Semitic Languages at the University of Pennsylvania, U.S.A., is now Professor of Bible at the Hebrew University of Jerusalem, Israel.

CHRISTIAN MAURER is Professor of New Testament on the Evangelical Theological Faculty of the University of Bern, Switzerland.

JÜRGEN MOLTMANN is Professor of Systematic Theology at the University of Tübingen, West Germany.

J. ROBERT NELSON is Professor of Systematic Theology at Boston University School of Theology, Boston, Massachusetts, U.S.A., and Chairman of the Working Committee of the Commission on Faith and Order of the World Council of Churches.

EUGENE A. NIDA is Secretary for Translations of the American Bible Society, New York, N. Y., U.S.A.

DAUD RAHBAR is Associate Professor of World Religions at Boston University School of Theology, Boston, Massachusetts, U.S.A.

DAVID A. ROBINSON is Director of the China Research Project and an associate of the Center for the Study of Development and Social Change, Cambridge, Massachusetts, U.S.A.

STANLEY J. SAMARTHA. Director for Dialogue with Men of Living Faiths and Ideologies, Programme Unit on Faith and Witness, World Council of Churches, Geneva, Switzerland.

BERNARD TOWERS, Fellow of Jesus College, Cambridge, England, is Professor in the Center for Health Sciences, University of California at Los Angeles, California, U.S.A.

The Chapters by Professors MAURER and MOLTMANN were translated from the German by Mrs. LEWIS WILKINS.

CHAPTER ONE

SIGNS OF MANKIND'S SOLIDARITY

J. ROBERT NELSON

I. *A Belief Shared by All?*

The cruelest irony of history is that men always talk of peace even as they make war. The fervent affirmations of human brotherhood are mocked by constant fratricide. Eternal hope for community springs in the human breast while enemies plot to stab in the back. The perennial question has now become existentially urgent: Is the possibility of human unity a reality or an illusion? Regardless of our sense of longing for validating signs of its reality, the goal of mankind's oneness is by no means self-evidently attainable. But of the universal longing there can be little doubt. Wherever people's minds rise above preoccupation with the immediately insistent needs of each day and reflect upon the condition of society, the longing finds expression.

So well fixed is this concept in the minds of men and women everywhere that it may seem presumptuous and irreverent for anyone to suggest that it may point to a mere illusion. For many millions of people it is virtually a religious dogma, that all belong to one another by virtue of their common participation in the primal quality called *humanitas*. What is more remarkable is the fact that this is a dogma on which people of many diverse religions and ideologies can concur.

The Jews have maintained their identity as a particular people through more than thirty centuries of hostile history. Yet out of their very particularity has emerged the universal faith in the one God who is creator and preserver of all mankind. It was promised to Abraham that "all the families of the earth" will be blessed because of him (Gen. 12:3). Throughout the Old Testament there is no relaxation of the theme of Israel's pre-eminence in the sight of Yahweh over all the nations; but the prophets realized that the purpose of Israel's enjoyment of the special favor of the Eternal was that all people to the ends of the earth might learn of him through

them. The dialectic between particularism and universalism of Israel and mankind is the contrapuntal theme which continues from
the biblical scrolls to the thinking of many Jews today (See Greenberg, Chapter Two). Relatively few Christian spokesmen are able to
match the fervor and eloquence of certain rabbis of liberal persuasion
in their exhortations to human brotherhood and their evocations of
the dream of universal peace. Frequently heard from Jewish lips are
the words of the passing notion of liberal Protestantism, "the
brotherhood of man under the fatherhood of God." Whether this
designation of the human condition can be validated by biblical and
theological warrant, either Jewish or Christian, is debated. When
used as a popular slogan, it provides a smooth and open detour by
which the mind can avoid the rough surfaces of both Jewish and
Christian particularism. By this route of universal fraternity under
a single divine paternity many persons have been led to valued
humanitarian attitudes and actions. It would be both ungracious
and unstrategic to quarrel with the formula, however, on the ground
that it fails to convey the distinctive understanding of brotherhood
under God which biblical faith teaches.

It is often and, for Christian faith, rightly observed that the intended universal scope of Judaism became actual in the Christian
church. Believing that traditional Jewish law, cult and ethnic
solidarity would restrict and stifle the universal message of love and
community which they learned from Jesus Christ, his earliest
followers, led by the Jewish Apostle Paul, felt compelled to transcend these limiting boundaries. The bitter dispute and the painful
break are described in detail by Paul (Gal. 2) and Luke (Acts of the
Apostles 15). In becoming the apostle to the Gentiles, Paul was
acting upon the faith and conviction that no human barriers,
whether natural or fabricated, could exclude any person from the
unbounded community of Christ. It is possible that he knew the
contrasting interpretations of the ancient myth of the Tower of
Babel and the apostolic account of the Holy Spirit's descent at the
first Day of Pentecost following Jesus' death and resurrection. In
this contrast was discerned how Yahweh's defense against human
pretensions at Babel was to "confuse the tongues" with many
languages, while at Pentecost the apostles, destined to inaugurate
an unlimited mission of the church from Jerusalem to the end of the
earth, were strangely empowered to be multilingual. If that reversal
of Babel had been wrought by God for the sake of the mission of

Christ to all persons, Paul did not speculate upon it in his letters. Nor is there very much explicit teaching of mankind's unity in the New Testament as a whole. Those who seek proof texts for world brotherhood usually turn to the address of Paul which he delivered near the Parthenon in Athens to an interested but skeptical audience of Stoic and Epicurean philosophers. It seems self-evident that his famous declaration, that God "made from one (note: not one *blood*) every nation of men to live on all the face of the earth," is an appeal to the natural unity of man which results from common origin (Acts of the Apostles 17:26). However, this assertion implies more than a reference to man's common creation. It is closely tied to Paul's characteristic preaching of the resurrection of Christ, in which the power for the *coming* unity of all persons is proclaimed. The philosophers who mocked him took no offense at the idea of the oneness of man, but at the preaching of a divine intervention by which that unity is to become actual.

These few references are not sufficient to account for the extremely intense belief of early Christians that the historical appearance of Jesus Christ constituted a new kind of indiscriminate human community, the church, with an open door to all humanity (See Maurer, Chapter Three). But history shows that by the second century the Christians of the Roman Empire were aware of their decisive importance for the whole of mankind. Despite their small and persecuted membership, the well-accepted claim was made for them in the Letter to Diognetus that they are the ones who hold the world together.

Through the centuries the church has not forfeited that conviction although it is surely faltering in the present time. Whether in times of the church's imperial power, as in Rome or Byzantium, or in periods of persecution or parochialism, this vision of the race united in Christ has been the patrimony of Eastern Orthodox, Roman Catholic, and Protestant Christians. Such faith falters today insofar as it is conceived in strictly ecclesiastical terms. But the vitality of an expectation of mankind's unity is registered by the literature of the Ecumenical Movement and especially of the Second Vatican Council. No other document has expressed so forcefully the Christian belief in man's unity as the *Pastoral Constitution on the Church in the Modern World*. Indeed, most of the council's pronouncements are addressed, not to Catholics alone nor even to all Christians, but to all men and women of the world. This is the same

practice as that of Pope John XXIII, when he directed his great
encyclical, *Pacem in terris*, 'to all men of good will.' So the council
refers often to 'the family of mankind,' 'the unity of man,' and other
variants of the idea (See Burrus, Chapter Four, for the openness of
the Catholic perspective in the sixteenth century). More recently in
1968 the World Council of Churches at its assembly in Uppsala gave
repeated emphasis to the same conviction. And its report deliberately appropriated the Vatican Councel's designation of the church's
place in this. The church may not any longer presume to be the
locus of human unity; it is rather the 'sign of the unity of all
mankind' and the instrument by which that purpose is served (See
Blakemore, Chapter Twelve).

In this new era of confrontation and cultural intercourse of
virtually all countries except China (See Robinson, Chapter Eight),
Western Christians and Jews have discovered that they have no
monopoly on the belief in the one humanity. Islam has its own
conception (See Rahbar, Chapter Six), which its adherents are
pressing especially in East Africa and among black people in America. The ancient cultural religion of India, Hinduism, with its
insatiable capacity for absorbing and appropriating foreign forms
of thought, is being carried to far countries with a message of universal harmony (See Arapura, Chapter Five and Samartha, Chapter
Seven). The Ramakrishna Mission, borrowing the missionary style of
Christianity, offers mankind an alternative basis for unity. And the
2500-year-old offspring of Hinduism, the religion of the Buddha,
has also been experiencing a subtle modification. Not only has the
idea of universal brotherhood been accepted by the adherents of a
religion and philosophy hitherto limited to the soil of Asia. There are
now Buddhists in Rangoon, Kandy and Bangkok, as well as those
sojourning in Europe and the United States, who charge that
Christianity has failed in its chance to bring about world brotherhood. They add that Buddhism is really equipped to effect this
global task. This may be only a bold claim, since Buddhism has
scarcely had an opportunity on a world-wide scale, as Christianity
has, to promote a sense of the human family everywhere; yet
growing numbers are convinced by it.

   To be a passionate advocate of human unity, however, one does
not have to be attached to any particular religion. He can sincerely
confess the doctrine on the basis of a strictly secular conviction. The
way of thinking which is often designated democratic humanism is

such a basis. This characterizes the viewpoint of countless sophisticated intellectuals, who have deliberately rejected Christianity or
religious Judaism, but have retained an influential residue of biblical
humanitarianism and Hellenic idealism. As steady readers of many
journals of culture and social ideas perceive, the democratic humanists regard the striving after an ever-widening human community to be the finest activity of any member of the species. This
worthy concern has become for some their surrogate for religion. It
is a religion whose god is humanity. As in every religion's circle,
there are sentimentalists, theorists and activists in this one. The
golden text for the sentimentalists is the illuminating line by the
17th century clergyman-poet, John Donne, who was made known to
the masses by Ernest Hemingway's felicitous choice of *For Whom
the Bell Tolls* as a book title. Thus we have learned that "no man is
an island" and "each man's death diminishes me." But while the
sentimentalists savor the analogy of being bits of soil on the shore
of the continent of humanity, there are reflective theorists in many
lands whose analysis of the human race leads them to conclude that
ascending degrees of tolerable order and peace among races, classes,
language communities and nations belong to its proper destiny on
earth. So the humanistic activists commit their money and energies
to the doing of all manner of good for the sake of the wellbeing of
their fellowmen. And no one with a distinctly religious motivation
for pursuing the same activity has justification for feeling conde-
scending towards these secular servants of mankind.

Not very different in its overt expression is Marxism's stance with
respect to the universal classless society. The thoroughgoing Marxist
responds instinctively to ringing words about humanity, even as the
ever-remembered Russian canine salivated at the ringing of Dr.
Pavlov's bell. In this there is nothing unusual. As the scholar of
Oxford, Robert C. Zaehner has observed, "Marxism is an eruption in
our time of the age-old, essentially religious, dream of human solidarity."[1] In our recent past the Stalinist and Maoist methods of
translating Marxist visions into political realities have scarcely
contributed to the upbuilding of world community. Ruthless
exterminations at home and xenophobic barriers against relations
with other peoples have been their dual defenses against opposing
ideas and movements. Even so, the new flexibility in Marxist philosophy represented by Roger Garaudy, Ernst Bloch and Milan
Machovec permits one to see the possibilities of the common quest

for human unity with religions and ideologies of the non-communist cultures.

In sum, this brief survey indicates that there is an intuitive knowledge of the unity of mankind found in religions and ideologies so diverse as Judaism, Christianity, Islam, Hinduism, Buddhism, democratic humanism and Marxism. No doubt the list could be legitimately extended to include more; but it would require more detailed documentation than is here possible to show which threads are common and which contrasting in these fabrics of thought and faith.

II. *Inconclusive Empirical Evidence*

Prophets, priests, professors and pundits speak about the given oneness of the countless descendants of Adam and Eve. How much truth is conveyed by their words? Can human unity be demonstrated, or merely asserted? We live in a time when empirical evidence is demanded in support of such lofty claims and convictions. If mankind is one, then prove it! Where is the evidence?

The biologists, of course, provide the evidence of human morphology. Clearly we all belong to that distinctive form of animal life known as *homo sapiens*. We are bipeds which walk upright, have four fingers opposed to the thumb, a relatively large cranial cavity, the ability to make noises which become communicative speech. We may not seem to be so *sapiens* all the time, but our structure is visibly that of *homo*.

Do these biological data substantiate the idea that as a whole race we are one family, one people, or one brotherhood? Not really. No more than comparable data on the morphology of cats support the theory that they form a universal feline family, with possibilities for distinctive community and a common dogless destiny.

To find such evidence we must seek it in the realm of human spirit rather than in the human organism. Unity is much more a relationship of spirit than of flesh. But when has it become apparent to all that the whole of mankind is at one in mood and purpose? Rare indeed is such a time, but when it comes there is a profound reality in the experience. Perhaps the universal sense of exhaustion, relief and rejoicing at the end of World War II was that kind of time. Or that black and terrible November day, still vivid in memory, when the whole world wept for John F. Kennedy. Then there was a brief suspension of animosity, distrust and hostility among the people of the earth as they pondered the meaning of this wonderful man's death. In the same way, through the instantaneous communication by television, the deaths of Martin Luther King, Jr., Gamal Abdul Nasser, and Charles de Gaulle have been world-events, provoking in sorrow the sense of man's oneness. And in the positive mood of excitement and common identity the millions of television watchers in many countries saw their first human representative touch his foot to the strange soil of the moon, while many more of the earth's family, too poor for either television or radio, learned of the achievement with amazement. These are not merely newsworthy events. Regardless of the ambiguities which surround them, such as the questions of war guilt, who killed the President in Dallas, or the legitimacy of spending billions of dollars on a 'lunar spectacular,' they are moments in man's corporate experience when subliminal yearnings and hopeful theories find a real but fugitive expression.

Beyond these unique and dramatic events, we look for other evidence of what the Vatican Council's Constitution calls man's 'communitarian vocation.' International organizations help to demonstrate this. The proliferation of specialized associations of an encompassing international character is an important mark of human civilization in this century. In these decades we have witnessed a veritable explosion of cultural, economic and political internationalism. Scarcely anyone knows how many thousands of these organizations exist, but it is patently inadequate to number them merely by the hundreds. An international organization concerned with international organizations has had to be established in the Hague. Through them we are experiencing not only a thriving inter-change among peoples and nations, but an irreversible inter-dependence. That is to say, we human beings literally hang upon one another in order to receive the necessary provisions for numerous aspects of our personal and communal livelihood. The common efforts and international alliances of physicists, chemists, engineering specialists, biologists and many other scientists indicate the growing need of the sense of human unity for sheer survival on the planet. (See Towers, Chapter Nine).

There are two ways of interpreting this unprecedented phenomenon. Either the forming of vast numbers of international and inter-cultural organizations is a demonstration of the given reality of human unity; or else, it is a vindication of the power of the idea

that mankind somehow ought to be one. There are two possible
causes, then: either the reality or the idea which provokes the desire.
But in both respects the effect is the same: an immense complexity
of structures serving numerous special purposes, which draw human
beings together into a semblance of unity.

In the forming, joining and supporting of international organizations, people of all nationalities are becoming most zealous. At the
top of the endless list of them are the United Nations, UNESCO, the
World Health Organization, the International Labor Office, and the
cluster of many nongovernmental organizations which are involved
in the vast work of the U.N. However vulnerable some or all of these
may be to criticism for failure to satisfy many persons' expectations,
however susceptible to the unrelenting human tendency towards
bureaucracy, however powerless to force upon dissident and recalcitrant nations the decisions of the majority, these interrelated
agencies of world order and cooperation are the practical and hopeful expression of man's new mood.

Beyond the United Nations' instruments for common work in the
world are all the other voluntary bodies of comparable purpose. The
lovely old city of Geneva was chosen by Woodrow Wilson to be the
seat of the League of Nations because of his Presbyterian penchant
for the idea of covenant in the theology of John Calvin. Since then,
there have been established the offices of more than four hundred
international associations, making Geneva the nexus for educational, commercial, religious, political, recreational and artistic communities of all nations. In this world of more than a thousand written
languages (See Nida, Chapter Ten), many races, and dozens of
burgeoning sovereign states, the cosmopolitan concept requires all
the official and voluntary international structures that men can
sustain.

In this new environment there has developed a new breed of
human being. His appearance in history is a factor of no small
importance. He is 'the cosmopolite.' His cultural roots go deep in no
particular soil, but they penetrate to a modest depth in many
patches of earth. This modern mutation thus finds himself at home
both nowhere and everywhere. He knows his way by Metro, tube
and underground under Paris, London and Moscow. At any given
time his body is clothed with garments bought in Hong Kong,
Caracas or Rome. His gastronomic taste has been refined by the
actual experience of eating in the places which the magazines of

tourism alluringly describe. Much of his life is spent aboard jet planes and in the glistening metal-and-glass airports which spangle the globe. His children attend international schools, learning several languages at a tender age; and they will grow up to become even more cosmopolitan than their parents. If we ask, then, how many people belong to this new breed, the answer is given in the hundreds of thousands. They are the avant-garde of many more, whose autochthonous provincialism will give way to a sense of at-homeness in many countries.

We asked for empirical evidence for the solidarity of the human race. Some current indications of the accelerating movement towards global unity have been offered. Do they not convince us that this unity is a fact to be accepted, a reality rather than illusion? No, not necessarily. For there is still another great block of evidence which speaks against man's unity. It seems to show that the chief preoccupation of man is with strategies for the destruction of his neighbors.

With honesty and candor we must turn to the catalogue of human divisiveness, strife and mutual hostility as we consider this theme. The validity of the idea of a natural human unity inexorably finding its expression in history is simply not self-evident. The cheerful signs of increasing brotherhood and the imminent reunion of the family of man are pleasing to behold. But they must be scrutinized in company with their opposites, which are the signs of rampant disorder and deterioration of the human community.

Each person is the center of many concentric circles of experience, moving outward from his personal affairs and relations to the daily events in his society and ultimately to the cumulative experiences of the whole human race. Within each of these centrifugal circumferences are found the deleterious data of human behavior which can make one feel only dismayed and dejected.

In the personal relations known to each one are discerned the diabolical devices by which the mutuality of individuals in a common humanity is subverted or denied. It is probably true, as Reinhold Niebuhr often stressed, that a single person is more ethically responsible than the whole society of which he is a member.[2] But even the moral man in the immoral society is seldom an adequate exemplar of the responsible self, much less of the good neighbor. Each man's inhumanity to man is calibrated on the scale which ascends from coldness and rudeness in relation to his family or immediate community to the defamation, injury or even murder of his neighbor. The daily papers convey the grim stories of the dreadful escalation of larceny, assault, rape and homicide in allegedly civilized and law-abiding lands. For a number of men and women, too large to contemplate with complacency, it is assumed in the United States that the constitutional right to bear arms implies the right to use these weapons at will. Nor does there seem to be sufficient respect for the law or dread of punishment to constrain the rising numbers of deliquents and criminals who are willing or constrained to destroy men's lives. Usually the stories of single or multiple murder seem remote to us, and we read them without being alarmed. However, eventually the bullet or the knife or the hammer strikes a close friend. Then the senseless wantonness of the act shakes one into realization of the horror of the millions of murders which have destroyed human life since the atavistic atrocity of Cain's slaughter of his brother.

There must be some truth in the thesis of Robert Ardrey, that the 'territorial imperative' is a law of nature, obeyed by all kinds of animals including man.[3] There is, he argues, an instinctive disposition to defend one's own territory, his nest, his home, his family, his native land. But the motive of defense still does not account for the impulsion to be aggressively rapacious and murderous. This is the deeper, darker spring of evil in the human heart which defies any rational accounting. It is the malevolent power which T. S. Eliot described as the serpent coiled in the pit of iniquity.[4] And virtually no man is immune to its venom.

In the bitter antagonism of racial blocs there is another form of the denial of the possibility of human community on a universal scale. Few people who really understand the conflicts of social dynamics in South Africa, Rhodesia, the United States or England today can be so sanguine as to predict an early and peaceful resolution of racial hostilities. Nor does it help the problem if it is shown that racism is more virulent and endemic in one of these countries than in others. Americans who are of white skin may derive no comfort from the fact that *apartheid* is a more thoroughgoing social policy in South Africa then it is in the United States. Neither are they entitled to a sense of morbid pleasure in watching the British, who have for long been critics of America's racism, falling into the same slough of prejudiced segregation. In white America's stubborn refusal to make adequate restitution and reparation for the sins of slavery and oppression of Negroes there is the same element of inhuman viciousness which keeps appearing in other forms: the slaughter of 10,000 of the Watusi tribe in Burundi; of 400,000 Christians in the Sudan; of half a million communist sympathizers in Indonesia; the recurring mutual destruction of Muslims and Hindus in India; and the apocalyptic devastation of human life wrought by German Nazis upon six million Jews of Europe.

The instances of racism and attempted genocide are just a few dramatic reminders of the massive atrocities which have been committed since 1940, and to which most people have become rather accustomed. Therefore the daily reports on mass media of the carnage in Vietnam, the Middle East or other lands of conflict cause scarcely any emotional response. But the combined weight of all these forms of human oppression and annihilation crushes any naively optimistic notion that human beings are finally learning to live happily with one another on this increasingly congested planet.

While reflecting upon these sombre reports and memories we can face still another set of frightful facts. These are the deathly destitution, constant famine, and proliferating population which obtain in many countries of the 'third world,' that is, Asia, Africa and Latin America. In terms of the blunt actuarial statistics, namely in the number of premature deaths, the riders of the pale and black horses of the Apocalypse, representing famine and pestilence, account for more than the conquering and warlike riders of the white and the red. What is the ultimate need of any human being, if not the indispensable food and drink which keep the body alive? Americans have been somewhat alarmed to discover the pockets of poverty and hovels of hunger in the Deep South, Appalachia, and the city slums. But what they call poverty would be considered almost bourgeois comfort by hundreds of millions of dwellers in the 'third world.' These are the people on the very boundary line of survival. They subsist on the unchanging diet of millet, corn or cassava, watching their little children slowly die of starvation even as they, the parents, continue to procreate more candidates for early death.

As one sensitive world traveller grimly observed, if the cries and shrieks of suffering and agony of the human race could be combined into one single scream, the force of the sound waves would be literally lethal.

Instead of worrying about the malnutrition of fellow human

beings, however, a great many prosperous people are constantly worrying about getting to be too fat on a surplus diet. To be sure, some help is rendered through public and private channels. No doubt the fact seems impressive to many that the United States government since 1954 has given away $12 billions in food products. But what is that as compared to the fantastic wealth which this nation has accrued and used for self-indulgence and military action during these years? On an annual basis, American gifts of food have been reported to be of the same value as the amount of goods which are stolen and sold by black marketers in Vietnam.

There is yet a more dire aspect of the maldistribution of the earth's food supply and of other essential commodites. It is the appalling fact that the rich minority of the world keep growing richer, while the poor majority become both poorer and more numerous; and the richer the affluent nations become, the less they share with the impoverished majority of the human race. In proportion to both the incalculable resources of the American people and the rising needs of mankind, this nation is actually contributing less and less each year.

In sum , without even mentioning a host of similar factors in man's present situation, we must look unblinkingly at the evidence before us and wonder if there is any realism at all in our ideas and hopes for the one world community.

III. *Unity in Christ—Unity of Man*

Again the question: is the unity of mankind a reality or an illusion?

The idea that it is merely an illusion must be rejected. It is easy to be seduced by naïveté, sentimentality or humanistic idealism into an illusory understanding of human unity. But after resisting that kind of seduction, we may still believe that there is a reality in the concept of human universal community. It is not a reality which is presently realized, however. Nor is it a reality which can be well demonstrated and illustrated at this stage of man's history. Like some of the elements of the Christian faith itself, the reality of human unity is a matter of faith. Its realization is still in the seminal stage as a matter of potentiality.

The unity of mankind, then, is no less an article of faith than the unity of the church is. Such empirical evidence as may be adduced lends support to that faith; but it cannot verify the assertions that mankind is a unity or that the church is a unity. The ceaseless flowing of historical events and phenomena may be viewed objectively by the comprehending eye of a Ranke or Toynbee without causing the historian to believe necessarily that these are elements of a divinely purposed historical movement. Likewise, we can note today how the ancient divisions within the universal church are being transcended, without having to judge this process as being more than the natural consolidation of certain religious groups having a common faith in Jesus Christ. Or, we may see the hundreds of signs of mankind's new interdependence, due to advances in technology, transport, communications, and political alignments, without necessarily attributing all of them to a grand doctrine of the brotherhood of man or of human solidarity. In short, any judgment concerning the meaning and purpose of human experience, whether it be a philosophical or a theological judgment, presupposes a certain attitude of faith in the unseen and the non-demonstrable.

Thoughtful Christians should have the intelligence and humility to recognize that their characteristic beliefs about the purpose and goal of human history are classed by most men among the other optional beliefs of Jews, Buddhists, Hindus, Muslims, Marxists, scientific humanists, and nihilists. Humanly speaking, then, the task of the Christian church is to make more credible the historic claims which it preaches concerning its role in the ultimate reconciliation of mankind. Can Christian faith really be made plain and credible: that the coming unity of man will not be the working out of a natural process, but the work of God as made known in Jesus Christ? (See Moltmann, Chapter Eleven). And further, that in the person of the perfect man, Jesus, and derivatively in the community of those who find life's meaning in him, there is given a foretaste and pattern of genuine human unity and community?

It is questionable and improbable that the avowed realist, who disavows all illusions about human affairs, can accept with seriousness this Christian affirmation about Jesus Christ, the church, and the unity of man. As Jesus himself taught, a kind of childlikeness or trusting attitude is a prerequisite of faith in a personal and purposive God.

However, uncritical naïveté about the church and the world is not a theological virtue. Indeed, we have to guard our minds against the simplistic notion that even so grand a phenomenon as the visible and tangible church with its recovery of inner unity in this era can bring into order, harmony, and peace the myriad tribes, communities, nations, and races of the divided human family.

If Christian faith today remains faithful to the message which has been proclaimed and taught in the past, it holds that the purpose of God the Father is to bring all persons into a state of personal reconciliation with himself and among one another. This was the meaning of the divine love as taught by Jesus and as incarnated and enacted in his life. So the primary task of the church in history is to be the bearer of that reconciling work in every generation. This is why there has to be concern about the manifest unity of the Christian churches. The message of reconciliation is scarcely believable to others when the people who bear the name of Christ are themselves at sharp odds with one another. Church unity and human unity are not identical; but the former serves the latter, and they are in-inextricably bound together in Christian faith.[5]

NOTES

[1] Paraphrased by Huston Smith in *Theology Today*, Oct. 1966, p. 368.

[2] Reinhold Niebuhr, *Moral Man and Immoral Society* (New York, 1932).

[3] Robert Ardrey, *The Territorial Imperative* (New York, 1966) and also *The Social Contract* (New York, 1970). It is debatable, of course, whether it is wholly legitimate to assume that human beings naturally behave as the animals do, as Ardrey thinks they must.

[4] T. S. Eliot, *Choruses from "The Rock,"* *Collected Poems, 1909-1935* (New York, 1936) p. 208.

[5] For a theological elaboration of this perceived connection between Christian unity and the unity of mankind, see the documents of the Commission on Faith and Order of the World Council of Churches. The present book was suggested by these ecumenical studies. Especially: "The Unity of the Church and the Unity of Mankind" in *Study Encounter*, V (1969), 163-181; and J. Robert Nelson, "The Unity of the Church and the Unity of Mankind," *What Unity Implies* (World Council Studies No. 7) (Geneva, 1969), pp. 101-114.

CHAPTER TWO

MANKIND, ISRAEL AND THE NATIONS IN THE HEBRAIC HERITAGE

Moshe Greenberg

If the needs of the hour seem to have outrun the resources of venerable religious bodies, this is due at least in part to a pious reluctance to sift critically the accumulated traditions they have received in order to distinguish the timeless and needful from the ephemeral and dispensable. The configuration of rites, ideas, and attitudes taught to the common man by today's religions often reflects a level of civilization and human interconnection long since past. Robert Redfield has described well the interaction of the moral and the technical orders and their relative progress:

> The unit of political life tends to become identified with a people who share a common moral life...So the tribe, the city-state, the nation are such approximate identifications of equivalent units of society, peoples that are both a technical and a moral unit. Yet as one looks at any one of these politico-moral societal types...one sees that the technical order, in the form of exchange of goods and in the conflict of war, has already gone beyond the politico-moral unit...; and one begins to look forward to the extension of the moral order to larger societal units, which will in turn call for political inventions. Today, some people recognizing that the technical order has gone far beyond the national state, and that its destructive power threatens everyone, begin to argue that the peace of the world must be planned by all the peoples of the world...and then, looking at the fact that these visions have come and begin to be transmuted into plans for action, one is required to admit that the fact that people speak as if world order and world peace must and will come about is itself influential in history... The idea that a world community is necessary is an idea created by developments in the technical order. This idea in turn influences the actual moral order to develop in its direction, and helps to bring about political inventions...that would both express and create the enlarging moral order.[1]

The heritage of Judaism from biblical times onward contains a series of adjustments to change: of enlargements and contractions of outlook in accord with the experiences of Jews in the world. The latest formulations of that heritage are now centuries old.[2] They presuppose compact, internally autonomous diaspora communities with no sense of a common destiny with the rest of pre-Messianic-age mankind. Attempts of 18th and 19th century European Jews to integrate their communities into the new nation-states by surrendering aspects of their distinctiveness injured their integrity without achieving the hoped-for results.[3] In the light of their twentieth century experience, Jews are torn between a deep doubt of the Gentiles' capacity to feel solidarity with them, and a need and desire greater than ever for harmonious relations with the rest of mankind. In this dilemma, work on the ecumenical front is promoted chiefly with the defensive aim of disposing Gentiles favorably toward Jews. However, as important as that effort is, it is equally necessary to consider what Jews as a religious community evisage as the ideal attitude toward the Gentiles. Unless Jews are aware of the terms on which, without loss of spiritual integrity, they can be at one with the world, such a union can hardly come about. These terms can be found in the received traditions of Judaism, but they must be highlighted and emphasized among the mass of inherited materials, while opposing conceptions must be recognized for what they are, and denied equal authority.

This essay attempts to delineate the Jewish conceptions of the unity of mankind and the postulates of Judaism's integration in the world. It draws upon the classic Hebraic sources: Scriptures and the rabbinic literature. The presentation is more conceptual than historical, and selective of what shows a constructive concern with the issue. Not an apology, it foregoes explaining (away) the anti-gentile elements of the tradition;[4] just so much of them as is needful for understanding the positive elements are adduced. By the same token, singular universalistic expressions are unnoticed except such as are attached directly to basic and pervasive notions. In sum, the testimonies offered here are believed representative of the essential Jewish teachings on our theme.[5]

I. *Adamites (bene 'adam)*

Hebrew history begins not with the patriarch Abraham, but with the father of the human race, Adam. Its proper subject is man as the self-conscious creature and subject of God; Israel arrives on the scene late, after several fruitless experiments with previous generations of men.

The Hebrew valuation of man grew out of reflection upon the implications of the story of his creation as told in Gen. 1:26-27 and 5:1-2. The first couple—Adam ("man," popularly connected with 'adama "earth"; i.e. "earthling") and Eve (ḥawwa, popularly connected with ḥay "living thing")—generated all mankind. Having a typical patriarchal viewpoint, the Bible depicts the entire human race as a family descended from a single father, and names it accordingly "Adamites" (children/sons of Adam/man; e.g. Ps. 115:16).[6]

The belief that man is in God's image serves as the rationale for regarding homicide as a capital offense. As the family of Noah started a new life after the Flood, God admonished them:

> Whoever sheds the blood of man
> By man shall his blood be shed;
> For in his image
> Did God make man.   (Gen. 9:6)

It must be borne in mind that this appreciation of man extends to all men; it attaches to the ancestor of the race, not to Israelites alone, who have not yet come upon the stage of history. The creation story inspired the Psalmist to wonder at God's favor toward man:

> What is man that you have been mindful of him,
> Mortal man that you have taken note of him,
> That you have made him little less than divine,
> And adorned him with glory and majesty;
> You have made him master over your handiwork,
> Laying the world at his feet...   (8:5-7)

God-like attributes attach to men at large; they are not a specifically Israelite property.

Man is the object of God's special care. The earth was designed as his home; Eden was to be his abode. Even after his offense, and having condemned him to expulsion from Eden, "the Lord God made garments of skins for Adam and his wife, and clothed them" (Gen. 3:21). After the Flood, he renewed his gracious relationship to mankind, promising never again to destroy the world and confirming his good-will by the token of the rainbow. Ever since creation God has sustained the world faithfully:

No man is alien   2

> The Lord is good to all
> And has compassion for all he has made;
> You open your hand graciously
> And give every living thing his fill.   (Ps. 145:9, 16)

The point of the book of Jonah is God's impartial concern for the well-being of all his creatures: "Should I not care about Nineveh, that great city, in which there are more than a hundred and twenty thousand persons who do not yet know their right hand from their left, and many beasts as well!" (4:11). That the repentant Ninevites remain pagans matters not.

Being his creatures, all men have access to God. Adam, Cain, Enoch, Noah were intimate with God. Abraham's contemporary, Melchizedek, was a priest of the Most High God (Gen. 14:18); king Abimelech of Gerar conversed with God in a night vision (20:4f.). The Mesopotamian wizard Balaam conversed with God and his angel (Num. 22:9ff., 31ff.). Jethro, the Midianite priest, sacrificed to God (Exod. 18:12); Solomon's temple was open to foreigners (I Kings 8:41ff.); and the Aramean officer Naaman undertook to worship God alone in his homeland (II Kings 5:17). The law allowed the Gentile to sacrifice in an Israelite sanctuary (Lev. 22:25 as understood by the Talmud, Temurah 7a), or—as the Talmud later put it explicitly—"to build himself a private altar and offer up whatever he wished on it" (Zebaḥim 116b).[7] That this actually occurred is the plain sense of the debated passage Mal. 1:11: "For from the rising of the sun to its setting my name is great among the nations, and in every place incense is offered to my name, and a pure offering: for my name is great among the nations, says the Lord of hosts."[8] In this spirit, a late midrash affirms the impartial outpouring of the Holy Spirit upon any and all deserving mortals:

> I call heaven and earth to witness that whether it be Gentile or Jew, man or woman, slave or handmaid, according to the deeds which he does, so will the Holy Spirit rest on him.   (Tanna de Be Eliyahu, 9 [p. 48])

The most profound expressions of the value of man are found in Tannaitic reflections upon the creation story.

> [Rabbi Akiba] used to say: Beloved is man for he was created in the Image; extraordinary is the love in that it was made known to him that he was created in the Image, as it is said, "For in his image did God make man"   (Gen. 9:6). (Abot 3.14[9])

In the course of admonishing witnesses in capital cases to tell the truth, the infinite worth of each human being was emphasized in this striking homily:

> For this reason was one single man created: to teach you that anyone who destroys a single life is as though he destroyed the whole of mankind, and anyone who preserves a single life is as though he preserved the whole of mankind;
> (and to foster harmony among men: that none might claim, "My ancestry is nobler than yours"...;)
> (and to show the greatness of God: for when man stamps many coins in one die they are all alike; but God stamped all men in the die of Adam, yet no two are alike);
> Therefore [since each of us is an Adam] everyone must say, "For my sake the world was created." (Sanhedrin 4.5[10])

The implications drawn from the creation story with respect to man are these: Man is dear to God, as his image; moreover, every man is equivalent to Adam, for whose sake the whole world was made; the multiplication of Adam's exemplars in no way diminishes the Adam-like worth of each exemplar. Hence arises the dignity of every man and the sanctity of his life. From the brotherhood of all men as common descendants of father Adam it follows that no man or group of men can claim to be racially superior to others, or essentially alien to or heterogeneous with their fellows: on this is founded the potentiality and the obligation of harmony among men. Individual differences are esteemed as testimonies to the creative greatness of God.

The essentials of a comprehensive doctrine of the unity of mankind are to be found in this passage. We proceed to inquire into its ramifications in classical Hebrew thought.

II. *Noachites and Righteous Gentiles*

After the Flood, God laid down to Noah and his sons the terms of a new order. Taking note of changed conditions, he now permitted them to eat animals (who owed their very existence to man)—on condition that flesh with its lifeblood still in it not be eaten. To take human life—cheap before the Flood and depreciated by it—was declared a capital offense, to be punished by a human agency; courts were thus authorized to execute killers (Gen. 9:1-7). The descendants of Noah—all mankind (Gen. 10)—were thus held accountable to a minimal number of divine commands.[11]

However, later divine punishments of men are neither justified by reference to these commands, not are they inflicted for violations of them only (cf. the offense of the Sodomites [Gen. 19:5ff.]). Throughout biblical literature, the Gentiles are required to answer for breaking elementary moral laws, though nowhere is the ground for their responsibility set out. The moral impulse of Gentiles, what we might call their conscience, derives in the biblical conception from "godfearing" (*yir'at 'elohim*)—a common human virtue that has no reference to knowledge of or revelations from the true God. It keeps them from murder (Gen. 20:11), adultery (39:9), and breach of faith (39:8f.; 42:18); lack of it accounts for Amalek's dastardly attack on Israel's stragglers (Deut. 25:18). Evidently this common property of all men is ground enough to make them accountable for wrongdoing despite their ignorance of God's laws (Ps. 147:20).

That the Gentiles' worship of 'false gods' was a sin came to be a common doctrine only in Second Temple times. Deut. 4:19 and 29:25 reflect the notion that the misdirected worship of the pagans was a divine ordinance. The first hints of a new attitude occur in Jeremiah 10:11, a polemical fragment against idolatry addressed to the pagans in Aramaic; in 50:38 idolatry appears to be held against a Gentile nation.[12] From here it is but a step to making the renunciation of false gods one of the minimal obligations of all men. This step was taken in the later formulation of the 'Noachite laws.'

Second Temple and rabbinic literature recognize universal standards of righteousness apart from the peculiar obligations of Judaism. The notion of Noachite laws binding upon all men becomes formalized while the 'fear of God' is credited to a broad class of non-Jews who gave up belief in the pagan gods, inspired by Jewish example.

The Book of Jubilees, dated variously between the third and first centuries B.C., depicts Noah teaching his sons "the ordinances and commandments and all the judgments that he knew":

> and he exhorted his sons to observe righteousness,
> and to cover the shame of their flesh,
> and to bless their Creator,
> and to honour father and mother,
> and love their neighbor,
> and guard their souls from fornication
>   and uncleanness and all iniquity ...
> Whoso sheddeth man's blood, and whoso
>   eateth the blood of any flesh,
> Shall be destroyed from the earth...   (7:20-39)

The Talmud and Midrash canonized this notion in lists of commandments believed to have been given to Adam and supplemented in a new revelation to Noah. The generally accepted list consists of seven items, with respect to (1) idolatry, (2) blasphemy, (3) homicide, (4) incest and adultery, (5) robbery, (6) eating the flesh of a live creature, (7) establishing a system of justice.[13] Although in theory these commandments were explicitly revealed to Adam and Noah, what they prohibited was thought to be self-evident to any human mind and conscience:

> "*You must keep my rulings*" (Lev. 18:5): This refers to injunctions of the Torah which, had they not been written in it, by right should have been written, such as (prohibition of) robbery, incest, idolatry, blasphemy, and homicide. (Sifra, Aḥare Mot, *ad loc.*)

During Hellenistic-Roman times there were many Gentiles who, disillusioned with paganism and attracted by the faith and mode of living of Jews, renounced the gods and adopted rudiments of Jewish observance. While in no sense regarded as Jews, such persons were esteemed as 'fearers of God' (*yir'e šamayim*), they were held beloved by God and assured of their ultimate reward.[14]

> *The Lord loves the righteous* (Ps. 146:8): Says the Holy One, blessed be he: *I love those who love me* (Prov. 8:17)...Why does the Holy One, blessed be he, love the righteous? Because they are not what they are through heredity or lineage. You find that priests are a family, Levites are a family—*O house of Aaron, bless the Lord! O house of Levi, bless the Lord* (Ps. 135:19f.). If someone wants to become a priest or Levite, he cannot, since his father was not of their family. But if a man wants to be righteous, even being a Gentile he can be, since the righteous are not a family. Hence it says, *O you fearers of the Lord, bless the Lord!* not, "O house of fearers of the Lord," but simply "fearers", since they are not a family, but came by their own impulse to love the Holy One, blessed be he. That is why he loves them... (Numbers Rabba, 8.2)

> R. Eliezer says: Gentiles have no place in the world to come; it says, *Let the wicked go back to Sheol, all the nations who have forgotten God* (Ps. 9:18)... R. Joshua replied: Had it said, "Let the wicked go back to Sheol, all nations" and stopped, I should agree. But since it adds "who have forgotten God," I infer that there are righteous among the nations who have a place in the world to come. (Tosefta Sanhedrin, 13, 2).

These ideas were synthesized in the definition of the resident alien (*ger tošab*)—the Gentile who may live in Jewish territory. Of various theoretical definitions (theoretical because formulated after loss of Jewish independence) the most widely accepted was: the Gentile who observes the seven Noachite laws (e.g., Aboda Zara 64b, 65a). An 8th century midrash sums up the discussion:

> The difference between the righteous Jew and the righteous Gentile is this: a Jew is not considered righteous unless he observes the whole Torah. But a Gentile is considered righteous if he keeps the seven commandments laid upon the Noachites—them and their ramifications,[15] and on condition that they understand their obligation to stem, through their ancestor Noah, from the command of God. If they keep them in this spirit, they have a share in the world to come just like Jews—despite their non-observance of Sabbaths and holydays, which they were never commanded to keep. If, however, they kept the seven commandments because they believed them instituted by some human authority, or as a dictate of reason; or if they ascribed a partner to God, they receive a reward in this world only.[16] (Mishnat R. Eliezer, vi [Enelow, 121])

Thus not only are all men as Adamites a single family, precious in God's sight, but by observance of the universal moral laws laid upon the Noachites they may be perfectly reconciled with God and enjoy the ultimate bliss. The consequence of the classical Jewish doctrine of man was that for his salvation neither Israel nor the Torah were, strictly speaking, necessary.

Historically, however, the Noachites had refused to accept their obligations; the nations were ignorant of the true God and barbarian in their conduct (cf. e.g. Aboda Zara 2b ff.). While the individual Noachite might be a Godfearer, for the salvation of the race a catalytic became necessary. That role was assigned to Israel.

III. *Israelites*

The effort of the builders of the Tower to defy God ended with the division of mankind into many nations and tongues; since henceforth the nations are depicted as idolatrous, a general falling away from God seems to have ensued. As the remedy to this frustration of his design, God chose Abraham to father a special nation—"to instruct his...posterity to keep the way of the Lord by doing what is just and right" (Gen. 18:19).[17] The special relation of Israel to God was announced to the assemblage of the people just before the Sinaitic theophany:

> You have seen what I did to the Egyptians,
> How I bore you on eagles' wings and brought you to me.
> Now then, if you will obey me faithfully
> And keep my covenant,
> You shall be my treasured possession among all the peoples;
> Indeed all the earth is mine,
> But you shall be to me
> A kingdom of priests
> And a holy nation.   (Exod. 19:4-6)

Comparison of the covenant laws of Israel with other law collections of antiquity reveals the sense of the phrases "kingdom of priests and holy nation."

> Religious laws are... rare in the Hittite law collection and altogether missing in the Mesopotamian ones. In contrast to Israel, these peoples did not consider themselves 'kingdoms of priests and holy nations'. The individual among them addressed the gods through the king, who was the chief priest, or through his priests, who served as his deputies. The community at large had only a small part to play in the public worship. A body of cult rules that bound every man did not exist among them, hence they saw no need to set out the details of such rules in legislation.[18]

In Israel, on the other hand, the very purpose of the covenant was to draw the whole people near to God—as he had intended all men to have been. Both the standard of conduct and ritual obligations elsewhere pertaining to priests were laid in Israel upon every man. Priestly food taboos (Lev. 22:8, Ezek. 44:31) were extended to all Israelites (Exod. 22:30; Deut. 14:21), with the same rationale: "You must be consecrated to me." Mourning rites banned to priests (Lev. 21:5f.) were forbidden to the laity for the same reason: "You are a people holy to the Lord" (19:28; Deut. 14:1).

A high moral standard of holiness was also imposed on Israel. Lev. 19 opens with the charge: "You shall be holy, for I, the Lord your God, am holy"; this was later understood as a call to imitate God:

> Abba Saul said: What is the duty of the king's retinue? To do what the king does.   (Sifra, *ad loc.*)

The chapter proceeds to spell out the meaning of holiness in moral and ceremonial terms: observance of the sabbath, reverence of parents, rejection of idolatry, leaving the due of the poor in field and vineyard, not lying or stealing or perjuring oneself, loving one's fellow as oneself, loving the stranger as oneself, and more.

What were the limits of the covenant group? Despite its name "Israel(ites)" the group in fact included anyone who wished to be included in it. The Exodus story mentions a "mixed multitude" (Exod. 12:38) who accompanied the Israelites; the passover regulations anticipate the presence of non-Israelites in the future community, and allow for their taking part in the celebration (vss. 43-49).

"There shall be one law for the citizen and for the stranger (ger) who dwells among you" (Exod. 13:49; Num. 9:14) is a recurrent injunction of the corpus of priestly laws (just where we might have expected the rigorous exclusion of aliens!) In Lev. 24:22 it concludes rules of civil and criminal responsibility; it recurs thrice in the sacrificial ordinances of Num. 15:15f., 29. Equation of citizen and resident alien occurs in Lev. 17, regarding sacrifice and the ban on blood; in 20:2, prohibiting Molech worship; in Num. 35:15, regarding the privilege of asylum in the cities of refuge.

The protection of the resident alien (ger) along with the native weak and needy is frequently commanded (e.g., Lev. 19:10, 33f.; Deut. 16:11ff.; 24:14f., 17, 19, 20, 21; 26:11f.; 27:19; or Exod. 22:20 23). Peak expressions of solicitude are Lev. 19:33f.:

> When a stranger resides with you in your land, you shall not wrong him. The stranger who resides with you shall be as one of your citizens; you shall love him as yourself, for you were strangers in the land of Egypt; I the Lord am your God.

And Deut. 10:18f.:

> For the Lord your God...shows no favor and takes no bribe, but upholds the cause of the fatherless and the widow, and loves the stranger, providing him with food and clothing. You too must love the stranger, for you were strangers in the land of Egypt.

Prophetic denunciation of social wrongs often includes the stranger among the native oppressed (Jer. 7:6; Ezek. 22:7; Zech. 7:10; Mal. 3:5).

According to Deuteronomy the strangers in Israel actually took part in the covenant ceremony concluded just before Moses' death (Deut. 29:10). As a consequence, in the septennial public recitation of the Torah, the stranger must be present alongside the native "to learn to fear the Lord, your God" (31:12).

Thus the covenant community of Israel was open to non-Israelites from the start. Doubtless, the resident alien suffered disabilities owing to his lack of family and precarious economic circumstances. He had no share in tribal land—an inequity which Ezekiel took care to remove in his ideal legislation for the future commonwealth (47:22f.). Nonetheless, Lev. 25:47 contemplates a stranger's rising above Israelites, and the historical books show that foreigners were particularly welcome in the royal courts and received high offices.[19]

Living within the community, the stranger gradually assimilated to it. Ruth's declaration of fidelity to Naomi epitomizes the process: "Your people shall be my people and your God my God" (Ruth 1:16). The discrepancy between Deut. 14:21 and Lev. 17:15 respecting the stranger's obligation to observe a food taboo bespeaks some vacillation with regard to the extent he was required to follow the finer points of the law. Yet there can be little doubt that within a generation or two his family was indistinguishable from native-born Israelites.

Even the exiled community of Judahites in Babylonia remained open to foreigners who wished to join it, and—what is more remarkable—there were foreigners who, in spite of the Judahites' low fortunes, actually entered the exilic community. We know this from Isa. 56:2-8, the germane parts of which merit full citation:

> Happy the man who does this,
> The Adamite who holds it fast:
> Who keeps the sabbath unprofaned
> And keeps his hand from doing any evil.
> Let not the alien who has attached himself to the Lord say
> "The Lord will separate me from his people (when he restores them
>   to their land)"...
> The aliens who attach themselves to the Lord, to minister to him,
> To love the name of the Lord and be his servants—
> Everyone who keeps the sabbath unprofaned
> And holds my covenant fast—
> I will bring them to my holy mountain,
> And make them joyful in my house of prayer;
> Their burnt offerings and their sacrifices shall be welcome upon my
>   altar,
> For my house shall be called a house of prayer for all the peoples.
> This is the oracle of the Lord God,
> Who gathers the outcasts of Israel;
> I will yet gather to them others
>   beside their own gathered ones!

The readiness of strangers to join this politically crushed community is not more astonishing than its accepting them; in the very
midst of a profound existential crisis, it would have been natural for
the exiles to have closed ranks tightly. That this did not happen
testifies to the radical hospitality of Israel to foreigners—a hospitality ultimately grounded on a self-conscious representation of God's
interest among men.

IV. *Proselytes*[20]

Even the earliest traditions ascribe to Israel's history a significance
transcending its national boundaries. Israel being the arena of
activity of the one, universal God, what happened in it had world-
wide repercussions and determined the reputation of the true God
among all men (Exod. 15:14ff.; Josh. 2:8ff.; I Sam. 4:8). On that
basis Moses appealed to God to renounce his plans to destroy Israel
in the desert (Exod. 32:12; Num. 14:13-16), the Psalmists pleaded
for help (e.g., 83:19; 115:1ff.), and Ezekiel assured his hearers that
God must restore his shattered people in their land (36:22-36).

The greater the devotion to God, the more intense the desire to
see his fame spread among men—in rabbinic terminology, "to
sanctify God's name." Foreigners were encouraged to "try" Israel's
God, to learn his power and responsiveness. A passage in Solomon's
temple prayer concerning the alien expresses this pious sentiment
and its ramifications perfectly:

> Then also as to the alien, who is not of your people Israel, but comes
> from a far country for your name's sake—for they shall hear of your
> great name, and your mighty hand and of your outstretched arm—
> when he shall come and pray toward this house, may you hear in the
> heaven your dwelling-place and do according to whatever the alien
> petitions you, that all the peoples of the earth may know your
> name, to fear you as do your people Israel...   (I Kings 8:41-43)

The spirit in which Elisha undertook to cure the Aramaean
Naaman's leprosy was the same ("Let him know that there is a
prophet in Israel!" [II Kings 5:8]); while Naaman's confession
upon being cured ("Truly I know now that there is no God in all the
earth but in Israel!" [vs, 15]) and his conversion to the sole worship
of Israel's God (vs. 17) are models of the desired effect of such a
trial.

So long as it was necessary to journey to the land of Israel to try

Israel's God, conversions of outsiders to his worship must remain few. With the creation of the Diaspora, Gentile contact with Jews became much commoner; Isa. 56 shows what effects the ardent faith of even a band of exiles could have on their surroundings. Accessibility of Jewish teaching was much furthered in Second Temple times by the canonization of the Torah (5th century B.C.), and the constitutional function of the Torah resulted in a definition of the Jewish nation as that whose life was directed by its teaching. Add to this the increase in individualism within as well as without Judaism in the Hellenistic period, and the ingredients of a new phenomenon, religious conversion (as opposed to ethnic-cultural assimilation) are all at hand.

The success of Judaism in winning converts during the centuries just before and after the turn of the era resulted from the propaganda efforts of considerable numbers of Jews—the Hellenistic-Jewish work produced in Egypt being the parade example[21]—and the receptivity of the Jews toward the newcomers. That propaganda for God was a duty is the message of a homily applying to Israel, as God's witnesses, the injunction not to suppress testimony (Lev. 5:1).

> *Though he is a witness* (Lev. 5:1)—"And you are my witnesses, says the Lord, and I am God" (Isa. 43:12);
> *whether he has seen*—"To you it was shown, that you might know" (Deut. 4:35);
> *or come to know the matter*—"Know, therefore, and lay it to your heart [that the Lord is God...there is none else]" (Deut. 4:39);
> *yet he does not speak, he shall bear his iniquity*—Said the Holy One, blessed be he, to Israel: "If you will not speak my Godhood among the nations of the world I will punish you for it"... (Lev. Rabba 6.6)

Attracting Gentiles to God was a manifestation of love of fellow man. Hillel urged to "love mankind and draw them to the Torah." (Abot 1.12) Abraham exemplified Hillel's saying:

> This teaches that one should bend men to and lead them under the wings of the Shekinah the way Abraham our father used to bend men to and lead them under the wings of the Shekinah. And not Abraham alone did this, but Sarah as well; for it is said, *And Abram took, Sarai his wife and Lot his brother's son, and all their substance that they had, gathered, and the souls that they had made in Haran* (Gen. 12:5). Now, not all the inhabitants of the world together can create even a single gnat! How then does the verse say, *And the souls that they had made in Haran?* This teaches that the Holy One, blessed be he, accounted

[the converting of Gentiles] to Abraham and Sarah as though they had made them.　(Abot de Rabbi Nathan A, 12 [trans. Goldin, 68])

Since the Septuagint renders *ger* mostly by "proselyte" (incidentally attesting the institution of religious conversion as early as the 3rd pre-Christian century), it is clear that all the ordinances favoring the alien and equating him to the native Israelite were applied to proselytes. Philo emphasizes the welcome given proselytes by the Torah:

> [The lawgiver] holds that the incomers too should be accorded every favor and consideration as their due, because, abandoning their kinsfolk by blood, their country, their customs, and the temples and images of their gods, and the tributes and honors paid to them, they have taken the journey to a better home... He commands all members of the nation to love the incomer, not only as friends and kinfolk but as themselves both in body and soul: in bodily matters, by acting as far as may be for their common interest; in mental, by having the same griefs and joys, so that they may seem to be the separate parts of a single living being... (*On Virtues*, 120-103)

Rabbinic homilies dwell upon proselyte's merits:

> Dearer to God is the proselyte, who has come to him of his own accord, than all the crowd of Israelites who stood at Mount Sinai! For had the Israelites not witnessed the thunders and lightnings, the quaking mountain and the blaring trumpet, they would not have accepted the Torah. But the proselyte without having seen any of these things comes and gives himself to the Holy One, blessed be he, and takes upon himself the yoke of Heaven. Can anyone be dearer to God than this man?　(Tanḥuma Buber, Lek Leka, 6)

On the basis of Deut. 29:15 it was affirmed that all future converts were present with Israel and entered the covenant from the first (Shebuot 39a).

The regnant view was that all men were welcome as converts: "The Holy One, blessed be he, disqualifies no man; he receives everyone. The gates are always open, and whoever wishes to enter may do so" (Exod. Rabba, 19.4). Biblical exclusions of certain peoples from marrying into the Jewish community were circumvented in behalf of proselytes. The test case and its landmark decision appear in Mishnah Yadayim 4.4:

> Judah the Ammonite proselyte appeared before [the scholars] in the academy and asked them: Am I permitted to marry a Jewess? [lit. "to enter the congregation"]. R. Gamliel replied, "You are not." R. Joshua replied, "You are."

R. Gamliel retorted: "Scripture says, 'No Ammonite or Moabite shall enter the congregation of the Lord; even to the tenth generation, etc.' (Deut. 23:4)."

R. Joshua said to him: "And are Ammonites and Moabites still in their homelands? Long ago Sennacherib king of Assyria came up and mixed all the peoples, as it says, 'I have removed the boundaries of peoples' (Isa. 10:13)."

R. Gamliel retorted: "But Scripture says 'But afterwards I will restore the fortunes of the Ammonites' (Jer. 49:6), and they have long since returned".

R. Joshua said to him: "Scripture also says, 'I will restore the fortunes of my people Israel' (Amos 9:14), and they have not yet returned."

So they permitted him to marry.[22]

Desirous of making the spiritual kinship of the proselyte supersede his genetic foreignness, the Rabbis, also interpret the term "your "brother" in the laws of the Torah as including the proselyte "since he is one of our brothers in the Torah and the commandments" (Midrash Tannaim, Deut. 24:7 [156]).[23] The institution of proselytism thus reflects a conception of Israel as a potentially universal people. By an act of will, any Gentile could be initiated into Judaism, and immediately be considered a Jew. The privileges (and obligations) of the Torah, with the promises held out by prophecy to Israel, were thrown open to all who wished to share them.

Jewish hospitality to proselytes fluctuated with the political status of the Jews. Pagan Rome sporadically, Christian Rome persistently persecuted Jews, forbidding proselytizing on pain of death.[24] Hard times impelled some converts to relapse, and some of these betrayed the resistance and disobedience of the Jews to their hostile governments. Such conditions advised careful screening of would-be converts and their initial discouragement (Yebamot 47a,b); they also account for the notorious adage of R. Helbo (first half of the 4th century, C.E.) that "Proselytes are as bad as the scab for the Jews" (Yebamot 109b).[25] Nevertheless, Jews continued to accept sincere converts, and even facilitated the acceptance of those who wished to marry into their community.[26]

The zeal for bringing the Gentiles under the wings of the Shekinah shown in the Second Temple and Tannaitic ages passed, and with it the eagerness of outsiders to join Israel's ranks. The misfortunes of the Jews had much to do with this, as did also the contraction of the field of proselyting endeavor due to the spread of Christianity and

Islam. Jewish proselyting had never been motivated by the notion
that outside of Judaism there was no access to God; hence the
dwindling number of converts was not regarded a failure of Judaism
to discharge its duty. Jews contined to believe that their primary
task was to be a holy nation, sanctifying the name of God. If for the
moment they were shunned and despised, vindication would surely
come in the Messianic age.

V. *Jews and Gentiles*

To be a holy nation meant, in the first place, to be separated from
the pollution of the nations. In biblical terms this pollution con-
sisted of idolatry and its concomitant moral corruption—the two
being indissolubly bound in biblical thought (cf. Lev. 18; 20: Deut.
12:31). Accordingly, the territory in which Israel lived must be
purged clean of idolatry and idolaters (pagan and Israelite alike;
e.g., Deut. 7:1-6; 13:13-19). Not even the private pagan cults of the
foreign wives of kings were to be tolerated (I Kings 11; 15:13;
16:31-33; 21:25). The dissolute character of the pagans is exemplified in the patriarchal contacts with them (Gen. 19:5-9 [Sodomi-
tes]; 39 [Potiphar's wife]), by the vicious Phoenician queen Jezebel
(I Kings 21 [Naboth's vineyard]), and by the corruption of Israelites who apostatized (e.g., Ahaz [II Kings 16:3]; Manasseh
[21:16]). To give sufferance to such persons was to risk learning
from them [Exod. 23:32f.; Deut. 20:18].

Intolerance of idolatry in territory controlled by Jews marked the
policy of the Hasmonean kings. Where they could, these kings
forcibly converted subject populations or destroyed them for
resisting conversion (Josephus, *Antiquities*, 13.9.1; 11.3; 15.4).
Later discussion of the subject was academic, since the Jews
nowhere could impose their will on Gentiles. It is nonetheless of
interest to note the final formulation of these discussions by Maimonides; it proves to be more moderate than ancient practice:

> When Jews are in control we may not tolerate an idolater in our
> midst. Even if he is a transient or a travelling merchant, he may not
> pass through our land until he accepts the seven Noachite com-
> mandments...If he accepts them, he is then a resident alien (*ger
> tošab*)   (Code, Idolatry, 10.6)

> Our teacher Moses bequeathed the Torah and commandments as the
> heritage of Israel and proselytes alone... If anyone else refuses them,

he is not to be coerced into accepting them. Moses, at God's behest, also commanded us to coerce all the inhabitants of the world to accept the seven Noachite commandments. Whoever refuses to accept them is to be put to death; whoever accepts them has the status of a resident alien... (*Ibid.*, Kings 8.9)

Having pre-empted for the proselyte all the favorable rulings of biblical law concerning the *ger* ([resident] alien), the Rabbis appropriated the relatively infrequent and undefined biblical term *ger tošab* to denote the Gentile who may reside in Jewish territory. His status was based on the principle that the Jewish community was obliged to provide him with sustenance (derived artificially from Lev. 25:35; cf. Pesahim 21b). From this, Nahmanides decided that he must be cared for when sick, and aided when in mortal danger (Supp. to Maimonides, *Book of Commandments*, Pos. Comm. 16), and Maimonides sweepingly equated him with a Jew in all matters ethical and charitable (Code, Kings, 10.12).

To sum up the academic discussion of the alien resident in Jewish-controlled territory: He is to be subject to the Noachite laws inasmuch as it is the duty of all men to obey those laws. But since observance of those laws entitled the Gentile to be called righteous (see above), it also creates an obligation of solidarity between Jews and such a righteous Gentile.

Relations with external Gentiles are hardly alluded to in the Torah, leaving them, in effect, subject to custom and prudential arrangements. Deut. 15:3 and 23:21 exclude the non-resident foreigner (*nokri*) from the benefit of the internal Israelite institutions of sabbatical cancellation of debt and interest-free loans. These aids to the poor were the expression of solidarity among Israelites; outsiders could neither be expected to share such obligations, nor expect to enjoy their benefits. A similar reciprocity is (according to some authorities) the reason for the Tannaitic exemption of a Jew from liability if his ox gored a Gentile's (Mishnah Baba Qama 4.3)—"because the Gentiles do not hold a man liable for the damages of his beast, and we judge them by their own laws" (Maimonides, *Property Damages* 8.5).

Other rulings however are frankly discriminatory, and reflect the mutual alienation and hostility of Jews and Gentiles. We may leave out of account the body of encumbrances to free intercourse with pagans, based on a repugnance toward promoting or participating in idolatry in any way (cf. Tractate Aboda Zara); these, after all,

spring from the sensibilities of monotheistic faith. More typical of
hostile rulings is the exemption of a Jew from obligation to restore
a Gentile's lost property, or to advise him of a business error he made
in a Jew's favor (Baba Qama 113b). Collections of these records of
enmity have been made and repeatedly discussed in anti-Jewish and
apologetic literature.

Our interest lies in the principles by which law and conduct rose
above such enmity. The very ruling cited above regarding lost
property is supplemented by the admonition that "in a case where
God's name would be dishonored the Gentile's lost article is not
forfeit." An exemplary tale goes further and shows how such a
situation is an opportunity for sanctifying the name of God among
the Gentiles.

> Simon ben Shetah [1st century B.C.E.] was a flax-merchant. Once his
> disciples said to him, "Master, take it easy! Let us buy you a donkey
> so you will not have to work so hard." They went and bought him a
> donkey from an Arab, on which a jewel was hanging. Then they came
> and said to him, "Now you will not have to work!" He asked, "Why
> not?" They replied, "Because we bought you a donkey from an
> Arab on which a jewel was hanging!" He asked them, "Was its owner
> aware if it?" They replied, "No." He said, "Then take it back to
> him—
> (But didn't R. Huna say...in the name of Rab: "... granted that
> robbing a gentile is forbidden; his lost article may, in everyone's
> opinion, be appropriated?")
> —What do you think, that Simon ben Shetah is a barbarian? Why,
> he would rather hear 'Blessed be the God of the Jews!' [from the
> mouth of the grateful Arab] than have all the rewards of this world!"
> (Pal. Talmud, Baba Meṣiʿa 2.2)

Another consideration that bridged the gap between Jew and
Gentile was obedience to the "ways of harmony (*darke šalom*).

> The Gentile poor are not to be prevented from gleaning in [Jewish
> fields] and vineyards on account of the ways of harmony... The
> Gentile poor are supported along with the Jewish, their sick visited
> along with the Jewish, their dead buried along with the Jewish, on
> account of the ways of harmony.   (Gittin 61a)

The sense of this phrase is illuminated by Maimonides' enlarge-
ment upon it: "It is said, 'The Lord is good to all and has compassion for all his works' (Ps. 145:9); it is further said, 'It ways are
ways of pleasantness and all its paths, harmony'" (Prov. 3:17).

Abaye's statement may also be compared: "The entire Torah too is on account of the ways of harmony?" (Gittin 59b). The proper aim of the Torah is to establish harmony among men; being the word of the universal God who cares for all his creatures, the scope of the Torah is no less than all men. Hence when a situation arises in which harmony between Jew and Gentile can be furthered, to do so becomes a dictate of the Torah.

Thus even when inter-communal hostility alienated Jews from Gentiles, Jewish thinkers and legists applied the grand principles of sanctification of God's name, imitation of God, and harmony among men to create unilateral obligations toward the Gentiles—obligations that did not depend upon reciprocity.

The Gentile of whom the classical Hebrew sources (Bible and Talmud) speak is a pagan, whose idolatry and immorality were an almost impassable barrier to feelings of solidarity.[27] The traditional image of the Gentile, however, became more and more incongruous with reality as Christianity and Islam spread in the lands of the Jewish Diaspora. The grounds for encumbering free intercourse with non-Jews and discriminating against them became inapplicable; actual relations with Christians and Moslems diverged from the talmudic prescriptions. At the end of the 13th century, an authority appeared in south France who cleared away the multitude of ad hoc harmonizations between law and life by stating a revolutionary hermeneutical principle. Rabbi Menaham HaMeiri laid it down flatly that the Gentiles of his time were not to be equated with those of the Bible and Talmud:

> [Biblical and talmudic rulings] apply to those times, and concern those nations who were idolatrous, filthy in their deeds and depraved in their character [he refers to Lev. 18:3]... But other nations who are disciplined by religion, and unsullied by those depravities —who indeed penalize them—are without question outside the purview of such rulings... (Commentary to Aboda Zara 22a)
> No discrimination may be practiced against such nations in ethical matters: It is forbidden to rob even idolaters and persons undisciplined by religion... Yet one is not obligated to take the trouble to restore their lost articles... since finding gives some title and restoring is an act of solidarity—and we are not obligated to show solidarity with godless barbarians... Still if he is aware of the facts, we must restore it...and so too in any situation where not to restore would result in a dishonoring of God's name.
> Hence you may infer that anyone belonging to a nation disciplined by religion, who worships God in any fashion—be it ever so different

No man is alien

from our faith—is not in the above category. As regards these matters, he is entirely like a Jew—in respect to his lost articles or errors
[made in a Jew's favor] or anything else—no distinction at all being
made [between Jew and Gentile]. (Commentary to Baba Qama
113b)

Elsewhere HaMeiri compares the religious Gentiles of his time to
observers of the Noachite laws, yet clearly distinguishing between
them (*ibid.* to 37b). Indeed, HaMeiri has broken with that traditional category of righteous gentiles in freeing his religious Gentiles
from any dependence upon biblical revelation. Their religio-ethical
virtue alone, whatever be its source, entitles them to fair and
equitable treatment.[28] A source of value independent of Judaism
and its Torah is acknowledged—a mediaeval version of the Gentile
'fear of God' known to Scripture.

Under the impact of the European Enlightenment this tendency
culminated in the elimination of every criterion but the ethical in
the definition of the Gentile to whom the Jew owes solidarity. The
development is highlighted by comparing an ancient and an
eighteenth century treatment of the biblical admonition, "You shall
love your neighbor as yourself" (Lev. 19:18). First, a Tannaitic
discussion of the verse:

> One should not think, "Love the sages but hate the disciples," or
> "Love the disciples but hate the ignorant," but love all of these and
> hate the sectarians, apostates and informers. So David said, "*Do
> I not hate them, O Lord, who hate you?*" (Ps. 139:21)
> But does it not say, *You shall love your neighbor as yourself: I am
> the Lord:* What is the sense? Because I (the Lord) have created him.
> Indeed! If he acts as your people do, you shall love him; but if not,
> you shall not love him (as though the sense were "you shall love your
> neighbor when he is as yourself").
>
> (The Fathers according to Rabbi Nathan A 16, in the
> translation of J. Goldin, p. 86)

And now a taste of the interpretation of Pinhas Eliah Hurwitz, a
pious mystic of the eighteenth century, whose *Sefer Ha-Berit*—a
scientific religio-ethical encyclopaedia from which the following is
taken—enjoyed great popularity among European and North
African Jews.

> The essence of neighborly love consists in loving all mankind, all who
> walk on two legs. of whatever people and whatever tongue, by virtue
> of their identical humanity, and their civilization—builders, farmers,

merchants, artisans...each serving the needs of men in his own way...
Human society is to be conceived of as a single individual composed
of many organs and parts; each person is like an organ or a part of
this individual... All men are interdependent and interconnected
like the links of a chain... The meaning of the scripture "You shall
love your neighbor as yourself" is not confined to Jews only, but the
sense is "your neighbor who is a human being as yourself"—men of
all nations are included, any fellow man... (*Sefer Ha-Berit* [Bruenn,
1797] II, 13)[29]

While the Tannaitic criterion is ethical (for by "acting as your
people do" is meant observing the Torah), it does not apply the
law of love beyond the bounds of Israel (although within Israel too
is explicitly excludes heretics, etc.)[30] The later statement, however,
with universalistic humanism typical of the age, conditions love of
fellow man only on his being a civilized human being, a contributor
to the common weal. For this Jewish son of the Enlightenment the
biblical admonition of neighborly love knew no boundaries short of
the whole human race.

V. *A Unified Humanity*

The kinship of all men as the descendants of one father and the
creatures of one Creator impressed itself upon the Hebrew imagination. How could I ignore the rightful claim of my servant, cries Job,
"Did not he who made me in the belly make him? Did not One
fashion us both in the womb?" (Job 31:15) This passage so worked
upon the Palestinian sage, R. Yohanan, that "whatever food he
partook of he shared with his servant" (Pal. Talmud Ketubbot, 5.5).
Ben Azzai and Rabbi Akiba argued over the most overarching
principle of the Torah; the latter put forward "You must love your
neighbor as yourself," the former, "This is the account of the generations of man" (Gen. 5:1). A late commentator explains: "While
'You shall love your neighbor' obligates one to love on the basis of
fellowship, 'This is the account' bases the duty on brotherhood—a
more absolute ground."[31]

The myth of one mankind under one God in primeval times—from
Adam to the Tower-builders—pressed for a complementary vision of
a reunited mankind under God at the end of time. The author of
that vision was the prophet Isaiah. The imperial success of Assyria
in imposing its yoke on the necks of all the nations on Israel's
horizon seems to have fired Isaiah's imagination to conceive of a

deeper unification of men under a greater than Assyria. The pagan empire was a preparation for God's universal kingdom; when Assyria had performed its allotted task, it would be broken on the mountains of Israel. The ensuing worldwide shock would be followed by a general renunciation of trust in human handiwork—in chariots, ships, towers, and idols; men would turn to Zion's hill for divine instruction. Wars would cease, for God would

> ...judge among the nations
> and arbitrate for the many peoples;
> and they shall beat their swords into plowshares
> and their spears into pruning hooks:
> nation shall not lift up sword against nation
> neither shall they experience war any more.   (Isa. 2:4)

Then Egypt and Assyria, converted to the worship of God, would be joined with Israel as a blessed triad, acknowledged by God as equally his own:

> In that day, Israel shall be a third
> with Egypt and Assyria
> as a standard of blessedness throughout the world,
> which the Lord of hosts will have established,
> saying, "Blessed be my people Egypt,
> my handiwork Assyria,
> and my heritage Israel."   (19:23-24)[32]

Isaiah's prediction that the nations would be converted to the worship of the one God was taken up by Zephaniah; annulling the punishment of the Tower-builders, God would "transform the speech of all the peoples into a clear language, that they may all invoke the name of the Lord and worship him in unison" (3:9). The idea recurs in Jeremiah (e.g., 3:17) and Habakkuk (2:14). It is a major theme of the second Isaiah:

> By myself I have sworn,
> From my mouth there has issued, triumphant,
> A word that shall not be thwarted:
> 'To me every knee shall bow,
> Every tongue swear allegiance'   (45:23)

Zecharaiah envisions a veritable frenzy of the nations to adhere to the God of the Jews (8:20-23; cf. 15:9, 16ff.).

These visions animated the messianic dreams of Judaism. Their promise of a glorious dénouement to human history, in which

Israel's faith and steadfastness to its covenant would be vindicated, and all men would join hands with it in subservience to their common Creator, were a beacon of hope in the vale of gloom and tears through which Israel walked for centuries. Some forms of this hope mirrored the animosity of the Gentiles by depicting the prelude to the messianic age as the destruction of the Gentile nations. But the form that entered the daily liturgy of the Jews was inspired by the noble vision of Isaiah. Originally composed for the New Year's liturgy, the following has, since about 1300, closed each of the three daily services of Judaism:

> We therefore hope in you, O Lord our God,
> that we may soon behold your glorious might
> when you remove the abominations from the earth,
> and the idols disappear;
> when the world will be perfected under the kingship of the Almighty,
> and all flesh invoke your name;
> when all the wicked of the earth will be turned to you.
> Let all the inhabitants of the world acknowledge and know
> that to you every knee must bend,
> every tongue swear allegiance;
> before you O Lord our God let them kneel and fall,
> and give honor to your glorious name.
> Let them all accept the yoke of your kingship,
> and may you reign over them soon for ever and ever.
> For kingship is yours
> and may you reign in glory to all eternity,
> As it is said, "The Lord shall reign for ever and ever" (Exod. 15:19);
> And again, "The Lord shall be king over all the earth; in that day the Lord shall be one, and his name one" (Zech. 14:9).

Classical Hebrew thought affirmed the basic unity of mankind in its creation myth, and complemented that myth with its messianic vision of a united mankind under God. It recognized access to God and saving virtue outside of Judaism, since its own covenant with God bound the covenant-community only. The rest of mankind was justified by observance of the Noachite laws or the discipline of religion. As for Israel, its task was to keep itself holy and sanctify God's name among men. Israel's relation to its neighbors was never merely reciprocal; something of its calling to witness the effect of God's word always tempered its external dealings. Its messianic fervor, never entirely cooled, has repeatedly flared up, in one form or another, at any suggestion of a movement to realize the brotherhood of man on earth.

NOTES

[1] Robert Redfield, *The Primitive World and Its Transformations* (Ithaca, 1953), pp. 74ff.

[2] See Louis Ginzberg, *On Jewish Law and Lore* (Philadelphia, 1955), pp. 180-183.

[3] See Salo W. Baron's summary in ed. Leo W. Schwarz, *Great Ages and Ideas of the Jewish People* (New York, 1956), pp. 315-390.

[4] Extensive, competent discussions of these elements are to be found in Michael Guttmann, *Das Judentum und seine Umwelt* (Berlin, 1927) and Joseph S. Bloch, *Israel and the Nations* (Berlin-Vienna, 1927).

[5] Important reflections on our theme are embodied in Isidore Twersky's "One World—One Ethics?: Judaism's Approach to Ethical Universalism," an unpublished paper of the 1959 Meeting of Fellows of the Conference on Science, Philosophy and Religion. I thank the Conference office, at the Jewish Theological Seminary of America, for allowing me to use Professor Twersky's paper.

[6] The variety of the races of men was later ascribed to environmental factors (e.g., climate); cf. the 19th century Mishnah commentary *Tif'eret Yisra'el* at Sanhedrin 4.5, note 38.

[7] Cf. E. J. Bickerman, "The Altars of the Gentiles: A Note on the Jewish 'ius sacrum,' *Revue International des Droits de l'antiquité*, V (1958), 137-164.

[8] This testimony to the effect of the Jewish diaspora on its pagan environment is preceded by a still earlier testimony in Isa. 56:3ff.

[9] Following Maimonides; cf. J. Goldin, *The Wisdom of the Talmud* (Chicago, 1957), p. 140.

[10] Printed editions read, in the first paragraph, "destroys/preserves a single life in Israel"; I follow the mss. and Albeck's note in his edition of the Mishnah. The significance of this passage is elaborated in my essay "The Biblical Grounding of Human Value," in *The Samuel Friedland Lectures, 1960-1966* (New York: The Jewish Theological Seminary of America), pp. 47-52.

[11] See the insightful comments of Gerhard von Rad in his *Genesis* commentary *ad loc.* (Philadelphia, 1961), pp. 126-129.

[12] Yehezkel Kaufmann, *The Religion of Israel* (Chicago, 1963), pp. 424f.

[13] Sanhedrin 56a and parallels; Gen. Rabba 16.16 and 34.19 (ed. Theodor-Albeck, pp. 149f., 316f., with important notes). For the relation of the Noachite laws to Christian "natural law," see N. Isaacs in ed. E. R. Bevan and C. Singer, *The Legacy of Israel* (Oxford, 1928), pp. 383-387; to the Roman *ius gentium*, Boaz Cohen, *Jewish and Roman Law*, 2 vols. (New York, 1966), Index, s.v. Noachian laws.

[14] See Bernard J. Bamberger, *Proselytism in the Talmudic Period* (Cincinnati, 1939), pp. 134ff.; Saul Lieberman, *Greek in Jewish Palestine* (New York, 1942), pp. 77ff.

[15] Some of which are given in the article "Laws, Noachian" in *The Jewish Encyclopaedia*, VII, 648ff.; comprehensively set out in the article *ben noah* in *Ensiqlopedia Talmudit*, III, 348-362.

[16] M. Guttmann ("Maimonides sur l'universalité de la morale religieuse," *Revue des études juives*, LXXXIX [1935], 34-45) observed that this passage was one of the sources of Maimonides' formulation in Code, Kings 8.11. That Maimonides requires the gentile to acknowledge Moses' agency in revelation of the Noachite laws accords with his exaltation of the prophet.

[17] G. von Rad, *The Problem of the Hexateuch and other Essays*, trans. E. W.

T. Dicken (Edinburgh and London, 1966), pp. 64-66; M. Buber, "The Mission of Abraham" (Heb.) in *Darko šel Miqra* (The Way of the Bible) (Jerusalem, 1964), pp. 65-81, esp. 68-71.

[18] J. J. Finkelstein, "Law, Ancient Near Eastern" (Heb.), in *Ensiqlopedia Miqra'it*, V (Jerusalem, 1968), p. 614.

[19] Cf. Alfred Bertholet, *Die Stellung der Israeliten und Juden zu den Fremden* (Freiburg und Leipzig, 1896), pp. 37-45.

[20] On the subject at large, see Bamberger (n. 14, above); W. G. Braude, *Jewish Proselytizing in the First Five Centuries of the Common Era* (Providence, R.I., 1940). Briefer treatments: G. F. Moore, *Judaism* (Cambridge, 1950), I, 323-353; S. W. Baron, *A Social and Religious History of the Jews*, I (New York, 1952), pp. 165-211. The classic discussion of the distinction between ethnic assimilation of resident aliens and religious conversion is by Yehezkel Kaufmann, *Gola veNekar* (Tel Aviv, 1934), I, 227-256.

[21] Cf. Bickerman (n. 7, above); R. H. Pfeiffer, *History of New Testament Times* (New York, 1949), pp. 197-230.

[22] Cf. Maimonides, Code, Prohibited Connexions 12.25: "When Sennacherib King of Assyria came up, he thoroughly mixed the nations and exiled them from their homelands. The Egyptians now living in Egypt are a different people, so too the Edomites in the Field of Edom. And since the four banned nations [cf. Deut. 23:4, 8] have been mixed up among the rest of the nations, who are permitted, all are permitted. For anyone who separates himself from them to convert to Judaism is presumed to have come from the majority. Hence anyone who converts nowadays from anywhere, be he an Edomite, an Egyptian, an Ammonite or a Moabite, an Ethiopian or any other nationality, male or female, is allowed to intermarry with us immediately."

[23] But not enough of a "brother" to qualify for kingship (cf. Deut. 17:15) or any other public office (Maim. Code, Kings 1.4). The Mishnaic disallowance of the proselyte to use "our fathers" in prayer was contradicted by the tanna R. Judah on the ground that Abraham was expressly called "father of a multitude of nations/gentiles" (*goyim*); thus the proselyte may claim Abraham as his father. The law was decided according to R. Judah against the Mishnah (Pal. Talmud, Bikkurim 1.4 end). Maimonides passionately defended the right of the proselyte Obadaiah to pray exactly as every other Jew, without changing a word; *Responsa*, ed. Blau, no. 293 [ed. Freimann, no. 42].

[24] James Parkes, *The Conflict of the Church and the Synagogue* (Cleveland and New York, 1961), Index, s.v. Conversion to Judaism: prohibited.

[25] See Braude (n. 20, above), pp. 42ff., 48.

[26] "If a man had intercourse with a Gentile woman...once she has converted and accepted Judaism we presume that pressure of necessity made her conversion sincere; for we have a rule that a man who converted to Judaism for the sake of a woman, or a woman who converted for the sake of a man are considered proselytes in all respects." (*Nimuqe Yosef* [Habiba, (15th century)], to Yebamot 24b).

[27] Yet the Rabbis recognized and esteemed virtuous pagans; cf. Lieberman (n. 14 above), pp. 68-90.

[28] See Jacob Katz's analysis of HaMeiri's position in ch. 10 of his illuminating survey, *Exclusiveness and Tolerance, Studies in Jewish-Gentile Relations* (London, 1961). A later version of HaMeiri's redefinition, designed specifically to bring Christians within the bounds of those to whom Jews owed ethical obligations, made biblical faith the determining factor: "These nations among whom we...are scattered...believe in the Creation and the

Exodus, and in several basic articles of faith, and have in mind the Maker of heaven and earth...We are duty-bound to pray for their welfare." (R. Moses Ribkas [17th c.] *Be'er HaGola at Šulḥan 'Aruk, Oraḥ Ḥayyim* 425).

[29] Cited from I. Zinberg, *History of Jewish Literature* (Hebrew) III, 323. My attention was originally directed to Hurwitz's *Sefer Ha-Berit* by n. 6 of J. Z. Lauterbach's "The Attitude of the Jew toward the Non-Jew," *Yearbook of the Central Conference of American Rabbis*, XXXI (1921), 186-233.

[30] Still valuable is the balanced discussion of the Rabbinic and Gospel statements on love and hate in C. G. Montefiore, *Rabbinic Literature and Gospel Teachings* (London, 1930), pp. 85-104. The writings of the Qumran sectarians now enable us to see the matter in a new light; see D. Flusser, "A New Sensitivity in Judaism and the Christian Message," *Harvard Theological Review*, LXI (1968), 107-127.

[31] Aaron ben Haim of Morocco (17th c.), cited from Lauterbach.

[32] See H. L. Ginsberg, "Isaiah in the Light of History," *Conservative Judaism*, XXII (1967), 1-18; for an appreciation of Isaiah's vision of peace, cf. Y. Kaufmann, *The Religion of Israel* (Chicago, 1963), pp. 386-395.

CHAPTER THREE

CHRISTIAN INSIGHTS FROM BIBLICAL SOURCES

CHRISTIAN MAURER

I. *The Old Testament*

The people of Israel never existed without relationships to the peoples around them. They were exploited foreigners in Egypt; they struggled with others for control of Canaan; they lived as a stateless people in Babylon and during the Persian period. Throughout there was lively economic, legal, cultural and religious intercourse which ought never to be underrated. Yet Israel always erected religious and cultural barriers, extending into all areas of life, which made community with the nations around it almost impossible. These barriers are directly related to Israel's relationship with God. Therefore, when we inquire into the interdependence of Israel and other peoples, the question takes on a strong theological character: How are we to judge the peoples whose common denominator is their opposition to the people of Jahweh but who, at the same time, belong with Israel to the creation of this very Jahweh?

Let us begin with the characteristic which, more than any other, gave Israel its peculiar position. As critical historical research has discovered, the confession of faith that Israel owes its existence to a God who has dealt graciously with his people belongs to the oldest stratum of Old Testament tradition. The very old, so-called "Small Credo" (Deut. 26:5-10) expressed the understanding that Israel's life depended on the gracious Jahweh who called them, a people without history, out of nothing and gave them existence and land, and in return expects grateful praise, as in the offering of the first fruits. The basis structure of this relationship can be traced throughout Israel's whole history. The birth of the nation, as various groups of foreign laborers came together in Egypt and in the gathering of the tribes at Sinai under Moses, took place as a miracle of the God who reveals himself as beyond human manipulation, yet faithful: "I AM, that is who I am" (Exod. 3:14). Israel saw itself as the least among the peoples; although it had no claim, it was chosen by the loving Jahweh (Deut. 7:7ff.).

This elective love determined the inner structure and order both of the individual tribes and of the people as a whole. Legal principles were taken over from the ancient Near Eastern environment, but they were adapted as the law of a faithful God who consistently turns his attention to the small and the weak: because the covenant is founded in the divine work of love, the life, marriage, and property of society's weakest members are placed under the protection of the divine covenant. This is particularly evident in the decalogue, Exod. 20:1-17. In the context of the conquest of Canaan, this principle had far-reaching social, economic, and legal consequences. Like the rest of existence, the land was accepted as a gift from the God of the fathers. Thus even though the Canaanite law of Baal vested ultimate ownership of the land in the reigning king, in Israel the individual's share in the covenant's land an legal rights could not be violated without justice being done. This economic and social premise, rooted in theological conviction, explains, for example, the story of Naboth's vineyard (I Kings 21), the Year of Jubilee with its provision for land reform every fifty years (Lev. 25:8ff., 27:17-24), and especially the prophets' protests against accumulation of great land holdings (Isa. 5:8-10; Amos 5:10-13; Mic. 2:1-5) and against violations of the rule of law (Isa 5:20;, 22-24; 10:1f.). The form this protest took shows clearly that prevailing conditions did not conform to this law of Jahweh, but that God repeatedly asserted himself against the will of Israel.

What does all this mean for the unity of the non-Israelite peoples? What do they have in common vis-a-vis the characteristic distinctiveness of Israel? We should mention here above all the important confession in Deut: 6:4f., which the pious Israelite prays daily: "Hear, O Israel, the LORD is our God, *one* LORD, and you must love :he LORD your God with all your heart and soul and strength." To acknowledge Jahweh as the one God is, first of all, to emphasize his exclusiveness: as a jealous God (Exod. 20:5), he does not yield his honor to another, he tolerates no other gods beside himself. Thus Israel's peculiar characteristic is to belong to the one God who, as a graciously electing God, does not allow himself to be confounded with other gods. This gives the non-Israelite peoples then a negative common property: while their right to existence is not denied in the name of God, they stand in the shadow of what they lack, of their not having a positive relationship with the gracious Jahweh, of their non-election. Thus the Hebrew *goyim* and the comparable Greek *ethnē* take on the meaning of 'people far from God.'

The same belief in the oneness of Jahweh who allows worship of no other God also opens the line to Israel's unity with other peoples. If Jahweh is really the only God there is, then he must also be the Creator of the whole world. So the nations, the whole creation and Israel, as well, live by the mercy of this one and only God! Thus the all-inclusive unity of all creation is a necessary consequence of Jahweh's exclusiveness.

This expansion of the Jahweh faith developed only in the course of Israel's history, however. In the early period, from the beginning down to the monarchy, concern for Israel's distinctiveness was paramount. But even so, this period includes a number of examples of Jahweh's mercy shown toward non-Israelites, as seen in the important roles played in Israel by the alien women Ruth, Rahab, and Bathsheba. The God of the covenant and the Creator of the nations were brought even closer together in the ancient confessions which locate the patriarch Abraham in relation to the nations round about (Gen. 11:10-33; Josh. 24:2f). Therefore it was only a logical further step when the Priestly tradition tells of the creation of heaven and earth and of the human race in order to establish the context of the covenant (Gen. 1), and when the editor of the Pentateuch later placed this creation story at the beginning of the Old Testament. This in turn demanded a clear statement of the incomprehensible intervention of evil, entangling man in a long chain of destruction (Gen. 3). The linkage between the confusion of languages and peoples in Gen. 11 and the call of Abraham in Gen. 12 discloses Israel's special role among the world's peoples: the blessing given to Abraham will become a blessing for the nations (Gen. 12:3). The words of Abraham's call combine both elements, Israel's distinctive status and its mission of blessing, and both are inserted in the dynamic of a future-oriented promise.

The Old Testament tells us little about where this promise leads. Its expectations are primarily concerned with the future of Israel and its salvation from the onslaught of its enemies. We do find in the later texts, however, hope for a peaceable kingdom which would embrace animals and men, nation and nation, and was expected in connection with the anticipated sprouting of the root of Jesse (Isa. 11:11). Second Zechariah expected a King of Peace who would rule the whole world (Zech. 9:10). Without question, however, the pinnacle of this development was reached in Isa. 2:1-4 (= Mic. 4:1-4): the nations will stream into Zion, there be instructed by God and, in consequence, make a complete shift from war to peace, from destruction to peaceful construction. At Babel (Gen. 11) the confusion of the peoples was produced by men; here it is the God of Israel who ordains the riches contained in that most pregnant of words, *shalom*, peace.

But how could the tiny nation of Abraham become a blessing to all nations? The Old Testament makes no effort to present Israel's government or religion or even its ethical standards as an enlightening example for others to follow. On the contrary, it speaks repeatedly of Israel's failure to do the will of God. So it is not just what Israel does but its whole existence, including its failure, which becomes the image in history of its experience with a merciful God. Second Isaiah makes this quite clear; he was even able to say that this little worm of a people, deported, stripped of its history by its own failures, would become a light for the nations. One may apply the so-called Servant Songs (Isa. 42:1ff.; 49:1ff.; 50:4ff., and 52:13-53:12) either to Israel as a whole or to another figure, although certainly an Israelite one. In any case, in the context of Second Isaiah they reflected Israel's last secret: God shows himself faithful, beginning anew where human failure has blocked off any future. If Jahweh, the creator of the world, can do such a thing with Israel, he will have no trouble letting the light rise from there to enlighten the nations far from God. Israel need not carry on a mission to the outside world; by its existence it uniquely represents the incomprehensibly merciful God to the whole world.

Without entering into the controversial detailed problems of the apocalyptic literature, we must, nevertheless, take note of one important point. In the midst of hopeless misery, as at the time of Antiochus Epiphanes IV, an awareness emerged that only a radically new order, which would include all nations, could bring salvation to scattered Israel. The apocalyptic prophet Daniel expected precisely such a new order, brought in by an eschatological intervention from beyond history, which would alter the whole course of the world and fulfill the boldest expectations of the ancient prophecy. Daniel's vision depicts the coming eternal sovereignty of God which will supercede all earthly authority (Dan. 2:44) and the Son of Man who will come from heaven to judge the world and to establish his eternal kingdom (Dan. 7:13f.). Jahweh will finish his saving work with his covenant people by reaching eschatologically beyond all history to show himself as the God who renews Israel, all nations, and even the whole creation.

II. *The Path of the New Testament Church*

It is an astonishing fact that the Christian church today can refer its sense of responsibility for all humanity back to the tiny band of first century Christians. How did it happen that a conscious responsibility for war and peace among nations today is derived from that unnoticed little fellowship? In the first place, we must simply observe that the New Testament church, even when it withdrew into itself, willingly or unwillingly triggered processes of social criticism beyond its own borders in society at large. This dynamic impulse can be shown at two points of historic decision which determined the course of the Christian church.

Jesus' interaction with his contemporaries was both personal and public in character. By allowing women of questionable reputation into his community of followers and providing them with his protection, he not only gave them individual forgiveness of sins but also raised fundamental questions about the values of a social and legal order which gave a man the power to repudiate his wife and so to discriminate against her (Mt. 5:32). When Jesus made disciples of tax collectors and sinners, that is, people who were discriminated against politically and religiously, he called into question the society which denied to such people a place of dignity. And finally, when he tolerated and encouraged sharp conflicts among his disciples, between revolutionary Zealots and the apolitical 'silent majority', between law-abiding Pharisees and libertine tax collectors, he opened up the basic question about the nature and boundaries of the people of God gathered about him. His answer was that the people of God goes beyond the previously recognized criteria for membership and includes the moral, religious, and political outsiders. Where does it lead when this inclusive tendency becomes a continuing and essential characteristic of the Christian church? Both Jesus himself and the leaders of the Jewish community knew very well, in any case, that this was an attack on the existing order and its relationships; if that were not so, they would not have found themselves in the conflict which led to the cross.

The so-called apostolic councils, too, made decisions about purely personal matters affecting the inner life of the church. Should belonging to Jesus be identical with belonging to the circle of those who obligated themselves through circumcision to keep as perfectly as possible the Torah as the Pharisees understood it? Gal 2:1-10 and the decree of the apostles in Acts 15:28 show clearly that this requirement was rejected. Although primarily a decision about the Church's internal order, it introduced a completely new dimension into the relationship between the church and so-called Gentile peoples. The dynamic of Jesus' position was accepted which drew the boundaries of the people of God much wider than any theology of maintenance of the status quo would want. After Easter the direction set by Jesus was definitively extended and broadened to include the whole world. This also removed those selfimposed limitations which the Old Testament people of God broke through only in exceptional cases, as in the prophet Jonah's mission to Nineveh. Now all nations could become partners, without discrimination, with whom the missionary church consciously entered into conversation and fellowship.

This world-wide missionary tendency, acknowledged by the Apostolic Council as a basic dimension of the Christian church, raised still further problems, however. The more pluralistic the entire church and each individual congregation became, the deeper were the conflicts which had to be overcome or at least controlled in order to create and maintain the fellowship. As the events which led to the Apostolic Council and Paul's struggle for the Galatians show, this was more than an internal problem: it was based on the mutual contempt between Jews and non-Jews which split the entire ancient world. The more the Gentile Christians came into leadership, however, the more the varied inheritance of these heterogeneous groups demanded a completely new conception of the foundations of human community. A vivid example is the first letter to the Corinthians. Here Paul develops the principles that determine what each individual and group had to give up and contribute in light of the religious and social viewpoints which had been thrown together in the Corinthian church. Even here the implications go beyond the internal form of Christian assemblies and into questions about basic human order. Thus what Paul says about eating meat offered to idols implies a critical examination of the official religious cults and systems by which meat was made available to urban populations

(I Cor. 8-10). The question of sexual ethics leads to judgments about the value and limitations of the state's jurisdiction (I Cor. 5). However cautious Paul may have been, questions about the internal order of the church lead inevitably to basic questions about human life, not just Christian life. The more ecumenical and world-wide the church became, even in the New Testament period, the more the external became internal and the more strongly universal human needs and questions entered the picture.

A. Jesus and the Evangelists

What is the basis of the dynamic which led the New Testament repeatedly to overstep its own boundaries? The historical environment certainly played a role, Palestine's position between Orient and Occident and its relationship to the world power of Rome, for example. Nevertheless, the church gets its momentum and direction from its own source. That source is related to the God-question as it appears in the New Testament message. The church understood its decision as a response to the will of God which it met in connection with the person of Jesus and which determined the disciples' strategy and tactics. These relationships are now to be examined.

If we begin with *Jesus*, we meet all the well-known methodological difficulties. Just as we cannot reconstruct a coherent and convincing 'life of Jesus' from the multiple strata of tradition in the Gospels, so we cannot create a unified and complete picture of his person. We must concede that the most we can do is to sketch in outline Jesus' thinking, his deeds and actions. There are many open questions, and not just those about the Easter event on which the church bases its message. At least one thing is certain, however. In regard to the unity of the nations, the post-Easter church shares with Jesus the dynamic toward overstepping boundaries which he began. Here are a few examples.

The starting point is Jesus' proclamation of the Kingdom of God. Mark 1:15 is certainly right in designating Jesus' preaching the intrusion of God's Kingdom and the call to repentence which it implies as his central message. This theme permeates the earliest parables, but it also is characteristic of Jesus' healings and his offer of liberation from loneliness and guilt. In order to see what was special in this message, we need to see Jesus' person against the Jewish background. The Jewish apocalyptic hope for the coming of God's Kingdom bore very disparate traits. For the Pharisees it was strongly religious and ethical, so that the yoke of the Kingdom of God was identical with acceptance of the Torah obligations; the Essenes from Qumran pictured future military battles; the politically active Zealots tied their hope for the Kingdom of God to revolutionary opposition to the anti-God Roman Empire. All shared a hope in a future eschatological act of God toward Israel and the nations which would bring help to his abandoned and humiliated people. As had been true in the time of the Maccabees, so too under Roman domination, this hope took the particular form of an expected apocalyptic destruction of the hostile powers.

Against this background, Jesus' message of the Kingdom of God stands out boldly in two ways that are important in our context.

First, Jesus speaks both in future and present tenses and even in the perfect about God's saving intervention: "The Kingdom of God is at hand." He thus ties this declaration to his own person, his preaching, and his deeds, and places before his contemporaries in a radical way the presence of the gracious God who has determined and undertaken to disclose himself anew as the liberating God of the covenant. Jesus thus understands his task to be that of the stronger conqueror of the Ruler of Darkness and who thus initiates the liberation of men (Mt. 12:28ff.; Lk. 11:20ff.). This is the basis of the Christian dynamic which was not broken off at the completion of Jesus' life by death and resurrection, but only then was fully inaugurated. Hope and action in his name lives in the belief that God's intervention has already begun, cannot be stopped, and will continue to involve ever widening circles.

Secondly, far more strongly than did the apocalyptic tradition, Jesus gives a personal thrust to the coming salvation, for he demands faith and conversion of the individual person. It would be a fundamental misunderstanding to view him as an individualist, however. The personal address serves to set the over-whelming intervention of God in new contexts. On the one hand, the personal invitation shakes the certainty of those who look backward to past promises of God: "... and do not presume to say to yourselves, 'We have Abraham for our father.' I tell you that God can make children for Abraham out of these stones here." (Mt. 3:9). Such a call to repentence indicates that a new light has fallen on men and nations outside Israel. A few examples will serve to substantiate this.

Among the sayings of Jesus preserved in Q, we find a statement which criticizes the self-confidence of the Jews he addressed: "Many,

I tell you, will come from east and west to feast with Abraham, Isaac, and Jacob in the kingdom of Heaven. But those who were born to the kingdom will be driven out into the dark, the place of wailing and grinding of teeth" (Mt. 8:11f.; Lk. 13:28f.). Jesus' rejection by the Israelites gives a new chance to the people who, by Jewish standards, were written off. This new chance is actually extended to individuals like the centurion from Capernaum (Mt. 8:5ff.), and it is potentially true of all the Gentiles that they can become first rather than last. Thus God establishes a new relationship between Israel and the nations.

The same intent can be seen in the threat about the sign of Jonah: "At the Judgement, when this generation is on trial, the men of Nineveh will appear against it and ensure its condemnation, for they repented at the preaching of Jonah; and what is here is greater than Jonah" (Mt. 12:41; Lk. 11:32). This recalls that prophet who was sent out into the world of nations. In dealing with the nations, Jesus, as the Son of Man and Judge of the world will be more generous, not more petty, than Jonah.

The passage about taxes for the Roman emperor is similar (Mk. 12:13-17). Jesus' answer contains primarily a rejection of the Zealot demand for an unconditional, radical struggle against Rome. When he instructs them to "pay Caesar what is due to Caesar, and pay God what is due to God," (v. 17), he surrenders neither Israel nor the Gentiles; he refuses to identify with the battle cry, "Death to the Romans!" To give God what is his also includes rejecting the opinion that one can have no dealings with Rome because it is a power in opposition to God. God is not only the God of the Zealots; he is also the God of the Gentile Caesar, whose service must also be viewed positively.

The parable of the last judgement goes one step further (Mt. 25:31-46). Again men of all nations, without exception but with equal chances, are placed under the judgement of the Judge of the world. Now, however, the law of love—which includes the care of the sick, the hungry, and the imprisoned—is clearly taken out of the limits of Israel and made universally applicable to all men everywhere. The same expansion is seen in the question of the lawyer, "Who is my neighbor?" and in the following parable of the Good Samaritan (Lk. 10:25-37). Here we should mention especially the antitheses of the Sermon on the Mount, the kernel of which certainly originated with Jesus. They not only catch the hearer in an ines-

capable choice; they also lead him into wrestling with the basic
structures of human communal life (Mt. 5:21-48). Jesus moves from
an absolute rejection of killing to mutual forgiveness as the basis of
human living; from rejection of divorce to recognition of mutual
faithfulness as the foundation of a sex ethic; from rejection of false
oaths to an uncompromising fight for truth as the life-giving
principle in human society. Thus he breaks out of an indifferent
co-existence to a pro-existence which, though it includes those who
hate, excludes hate itself. The desire which is expressed here implies
the dynamic which presses on to personal engagement and to universal expansion, and therefore stops at no borders, but works
creatively until new institutions are formed in church and state.

The tendency toward expansion beyond all visible and invisible
boundaries had its effect on the course of the church after Good
Friday and Easter. We can see this in the Gospels.

It is helpful to understand the Gospel of Matthew in the context
of Judaism's difficult decisions, after losing the Temple and its
existence as a state in 70 A.D., when a new course had to be chosen
for the old covenant people. The Pharisees, who had risen to be the
dominant party, decided to gather the people about the Torah,
which was to be strictly preserved, and at the same time to exclude
all alien influences. This decision pointed the way to the ghetto,
where the Jewish people have tried to protect their existence until
modern times. Jesus' church, however, consciously chose the alter-
nate course: in obedience to their Lord, they became the executors
of the Old Testament inheritance, they delivered themselves to the
Gentiles and thus ran the risk of a breakthrough to universalism.
Matthew took this course by starting his gospel with Abraham and
ending it with the commandment to evangelize the nations; by
applying to Jesus the prophecy of the Servant of God whose task is
to proclaim God's justice to the nations (Mt. 12:18-21), and by
especially emphasizing Jesus' insistence that the gospel was to be
brought to all the nations despite all persecutions (Mt 10:18;
24:14).

One sees in the conflict with Pharisaic Judaism that the gospel of
unifying the peoples leads not only to unity but also to very deep
divisions; this phenomenon has appeared over and over in various
forms. In the schism between the Jewish and Christian branches of
the Old Testament people of God, we see clearly that Matthew's
goal was to move from narrow particularism into the breadth of

universality in the name of Jesus Christ. The criterion of Christian decision-making is not that it shuts one off from the world, but that it is on guard against being cut off from solidarity with the world around.

In *Luke*, the Kingdom of God moves into an indefinite future and becomes more strongly other-worldly; in this the delay of the Parousia and the church's discovery of temporal duration play a role. Nevertheless, by including the great interim period of mission, Luke does not overlook that aspect of the gospel of the coming kingdom which unites the nations. The first of Luke's two volumes climaxes with the promise that the forgiveness in Christ, which creates peace, will be offered to all men (Lk. 24:47). Similarly the Resurrected Lord answers the question about the kingdom of Israel with a commission to include the whole inhabited earth (Acts 1:6ff.). The kingdom and the Parousia of the Son of Man who will come on the clouds as the judge of the world (Acts 1:11) have to do with all nations; God is Lord not only of time but also of space.

John seems to offer a theology which is introverted and turned away from the world. But the appearance deceives. In analogy to the one comprehensive God of the Old Testament, John's Christ bears the exclusive trait of the good shepherd who rejects all the alien savior figures as hirelings (Jn. 10:11ff.) and at the same time will call his flock together across all borders (Jn. 10:16f.; cf. 17:20ff.). In addition, the prologue recalls that the Logos who became flesh is one with the creator God before whom the cosmos came together into a unity (Jn. 1:1ff.). Thus in the Fourth Gospel we see the universalism which reappears in the Apocalypse of John as the church of the coming Son of Man confronting the world of nations with the gospel.

B. Paul

Paul developed explicitly the universal dynamic which we have seen in a more implicit way in Jesus. However, the apostle did not understand himself as the perfecter of a work which Jesus began, but as a messenger who obediently announced the breakthrough Jesus had brought about by his sacrificial death and resurrection. Acts and the Pauline letters we still have reveal the immense life work of the missionary to the Gentiles. Within a few years he dotted half of the then-known world with a network of missionary beachheads in the major cities. Yet the whole is no more than an in-

complete fragment. Such a judgment is not only based on our scanty
information about Paul—we know about little more than a single
decade of his life. His letters testify that he himself understood his
work as fragmentary. He places it within the over-arching context
of a comprehensive, divine Whither and Whence from which he and
his churches take their cues. Thus the massive missionary work of
Paul points beyond itself to a far broader horizon.

The starting point for the apostle's life work is determined by the
name of Jesus Christ. As a Pharisee, he at first passionately opposed
the message of this Christ as the abolition of Israel's privileged
position and of God's revelation in the Torah. In the light of the
Crucified One, he recognizes, however, that all the dividing walls are
down, that the last will be first and those farthest away have been
brought most near. Therefore he interprets Jesus' behavior toward
the outsiders of his own people as the model for the relationship
between Israel, which is close to God, and the Gentiles who are far
away. Thus the radical Pharisee, concerned only with the salvation
of Israel, becomes the equally determined missionary to the nations,
going out to those places where the Gospel has not yet been heard.
Thus began to emerge the vast outline of a new humanity, a horizon
so spacious that the apostle's missionary work seems like only a
small down-payment. What began in Antioch and Rome, the missionary bases used by Paul, is merely the beginning of renewal of
the world of men under the sign of reconciliation.

How does Paul conceive of the unity of mankind in this context?
In the following we shall show this in Paul's use of older confessional
formulas, in his construction of the Letter to the Romans, and in his
treatment of the theme of the body of Christ.

1. Paul's Use of the Old Confessional Formulas

As form-critical and tradition-history studies have shown, Paul
draws upon and restates traditional formulations in fashioning his
own theological statements at decisive points in his letters. He takes
old hymns, bits of liturgy—like the words of Jesus at the Last Sup-
per, for example—or older confessions and makes additions to make
them conform to his own personal views. Such texts allow us to make
an important observation.

On the one hand, formulations appear—primarily Christological
confessions—which describe the salvation event grounded in Jesus

by means of individual statements about the Christ or by means of Messianic titles. The apostle's additions to such statements tend to emphasize their universal significance. For example, in Rom. 1:3ff. the traditional confessional formula identifies Jesus as the Son of David according to the flesh and the Son of God according to the spirit. By adding that this Christ has called him to be the apostle to all nations, Paul elevates the traditional titles to a universal plane. Rom. 3:24ff. is similar. Probably an already traditional confessional formula expressed the justification of sinners wrought by the sacrificial offering of the crucified Christ. Again Paul enlarges the statement by placing it in world perspective. Vv. 25ff. speak of the history of salvation before and after the appearance of Christ. In vv. 27f. God's new justice goes beyond every boundary between Jew and Gentile. Vv. 29f., finally, reveal where Paul finds the source of the unity of humanity, that is, in the quintessential Jewish faith in the one and only God (Deut. 6:4). As the one God, the father of Jesus Christ is also the All-encompassing before whom the whole creation appears as his single counterpart. This dual view of God as exclusive and total is one which Paul shares with the Old Testament. What is new is that the grace revealed in Christ precludes any human group's priding itself over another, and that the justification of sinners does not just create dull uniformity, but a mutually enriching, pluralistic community. I Cor. 15 shows an analogous expansion. In v. 3f. Paul used the traditional confession about the Christ who died and was raised for our sins in order to remind the Corinthians of the basis of their own faith. As he continued, he likened the once-for-all of the resurrection event to the general resurrection of the dead (vv. 20ff.). Thus an old confession was broadened to an assertion about the universal history of humanity.

Paul also uses hymns, which already contain the universal component, in order to place the congregation he is addressing in a world-wide context. This is what happens in Philippians 2. The *kyrios* title in v. 11 already expresses Christ's dominion over heaven and earth. It introduces the hymn which ties the daily life of the congregation to this dominion of the humiliated and exalted Christ: "Let your bearing towards one another arise out of your life in Christ Jesus" (Phil. 2:5).

Finally we will mention the extremely important passage 2 Cor. 5:17-21, where the traditional formulation probably already contained the polarity between the personal, invisible, and the universal, public, aspects of the event of reconciliation in Christ. The universal new creation which takes the place of the old is founded on one person, Jesus Christ, through whom God has brought the whole world into the reconciliation (vv. 19, 21). The Corinthians are addressed where they are, within this polarity between the one Christ and the totality of the world (v. 20b). The existence of the apostle's and the church's ministry of reconciliation, which receives its meaning and concrete task in such polarity, comes from God, who in all secrecy has performed the decisive act for the world public.

2. The Outline of the Letter to the Romans

Paul's view of the totality and unity of men and of nations reveals itself particularly in the outline of the Letter to the Romans. The declared intention is to convince the Roman congregation to serve as the base of operations for the projected evangelization of the western Mediterranean (15:24). Therefore Paul takes up the basic theme of God's justice toward the whole world (1:16).

As in the Old Testament and in Judaism, Romans does not raise the question whether the unity of men exists or should be created. This theme is pre-supposed as self-evident and for Paul is a given which established the context for reflection. The question, rather, is one of the intent, and thus the content and character, which such presupposed unity has or should be given. This is apparent when the first part of the letter is compared with the second, which begins with the major statements in 3:21.

A certain commonality of all nations and men is presupposed in 1:18-3:20, in that all have part in God's anger about human sin (1:18). The charges leveled against the Gentiles and the Jews in the first and second chapters concern not only individual evil-doing, but also perversion of the religious (1:20ff.; 2:17ff.) and ethical (1:24ff.; 2:21ff.) foundations of both social orders. What both groups share is their falling away from God and dissolution of human society, manifest especially in the mutual hatred and contempt between Jews and non-Jews. So, paradoxically, their unity is that all live on their own resources and therefore are in universal conflict with all others and are given over to the annihilation and judgement (3:17f.).

The "now, however" in 3:21 opens the way to a new unity. Out of justification by faith, which frees from personal glory, comes a unity in which one is for all and all are for one, and therefore there is not only unity but also living and life-promoting community.

The change from one sort of unity to another is grounded in Jesus Christ, through whose sacrificial deed is created anew the fellowship between men and God and also among men. This dynamic moves in ever expanding circles. Thus the figure of Abraham is introduced as the promise for the future (ch. 4), the present affliction becomes the overture to the coming salvation (5:1ff.), obedience leads to new service of justice (ch. 6). Most important, there dawns the freedom of the children of God which leads from the perverted law, which also perverts reality (ch. 7), to the renewal of the whole creation (8:19ff., 38f.). Thus in Christ the hope arises that men can be led from a unity in self-destruction into a new unity of constructive community.

Therefore the much-discussed passage about the old and new Adam in 5:12-21 is not to be interpreted primarily or only on the basis of contemporary parallels; it has its own intention and specific content. It has always been noticed that the apostle breaks off the parallel statement which starts with 5:12, and picks it up again only in v. 18. The reason for this anacoluthon is that Paul is not primarily interested in the parallel between the old and new Adam, each including all men, but that against the background of the existing parallel he wants to emphasize the differences between the two figures (5:15-17). The theme of the altered sign has priority over the theme of unity. The question of whether any unity exists at all is superceded by that about the qualities of the new unity in contrast to that unity which is passing away.

Did Paul expect the future unity which will join together the whole creation, including mankind, in a new peace (8:19ff.) as an event within human history, or did he have in mind the intervention of an eschatological event which is entirely other-wordly along the lines of Jewish apocalyptic? According to I Cor. 15:20-28, 50-53, he envisioned a sharp break between the totally new order and the course of history. Yet in Romans 8 one finds no trace of this. This inconsistency suggests that while Paul was aware of the problem, he did not consider it crucial. He would not and could not systematize; his thought is based on Christ, resurrected from the dead; in him all rational systems find their limits, yet he awakens new hope where human eyes can see only blank impossibility. Paul leaves ultimate riddles unsolved; he understands himself, however, to be placed in a

future-oriented hope by the revelation of Christ, and it is this hope
which spurs him on to hope and try for new and impossible things at
those points other men see themselves trapped by walls with no
exit.

The relationship between Israel and the nations is considered in
Rom. 9-11. This passage is an extremely good example of how Paul
leaves many particular questions unresolved, yet out of his lively
hope in the future, engages in decisive and concrete action in the
present. Paul's question here stirs up a host of ultimate problems.
What is the relationship between the one chosen people of God and
the Gentile nations who have no share in this election? What about
the new schisms which are enkindled by the message of the gospel?
Why does the church of Christ now see itself caught between Israel's
rejection and the Gentile world's reservation about the gospel?
Starting from the position that the justification of the sinner is the
central core of the gospel of Christ, Paul finds his way to a single,
decisive prophetic insight within the whole maze of questions: when
"the Gentiles have been admitted in full strength... the whole of
Israel will be saved" (11:25f.). It would lead us too far afield to
discuss the meaning of these two expressions. Briefly we can note,
however, that Paul is thinking here not about single individuals,
but about nations. Paul's hope in the power of God's world-wide
faithfulness to the covenant excludes none of these peoples from
solidarity with him. Precisely at the point where his Jewish brothers'
solid line of defense condemns Paul to complete failure, his believing
and hoping eye discovers the hidden path of God's purpose. The
unity of the Gentile nations made possible by reconciliation will
also lead to the unity of these nations with the original covenant
people who are now on the sidelines. It is an open question whether
this unity will exemplify 'churchly' or 'secular' ecumenism.

If Paul offers this vista of a universal new world, how can we
understand the conspicuous fact that his admonitions are addressed
specifically to the Christian community and to no one else? Does this
mean that Paul really thinks only in particular terms or that he
limits himself to the evangelistic gathering of individual converts
who have nothing to do with the non-Christian world? This question
calls—as a part of our reflection on the outline of the Letter to the
Romans—for an examination of the basic structure and breadth of
Paul's paranesis.

We should recall once more that Paul's view of his entire missionary work stands under an eschatological reservation and that he therefore sees it as incomplete, open to all quarters. This fragmentary openness yields a number of criteria for the nature and function both of the church and of Paul's paranesis itself. One dimension is certainly that because the Christian church yields itself to the Father of Jesus Christ, both as a whole and as individual members, it is drawn into the dynamic which leads from doubt to faith, from division to community, from curse to thanksgiving, from resignation to active courage and thus, in the eschatological realm, from death to life. And because this God bears universal characteristics, the life of the church cannot exhaust itself in an isolated self-sufficiency, but it is set within the broadest possible context.

The church in which Jesus Christ understands God's mercy as the *only basis* for its own and the world's existence necessarily comes into conflict with the ideological idols and taboos of certain situations and powers which lead to discrimination, hatred, and disdain for certain men and groups of men. Because Christ's exclusive claim does not stop at the boundaries of the church, decisions made inside the church about the bases of human behavior toward other humans reach out into the general social and political spheres. Belief in the exclusive, merciful God necessarily leads to encounter with the existing orders, even those outside the church, encounters fraught both with conflict and with promise.

The church, which proclaims the Father of Jesus Christ as the one and the *universal God*, is placed *nolens volens* in an inalienable and world-wide solidarity with all men by virtue of its own decision in response to its election. It cannot celebrate its freedom and hope and ignore the men outside its walls—all mankind—who also are called to participate in the same liberation and hope; this church after all is the down-payment and eschatological example of God's worldwide decision. Therefore the church will intervene with all possible and appropriate means among all men and all nations against destructive hatred and war and for life-sustaining reconciliation. It will even discover that involvement on behalf of God's mercy outside the church's boundaries often is more concrete than among its own members.

A further element comes into play at this point. The church, which yields itself to the God who is both exclusive and universal, finds itself in a realm of will characterized by *integral intensity*. The merciful Father demands that he be loved with man's whole heart, soul, and strength (Deut. 6:4f.). Because this one God is also the creator of all men, Jesus applies this same totality of personal response to relationships between men; he includes the love of neighbor, whoever that may be, in the commandment to love God (Mk. 12:28ff., par.). Therefore an integral component of the freedom and vocation of the Christian church is that its members suffer, hope, act in solidarity wherever men's freedom or honor is violated by other men or by the pressure of institutions on their lives. As with Jesus so too with Paul, we need to notice the character of this intensity: the double commandment to love God and neighbor engages the addressee so radically and integrally that the definitions of the neighbor and the places where he is to be found become limitless; the law of love is no longer limited to members of one's own nation or even one's own church (Lk. 10:25-37). Because the hearer is placed unconditionally under the law of love, he is at the same time freed to offer what is appropriate and helpful to particular persons and circumstances. The radical demand always to be in solidarity with one's neighbor is unconditionally valid in all places and circumstances, from the sphere of personal love between two individuals to that of political or social justice between different groups of men.

These three aspects of the exclusive, universal, and integral God of mercy can be seen even at the beginning of the paranetic portion of the Letter to the Romans (12:1). Paul addresses himself, to be sure, to a particular congregation which is embraced by God's mercy, but he moves directly to the integral intensity of his demand by speaking of living sacrifice and reasonable service. The warning not to conform to the world corresponds to the exclusiveness of God. Yet the will of God, which is to be discerned and done, does not lose its universal thrust.

This universal thrust pervades the entire paranetic section, Rom. 12:3-15:33. The admonitions to sobriety, which should correspond to the measure of faith one has been given, at first seem to be limited to life within the body of Christ, that is, within the church (12:4f). Likewise the admonitions to sincere love and hospitality are placed primarily in the context of providing for the needs of Christian travelers (12:9-13). But at the latest by v. 14, and without any evident transition, it becomes clear that the intensive engagement of such life and action goes beyond the boundaries of the congregation: Paul moves there to deal with how Christians should react to persecutions and with the relationship between the church and its Gentile environment. It is not accidental that the following passage, 13:1ff., again without any transition, goes on to treat the position of the Christian church over against the anti-Christian policies of the Roman empire. To understand it rightly, we must free Rom. 13 from romantic notions of obedience to the state which have obscured the text's original intention. Then it becomes even more clear that Paul defines the attitude of the Christian toward the state and as a citizen within the state on the basis of the eschatological future, which the order of the state also has to serve (cf. 13:11-14). This position laid a solid foundation of principle for the view that Christian responsibility cannot stop short of involvement with political questions, but must hold to the claim of the merciful God, no matter how much the specific problems may change through the centuries.

This line of thought comes even more strongly to the fore in chapters 14 and 15. At first the discussion of the relationship between the 'strong' and the 'weak' is concerned with dealings between scrupulous Jewish Christians and free-living Gentile Christians in one congregation. By 15:7ff. at the latest, however, it is set in the context of the Christ through whom Jew and Gentile are to be brought to a new, universal fellowship. Therefore Paul is not changing the subject when he calls upon the Gentile Christians to contribute to the Jewish Christians in Jerusalem in the middle of a report on his travel plans (15:23 ff.).These internal ecumenical bridges between Christians as Jews and Gentiles concretize at a decisive point the fact that the cleavage between various religions and peoples, as well as the division between the elected people of God and the Gentiles outside, has lost its importance.

The intra-churchly, ecumenical, and finally universal aspects of the single paranesis are here closely intertwined. In Romans, as in Paul's other letters, the direct address to the Christians includes a total claim on the church to live out of the merciful will of God without reservation and to allow itself to be directed by it in all areas. This personal urgency had to lead eventually to broader reflection on the formation of common life in the light of the gospel in various political, national, and social spheres and to increasingly wide-ranging implementation of the conclusions reached.

3. The body of Christ

The concept of the body of Christ, which plays such an important role in the Pauline and sub-Pauline letters, merits particular consideration. We are not concerned with its origin, whether Old Testament or Hellenistic. Nor are we concerned with Paul's own contribution to its development. We will merely underscore some of the changes on the theme within the New Testament which are important here.

Within the undisputed Pauline letters, I Cor. 12:12ff. and Rom. 12:4f. speak of the body of Christ. Both passages are concerned with the sphere of the church's existence as the basis for ordering the mutual interdependence of the individual members and their actions for the upbuilding of the whole. Membership in the body of Christ has constitutive and regulative power over the construction of the church. It is not simply a comparison with the human body; rather the body is identical with the reality created in Christ: "Now you are Christ's body, and each of you a limb or organ of it" (I Cor. 12:27).

How far-reaching is this existence as body and members? In I Cor. 12, the statements and instructions touch only relationships within the church. The weaker members are to be protected from being overwhelmed by the Gnostic spiritualists. Was this limitation derived from the theological conceptuality of the body of Christ, or was Paul motivated in his dealing with this situation in the church by pragmatic considerations? Rom. 12 takes us a step further. As we have seen already there, the limitation to events and relationships within the church is of no particular consequence for Paul because he always has in mind the world-wide function of everything the church does. Therefore a completely new potential dimension of the body of Christ comes into view. The members of the body of Christ do not serve each other only in mutual self-satisfaction; they become tools through whom the Lord reaches out into the surrounding world where Christians are always participating.

Therefore the two post-Pauline letters to the Colossians and the Ephesians are more a logical extension than a break with Pauline theology. Here the idea of the body of Christ is placed *expressis verbis* in new contexts: Christ becomes autonomous as the head who gives life to and governs the body, and he is also identified as the mediator of creation (Col. 1:16ff.; 2:10; Eph. 1:22ff.; Cf. Jn. 1:1ff.,

Heb. 1:1ff.). This double function of Christ as Lord of the cosmos and of the church redefines both the relationship between the church and its head and the relationship between the church and the surrounding world.

In Colossians, this relationship is first presented as one of diacritical distance. Because Christ has deposed the powers which oppose God, the church can stop respecting them and live the freedom it has been given (2:8-33). At the same time, a new openness to the world appears: Christ, whose mystery encompasses the whole world (1:6, 26f.) reaches out through his Gospel to every man, and therefore to all men (1:28). The hope which has burst forth is seen in the fact that among those reached by Christ, mankind's religious, racial, and social divisions appear overcome (3:11). Such a new community is formed even where only a part of the people are members of the church.

We see this in that Colossians is the first New Testament book to take over the pagan household instructions (3:18ff.). Here Christians are called upon to let their own actions be determined by Christ even when they find themselves in social structures in which non-Christians also participate. By proclaiming Christ to be Lord of all creation and all creatures, they also call into play a criterion which at first only determines personal relationships within the existing orders of life, but necessarily leads to critical analysis and new structuring of the present orders of the public 'secular' institutions.

The Letter to the Ephesians also identifies the Lord over all the powers and all the world as the head of the church (1:22f.). Nevertheless, the church's task toward the world seems at first glance to take second place to the theme of ecumenical unity (4:1-16). But this unity also turns out to be founded on the Lord who fills the universe (4:10). When, in the context of the household instructions, the close parallel between Christ's relationship to the church and the relationship between marriage partners is set forth (5:22), we again see how the nature of fellowship not only among Christians but among all men is illuminated by means of an innermost secret of faith. Similarly, the unity created in Christ between Jews and Gentiles is placed in the context of the freedom which Christ has created, for all men and between heaven and earth, when he broken down "the enmity which stood like a dividing wall between them," between God and men and among men (2:14). Thus according to Ephesians, the ecumenical expansion of the church is both the beginning and the likeness, which is filled with promise, of that unity which reaches far beyond the limits of the Christian community and into the realm of the whole creation.

Between I Corinthians and Ephesians we can see the concept of the body of Christ change as the church is led out of introverted narrowness into ecumenical breadth and responsibility for universal problems.

III. *The Biblical Directions for Today*

This essay has sketched the dynamic and main tendencies of Biblical statements about the unity of mankind. In conclusion, we will look at some contemporary implications of those impulses.

The unity of men is not a theme in and of itself in either the Old or the New Testament; the remembrance is ever present that the whole creation stands over against its God as a unity. Interest is concentrated, however, on how a new unity in the sense of the Hebrew *shalom*, a fullness in mutually constructive and consciously formed community, comes forth from the universal, paradoxical unity of destructive sin. The people of God in the old covenant, and even more so those in the new, know they are on the way from the world which is passing away to the coming world made whole. Therefore the church is doing its own work, not someone else's, when it turns from evil to good, from sin to repentance, in solidarity and engagement with the history of men and nations.

If the church takes the Bible seriously, it will always be confronted with the claim that the name of Jesus Christ is the Archimedean point which has triggered the movement from the past of evil into the future of salvation and keeps it in motion. This claim insists that in the crucified, exalted, and living Jesus, God has revealed himself as the God who has adopted the renewal of men as his own cause—in an exemplary way in the old covenant and once for all in the Messiah of Israel. This claim also discloses that the root and essence of destructive power are tied to human responsibility and human guilt and sin, and that the salvation is rooted in God's once for all decision to be and to remain in solidarity with these godless men and to suffer by, with, and for them until it comes out all right in the end. Therefore the church gathered around the Bible is invited to proclaim reconciliation at all times and everywhere as the one, all-inclusive message of good news which lays the foundation for human life, justice, honor, and freedom, *i.e.*, human community. Therefore the church of Jesus Christ is always invited in hope and obedience to its Lord to endure, to hope, and to risk the formation of this new unity in partnership with all fellow human beings.

The Bible and church history show clearly how the single and central reconciliation event continues to take on new and unforeseen forms as the historical circumstances change. In our century the Gospel encounters a mankind which stands before a new and unprecedented task. It must give form to a community with worldwide dimensions. Modern science and technology have created a cultural, economic, and political interdependence which finds all men for the first time in a single, life or death destiny. To be or not to be really is the question; will we break through from world war to world peace, from world hunger to world economic justice?

This situation broadens further than ever before the promise and task of the Christian church. The ecumenical movement cannot be just a matter of bringing together within the church Christians from various nations and races, spiritual traditions and moral customs, into a fellowship which remains aware of its responsibility while dealing with its own inner tensions. As members of the body of Christ, we are called to live in the tensions of our century, firmly grounded in that reconciliation which leads from anxiety and aggression to courageous renunciation of nationalism and to a new ordering of national and international relationships.

This means, however, that the Christian church must examine all things in order to judge what must be applied to the future. Its concerns about the use and misuse of power cannot merely exhaust themselves in theoretical studies but must engage real economic and political power relationships and place them in the service of men. It must know the facts about the threat of military technology and arbitrary use of power in order to awaken genuinely human freedom and to allow it to flourish. All of these actual relationships push Christians to make common cause with non-Christians in order to become active partners in the new humanity which is in process of formation. In the process, many treasured traditions and rigid theologies may undergo radical transformation. Therefore a church which is serious about renewal of the world-wide human community will pray again the old petition: Lord, renew thy people, beginning with us!

CHAPTER FOUR

MUHAMMAD AND ALL MEN

DAUD RAHBAR

Four Quotations from the Holy Qur'an:

> For each one of you have we made a law and a pathway; and had
> God willed He would have made you one nation, but He will surely
> try you concerning that which He has brought you. Be ye therefore
> emulous in good deeds; to God is your return altogether; and He
> will let you know concerning that wherein ye do dispute.   (5:52-53)
> And view with one another for pardon from your Lord, and for
> Paradise, the breadth of which is as the heaven and earth, prepared
> for those who fear;—for those who expend in alms, in prosperity and
> adversity, for those who pardon men; God loves the kind.   (3:127-
> 128)
> Fight in God's way with those who fight with you, but transgress
> not; verily, God loves not those who do transgress.   (2:186)
> Men were one nation once, and God sent prophets with good tidings
> and with warnings, and sent down with them the Book in Truth, to judge
> between men in that wherein they disagreed; but none did disagree
> therein save those who had been given it after that manifest signs
> had come to them, through greed amongst themselves;... (2:209;
> see also 10:20)

I. *Presenting the Prophet*

Before turning to the evidence of Muhammad's teachings related
to the subject of unity of mankind, we should consider briefly the
impact of his career on world history.

Muhammad was a man of refined culture. His social reform aimed
at converting the impatience, short temper, and vanity of his society
into forbearance, prudence and harmony. In order to achieve this,
he educated his fellow men by the charisma of personal example,
conversation and political action. In all of this, he was evidently a
man gifted with boundless energy, charm, charity, patience, sagacity, and friendliness. Division, revenge, deceit, and hypocrisy
repulsed him but he confidently saw in those exercising them the
possibilities of conversion. He was a man of peace. We must un-

derstand with sound reason the rationale of his wars. That his wars were not instruments of revenge and spite, is clear from the event of the Amnesty of Mecca.

We have to be on our guard against brashness when attempting to see what accounts for the global fireworks of Muslim warfare after the Prophet's death. Were they a direct result of Muhammad's teachings and example as a warrior?

The Prophet regarded his repatriation in Mecca and the establishment of a Kingdom uniting many tribes as a goal worth a protracted effort full of danger. His opponents were already at war with him by forcing him out of his hometown and by 'refusing to allow' his ideas to spread.

Did an alternative to war exist for the Prophet to act creatively for the promotion of peace in Arabia? Did circumstances contain greater possibilities of setting afoot in those environments the forces of peace by some method avoiding war?

What would have been the course of Arabian history if a Confucius, a Buddha, an Asoka, a Jesus or a Gurn Nanak had been made a messenger by God in the midst of the same Arab tribes of the seventh century?

We are raising hypotheses so large that we can respond to them only by silence.

By sending envoys to rulers of neighboring states, the Prophet did indeed impress upon his followers that he meant his teachings to spread all over the world. He died only two years after this initiative of mission to some non-Arab nations.

Is the action which his followers took after his death identical with the action which he himself would have taken if he had lived longer? How much of a span of time do we have in mind when we say "if he had lived longer"? Half a century? A century? Or more? Raising these latter questions brings into focus the observation that no single human being can remain to participate in the steering of history forever, and that the unseen hand of Providence is there as the ultimate power during and after the lifetime of the man of great influence. Even at the peak of his success, Muhammad would not boast of having changed all Arabs into veritable saints and the environment into Paradise. He inspired many, outraged many, and puzzled many. All those involved in his religious movement were creatures caught in their personal circumstances, with assets of personal gifts, and liabilities of personal shortcomings. The spirit of the Prophet's work and word did indeed become a major force of history which interacted with countless dispositions of individuals and groups responding and reacting in different ways.

II. *Muhammad's Example*

Islam began at a time in history when Middle Eastern society had tasted the experience of composite civilization. The Byzantine and Sassanian empires had promoted cultural cross-fertilisation and international trade. Both the empires could boast of having sophisticated religious traditions. With these two large administrative units providing limited means of expansion of culture and thought, the restless Middle East was ready for an adventure of bigger dimensions. The more interesting development is not that so many Asian and African countries succumbed before the rolling forces of Islamic expansion but that they were not persistently resistant to the religious thought of the new movement. There was certainly something impressive, constructive and integrative about Islam in the context of the early centuries of its growth.

The Prophet of Islam was a realistic visionary and a remarkable missionary. He was born in the rather secluded society of Mecca, the urban life of which was hardly in the making before he began his work of reform. It was a cluster of tribes whose hearts beat with the unbridled freedom of the desert wind. Extremely flammable and haughty, these people lived by a sense of honor that was bloodthirsty and reckless. Exploits of retaliation were a never ending chain, making life thrilling for the gallant knights but extremely insecure for the weak. The Prophet's trips-for-trade in the Middle East served as a preparation for his revelation which confirmed his conviction in the values of compatibility, reconciliation, forgiveness, charity, humanity and politeness. Before declaring himself a Prophet, he had experienced both tribal and urban societies and his peace-loving nature had helped him see with concern the weakness and corruption of man.

His mission work extended over twenty-three years. The first thirteen of these were spent in Mecca, where his fellow-tribesmen persecuted him and his small number of devoted followers ceaselessly. Nearly a decade thereafter he lived in exile in Medina where his life was one of anxious leadership. The Meccans marched against him and subversive men in Medina made his life difficult. His survival through all this was almost miraculous. The only offensive war he fought was when he finally marched to Mecca at the head of a large force of his followers to end his exile and assert his right of repatriation. His victory made him King of Arabia. His nature found persuasive talk and friendly negotiation really congenial and he resorted to warfare with sagacious discretion to accelerate the unification of Arabia and to preserve his reform movement from extinction.

His followers unanimously remembered him for his phenomenal capacity for forgiveness, self-control and gentle humanity.

We see Muhammad, before he was twenty-five years of age, as the bearer of the popular title of *al-Amin* (the Trustworthy). He won admiration of the haughty tribal chiefs by becoming the agent of peace in a most explosive situation. The occasion was the reconstruction of the Temple of Ka'ba. All building work was accomplished except the laying of the sacred Black Stone on its chosen spot in a wall. Rival tribes claimed the crowning honor of this act of pious masonry. Unless some inspired solution were provided by someone trusted for wisdom and pure motivation, the tribes were sure to plunge into a ruthless civil war. Muhammad assumed the mighty role of arbitrator by being the first to enter the temple on that historical morning. A sheet of cloth was brought at his request. He put the Black Stone in it and requested the representatives of each tribe to join in lifting the sheet up to the level of the spot fixed for laying the Stone. When this was done, he himself took the Stone and fixed it in the wall. Thus he averted the bloodshed and won hearty acclaim from the people.

He warned his people of God's punishment, but was soft-tongued and gentle in conversation of business and of companionship. Disconcerted by his growing fame in Arabia, his fellow-tribesmen tried to dissuade him from his mission. Their arguments often turned angry and they accused him of sorcery, untruth and called him insane. For thirteen years he suffered persecution, humiliation and violence in his hometown. The non-Muslim Meccans denied the few Muslims food and drink and made their life unbearable. At fifty-three, the Prophet faced threat of assassination and decided to migrate from Mecca.

He thought of trying the town of Ta'if for his new abode. His arrival there aroused much hostility. He was pelted and abused. He bled but refused to be provoked. His reply to this violence was prayer for the guidance of the ignorant people.

The Prophet's migration (*hijra*) to Medina was, however, warmly welcomed by the war-weary town, two hundred miles from Mecca. The small population of that town had ambitious, capricious and conceited tribal chiefs competing for supremacy but lacking in conclusive strategy and stable diplomacy. To the Prophet the citizenry looked with hope of constructive leadership. He appeared on the scene with a will to reconciliation and a disposition committed to negotation and peaceful covenants. The revolutionary character of his idea of creative society was in terms of a community (*ummah*) united by the bond of a common faith. The tribal basis of society was unacceptable to him.

The illiterate Prophet demonstrated amazing statesmanship by signing at once a treaty with the people of Medina, particularly the Jews of that town. This was a document of his own authorship prepared in a spirit of mutual consultation. The treaty instituted the transition to the new society of his dream. The terms of the treaty evidence respect for the principles of trust, religious freedom and equality of human beings. An English translation of some of the articles of this noble document is as follows:

> In the name of God, the Merciful, the Compassionate! This is a writing of Muhammad the Prophet between the believers and Muslims of (Meccan) Quraysh and Yathrib* and those who follow them and are attached to them and who crusade (*jahadu*) along with them.
>
> 1. They are a single community (*ummah*) distinct from other people.
> 2. The emigrants of Quraysh, according to their former condition, pay jointly the blood-money between them and they (as a group) ransom their captives (doing so) with uprightness and justice between the believers.
> 3. Banu 'Auf,** according to their former condition pay jointly the previous blood-wits, and each sub-clan *(ta'ifa)* ransoms its captives, (doing so) with uprightness and justice between the believers.
> 11. The believers do not forsake a debtor among them, but give him (help), according to what is fair, for ransom, or blood-wit.
> 12. A believer does not take as confederate (*halif*) the client (*maula*) of a believer without his (the latter's) consent.
> 13. The God-fearing believers are against whoever of them acts wrongfully or seeks (plans) an act that is unjust or treacherous or hostile or corrupt among the believers; their hands are against him, even if he is the son of one of them.

* Banu Quraysh is the name of the Prophet's tribe. Yathrib is the name of the city of Medina.
** Banu means "the descendants of."

14. A believer does not kill a believer because of an unbeliever; and does not help an unbeliever against a believer.

15. The security (*dhimmah*) of God is one; the granting of 'neighborly protection' (*yujr*) by the lowliest of them (the believers) is binding on them; the believers are protectors (or clients = *mawali*) of one another to the exclusion of (other) people.

16. Whoever of the Jews follows us has the (same) help and support (*nasr, iswah*) (as believers) so long as they are not wronged (by him) and he does not help (others) against them.

17. The peace (*silm*) of the believers is one; no believer makes peace apart from another believer, where there is fighting in the way of God, except in so far as equality and justice between them (is maintained).

19. The believers exact vengeance for one another where a man gives his blood in the way of God. The God-fearing believers are under the best and most correct guidance.

21. When anyone wrongfully kills a brother, the evidence being clear, he is liable to be killed in retaliation for him, unless the heirs of the murdered man agree and are satisfied (with payment). The believers are against him (the murderer) entirely; nothing is permissible to them except to oppose him.

22. It is not permissible for a believer who has agreed to what is in this document (*sahifah*) and believed in God and the last day to help a wrong-doer or give him shelter. If anyone helps him or gives him shelter, upon this man is the curse of God and His wrath on the day of Resurrection, and from him nothing will be accepted to make up for it or take its place.

23. Wherever there is anything about which you differ, it is to be referred to God and to Muhammad (peace be upon him).

24. The Jews share the expenses with the believers so long as they (Muslims) continue at war.

25. The Jews of Banu 'Auf are a separate community (*ummah*) as the believers. To the Jews their religion (*din*) and to the Muslims their faith. (This applies both to their clients and to themselves, with the exception of anyone who has done wrong or acted treacherously; he brings evil only on himself and on his household.)

23. It is for the Jews to bring their expenses and for the Muslims to bear their expenses. Between them (that is, to one another) there is help (*nasr*) against whoever wars against the people of this document. Between them is sincere friendship (*nas'h wa nasihah*), and honourable dealing, not treachery. A man is not guilty of treachery through (the act of) his confederate. There is help for (or, help is to be given to) the person wronged.

46. The Jews of al-Aus, both their clients and themselves, are in the same position as belongs to the people of this document while they are thoroughly honourable in their dealings with the people of this document. Honourable dealing (comes) before treachery.

47. A person acquiring (? guilt) acquires it only against himself. God
    is the most upright and truest fulfiller of what is in this document.
    This writing does not intervene to protect a wrong-doer or
    traitor. He who goes out is safe, and he who sits still is safe in
    Medina, except whoever does wrong and acts treacherously.
    God is ' protecting neighbour' (*jar*) of him who acts honourably
    and fears God, and Muhammad is the Messenger of God (God
    bless and preserve him).

The importance of the unity of *ummah* (= community united by
common faith) is much emphasized in the treaty. The fair spirit of
cooperative trust between the Muslims and Jews is recommended in
forthright language. Tribal loyalty is openly rejected.

The treaty was the crystallization of a historical challenge to a
tribal culture of frequent feuds, bloodshed and chains of retaliation.
The tribal morality was the morality of *murū'a* or manliness. A
highly flammable sense of honour made the Bedouin knights relish
banditry and killing of rival tribes. Even the cherished values of
generosity and hospitality were cultivated with reckless abandon
and excessive eating and drinking. Conduct was capricious as a rule.

The Treaty of Medina forbade confederacy (*hilf*) within the
Muslim community; no two groups were to establish a subversive
pact. The Treaty was the constitution that all undersigning parties
were to abide by. A small commonwealth was established.

The Prophet lost no time in following up the initial steps to con-
solidate the new society of Medina. The community there was full
of subversive elements. The internal danger was serious. On top of
it the Quraishites of Mecca hastened to attack Medina. Only a little
over three hundred Muslims formed the little army to be encountered by the foe. During this encounter two Muslims managed to
reach the Muslim camp from the town of Mecca. They had been
intercepted by the non-Muslims and released upon their pledge not
to take part in the imminent Battle of Badr against the invading
Quraishites. Upon arriving at Medina both of them volunteered to
take up arms and join the small Muslim force. The Prophet firmly
bade them honour their pledge. The miraculous victory of the
Muslims in the Battle of Badr was followed by a policy of peace and
forgiveness on the part of Muhammad.

At the conclusion of the subsequent Battle of Uhud a year later,
Muhammad gave thanks to Allah for a victory won not without
hazardous reverses. He maintained tolerance and friendliness
toward the malicious opponents.

Six years after his migration to Medina, Muhammad signed a treaty with the Meccans, another major event of negotiation under very dramatic circumstances. This is known as the Treaty of Hudaibiya.

In February 628, Muhammad camped with about fourteen hundred Muslims in the small village of Hudaibiya, only a few miles north of Mecca. He had come not to militate but for peaceful participation in 'Umra (= Little Pilgrimage). It was the sacred lunar month of Dhu'l-Qa'da. The law of custom entitled the Arabs to perform the 'Umra. In coming to Mecca just then, Muhammad expected a meaningful development. The Arabs of Mecca were both perplexed and provoked and were on the verge of violating the tradition of abstention from fighting during a sacred month. Hearing about these preparations, Muhammad conveyed to the Meccans through a friendly tribal chief that he and his followers had come on a pilgrimage and not with any hostile intentions. He proposed a treaty of peace for a fixed period. In the talks on it he indicated that he would not desist from war if his offer of peace were declined. The Arabs of Mecca arrogantly turned it down. At this a very old Quraishite leader, whose name was 'Urwa, came forward as a mediator and by persuasive words pacified the Arabs. They gave him full powers to negotiate. 'Urwa was insolent in his talks. Smiling, the Prophet assured him of the peaceful reason for the Muslims' visit to Mecca. 'Urwa was greatly surprised at the spirit of devoted loyalty of Muhammad's followers and upon return to the Meccans reported all this. He failed to return to Muhammad's camp for continued talks. Muhammad sent an emissary for enquiry who rode a camel owned by Muhammad. This camel was killed by the Meccans. Some Quraishite soldiers dashed out to attack the Muslim camp. They were captured and the battle was averted. The Prophet was not provoked and continued the effort to arrive at a friendly agreement. He freed the prisoners captured by his men.

Now he moved on by sending 'Uthman ibn 'Affan, a dear companion, to resume talks with the Meccans. 'Uthman was detained for several days and rumor spread that he had been killed. The Prophet now resolved to take up arms and march against Mecca. He took the Pledge of Fealty from his followers at a solemn ceremony.

Muhammad's persistence to settle the dispute by peaceful negotiation had already served an educative purpose. The Meccans were themselves learning to deliberate and in the process were becoming conscious of portents of unprecedented changes around them. The movement of Muhammad was gaining strength and they sensed that impulsive warfare would fail to accomplish sustained victories. The news of Muhammad's resolve to march against them changed their attitude and they sent an envoy to him. The draft of a treaty was presented for discussion.

Suhail, the envoy of the Quraish, objected to the opening words of the draft, "In the name of God, Most Gracious, Most Merciful." He demanded that these words be replaced by the traditional formula, "In your name, O God." The prophet accepted the change. Although Rahman (= the Merciful) was the name of Allah specially introduced by the Prophet in his teaching, he answered tactfully, "Call Him Allah or Rahman, by whatever name He is called; to Him belong all the beautiful names." The change of the words did not compromise conviction.

Another among objections from Suhail was that to the use of the words, "Muhammad, the Apostle of God." Muhammad declared "By God, I am the Apostle of God, even though you believe not my claim." With this clarification, however, he told 'Alī, the scribe of the treaty, to change the words to "Muhammad, son of Abdullah."

The form in which the Treaty was accepted by the two parties is as follows:

> With Thy name, O God! This is what was agreed upon between Muhammad, son of 'Abdullah and Suhayl, son of 'Amr.
> They both agreed to put down fighting on the part of people for ten years, during which period the people were to enjoy peace and refrain from fighting with each other.
> And whereas whoever of the companions of Muhammad comes to Mecca on Hajj or 'Umra pilgrimage, or in quest of the bounty of God (i.e. commerce, cf. Qur'an lxii. 10), enroute to Yemen or Ta'if, such shall be in security regarding his person or property. And whoever comes to Medina, from among the Quraish, enroute to Syria or Iraq (variant: Egypt) seeking the bounty of God, such shall be in security regarding his person and property.
> And whereas whoever comes to Muhammad from among the Quraishites without the permission of his guardian (*maula*), he (i.e. the Prophet) will hand him over to them; and whoever comes to the Quraish from among those who are with Muhammad, they will not hand him over to him.
> And that between us is a tied-up beast (i.e. bound to fulfill the terms), and that there shall be no secret help violating neutrality, and no acting unfaithfully.
> And that whosoever likes to enter the league of Muhammad and his

alliance may enter into it; and whosoever likes to enter the league of the Quraish and their alliance may enter it.

And that thou (Muhammad) shalt return from us (Quraish) in this year and enter not in our midst; and that when it is the coming year, we shall go out from thee and thou shalt enter with thy companions and stay there three nights, with thee being the weapon of the rider; having swords at the side, thou shalt not enter with what is other than them (swords).

And that the animals of sacrifice (brought by thee) will be slaughtered where we found them (i.e., in Hudaybiya), and thou shalt not conduct them to us (in Mecca).

(Probably Seal of Muhammad and Seal of Suhayl) WITNESSES: Muslims: Abu Bakr, 'Umar, 'Abd al-Rahman ibn Auf, 'Abdullah ibn Suhayl ibn 'Amr, Sa'd ibn Abi Waqqas, Muhammad ibn Maslamah, etc.

Meccans: Mikrad ibn Hafs, etc.

SCRIBE AND WITNESS: 'Ali ibn Abi Talib.'

The fourth paragraph of the text above contains a compromise which sounded to Muhammad's followers as a dishonourable surrender of rights and made them disheartened and angry. Soon another incident made them even more dejected. Abu Jandal arrived at the Muslim camp in chains after suffering tortures at the hands of the Meccans. This youth was the son of Suhail, the envoy who had negotiated the Treaty of Hudaibiya. Only the son was a Muslim while the father was an opponent of the Muslims. Abu Jandal had escaped from imprisonment in Mecca. Against the clamor of protest from fellow-Muslims, the Prophet surrendered Abu Jandal at the demand of the latter's father who was still at the Muslim camp. Even entreaty by 'Umar failed to alter the Prophet's decision. In the midst of peace talks he would not demonstrate any unsolidity of integrity. He ordered Abu Jandal in a voice filled with compassion to return to Mecca with the latter's father. Abu Jandal screamed in protest. The Prophet counselled him to be patient and hope for relief from God. Abu Jandal obeyed while most of the Muslims muttered angrily.

The Muslims marched back to Medina soon after the signing of the treaty. They were grief-stricken. The Prophet recited to them the newly received revelation, "Lo! We have given thee (O Muhammad) a signal victory." The listeners wondered what sort of a victory this was. The Prophet had prophetic foresight which others did not have. By concluding this treaty the Prophet had secured the prospects of continued contact with Mecca. The treaty was signed in A.H. 6.

Muhammad conquered Mecca in A.H. 8. In the two years between the events, many Muslims were able to visit Mecca under the protection of the treaty. The clause of para. 4 of the treaty worked out to the Muslims' advantage; their detention multiplied Muslim population of Mecca. The treaty did turn out to be a way to victory. 'Umar who criticized the treaty in A.H. 6 admired its sagacity in later years.

The exile of less than a decade was a period of hardship and achievement for Muhammad. His physical and spiritual stamina as well as his safety from assassination among so many impetuous characters was amazing. His followers multiplied so much that, when finally he took Mecca by surprise, his followers outnumbered the Meccans. When the victorious Prophet entered the town, a herald proclaimed aloud, "O Quraish, this is Muhammad who has come to you with a force you cannot resist. He who enters Abu Sufyān's house is safe and he who locks himself up is safe." A bitter foe of Muhammad, Abu Sufyān himself had been pardoned by the Prophet on the eve of the conquest of Mecca. His house was specially mentioned in the proclamation to augment the dramatic impact of a general amnesty, the first beneficiary of which was Abu Sufyān.

As victor, Muhammad entered his hometown, riding a horse, humbly, with his head lowered in submission to Allah. His address to the people of Mecca was a moving message of compassion. He stood at the door of the Ka'ba and spoke thus, "There is no God but Allah alone; He has no associate. He has made good His promise and helped His servant. He has put to flight the confederates alone. Every claim of privilege or blood or property are [sic] abolished by me except the custody of the temple and the watering of the pilgrims...O Quraish, God has taken from you the haughtiness of paganism and its veneration of ancestors. Man springs from Adam and Adam sprang from dust." Then he recited to them from the Qur'an, "O men, We created you from male and female and made you into peoples and tribes that you may know one another: of a truth the most noble of you in God's sight is the most pious." He went on and then asked, "What do you think I am about to do with you?" They said, "Good. You are a noble brother, son of a noble brother." The Prophet proclaimed, "Go! You are relieved; no more responsibility burdens you today; you are the freed ones."

There are many other illustrations of the Prophet's exemplary clemency which earned him the title of "A Mercy for the Worlds." Of these we have presented some that represent 'Muhammad's action in the most decisive moments of his life. After his victory, he received numerous deputations with whom he dealt with masterly diplomacy and consideration. The deputation from Hunain came with entreaty for return of six thousand captives taken by the Muslims at the Battle of Hunain. The Prophet granted the request and spoke words of spiritual counsel to the envoys.

When the time came for distribution of the large amount of booty, the Prophet gave away most of it to the more recent Meccan converts. The helpers from Medina who had given shelter to Muhammad a decade earlier and had supported his movement in earlier years, were offended by the favor to the Meccans. In a moving speech the Prophet consoled them saying, "Are you not satisfied that men should take away flocks and herds while you take back with you the Apostle of God?" Many among the helpers wept as they heard these noble words. He explained later that the favor to the Meccans was motivated by his concern to strengthen the loyalty of the new converts.

The Prophet's dealings with several other deputations evidence his thoughtfulness and foresight. The demands of the deputation from Tā'if involved compromise on some of the most serious tenets of Islam. The representatives wanted exemption from the prescribed daily prayers, alms-tax and the responsibility to take up arms in alliance with the Muslims. Knowing them to be hardened in their perversions, the Prophet did not insist on their abstention from adultery, usury and drinking alcohol. He had a prophetic foresight about the nature of these people: coercion would not help and accommodation would win them soon. His prediction came true. Within two years the people of Ta'if caught the contagion and began to see the rationality of the new injunctions.

The only obligation on which the Prophet insisted at the negotiations was daily prayers to Allah. This meant the rejection of al-Lāt, the idol-god of the people of Ta'if. The idol, the Prophet demanded, should be broken to pieces. An agreement was reached that this would be done by a Muslim to be nominated by Muhammad and that the people of Ta'if should be spared the pain of the act.

The deputation of the Christians of Najran was an occasion of debate on the divinity of Christ. The proceedings were marked by a decorum maintained by both parties. The Prophet's presentation was unacceptable to the envoys but it was made with his habitual politeness and he expressed veneration for Jesus.

The deputation from Banu Tayy was led by 'Adiy ibn Hatim, an arrogant man. The Prophet escorted him to the former's house and made him sit on a leather cushion and himself sat on the ground. This humility touched 'Adiy and the Prophet won his heart by soft words.

The envoys from Banu Tamim were boastful, frivolous and insolent. Their representative poet recited a boastful poem. A gentle reply in verse was declaimed by a Muslim poet. The Prophet spoke gently and showed no anger at the impoliteness of the visiting group.

The deputation from Banu Hanifa was a strange affair. The impostor Musailima, who claimed to be a prophet to contest Muhammad in A.H. 10, did not accompany the envoys and stayed away. However, after hearing an account of the meeting from the envoys, he entertained a design to declare himself a partner with Muhammad in prophethood and began to recite his own thoughts in a style intended as the Qur'an's imitation. He then sent two men back to Muhammad with a letter that read. "From Musailima the apostle of God to Muhammad the apostle of God. Peace be upon you. I have been made a partner with you in authority. To us belongs half the land and to Quraish half, but Quraish are a hostile people." The Prophet's reply read thus, "From Muhammad the Apostle of God to Musailima the liar. Peace be upon him who follows the guidance. The earth is God's. He lets whom He will of His creatures inherit it and the result is to the pious."

To the kings of Himyar in South Arabia who sent to the Prophet a messenger, with assurance of their loyalty to Islam, the Prophet wrote a reply instructing them on the subject of alms and taxes. The letter contained also the sentence, "If a Jew or a Christian becomes a Muslim, he is a believer with a believer's rights and obligations. He who holds fast to his religion, Jew or Christian, is not to be turned from it. He must pay the poll-tax (*jizya*)—for every adult, male or female, free or slave, one full dinar...or its equivalent in clothes..." He enjoined them "not to be false and treacherous, for the apostle of God is the friend both of your poor and your rich. The alms tax (*zakat*) is not lawful to Muhammad or his household; it is alms to be given to the poor Muslims, and the (poor) wayfarer (*ibn al-sabil*).

The nature of the missionary spirit of the Prophet is consistently one of urgency governed by persuasiveness of a wise educator. In the last two years of his life he sent envoys to several rulers including those of Bahrain, al-Yamama, 'Uman and to the governors of Damascus and Alexandria. He also sent messengers with letters to the Roman and Persian Emperors. All the messages contained claims of his Prophetic status and an invitation to repent. The envoys were instructed to observe restraint, gentleness, abstention from bad temper and haste. They were to teach veneration for former prophets, the value of the five daily prayers, the obligation of the rich to give alms to the poor, to condemn injustices and to encourage the study of the Qur'an. The accounts of these envoys and the text of the letters sent can be read in Alfred Guillaume's English translation of Iban Ishāq's *Siratu Rasul Allāh* (Oxford, 1955).

III. *The Struggle of Implementation*

Factions emerged immediately after his death. Apostasy asserted itself. The Caliphate became a source of contention and violence. Three out of the four Orthodox Caliphs were assassinated one after another. Their period was followed by the Umayyad dynasty of Caliphs who inherited a huge empire to manage. Ambition and economic interests were active in the political game of this early period. Subversion was motivated by love of traditional nomadism, race difference, clash of clans while unwieldiness of the empire remained a constant challenge to the administrators. The overthrow of the Umayyads (the first dyasty of Caliphs) in A.D. 750 was engineered substantially by the Iranian supporters of the Abbasids (the second dynasty); the Iranian converts to Islam struggled to secure equality with the Arabs as the first step and under the Abbasids brought about political, social, and doctrinal changes in Islamdom to strengthen their national life. By inducing the Abbasids to intermarry with Iranians, and by securing large participation in administration they achieved strong influence and reduced the Caliphs to puppets. The devastation brought to Baghdad by the Tartars in the middle of the thirteenth century served as the final blow to Arab dominance and non-Arab sultanates cropped up along with rival seats of Caliphate.

The sectarian life of early Islam changed to an orthodoxy, which facilitated intersectarian compatibility and integration of Muslim psyche. Much of doctrinal thought was born out of psychological and political needs of groups. The Murji'a, the Kharijites, the Mu'tazilites and above all the Shi'ites—these were the prominent sects of early Islam—were politically active and divisive. Yet they contributed to the integration of Islamic society and culture by offering exciting variety in thought and a feeling of the vast expanse and possibility of human experience.

The missionary methods of Muslims combined preaching and education with coercive tendencies. The acceptance of Islam by varied peoples, however, was facilitated by flexibility in exegesis and accommodation to an immense amount of ideas, creeds, customs and rituals. While cherishing the anchorage in an orthodoxy promoted by government and endorsed by consensus (*ijmā'*), the leadership of Islam did not excommunicate professing Muslims on grounds of religious accretion. The tribal Muslims of North Africa blended Islam with animism. The Muslims of Iran created a place for Zoroastrianism within their Islam. The Abbasid Caliphs introduced the venture of integrating the teachings of the Qur'an with Greek thought and sciences and invited a Nestorian to supervise the work of translations from Greek. Standard Muslim theology is highly Hellenized in character.

In India, Muslims adopted the sacred music of Hindu temples for entertainment. The elements of Hindu thought in Islamic pantheism are an important example of the assimilative character of Islam.

Mediaeval Muslim society served as a custodian of Greek science and philosophy.

The concepts of *ra'y* and *'urf* are sources of flexibility in Islamic Law. *Ra'y* means personal opinion and is the principle of applying one's faculty of reason in interpreting the sources of law on a given issue. *'Urf* means local custom and its recognition as a practical source of law in Muslim administration enabled very different societies to integrate themselves with Islam as a world religion.

In the recent centuries, mysticism has prevailed throughout the Muslim world. Pantheism has been the most popular doctrine in Sufism. The psychology of pantheism is other-wordly and unitive. So strong did the pantheistic thought become in Indian Islam that it began to dilute the distinctness of Islam and the communal solidity of the Muslim community there. In the seventeenth century, the mystic Sarhindi reformed the Muslim mysticism of India to free it from pantheistic relativism. Sarhindi's work was continued by the twentieth century poet, Muhammad Iqbāl.

Ibn al-'Arabi, Rūmī, Hāfiz Amir Khusrau and Ghalib are outstanding examples of Muslim mystics free from communal bias.

Internally, the Muslim community has demonstrated the will to
unity and disunity simultaneously. The Shi'ites and the Sunnites
have quarreled and cooperated over the centuries. The respective
thought of both has enriched the psychological experience of the
Muslim community as a whole.

The exlusivism and dogmatism of the Muslims should not be
exaggerated. The Qur'an is full of biblical allusions. Muslim Christo-
logy is not identical with the Christology of the Christian Church.
However, the Qur'an places Christ on an exceptional prophetic level.
The respect for Socrates, Plato, Aristotle, and Pythagoras among
Muslim thinkers is not casual.

The Emperor Abkar in India married a Hindu princess and made
her queen without forcing her to accept Islam. Akbar's thought is
regarded as heretical and is mildly condemned by Muslim divines
but hardly anyone among them has declared Akbar categorically an
infidel. Akbar's great-grandson, Dara Skikoh, wrote his work
Majma' al-Bahrain as an attempt to show the sameness of the best
of Hindu and Muslim thought.

As we look at the Muslims of our own times, we find them willing
enough to participate in the shaping of a more unified world. The
Agha Khan was the President of the League of Nations. Muhammad
Zafrulla Khan contributed to the world's respect for the negotiating
table by his earnest and learned speeches at the United Nations
General Assembly and is now Chief Justice of the International
Court of Justice of the Hague. Muslims in a large part of the world
have changed their weekly holiday from Friday to Sunday. Democracy is replacing monarchy. Muslim nations are not rejecting
Western education and are maintaining an influential status of some
European languages in their national life. In economy they are fully
involved with non-Muslim nations. The Suez Canal was built, after
all, with the cooperation of the Egyptian and the Ottoman authorities. Indian Muslim soldiers fought against Germany and Italy under British command in World War II.

In a rethinking about Islam's place in world-history, Muslims are
not reluctant to read and quote Western scholars. *The Encyclopedia
of Islam*, published in Leiden, has been translated into four Muslim
languages under state sponsorship.

The Azhar University has been revising its curriculum for several decades and today its faculty includes numerous Shaikhs trained at European Universities.

In India, Sir Sayyid Ahmad Khan did unique work in reconciling Muslims and Christians. He persuaded the English rulers to be gentle to Muslims and persuaded Muslims to stop blind rejection of Western ideas. He wrote extensively to show that the teachings of the Bible and the Qur'an are not really divergent. The sincerity of his effort has been recognized internationally. Even the passionate defender of Islam, Sir Muhammad Iqbal, made great contributions to the cooperation of Islamdom and the West by his profound study of Western philosophy.

In every generation of Muslims since the advent of Islam, there have been innumerable individuals with no malice toward non-Muslims. They have been average breadwinners who have concentrated on the faithful toil of taking care of their families. Their preoccupation was not hostility to non-Muslims. They had too much of a struggle to survive to afford the luxury of hostility toward non-Muslim communities.

No single reformer can do anything in history guaranteeing perpetual peace. Each generation has to take care of its spiritual life anew, making fruitful use of the best in human legacy. Islam as one of the major integrative movements in human history has been an instrument of much creativity. Its sacred literature, scholarship, historiography, artistic expression and social organization are part of man's experience. The future of the world will be enriched by reflection on the nature of the Islamic venture. The neglect of Islamic studies will impoverish world civilization.

IV. *Islam in Review*

We opened this essay with some quotations from the Holy Qur'an. In these there are three revelations: first, forgiveness is meritorious; second, the act of war is justifiable only when defensive; third, the origin of mankind is the same and conflict arose when men were confronted with the obligation to obey the law of God.

There is another quotation from the Qur'an that will help us:

> There is no compulsion in religion; the right way has been distinguished from the wrong, and whoso disbelieves in Taghut* and believes in God, he has got hold of the firm handle in which is no breaking. (2:257)

* The idols and demons of the Ancient Arabs are called Taghut.

Inspite of the fact that the Muslims, after the Prophet's death, often failed to adhere to the principle of persuasive talk and peaceful negotiation, historians recognize that Islam developed as an integrative force in the history of mankind. After the initial military activity of about a century, the Muslim community, while never being free of conflict of ideas, nationalities, and ambitious adventurers, began to evolve a transworld culture of its own. The spread of the Arabic language over a large number of Muslim lands facilitated international travel. The growth of classical Arabic and Persian literature made learning a common heritage of many Muslim lands. Standard religious obligations like the five daily prayers, the pilgrimage of Mecca, and fasting insured some sustained familiarity for travellers and immigrants. Acceptance of the sacred literature of Arabic and Persian as well as *belles lettres* of these two languages made the Muslim nations outside Arabia and Iran dependent upon the scholarship of these countries and thus internationalism became the spirit of Muslim scholarship.

Libraries all over the world today contain evidence of the phenomenal literary creativity of the Muslim community. As a producer of a great tradition of literature of historiography, mysticism, poetry, biography, philosophy and theology, the Muslim community has made available to us immense food for thought about human existence. The fine arts of calligraphy, architecture, carpet-weaving and garden-making are outstanding features of Islamic culture. Above all, Islamic society perhaps is foremost in developing the art of conversation, an art so vital to human fellowship. All this heritage is there to enrich human wisdom, fellowship and insight. Now that the dream of uniting the world-society is talked about everywhere, it is up to the makers of the future to benefit from or dispense with the study of the Muslim venture of the craft of civilization.

Nine thoughts, finally, may stimulate appreciation of Islam:

1. Muslims are traditionally hospitable and therefore extravagant. They are not keenly budget-minded in matters of domestic or national economy.
2. Islam resists nationalism. Therefore ruthless, patriotic nation-building is not the usual Muslim pursuit.
3. At the core of Islamic teaching is the idea of benevolent kingship. Traditional Islamic thought therefore is not very conducive to the flourishing of democracy.

No man is alien   6

4. Mysticism has prevailed in the Muslim world for the last eight centuries because it provides the most helpful mode of meeting the psychological needs of man in response to the Qur'an's teachings. As a result of this, rationalism has been declared barren by many influential mystics.

5. In the mysticized Muslim intellect, there is still a tremendous residue of poetical orientation which does not allow the Muslims to develop that reckless commitment to technology which marks the prosaic Anglo-Saxon civilization of our times.

6. The military career of the Prophet and the first four Caliphs predisposes Muslims to have a disdain for sustained obliqueness in diplomacy. There is a spontaneous openness in Muslim commentary on the behavior of offenders. In the midst of the cocktail diplomacy of the modern world, Muslim diplomacy seems tactless and blunt.

7. The mystics of Islam, due to the wonder-inspiring message of the Qur'an, have responded to the mystery of life and death with a delightful kind of devotional humor, developing particularly in the massive output of *ghazal* poetry, a light-hearted language of informal, loving conversation with God. Muslim lovers of *ghazal* poetry are seldom embittered by the hardships of life and react to them with an amused wistfulness.

8. There have been more wars within Christendom and within Islamdom than between Muslims and Christians.

9. The traditions of Buddhism, Christianity, Hinduism, and Islam are assets for world unity if together all of us decide to benefit from them as such. They can become liabilities if we continue to exploit them for fanatic pride and destructive activity. All major religious traditions can be turned into monsters if cultivated with perverse and sick motivation. Such motivation can be transformed into peace-loving motivation by habits of soul-searching introspection, warm and imaginative conversational, cultivation of charm in personality, love of dream and drama. The educational system throughout the world has to develop an orientation conducive to sincere and warm fellowship. Worry about the world-economy of tomorrow and peace in the whole world can easily become a cause of evasion of the problems of today's thanklessness, emptiness, and lack of faith. A frustrated and discontented life is a soldier of the devil's army.

To close, we cite two verses of the great Indian Muslim poet,

Asadullah Khan Ghalib (d. 1869), may God rest his soul:

Stable fidelity is the true essence of faith.
If the Hindu priest dies in an idol-house,
Pay homage to him with a burial at the Sanctuary of Mecca.

We are Unitists;
Our creed is the dismissal of fanatic conventions.
When communities unite, then alone
They are truly participants in faith.

BIBLIOGRAPHY

Any student of Islam who is eager to pursue a sympathetic study of its history should first get acquainted with the following books:

Carl Brockelmann, *Geschichte der Arabischen Literatur*. Vol. I (Weimar, 1898); Vol. II (Berlin, 1902). Supplement 3 Vols. (Leiden, 1937-42).
Encyclopaedia of Islam (Leiden, 1908-36).
C. A. Storey, *Persian Literature; A Bio-Bibliographical Survey* (London, 1927-).
The Catalogue of Arabic Manuscripts in the British Museum.
The Catalogue of Persian Manuscripts in the British Museum.

Major sources for the pursuance of the observations of this essay:

Ameer 'Ali, *The Spirit of Islam* (London, undated).
A. J. Arberry, *Sufism* (London, 1956).
Sir Thomas Arnold (and Alfred Guillaume), *The Legacy of Islam* (Oxford, 1931).
T. W. Arnold, *The Preaching of Islam* (London, 1913).
Faridu'd-Din Attar, *Muslim Saints and Mystics*, translated by A. J. Arberry (Chicago, 1966).
Abu Mansur al-Baghdadi, *Moslem Schisms and Sects*, translated by K. C. Seelye (New York, 1920).
Gertrude Lowthian Bell, *Poems from the Diwan of Hafiz* (London, 1897).
E. G. Browne, *Literary History of Persia*, Vols. I & II (London, 1909, 1915); Vols. III & IV (Cambridge, 1920, 1924).
Kenneth Cragg, *The Call of the Minaret* (Oxford, 1956).
T. J. De Boer, *The History of Philosophy in Islam*, translated by Edward R. Jones (London, 1933).
Dwight M. Donaldson, *Studies in Muslim Ethics* (London, 1953).
Richard N. Frye, *Islam and the West* (The Hague, 1957).
Sir Hamilton Gibb, *Mohammedanism* (Oxford, 1957).
Philip K. Hitti, *Islam and the West* (Princeton, 1962).
Afzal Iqbal, *Diplomacy in Islam* (Lahore, 1962).
T. Izutsu, *Ethico Religious Concepts in the Qur'an* (Montreal, 1966).
God and Man in the Koran. (The Keio Institute of Cultural & Linguistic Studies, Tokyo, 1964).
Muhammad Zafrulla Khan, *Islam; Its Meaning for the Modern Man* (New York, 1962).

Reuben Levy, *The Social Structure of Islam* (Cambridge, 1962).
Bernard Lewis and P. M. Hold (eds.), *Historians of the Middle East* (Oxford, 1962).
D. B. Macdonald, *Development of Muslim Theology, Jurisprudence and Constitutional Theory* (London, 1903).
De Lacy O'Leary, *Arabic Thought and its Place in History* (London, 1922).
———, *How Greek Science Passed to the Arabs* (London, 1948).
Constance E. Padwick, *Muslim Devotions* (London, 1961).
Fazlur Rahman, *Islam* (New York, 1968).
Jalalu'd-Din Rumi, *The Mathnawi*. Translated with commentary by R. A. Nicholson. E. J. W. Gibb Series. 9 Vols. (Cambridge, 1925-40).
Joseph Schacht, *An Introduction to Islamic Law* (Oxford, 1964).
Wilfred Cantwell Smith, *Islam in Modern History* (Princeton, 1957)
Gustave E. Von Grunebaum (ed.), *Unity and Variety in Muslim Civilization* (Chicago, 1955).
W. Montgomery Watt, *Islam and the Integration of Society* (Evanston, 1961).
———, *Muhammad at Mecca* (Oxford, 1960).
———, *Muhammad at Medina* (Oxford, 1962).
R. A. Nicholson, *Literary History of the Arabs* (London, 1914).

The author of this essay is particularly indebted to the eloquent and most thoughtful book by Afzal Iqbal entitled *Diplomacy in Islam* (Lahore, 1962).

CHAPTER FIVE

THE IMPACT OF NEW WORLD DISCOVERY UPON EUROPEAN THOUGHT OF MAN

Ernest J. Burrus, S.J.

It would be tempting to try to parallel the discovery of the New World with the landing of the first men on the moon. When scholars and statesmen began to realize the consequences of Columbus' voyages, they wrote, "This is the greatest event since the birth and death of Christ."[1] Modern scientists and national leaders have been even bolder in qualifying the lunar landing as "the greatest event in the history of mankind."[2]

Hundreds of millions of people watched on television as Armstrong and Aldrin emerged from the space capsule almost at the very instant they made their historic move. Newspapers and other media of communication reinforced the first and instantaneous impact upon men throughout the world.

It would be all too easy for us moderns to imagine something similar in regard to the discovery of two vast continents—a truly New World. Closer study, however, shows that precisely because the discovery was such an unexpected and overwhelming event, it took several generations to grasp its real significance. But, for the very reason that it took Europeans so long to realize its full import, its effects were all the more profound, extensive, and enduring.

In the course of two centuries, the discovery, exploration, settlement, and exploitation of the New World succeeded in exerting their deep and lasting influence upon every phase of European thought and life—religious, social, political, intellectual, economic, and countless others. Inasmuch as it is impossible, in such a brief study as this, to consider these numerous and disparate effects, I shall limit my attention to the most important; namely, to the religious impact upon European Christian thought, especially the Hispanic, of the opening up of the New World in the sixteenth and seventeenth centuries as this had a bearing on the concept of human unity.

The New World enterprise possessed a dimension thus far lacking

in our modern space voyages—the discovery of fellow men. Consequently, Europeans took an interest not only in the natural resources of the new lands, but also in their inhabitants. Very early
in the history of the dealings of Europeans with the American
natives, two problems emerged which had the most profound effect
upon European Christian thought: the origin of the inhabitants,
and their rights. At the very time answers to these two questions
were being sought, discoverers, explorers, settlers, and especially
missionaries, reported that the Indians were intelligent, and that
they were also capable and worthy of receiving the Christian Faith.

I. *The Origin of the Indians—a Riddle*

In order to understand more fully the centuries-long discussion
on the origin of the American Indians, it will help if the reader keeps
in mind the evolving geographic concepts of the time. As Europeans
probed the new lands to the north and south in order to find the
Asia they already knew, or to discover at least a passage to it, they
gradually came to realize that the regions discovered by Columbus
were not a prolongation of Asia but two new continents lying
athwart the route to the Far East.[3]

Here is a very brief conspectus of the key discoveries which
established this fundamental reality. The Portuguese Gonzalo
Coelho explored, in 1501-1502, the lands south of Brazil, entering
the estuary of La Plata and then sailing around to Patagonia at the
tip of the southern continent. One of the participants of the expedition, the Florentine Amerigo Vespucci, on returning to Europe
and realizing that such an area could not constitute any portion of
Asia, wrote, in 1502, a booklet with the significant title of "New
World" (*Mundus Novus*). It was first published in 1503, and it
immediately became a best-seller throughout the Old World,
completely revolutionizing the geographical concepts hitherto held
about the lands discovered by Columbus.[4] Vespucci's conviction
was recorded cartographically in 1507 by Martin Waldseemüller in
his *Cosmographiae Introductio* (Saint Dié, Lorraine), where for the
first time the southern land mass is represented as a continent and
is called "America." This "Fourth Part" (*Quarta Pars*) of the world
now takes its place besides Europe, Africa, and Asia. More than two
and a half centuries will have to pass before man can add the fifth
and sixth "parts"—North America and Australia.

Vespucci's conviction was confirmed by Balboa's discovery of the Pacific in 1513, and the voyage of Magellan and Cano in 1519 to 1521, which was not merely the first circumnavigation of the globe but also furnished experimental proof of the presence of a vast ocean lying between the southern part of the New World and Asia.

None of these discoveries, however, clarified the extent of the northern land mass and its relation to Asia. For more than two centuries—until 1728, when Vitus Bering sailed through the strait which now bears his name—map-makers continued to represent North America as extending far northwestward to link up with northern China or some other part of Asia.[5] Their next step was to separate the northern portion of the New World from Asia. The strait dividing the two land masses was called "Anian." This mythical passage was usually located several thousand miles west of the real strait separating North America (Alaska) from Russia.

The first question—the origin of the Indians of the New World—might seem to be, at best, of scientific interest to a very few scholars. In attempting, however, to find a satisfactory solution to the problem, an important truth was postulated that had a revolutionary implication: all men formed one and the same community. The lands discovered were a new world, but not a totally different world; their inhabitants, in turn, must have come from one or more of the other continents, inasmuch as no one held seriously that the Indians were autochthonous or indigenous in the sense that they had their ultimate origin in the New World. Accordingly, Europeans reasoned that the natives of the Americas had come either across the Atlantic from Europe or Africa, or that they had migrated across the Pacific, or that they had come by land from Asia. For more than three centuries, Europeans discussed the problem and debated its implications with an intensity we cannot fully appreciate today.

The books by Acosta, García, Grotius, Laet, and many others, dealing with the origin of the Indians, were published in every European country and language.[6] Their theories as to who these natives were, whence they had come, and how they had reached the New World, were taken over and widely diffused by more popular writers. Regardless of the theories held, all writers—scientific and popular—agreed in proclaiming the unity of the hunam race.[7]

II. *The Equality of the Indians*

Such accord, however, in regard to the unity of the human

family, did not always lead to an acknowledgment of equality of rights. The discussion of this second problem had a vastly greater impact on European Christian thought. The ultimate theoreticals answer, as we shall see, was that they did have the same rights as Europeans. This equality of rights derived from intellectual and moral equality. Such seemingly obvious answers were not readily found nor conceded, because far too much was at stake. Thus, if the *conquistadores* and settlers admitted that the Indians had the same rights as the Europeans, then, of course, they would not be allowed to enslave them, force them to toil in the mines, workshops, farms, ranches, and homes, take away their personal belongings, despoil their places of worship, and deprive them of self-government.

Let us look at the steps taken to arrive at this principle of equality and its difficult implementation. The defense of the Indians before 1700 was undertaken by numerous Christian humanitarians. Their efforts constitute an important chapter in the struggle to effect a sense of universal Christian unity based on justice and charity. These champions of the natives' equality and, consequently, of their freedom had a discouragingly difficult task to face; nor are we to imagine that they were always and everywhere successful, even in theory. I think that we moderns can most easily follow their efforts if they are seen both chronologically and thematically, despite partial overlapping: A. *Before Las Casas (1492-1514)*; B. *Las Casas, Vitoria, and Vera Cruz (1514-1584)*; C. *Spanish Legislation in behalf of the Natives (1504-1681)*; D. *Brazil (1500-1700)*; E. *European Knowledge of and Attitude toward the Evangelization of the Indians (1493-1700)*.

A. Before Las Casas (1492-1514)

So desirous was Columbus to inform Europeans of his extraordinary discoveries that he did not wait to set foot on the Spanish soil from which he had sailed; but, as soon as the returned to the Canaries, he sent ahead an account of his successful voyage. When he landed in Lisbon, he dispatched a second message. Already on March 30, 1493, Isabel and Ferdinand answered his letters. A few days later, he gave them a personal account at their court in Barcelona, Spain.[8]

How rapidly the Holy See learned about the epochal discoveries and how quickly it reacted to them is evident from the solemn declarations issued by Alexander VI: the *Inter caetera*, dated May 3, 1493, and the *Eximiae devotionis*, proclaimed the next day.[9]

In the first document, the pope praises the Spanish sovereigns for their zeal in promoting the Christian Faith, as evidenced by two historic events: their liberation of the province of Granada from the Saracen yoke and promotion of the voyage of Columbus. He, in turn, is credited with discovering islands inhabited by natives who believe in a universal Creator and are anxious to embrace the Faith.[10] The pontiff exhorts the sovereigns to continue in their zeal for the Faith; and, in order to encourage them to do so, he grants them the islands and the mainlands already found, and those still to be discovered to the west of a longitudinal line drawn around the globe at 100 leagues west of the Azores and Cape Verde Islands.

In the second document, Alexander VI grants to the Spanish sovereigns, for the conversion of the natives of the new western lands, the same graces, privileges, and powers as already conferred on the Portuguese king for Africa and the Orient.

Two additional papal documents were issued before the close of 1493: *Piis fidelium*, June 26, 1493, and *Dudum siquidem*, September 27, 1493.[11] In the first message, the pope grants to the first missionary to the New World, Bernardo Boil, and his companions, the spiritual powers necessary to effect their work of evangelization. In the second document, the pontiff clarifies and extends the concessions made to the Spanish sovereigns in the *Eximiae devotionis* by granting to them the islands and other lands 100 leagues west of the Azores, not only in the west but also in the east, to be discovered by sailing westward and southward.

While Columbus prepared his second voyage, the Spanish sovereigns were busy making certain that the evangelic aspect of the enterprise would not be forgotten. They wrote to their official representatives in Rome in order to secure spiritual authorization for the missionaries designated to accompany the discoverer. They also drew up a detailed instruction emphasizing the preaching of the Gospel to the natives and treating them with all kindness —transgressors were to be punished severely. Columbus set sail on September 24, 1493, accompanied by four priests and two brothers— the first Christian mission from Europe to the New World.

Before the year 1493 was out, Fray Román Panes, a Hieronymite missionary, compiled at Columbus' request a treatise on the natives of the islands, stressing their origin and religious beliefs. Its twenty-six short chapters constitute the first ethnographic report on the inhabitants of the New World.[12]

During the next two decades, three thoughts were to dominate the correspondence of the Spanish sovereigns with Columbus, and with the respective civil and religious authorities: none of the Indians—not even those brought by the discoverer to Spain—were to be enslaved, rather they must be taught to believe and live as true Christians, and finally Spaniards in sufficient numbers were to make the overseas dominions their new home.

The missionaries working in the islands sent in first-hand reports, emphasizing the favorable disposition of the natives towards the Faith, and then pleading for fellow helpers in the harvest.

Papal documents encouraged the efforts of the Spanish sovereigns and of the missionaries by stressing the importance of the evangelization of the new lands and by applying the ecclesiastical tithes to the building of churches and the maintenance of the preachers of the Gospel.

It was not easy for the Spanish authorities to know what was taking place at such a vast distance. Already in 1503, a decree was issued which could be used later on as a pretext to enslave the natives. Word had reached Spain that some of the islanders were cannibals. The question arose as to how the Spanish soldiers were to deal with "these offenders of the natural law"? The decision arrived at in Spain read: "Those who refuse to be dissuaded from their practice are to be made prisoners and brought to Spain."[13]

Fifteen hundred and four is an important date in the evangelization of the New World. On November 15, Julius II established the first three episcopal sees in the Americas and appointed bishops to them.[14] Unlike England, which was never to allow her American colonists a bishop of their own, Spain insisted at this early date on the constitution of a separate hierarchy for her overseas dominions, just as later she would encourage the establishment of printing presses and the founding of universities. Spain looked upon her new lands across the sea as an extension of the homeland.

Queen Isabel, in drawing up her last will and testament in 1504, the year of her death, wished to insure the evangelization and good treatment of the Indians. Las Casas would later often cite the document in their defense, and the definitive Spanish legislation (1681) would incorporate its key passages.[15]

On July 28, 1508, Julius II, through the *Universalis Ecclesiae,* granted to King Ferdinand and his successors universal patronage over the Church in the New World.[16] The pontiff's intention was to insure royal protection and assistance for the evangelization of those extensive lands.

The law itself, as we have seen, was on the side of the natives' freedom; greedy and unscrupulous *conquistadores* and settlers, however, only too often disregarded law in order to subject them to virtual slavery. On December 20, 1511, the Dominican Friar Antonio Montesino "preached a violent sermon in Santo Domingo against the cruelties of the Spaniards and their mistreatment of the Indians...Montesino gave the King such a shocking account of conditions that Ferdinand immediately called a junta to consider the matter."[17] The commission declared that the natives were free, that they were to be instructed in the Faith with all possible diligence, that their work was to be remunerated and was not to interfere with the instruction in and practice of the Faith, that they were to have property of their own, that they were to have contact with the Spanish settlers so that they might be better and more rapidly instructed in the Faith.[18]

B. Las Casas, Vitoria, and Vera Cruz (1514-1584)

For seventy years, the Indians found tireless protectors in these three outstanding champions of their rights. All three wrote treatises which influenced Europeans to sympathize with the plight of the American Indians and to regard them as fellow men with basically the same rights as their own.[19]

The Dominican Bartolomé de las Casas was responsible, in very great part, for creating the Black Legend against Spain. His intention in his writings was to defend the Indians he loved and to awaken the conscience of his countrymen against the terrible injustices of some of the soldiers and settlers. His publications, however, were taken over by the enemies of Spain and used as mighty weapons of propaganda against her. Most Europeans forgot to reflect on the great freedom allowed to Spanish writers in defending the natives so openly, a freedom other colonial powers would not permit when they attained to a similar position; later, they would also forget very conveniently that their own treatment of the natives was not as benign or just as Spain's.

This widespread campaign of hatred against Spain served at least one good purpose: Europeans were made aware of the plight of the Indians and their need of a more humane and Christian treatment. The Old World reacted in their favor, coming to regard them as fellow Christians.

For more than half a century—from 1514 until his death in 1566—Las Casas was tireless in his efforts. He could cite his own experience and observation in the islands, in Mexico, in Vera Paz (Guatemala), and in South America. He could rightly claim the approval of his basic convictions by both ecclesiastical and civil authorites, even by Charles V and Philip II. He was made bishop of Chiapas. His influence was so great that the New Laws (1542-1543) in behalf of the Indians were proclaimed at his insistence.[20] His prolific writings —fierce invectives against Spanish destruction and cruelty, treatises suggesting a more humane treatment of the natives and a more effective way of converting them, his disputations against Sepulveda in behalf of the natives' rights, an extensive history of the Indies from the discovery of the New World to his own times—were in part widely diffused throughout Europe during and after his own long lifetime and in part are being published in our own day. In all his writings he refuted the claim of some Spaniards to a natural superiority over the Indians.[21]

No one ever regretted more than Las Casas himself the illogical injustice he once committed by suggesting the importation of more Negro slaves to perform the heavy tasks which were killing off the natives. His love for the Indians led him to suggest the use of Negro slaves, so common at the time in Europe.[22] Here, again, the Spaniard was extending to the overseas dominions an institution accepted in the homeland.

Unlike Las Casas and Vera Cruz, the Dominican Francisco de Vitoria was never in the Indies. In formulating his classic defense of the natives, he had to rely on the reports from missionaries and officials who had worked among the American Indians. The question proposed to him for an answer was the justice or injustice of Spanish dominion over the natives. Unlike Las Casas, he did not try to solve numerous other problems linked with Spain's claim to the Indies, e.g., how best to effect the evangelization of the Americas.

Whether one grants that Vitoria is the founder of international law or not, his great merit derives from the undisputed originality and systematic study of the juridical position of the Indians as equal members of an international community.[23] Making use of all the traditional sources to solve his central problem, he came to the same conclusion as the scholars who had investigated the origin of the Indians: they formed part of the world-wide human family; and like Las Casas, he insisted on their equality, rejecting the Spaniards' claim to natural superiority over them. Vitoria now brought the two conclusions together: the natives of the New World are the equals of Europeans as members of a universal community. Had Vitoria's contention been accepted at the time, Spain's enterprise would have been more humane in practice, and advantageous to both conqueror and conquered.

Vitoria gave both of his series of public lectures on the Indians at the University of Salamanca in 1539, but they were not printed until 1567. Their broad scholarship and cogent reasoning had a profound effect on European thinkers in general and on Spanish lawgivers in particular. Even before they appeared in print, manuscript copies had left their mark, especially on the Las Casas-Sepulveda dispute of 1550.

Vitoria had planned on studying three fundamental themes of the conquest and settlement of Hispanic America: (1) the right which the Spaniards had to take over the natives, (2) the temporal and civil rights which the Spanish sovereigns had acquired over them, (3) the rights which the same sovereigns or the Church had over them in the religious and spiritual spheres. In his two treatises, Vitoria took up only the first of these three themes, never finding the opportunity to deal with the other two.[24]

The Augustinian Friar, pupil of Vitoria, and close friend of Las Casas, Alonso de la Vera Cruz, discussed all three of Vitoria's problems in his political-science treatises, and in the lengthy volume, *Speculum coniugiorum*. The latter work, which extols the intelligence and morality of the natives of Mexico, especially the Tarascans, first appeared in Mexico City in 1556, and was reprinted thrice in Spain and Italy before the end of the century.

Vera Cruz's first treatise was a three-fold defense of the rights of the natives: their personal freedom, their self-government, and their personal ownership of property. His second treatise set forth and defended the privileges to be accorded to the natives, in particular exemption from the payment of tithes.[25]

The first treatise, *On the Rights of the Indians*, the earliest extant university course in the Americas, was discussed in his inaugural classes at the University of Mexico (1553-1554) and given in briefer form to a general audience in 1554. It was incredibly bold for the Augustinian to begin his university teaching with a defense of the Indians and a public condemnation of the injustices committed against them by many of his hearers. Particularly remarkable was his insistence that the natives should not be deprived of their lands; in this he was far ahead of his times.

The second treatise, *On the Privileges of the Indians*, was explained in his university classes in 1554-1555, but civil and religious authorities intervened to prevent his repeating its contents to a larger audience in 1555.

His attempts to get the two treatises published ultimately led to his being summoned by Philip II in 1562 to Spain, where he remained until 1573. He spent these eleven years in Spain in behalf of the American Indians, insisting personally with Philip II on their just treatment and writing to Pius V in their behalf. He continued to keep in touch with Las Casas and did not shrink from embracing the just cause of Fray Luis de León, fellow Augustinian and professor at the University of Salamanca, his own alma mater.[26]

With greater calm and scientific depth than his Dominican friend, Bartolomé de las Casas, Vera Cruz defended the rights and privileges of the natives and condemned the injustices committed against them. He was careful not to make sweeping and unfounded claims of Spanish cruelty. He was not the proponent of either a black or a white legend: he strove to find out the facts and to correct the undeniable and tragic abuses. He was not so narrow-minded as to think that all Spaniards who crossed the Atlantic were necessarily evil. He was deeply convinced that each of the two ethnic groups had much to give and share with the other; it was to their mutual advantage to live and work together—even to govern, and to own and till the land together.[27]

Vera Cruz had an evident advantage over his better-known professor of theology at the University of Salamanca, Vitoria, a theorist who depended on others for his knowledge of the New World. Vera Cruz had been living and working among the Indians for some seventeen years before he composed the treatise in their defense. He had seen the injustices which he related, but he did not exaggerate them nor did he forget the advantages which European culture and Christianity could bring to the Indians. As a result of this experience and attitude, his treatise is more objective than the syllogisms and distinctions of Vitoria. His statements could be easily checked for their scrupulous accuracy, and they could be readily applied to actual conditions in the Americas.

Las Casas, Vitoria, and Vera Cruz were not the only defenders of the natives whose writings helped to form, among Europeans in general and among Spaniards in particular, a consciousness of a universal human family possessing equal rights; but the principles they set forth and defended are typical of the period and most profoundly influenced other persons.[28]

An important by-product of the writings of these and other political scientists who defended the rights of the American Indians was the increasing European awareness of the need of a broader re-interpretation of the old law of nations (*ius gentium*)—one which, if it did not completely coincide with our modern concept of international law, at least came very close to it.[29]

C. Spanish Legislation in behalf of the Natives (1504-1681)

The patronage of the king of Spain over the Church in the Indies resulted in the closest if not always the most harmonious cooperation of State and Church. It is not surprising, then, that the laws and regulations emanating from the two jurisdictions should so closely resemble each other.

The more personal attention given to the problems of the Indies by Isabel and Ferdinand could not continue with the growth of the Spanish dominions, but had to be entrusted first to the Council of Castile and then to a special department or ministry, the Council of the Indies. This ministry, constituted by a president and counsellors, was directly responsible to the king.[30] It supervised every activity in the Indies: directly, the temporal (economic, military, political, etc.); and, indirectly, the spiritual.

We are concerned here with Spanish legislation, both civil and ecclesiastical, only insofar as it dealt with the rights of the natives and came to the knowledge of the European public. Because of the progressive or evolving nature of the laws for the Indians, they can best be studied chronologically, especially since subsequent codes usually included earlier legislation.

We find the first important set of decrees in behalf of the natives promulgated in 1504. Their very title is significant: "Laws and ordinances issued recently by his Majesty for the government of the Indies, the good treatment and conservation of the Indians."[31]

The 1512-1513 laws are the earliest attempt at a basic and more general legislation to protect the natives and to promote their evangelization. "The royal ordinances for the good government and treatment of the natives" are commonly termed the "Laws of Burgos" from the city where they were first drawn up. They were promulgated by Queen Juana, and were published several times.[32]

The expressed purpose of this pioneer code was the conversion of the natives. One of the principal means specified was for the Indians to live in the towns of the Spanish colonists. This arrangement, it was argued, would bring them important advantages: better religious instruction in and practice of the Faith; more effective protection, especially for the sick and weak (women and children). As is obvious, such a stipulation implied the acceptance of an institution fiercely opposed by Las Casas—the *encomienda* and its concomitant *repartimiento*.[33]

The expedition of Cortés to Mexico in 1519 and the fall of its principal city in 1521 radically changed the Spanish overseas enterprise from sporadic attempts at colonizing a few primitive islands in the Gulf of Mexico to the conquest and settlement of a vast land mass with a relatively advanced civilization. Cortés and later Pizarro were the conquerors of two continents for Spain.

The first important civil legislation for this changed situation was the code issued by Charles V on December 4, 1528, addressed to the *Audiencia* of New Spain and to its two bishops, Julián Garcés of Tlaxcala, and Juan de Zumárraga of Mexico City.[34]

On July 2, 1524, less than three years after the capitulation of Mexico City, the first ecclesiastical meeting was held there to determine several urgent problems regarding the conversion of the Indians and the administration of the Sacraments to them. The missionaries wanted to know in particular whether native marriages contracted before the reception of baptism were to be regarded as valid. When the local ecclesiastical junta could not decide the question, it was submitted first to Cardinal Cajetan and then to Paul III.[35]

The Second Mexican ecclesiastical gathering was held in 1539. The three bishops of Mexico, the commissary general of the Franciscans, the provincial superiors of the three religious Orders (Franciscans, Dominicans, and Augustinians), and many theological experts attended the discussions, which dealt mainly with the administration of baptism.[36] All children in danger of death, obviously, were to receive this Sacrament; but under what conditions was it to be administered to adult natives? How much instruction and knowledge of the Faith was to be demanded of them before they might receive it?

In 1538 Las Casas again returned to Spain in order to defend the rights of the Indians and to secure additional missionaries. In a conversation with Cardinal Loaysa, president of the Council of the Indies, Las Casas pleaded so insistently in behalf of the suffering natives that the prelate ordered competent officials to meet and discuss the problem in Valladolid (1541-1542). Las Casas himself submitted memoranda on the destruction already wrought and the remedies to be adopted. The practical result of the Valladolid meeting was the promulgation of the 1542-1543 laws.[37] So violent, however, was the reaction in the colonies over the attempted abolition of the *repartimiento* ordered by this code that it was thought more prudent to suspend it in most regions. After the vision of such bright hopes for better treatment of the natives, this reversal of policy was a heart-breaking defeat for Las Casas.

The 1551-1552 Lima Council was the first of its kind to be held in the Indies. Some of the key topics discussed and determined by it were the following: the religious instruction to be imparted to the natives, their freedom in the acceptance of baptism, what Sacraments were to be administered to them, how to promote the work of the missionaries and of parish priests.[38]

In 1555 a similar council was held in Mexico City. It took up much the same problems as the Lima Council but dealt with them at far greater length.[39]

Archbishop Montúfar convoked the second Mexican Council in 1565. After ordering the exact observance of the Tridentine decrees in the dioceses under its jurisdiction, it took up the administration of the Sacraments to the Indians; it also insisted that parish priests learn the native languages. The greater part of the enactments and decrees, however, unlike those of the First Mexican Council, had to do not with the Indians but with the Spanish colonists.[40]

The earliest codification of the Spanish colonial laws appeared in Mexico City in 1563. It contained all the laws regarding the Indians promulgated by the home government from 1525 to 1563. The edition was prepared by Vasco de Puga and was re-issued at least twice. The newly published code bore eloquent witness in Europe to the efforts of the Spanish government in behalf of the native population of New Spain.[41]

The second council of Lima was held in 1567-1568. It stressed the qualities to be required of the ministers to the Indians, their practical mastery of the native languages, the importance of personal good example to be given to their charges, their obligation not to demand too much from the natives (the administration of the Sacraments was to be gratuitous); the conferment of the Sacraments in general, and of baptism, confession, confirmation, communion, matrimony, and extreme unction, in particular; the building and maintenance of adequate churches for the Indians; and the extirpation of idolatory and superstition.[42]

A new code of civil laws for the Indians was drawn up in 1571. As was the case with preceding governmental legislation, this code also dealt with the work of evangelization, conversion, and religious administration of the natives.[43]

The most important Church legislation in Spanish colonial history emanated from the Third Councils of Lima (1582-1583) and Mexico City (1585). The decrees of the Lima assembly regulated the religious life of the Spanish colonists and the Indians of South America (Brazil excluded) until the close of Spain's dominion. Those of the Mexican council governed the rest of the Spanish overseas countries, the Philippines and Marianas inclusive, during the same period.[44]

The enactments of the two councils in behalf of the Indians were more particularized and extensive than those of the preceding councils. In the light of longer experience, they dealt with every phase of the religious life of the natives and of the work of the missionaries serving them. Both councils specified what elements of Christian doctrine and ritual should be stressed in the apostolate of the Indians; the councils dared to contravene numerous royal decrees which ordered that all instruction in the Faith should be given exclusively in Spanish, by insisting that the natives should be taught in their own languages. Much attention was given to the education of the Indian children. More specific instructions were given for the administration of the Sacraments with insistence that it should be gratuitous. Discussed, too, was the all-important question of ordaining natives to the priesthood.

Already in 1570, the Spanish government had ordered the more systematic and complete codification of all its laws concerning the natives, but it was not until 1596 that the first four volumes of this extensive compilation (1,845 pages) appeared.[45] It was a monumental testimony of Spain's solicitude for the natives at the very time

Europeans were scandalized at the destruction and cruelty claimed by Las Casas.

The productions of few Spanish jurists had as wide an influence as the published writings of Juan de Solórzano Pereira, professor of law at the University of Salamanca, his alma mater, *oidor* of the Lima *Audiencia* (1609-1627), and counsellor of the Councils of Castile and of the Indies (1629-1644). He wrote two huge folio volumes to establish Spain's just claim to the Indies and to prove her humane treatment of their inhabitants. The first volume appeared in Madrid in 1629, and the second in 1639; a complete second edition in two volumes was issued in Lyons, France, in 1672; and a third in Madrid in 1777. A Spanish translation in one volume followed in 1648, and was re-issued in three subsequent editions. The work not only summarizes, with indication of sources and authorities, the abundant Spanish legislation in behalf of the Indians, but also includes the texts of numerous pertinent documents.[46]

The last official and most important code of colonial laws was the "Digest of the laws of the kingdoms of the Indies" (*Recopilación de leyes de los reynos de las Indias*), first published as a three-volume work in Madrid in 1681, and frequently re-issued. Whereas the entire compilation in nine books is pertinent to our theme, it is the sixth which is wholly dedicated to the rights, obligations, and activities of the natives.[47] An entire section has to do with their freedom; another deals with their protectors or defenders; four sections regulate their dealings with the colonists through the *encomienda* and *repartimiento*; the twenty-three laws of section ten insist on the good treatment to be accorded to the Indians; one of the longest sections (forty-nine laws) regulates in general the vexed problem of the personal service to be performed by them; and six sections deal with more specific problems having to do with Indian labor.

No one will want to pretend that the Spanish laws, published for exclusive application in the New World but also in order that all men everywhere might see what rights were officially recognized in regard to the natives, were perfect. It is easy to detect two flaws in such legislation: first, it did not insist on absolute and complete legal equality of the Indians with the Spaniards; secondly, even these compromise laws, once promulgated, were not always put into practice.

These laws, however, did recognize in the natives fellow Christians and dared to proclaim this truth to all. This step forward toward more perfect equality of all men before the law and a more profound sense of Christian unity was due to the insistence of churchmen and missionaries such as Paul III, Pius V, and Clement VIII, Garcés, Montesino, Vasco de Quiroga, and Kino; of political scientists such as Las Casas, Vitoria, Vera Cruz, Focher, and Acosta; of rulers such as Isabel, Ferdinand, Charles V, and Philip II in Spain, and Mendoza, Velasco, and Toledo in the colonies.[48]

D. Brazil (1500-1700)

We have thus far restricted our attention to the Spanish enterprise in the Indies. We must not, however, overlook Brazil, the Portuguese colony and the largest country in Latin America. In the next section of this study, where we come to speak about the European knowledge and attitude toward the evangelization of the Indians from 1493 to 1700, we shall include the key publications which dealt with both Spanish and Portuguese America; in the present section we want to discuss merely the same two points we have already considered in regard to Spain's overseas dominions: first, the origin of the Brazilian Indians; secondly, their equality before the law with Europeans.

1. Origin of the Brazilian Natives

As with the natives in Spanish America, so also in regard to those of Brazil, we are not trying to determine with scientific accuracy when they came or from where they came, but are only pointing out that the theories propounded in colonial times as to their origin helped to form in the minds of Europeans a concept of unity of mankind. This came about through the insistence of those writers who dealt with the problem that all the Indians of the New World had migrated there from one or more of the "old continents," and hence were a part of the human family.

The classic writers on the origin of the American Indians, from Acosta to Laet, made no distinction between the natives living in the Spanish and in the Portuguese overseas dominions, and accordingly incorporated all of them into the world community.

2. Equality of the Brazilian Indians

Continental Portuguese America was discovered and very partially explored at an early date. Pedro Alvares Cabral, in March of 1500, shortly after the return of Vasco da Gama from his epochal discovery of the route to Calicut, India, set out for the same Orient via the New World. Cabral reached Brazil at about eighteen degrees south latitude, near the present Porto Seguro. Between 1500 and 1503, Portugal sent out four unsuccessful expeditions to the Brazilian coast in order to follow up the discovery made by Cabral.[49]

Her great overseas empire was to be built elsewhere—in the Far East—although later she would settle along the coastal fringe of her American colony and ultimately establish her sway far inland. As in Spanish America, so also in Brazil, the activity of the Church was under the patronage of the colonizing sovereigns.

The settlement of Brazil followed a pattern partially different from that of Spanish America. No universities or printing presses were established during the centuries we are studying. Thus, Brazil was far more isolated from European awareness than the Spanish overseas dominions. Portuguese America, however, did not lack zealous and competent defenders of the rights of the natives; but their defense could not receive the attention given in Europe to Las Casas, Vitoria, Vera Cruz, and others who published their treatises.[50]

The Jesuit missionary Manuel da Nóbrega's "Dialogue on the Conversion of the Natives", written about 1557-1558, was not published until 1880, although manuscript copies may well have exerted considerable contemporary influence on missionaries, ecclesiastical authorities, and civil leaders. Nóbrega defends the intellectual and moral aptitude of the Indians for the reception and practice of the Christian Faith. He urges gathering them into centers and preventing them from warring on each other and continuing in their cannibalism. His greatest hope lay in the education of the native children to a better way of life.[51]

On May 8, 1558, Nóbrega sent his "Observations on Conditions in Brazil" to Father Miguel de Torres, provincial superior of the Portuguese Jesuits and confessor of the Queen. He suggested a six-fold law to be observed by the Brazilian Indians: forbid them from engaging in wars and eating human flesh, insist that they have only one wife, oblige them to wear clothes, banish their medicine men, demand that they act justly towards one another and towards the Christians, and have them come together in villages adjoining sufficient land for their needs.[52]

In both of his writings Nóbrega insists on the capacity and worthiness of the Indians to become Christians; in his opinion, not innate racial inferiority but lack of opportunity and environment have kept them from the benefits of a higher culture and a nobler way of life.

The defense of the natives undertaken by the later Jesuit missionary, António Vieira (1608-1697), had a far greater influence on European thought because he returned several times to Portugal to plead in their behalf; he preached numerous sermons in their defense, some of which were published during his lifetime or shortly afterwards. Through his tireless correspondence with the Portuguese king and queen and with the highest civil and ecclesiastical authorities of the land, he obtained favorable legislation in behalf of the Brazilian Indians.[53]

E. European Knowledge of and Attitude toward the Evangelization of the Indians (1493-1700)

In this concluding section I should like to point out the main types of publications which recorded the evangelical apostolate among the Indians and were most influential in informing Europeans about a "Christendom across the seas." Such publications belonged predominantly to the following categories: current events; mission reports; histories of the European enterprises in the New World; ecclesiastical histories and problems; religious chronicles; and, finally, biographies of apostolic workers.

1. Current Events

Throughout the colonial period, most of the key discoveries and events were quickly recorded in print. Thus, Columbus' letters of his first voyage were published several times in 1493, that is during the very year of his return to Europe. The Italian Pietro Martire, soldier, priest, legate of the Spanish King to the Egyptian Sultan, and official chronicler of Spain, wrote and published numerous works on the exploits of the Spaniards and Portuguese in the Americas and the Orient. He may well be termed "Europe's pioneer reporter of the overseas enterprise." Las Casas began his influential publications on "history in the making" with his 1552 Seville edition of the "Summary of the Destruction of the Indies."

2. Mission Reports

Although current events in Portuguese and French America were not reflected in printed works as fully as those in Spanish America, Europeans did learn about them from other types of publications, in particular from mission reports. Today such accounts interest the scholar for the light they throw on the history of the period, the character of the natives and their reaction to a different way of life, the languages used by them, the natural resources discovered, the voyages and explorations undertaken, and other similar topics. The mission reports reaching Europeans during the sixteenth and seventeenth centuries, however, aroused a very different interest at the time: the interest was actual, not historical. The missionary letters and other accounts told of events still in the course of development; they revealed a new and fascinating world; they were looked forward to with the most intense anticipation; and they were read with the greatest attention and interest.

3. Histories of the European Enterprises in the New World

The pioneer general history of the Americas was by the first official chronicler of the New World, Gonzalo Fernández de Oviedo y Valdés, who published his "General History of the Indies" at Seville in 1535. Oviedo had traveled extensively in the New World and could write with the authority of an eyewitness. He devoted many pages to the evangelization of the natives. This popular work took on European dimensions through two early translations: a French version appeared at Paris in 1556, and Ramusio included the history in his Venice edition of that same year.

Considering the relatively late start of the French in the New World, it is most surprising to find so early a general history of their undertaking as Marc Lescarbot's *Histoire de la Nouvelle France*, which first appeared at Paris in 1609.

Due to their exceptionally wide diffusion and intense interest, such books helped to awaken and increase a European awareness of the evangelical enterprise in the New World and the conditions of its inhabitants.

4. Ecclesiastical Histories and Problems

Instead of exclusively historical accounts of the universal Church, scholars of the period we are reviewing preferred a more juridical approach by studying specific problems. Even ecclesiastical histories of an exclusively national character were extremely rare and comparatively late.

The official Spanish chronicler, Gil González Dávila, published in two volumes (Madrid, 1649-1655) his *Teatro eclesiástico de la primitiva Iglesia de las Indias*. The work revealed to European readers a well-organized and progressive Christian community across the seas.

A popular and extensive study of the relations of non-Christians with Christians was Marquardus de Susannis' "Treatise on non-believers," first published at Venice in 1558, and frequently reprinted. The author dealt specifically with the Spanish conquest of the Indians and of the coercion permitted in order to bring them into the fold of Christ.

The numerous treatises and manuals on the administration of the Sacraments to the Indians helped to impress Europeans with the unity of the Christians in the Old and New Worlds. If the natives were worthy to receive the Sacraments—especially the Eucharist—then they were obviously to be regarded as fellow Christians.

5. Religious Chronicles

During more than two centuries, the religious Orders rather than the diocesan clergy carried the main burden of teaching the Indians of the Americas Christian doctrine, ritual, and a new way of life. Franciscan, Augustinian, Dominican, and Jesuit missionaries preached in the native languages to their charges in country or city churches and chapels, and taught the Indian children in elementary schools.

The numerous histories of their world-wide activities called increasing attention to their apostolate in the Americas and helped to inform Europeans of a growing Christian Church across the seas.

6. Biographies of Apostolic Workers

No other type of publication we are considering found such a popular demand or wide diffusion as the biographies of the missionaries working in the New World. The zeal of these men in behalf of a cause considered most noble and sacred appealed to fervent European Christians: for them the missionaries were Crusaders in the sublimest sense of the term. Through the biographies of such workers, high ideals were removed from the realm of abstraction and were incorporated in individuals whom they admired and even reverenced. This was particularly true of such missionaries as were considered or officially declared saints and martyrs of the Faith. Hence, the Church in the New World, especially during the first two centuries, was often equated with Christianity in its primitive fervor.

III. *Conclusion*

An important link between Europe and the overseas dominions was the constant flow of goods and wealth across the seas. A still more vital contact between the two worlds was the presence in the Americas of the most enterprizing citizens from the colonizing nations. Many policies of sovereigns and popes were determined or at least considerably modified by events in the Americas.

The historian who would deal more adequately with the present theme would have to analyze how profoundly the New World enterprize affected every phase of European life; even, as in turn, all European learning was called upon for the solution of the problems arising in the Americas.

NOTES

[1] See, e.g., M. Bataillon, "L'idée de la découverte de l'Amérique chez les Espagnols du XVIe siècle," in *Bulletin Hispanique*, LV (1953), p. 48: "Si, pour ces Espagnols, 'le plus grand événement depuis la création du monde, en mettant à part l'incarnation et la mort de celui que le créa, c'est la découverte des Indes'? Cette admirable formule, frappée en médaille, est de [Francisco López de] Gómara. Comment un événement de ce calibre échapperait-il à la Providence divine"?

[2] Cf. *Time* (August 1, 1969), p. 9, under the caption "Greatest Since Creation," the editors wrote: "To describe the feat, Nixon reached for a superlative and found a big one. 'This,' he announced, 'is the greatest week in the history of the world since the creation.' That seemed somewhat sweeping for a President who has instituted weekly religious services at the White House: in the Christian view, the birth of Christ surely must rank as a greater event in the world's chronology since *Genesis*." The Parisian *Le Monde* (October 10, 1969), p. 14, reported on the visit of the three astronauts: "Je suis heureux, leur déclara M. Pompidou, de saluer en vous les héros de la plus grande aventure humaine."

[3] I discuss these notions in my monograph, *Kino and the Cartography of Northwestern New Spain* (Tucson, Arizona, 1965), p. 28.

[4] On the discoveries of Vespucci, consult R. Levillier, *Americo Vespucio* (Madrid, 1966). The same author published a critical edition of the "New World" in *Mundus Novus : La carta de Vespucio que revolucionó la geografía* (Buenos Aires, 1956). Whether Columbus really deserves to be considered the discoverer of the New World and what precisely he did accomplish are questions which lie beyond the scope of the present essay; see E. O'Gorman, *La idea del descubrimiento de América* (Mexico City, 1951); also M. Bataillon and E. O'Gorman, *Dos concepciones de la tarea histórica con motivo de la idea del descubrimiento de América* (Mexico City, 1955).

[5] Numerous sea expeditions in the sixteenth century furnished a more accurate idea of the Pacific Coast of North America; cf. H. R. Wagner, *Spanish Voyages to the Northwest Coast of America in the Sixteenth Century* (San Francisco, 1929).

[6] Many others besides the four listed here wrote on the origin of the Indians. Outstanding among them was the Carmelite Antonio Vázquez de Espinosa, whose *Compendio y descripción de las Indias Occidentales* was not published until modern times (Washington, D.C., 1942, 1948).

[7] The unfavorable and bizarre opinions about Americans held by some Europeans belong, for the most part, to a later period; see A. Gerbi, *La disputa del Nuovo Mondo : Storia di una polemica, 1750-1900* (Milan and Naples, 1954).

[8] Consult R. Streit, *Bibliotheca Missionum*, vol. II, 1-2. Henceforth this work will be cited as B M. The first three volumes—the only ones to be referred to—were published in Münster-Aachen, 1916-1927.

[9] Details are given in B M, II, 2-4.

[10] See the pertinent text in F. J. Hernáez, *Colección de bulas*, 2 vols. (Brussels, 1879), I, 12.

[11] Cf. B M, II, 7, 9.

[12] For a summary of its contents and various editions, consult B M, II, 9.

[13] See B M, II, 14, § 44.

[14] The two papal documents are cited and analyzed in B M, II, 14-16.

[15] The important document is explained briefly in B M, II, 16; B M, I, 41, § 93, shows that it was already incorporated into the 1563 laws.

[16] The complete Latin text with a Spanish summary is given by Hernáez, *op. cit.*, I, 24-26.

[17] Quoted from H. R. Wagner and H. R. Parish, *The Life and Writings of Bartolomé de las Casas* (Albuquerque, N.M., 1967), p. 8.

[18] Explained in *op. cit.*, pp. 8-9.

[19] Dr. Lewis Hanke has written extensively on Las Casas. Unless stated otherwise, I shall cite his unpublished "All the Races of the World are Men," which synthesizes the ideas of Las Casas and the controversies they occasioned; this work is to appear as the Introduction to S. Poole's edition of Las Casas, *Apologia adversum Sepulvedam*. A handy edition of Vitoria's treatises is by T. Urdánoz, *Obras de Francisco de Vitoria : Relecciones teológicas* (Madrid, 1960). I am editing the unpublished works of Vera Cruz in five volumes, of which three appeared in Rome in 1968; the series bears the title of *The Writings of Alonso de la Vera Cruz*.

[20] A facsimile edition of the manuscript of these laws with a transcription is given by A. Muro Orejón, *Las leyes nuevas, 1542-1543* (Seville, 1945); for a study of these laws, see Wagner-Parish, *op. cit.*, pp. 108-120.

[21] Consult Hanke, *op. cit., passim*, especially section IV. On Sepúlveda's contrary conviction, see A. Losada, *Demócrates Segundo* (Madrid, 1951).

[22] See the numerous references in Wagner-Parish, *op. cit.*, p. 310 (Index, under "Slavery, Negro").

[23] Most editors of the works of Vitoria give him the title of "Founder of International Law;" but cf. B. Hamilton, *Political Thought in Sixteenth-Century Spain* (Oxford, 1963), p. 98: "The ancient concept of the *jus gentium* received new life in Spain through the discovery and conquest of the Americas. It would be absurd to credit any of these writers with being the 'founders' of international law, or even with having a clear notion of it in the modern sense. But their consciousness of living in an expanding world made them more aware of the unity of mankind and more anxious to assert it."

[24] See my edition of *The Writings of Alonso de la Vera Cruz*, 3 vols. (Rome, 1968), II, 65.

[25] Vol. IV of *op. cit.* will contain Vera Cruz's treatise on the privileges of the Indians.

[26] Details in *op. cit.*, I, 180.

[27] Discussed in *op. cit.*, II, 7.

[28] L. Hanke and A. Millares Carlo edited many such treatises and refer to others in *Cuerpo de documentos del siglo XVI sobre los derechos de España en las Indias y las Filipinas* (Mexico City, 1943).

[29] Consult *supra*, note 23.

[30] See E. Schäfer, *El Consejo de Indias*, 2 vols. (Seville, 1935-1947), I, 43-50.

[31] Details in B M, II, 17, § 50.

[32] A facsimile and Spanish text were edited by A. Muro Orejón, *Ordenanzas reales sobre los indios: Las leyes de 1512-13* (Seville, 1957). There is an English translation: L. B. Simpson, *The Laws of Burgos* (San Francisco, 1960).

[33] Hanke, *op. cit.*, section II, deals with Las Casas' opposition to these institutions. Through "encomienda" the Indians were entrusted to the care of Spaniards to be instructed in the Faith and taught a European way of life; "repartimiento" was the apportioning of the natives to work for the Spaniards

[34] Details in B M, II, 59, § 221.

[35] F. A. Lorenzana, in his edition of *Concilios provinciales primero y segundo de México* (Mexico City, 1769), pp. 1-10, published all extant documents concerning the first ecclesiastical meeting; cf. also B M, II, 53-54. On Paul III's 1537 defense of the Indians in reply to the letter of Julián Garcés, bishop of Tlaxcala, Mexico, see Hanke, *Estudios sobre Fray Bartolomé de las Casas* (Caracas, Venezuela, 1968), pp. 57-88.

[36] Details and sources in B M, II, 107-108.

[37] See *supra*, note 20.

[38] R. Vargas Ugarte, S. J., published the official acts and history in *Concilios Limenses*, 3 vols. (Lima, 1951-1952, 1954); on the first council, see I, 1-93; III, 1-24.

[39] Cf. Lorenzana, *op. cit.*, pp. 35-184.

[40] See *op. cit.*, pp. 185-208.

[41] Details in B M, I, 41, § 93.

[42] Official acts and history in Vargas Ugarte, *op. cit.*, I, 95-257; III, 25-53.

[43] Although these laws had their practical effect in Spanish America, they did not appear in print until 1871; see B M, II, 206, § 879.

[44] For the Third Council of Lima, see *op. cit.*, I, 259-375; III, 54-113; for the corresponding Mexican Council, cf. Juan de la Serna, *Sanctum Provinciale Concilium Mexico* (Mexico City, 1622). Less important than either of these two councils was the Fourth Council of Lima, held in 1591.

[45] Details in B M, I, 97, § 222.

[46] On Solórzano and his publications see J. de Ayala, *Ideas políticas de Juan de Solórzano* (Seville, 1946); his editions are commented on briefly in B M, I, especially p. 191.

[47] *In Recopilación*, 3 vols. (Madrid, 1781), II, 189-343. This edition is the most readily accessible inasmuch as it has been re-issued recently in facsimile.

[48] Had space permitted, I would have devoted far more attention to the papal documents which helped to make Europeans aware of the rights of their Christian brothers across the seas. On Paul III's efforts, see Hanke's study cited *supra*, note 35. Paul V's letters in the defense of the Indians are scattered in numerous publications, e.g. G. Catena, *Vita del gloriosissimo Papa*

Pio Quinto (Rome, 1587), pp. 104-107; L. Lopetegui, S. J., "San Francisco de Borja y el plan misional de San Pío V," in *Archivum Historicum S.J.*, XI (1942), 1-26. In 1605, Clement VIII forbade under penalty of excommunication the enslavement of the Indians; the original Latin text and a Spanish summary of the document are given by Hernáez, *op. cit.*, pp. 109-110.

⁴⁹ Consult J. F. Bannon, S.J., and P. M. Dunne, S.J., *Latin America* (Milwaukee, 1947), pp. 74-75.

⁵⁰ Cf. S. Leite, S.J., *História da Companhia de Jesus no Brasil*, 10 vols. (Rio de Janeiro and Lisbon, 1938-1950), especially IV, 3-94; VI, 306-354. A briefer account can be found in the same author's *Suma histórica* (Lisbon, 1965), p. 279 (Index, under "Liberdade dos índios").

⁵¹ See S. Leite's edition of Nóbrega's *Diálogo sobre a conversão do gentio* (Lisbon, 1954).

⁵² Discussed in *op. cit.*, pp. 27-28.

⁵³ See especially Leite, *História*, IV, 432 (Index, under "Vieira: lutas a favor da liberdade dos índios").

CHAPTER SIX

THE EFFECTS OF COLONIALISM UPON THE ASIAN UNDERSTANDING OF MAN

J. G. ARAPURA

This essay is confined to the history of three centuries, from the beginning of the seventeenth to the end of the nineteenth. This limitation might appear unduly severe. Nevertheless, it is not arbitrary to treat this block of time as a distinct historical unit. On the one hand, the year 1600, round number that it is, is in many ways an effective divider between the late medieval and modern ages; and on the other, the year 1900 marks the culminating point of a long era of preparation, ushering in the most crucial and eventful segment of time in all secular history, the twentieth century. Historians have conventionally treated the first of these dates as a significant point of transition in Europe and Asia separately as well as in their mutual relation. Donald F. Lach, in a work entitled, *Asia in the Making of Europe,* ends the first volume on the year 1600, giving the following explanation: "The final years of the sixteenth and the beginning years of the seventeenth century saw fundamental changes in both Europe and Asia which altered basically their earlier relationship!"[1] The changes which affected this relationship were signalled by the end of the Portuguese monopoly of the sea trade with Asia, the entry of England, Holland and France into that trade, and such epoch-making changes in Asia itself, as the rise to its zenith of the Moghul empire under Akbar. Even Shakespeare will bear witness to the fact that about this time the geopgraphic reality of Asia took firm roots in European consciousness: "He does smile his face into more lines than are in the new map with the augmentation of the Indies."[2] As for the second of these dates, 1900, there is no doubt that we, who live in this present century of apocalyptic turmoil, must look back to the epoch culminating at that point as if a period of pregnancy had ended and birth pangs begun. Taking the Hegelian theory of the self-manifestation of the Absolute seriously, we can conclude that the spiritual seeds of much that we reap today, including dialectical materialism, had been sown in the century that has gone by.

I. *Large-scale European Movements into Asia*

It is well-known that the Portuguese had opened the way for European movement into Asia via the sea route. Trade with India and the Far East had been completely dominated by the Portuguese for a whole century since Vasco da Gama's arrival at Calicut in 1498, having virtually replaced the Arab hegemony of the seas with their own.

Four Dutch vessels sailed to Java in 1595 under the command of Cornelius de Houtman and returned after two and a half years, laden with goods. Consequent on this successful expedition, the United East India Company of Holland was chartered with the signature of the States General on March 20, 1602. The Charter conferred on the Company not only trade rights but also power to conclude treaties and to enter political alliances. The first treaty the company signed was with the Zamorin of Calicut, the arch-foe of the Portuguese. But the Dutch moved further on, south to Ceylon and east to Java and concentrated their energies more on those islands than on India. Jan Pieterz Coen seized Jakarta, the capital of Java, in 1619, reporting his exploits to the directors of the company in these words, "The foundation of the rendezvous so long desired now has been laid. A large part of the most fertile land and the most prolific seas of the Indies is now yours;... Behold and consider what a good courage might accompany and how the Almighty has fought for us and blessed your Honoures."[3] By the middle of the seventeenth century the Dutch power was firmly established in the Indonesian islands, from which they extended their trade to China and Japan.

The English came to India in the wake of the Dutch, although the English East India Company had been established a year before the Dutch company. The company's first vessel sailed East on January 24, 1601, under the command of Captain Lancaster; after reaching Achin in Sumatra, it returned laden with cargo, terminating a voyage of two and a half years. Their primary need was spices,[4] and being short of cash commodities to pay for them, they facilitated their trade by selling Indian textiles in the East Indies. In order to buy the textiles they established a trade center at Surat on the West coast of India. This was the beginning of the English presence in India. Soon they built forts at Madras, Bombay and Calcutta, guarded by garrisons in order to protect their trading interests. In course of time these commercial activities took on political character with the result that new settlements arose all over India. In 1668, King Charles of England transferred to the East India Company full jurisdiction over these settlements, a state of affairs that led eventually to the company's rule of the whole of India. This was terminated, as a result of the Great Indian Mutiny (1857), by the direct assumption of power by the British Sovereign as presumed successor to the Moghul Emperors.

The French followed suit in efforts to impose their presence on Asia. Although in 1601 Henri IV of France had tried to establish a French East India Company, his effort was not soon crowned with success. The French dream materialized only in 1664 with the sailing of a fleet under Captain de lay Haye. The French had to fight their way through stiff opposition from the then dominant colonial powers, but eventually established themselves in Pondicherry on the east coast of India and subsequently in Indo-China.

The European maritime powers developed an altogether different pattern of expansion in China and Japan from that which they followed in India, Ceylon, Java and Indo-China. Neither of these two countries was conquered by Europeans, thanks to the strength and vigilance of centralized imperial authority in their capitals. For about two centuries, that is, from the beginning of the seventeenth to the nineteenth, Jesuit priests were employed by the emperors in Peking in different advisory capacities, mostly related to science, not excluding the forging of weapons. However, this kind of mutually advantageous relation assured for the Portuguese a favored place in trade. The English and the Dutch deeply resented the Portuguese monopoly and, though bitter mutual enemies themselves, joined hands to dislodge them from their privileged position. This uneasy alliance soon gave place to an equally curious alignment of the English and the Portuguese against the Dutch. All this, however, bore very little fruit. China, meanwhile, remained essentially a closed land although in 1685 the city of Canton was opened to the English. The English used their powerful position in India to secure a commanding share of the China trade and to compel the reluctant Chinese to engage in wider commerce with them. This situation prevailed until the English were joined by the Americans and other Western nations in the nineteenth century, culminating in the famous 'open door policy' implemented under pressure from the Americans. As a result, East Asia became the scene of unrestricted exploitation by all Western nations. The British, meanwhile, used India as a base from which to conquer Burma, Malaya and Singapore.

Western navigators and missionaries had had contact with Japan from 1542, the year in which Antonio Galvano, governor of Malacca reached her shores. However, from the ascendancy of the Tokugawa Shogunate (1600) for a period of two and a half centuries, Japan preferred to remain in a state of watchful isolation from the rest of the world. But even during this era of jealous seclusion missionaries and traders kept up some limited contact with that country. In the long run, whether as a result of her policy or not, Japan remained the only truly free country in Asia. Ironically enough, towards the end of the nineteenth century, she herself launched out on a career of imperialistic activities. Having siezed Ryukyu Islands and Formosa (1874) and having engaged in a successful war against China (1894-95) with the result that Korea was detached and proclaimed a "free state,"[5] Japan opened the era of modern inner-Asia colonialism. In short, no country in Asia except one escaped colonialism of one kind or another; the one country that did meted out a colonialism of its own.

A. Material effects of Western expansion

The impact of modern Western nations upon Asia has caused an unprecedented and unique chapter to be written in world history. In its devastating power it is comparable to a hurricane.[6] Its effect upon Asian civilizations, in terms of intensity, durability and extensiveness, is somewhat like what earthquakes and volcanoes do to the crust of the earth. In Panikkar's words it "covers an epoch of the highest significance of human development. The changes it brought about and the forces it generated in the countries of Asia... have effected a transformation which touches every aspect of life in these countries."[7] Panikkar rightly surmises that although we cannot predict the net result of it all for the future, "there is no gainsaying the fact that the massiveness of the changes that have already taken place, the upsurges which have already transformed their ancient societies, and the ideas that have already modified their outlook, involve a qualitative break with the past which justly entitle the changes to be described as revolutionary."[8]

B. The Spiritual power behind Western expansion

While explaining "the religious urge of European expansion," a fact well known to many Western writers but seldom recognized by Eastern historians, Panikkar writes, "indeed it might be appropriately said that political aggrandisement was the work of governments and groups, and commerce the interest of organized capital, mission work was the effort of the people of the West to bring home to the masses of Asia their views of the values of life."[9] Like most Eastern authors, however, he fails to see that the interest in missionary activity cannot be separated from the forms of political life or from the economic developments which seized Europe. Max Weber and R. H. Tawney are perhaps the most outstanding exponents of the "influence of certain religious ideas on the development of an economic spirit, or the *ethos* of an economic system."[10] One of the principles Weber has tried to deal with is "the connection of the modern economic life with the rational ethics of ascetic Protestantism."[11] Tawney, while contending that capitalism is not "the offspring of Puritanism," nevertheless also argues, "But it found in certain aspects of later Puritanism a tonic which braced its energies and fortified its vigorous temper."[12] More must be said on this subject later.

Now to return to the missionary activities of Europeans in Asia, there is little doubt that there was often manifest an excessive spirit of self-assertiveness and a remarkable inability to separate the spiritual from the temporal. The concluding statement of a letter sent by the King of Portugal to the Zamorin of Calicut (beginning of the sixteenth century) through Admiral Pedro Alvarez Cabral reflects to a greater or lesser degree the spirit that has prevailed ever since. It reads as follows: "And if it should happen that...we find you the contrary of this...our fixed purpose is to prosecute this affair and continue our navigation, trade and intercourse in those lands which the Lord God wishes to be served by our hands.[13] The first missionaries from the modern West to make contact with Asian peoples were the Dominicans and the Franciscans, who followed in the wake of Portuguese expeditions. Then came the Jesuits, whose work in India, China, and Japan, as elsewhere, constitutes one of the most romantic and adventure-filled epics of all religious history.[14] The Protestant missionaries were the last to arrive, having had to overcome such obstacles as official discouragement by the English East India Company for one. Though late in arriving, they soon fanned out in all directions and became firmly entrenched in most parts of Asia by the middle of the nineteenth century.

C. Christianity and Western ideologies in Asia

The inner urge of Christianity to spread to the whole world may itself have been partly instrumental in instilling that propensity for self-expansion so visibly manifest in modern Western culture. Conversely, the fierce energy that has characterized the culture became a vehicle for the religion. The attitude of freedom and openness towards time, and therefore towards the future, and of freedom and openness towards space, and therefore towards the universe, which has been the dynamo behind the Western spirit of exploration and expansion, has unquestionably emanated from the idea of the Kingdom of God. It is in that idea that one might find the ultimate sources of modernity itself. Science and the tendency towards expansion had indeed been present elsewhere too; but with the alchemy provided by Christianity they became expressions of ideologies,[15] the means for actualizing some vision of the end of history. We may say that either there have been several Western ideologies or that there is one single Western ideology which has taken several forms such as communism, anti-communism, capitalism, liberalism etc. Ideology is possible only when the reality of society is taken with the utmost seriousness, as something obviously concerned with individual human beings but also distinct from them.[16] Modern Western civilization itself is thoroughly ideological in character and Christianity can hardly be separated from it,[17] facts with which a keen student of comparative religion cannot escape being impressed. Further, in speaking of Christianity and ideology together one must consider the following facts: (1) The kernel of all-embracing universality which is native to Christianity, when transferred to a secular ideology devoid of grace, tends to acquire traits of incipient totalitarianism. These latent traits become patent when the ideology develops into a fully self-conscious state as in the case of dialectical materialism, which, let it not be forgotten, is the most extreme form of Western ideology, although in the hands of its oriental adherents it puts on an anti-Western aspect. Dialectical materialism like other forms of Western ideology could not have had its genesis without Christianity. Hendrik Kraemer is quite right when he points out that "Communism and the Marxist-Leninist doctrine of salvation are a gigantic off-shoot of Western idealism," constituting a "Western invasion" of "extreme severity in Asia" today.[18] (2) Christianity in the guise of secular Western ideologies, rather than directly as religious faith, has provided the most potent factors of transformation in the modern West and through it the Orient. (3) There has remained a purely religious residuum in Christianity which has resisted translation into ideology. This has been maintained by symbolic devices of belief. (4) Even this purely religious Christianity has been subjected to an incessant process of secularization so that, under tremendous pressure, the transcendent end of salvation itself has been progressively transformed into proximate and immediate goals in conformity with the requirements of fully secular ideologies. Even the highest purposes of evangelism have been, for good or for ill, constantly secularized. They have become enmeshed with programs of worldly redemption, good works, reform, revolution, and social service. In the field of mission in the past they were often entangled with less humble programs of power-equations and paternalistic domination over others for what was probably honestly thought to be their good. (5) Now in respect to the Asian peoples' response, we can easily see that they have accepted most elements of Western ideology although there persists a certain degree of ambivalence. The last three centuries laid the groundwork for this response by a series of cultural invasions. In respect of Christianity we can notice that its influence upon Asia is a partial and one-sided (and sometimes even lop-sided) shadow of its influence upon the West exerted in the course of forming Western ideology or ideologies. The evidence for this assertion is the perceptible desire in the East to imitate and incorporate Western socio-political and economic examples, coupled with a wide-spread, ostensible determination to ignore or underplay the specifically religious aspects of Western tradition. The nineteenth century was the period in which these attitudes were formed. As Panikkar observes: "Though the Hindus, the Chinese and the Japanese liked to believe that their own cultures were superior they could not deny either the superiority of Western knowledge or the greater strength—though not the stability—of European social and economic organization. They were convinced, after a short period of intoxication, that their own religious and moral systems were superior but they had ample proofs to satisfy them that Europe was intellectually centuries ahead."[19]

II. *The Different Areas of Western Impact*

Asian historians rightly say that there was no discernible impact of Europe upon Asia before the middle of the eighteenth century.[20]

For all practical purposes the late eighteenth and the nineteenth centuries constitute the really important period of decisive influence of Europe on Asia. It was during that time that capitalism was reaching its height in Europe and technology was becoming mature enough to be exported. Capitalism and technology are the result of a causal chain that ultimately reaches back to a revolution in man's self-perception, a religiously grounded revolution. As Tawney observes, with respect to Calvin's influence on the economic and social spheres of life, "So little do those who shoot the arrows of the spirit know where they will light."[21] In the estimate of many important scholars the Puritan was the principal author of that revolution in self-perception which has destined to change everything. Tawney describes the Puritan thus: "A spiritual aristocrat, who sacrificed fraternity to liberty, who drew from his idealization of personal responsibility a theory of individual rights, which, secularized and individualized, was to be among the most potent explosives that the world has known."[22]

Asians were exposed to the eddies of these momentous developments in the West and were henceforth subjected to capitalism and technology. Capitalism was freely admitted but it worked as a rapacious and unconscionable system of exploitation; and technology was imported only through rigidly controlled channels. They also came into contact, inevitably, with the political and ideological expressions of the European revolution in self-perception; but this influence was rather ineffective, inasmuch as the missionaries and colonial educators who conveyed the ideas had not been themselves deeply involved at the center of European intellectual and spiritual ferments.

Because European spiritual movements have remained beyond the vision of Asian eyes, Asian writers tend to treat socio-political and economic manifestations of Western life as the sole causal factors. In their selection of methods of historical analysis they tend to choose as models those liberal, utilitarian or pragmatist Western writers with whom for a combination of reasons they feel a certain pre-established affinity. Such men are Bertrand Russell, John Dewey, H. G. Wells, and John Stuart Mill. But in so far as these confine themselves to the areas of impact on Asia they are to a considerable degree right. Accordingly, Panikkar thinks that nationalism is for Asia the most significant manifestation of the European revolution.[23] However, nationalism in Asia is not simply a transplantation of the European idea. Rather it is a fusion of a spirit of rational liberation with that from which one has been liberated, a concrete example of the latter being the magical-empirical self-perception of societies classically obtaining in the caste system of India. There is indeed a certain degree of rationalization[24] in this process, over which also broods a catalytically-produced new self-consciousness. Even in the narrow sense of pride in one's own culture and heritage, nationalism in Asia, as Panikkar would freely admit, "is due to the recovery and interpretation of the culture of India and China by Western scholars."[25] A perusal of Max Müller's inaugural lecture at Oxford (October 27, 1878) will bear testimony to this fact.[26]

Shifting emphasis from nationalism, Panikkar further observes, "The first and perhaps the most abiding influence is in the sphere of law."[27] More clearly belonging to the rational side of life than nationalism, law in the modern Western sense of the word, consisting of what Weber calls "a calculable legal system and of administration in terms of formal rules,"[28] has indeed been a radical innovation in Asia. The introduction of such rational law, particularly in India, is "the establishment of the great principle of equality of all before law in a country where according to Hindu doctrines a Brahman could not be punished on the evidence of a Sūdra, and even punishment varied according to caste, and where according to Muslim law, testimony could not be accepted against a Muslim, was itself a legal revolution of the first importance."[29] The legal position of women has also been much affected by modern enlightened laws in Asian countries. Obviously a universal concept of what is human, as distinct from some precise, empirically identified entity as man or woman or Brahman or Sūdra or Muslim or unbeliever finally gained ascendancy, at least in the eyes of the law. Not only India and the countries directly ruled by colonial powers, but China and Japan also patterned their law more or less after the new Western models. The introduction of the extended jury system in Japan "is itself a demonstration of the influence of the British judicial practice."[30] Some Asian writers, however, fascinated by the French revolution, on account of its obvious non-religious character, tend to assign too great an importance to it in the formation of Asian laws.[31]

Another area of great importance is urban life. Along with new cities like Calcutta, Bombay, Shanghai, Tientsin, Hong Kong, and Colombo, there grew up the new concepts of civic life and citizenship which were not, however, the automatic result of the fact of there

being cities. There had been, no doubt, cities like capitals of kingdoms and empires and religious centers in Asia before the advent of
Western ideas, but the new cities that sprang up in contact with the
Europeans transmitted a wholly new principle. The absence of
words in Asian languages conveying the meaning of 'citizen' is note-
worthy. Panikkar himself explicitly points out that even the Sanskrit word '*nāgarika*' (from *nagara*, city), describing a state of being
cultured, did not translate it.[32] This bears out Weber's statement that
"although there have everywhere been civic market privileges,
companies, guilds, and all sorts of legal differences between town and
country, the concept of citizen has not existed outside the Occident,
and that of the bourgeoisie outside the modern Occident."[33]

Nationalism, rational law and the concepts of citizenship and
civic life are among the outward results of the revolution in self-
perception. The more interior results are those affecting the ideas of
class, the individual and labor, all of which underwent a revolution
concurrently. This would not have been possible outside the religious
context in which they took place in Europe. Karl Marx himself
points out that "for such a society" (in which all those things took
place), "Christianity with its *cultus* of abstract man, more especially
in its bourgeois developments, Protestantism, Deism, etc., is the
most fitting form of religion."[34] Other societies including Asian,
could not have engendered such revolutions. To quote Marx,

> [But] they are founded either on the immature development of man
> individually, who has not yet severed the umbilical cord that unites
> him with his fellow men in a primitive tribal community, or upon
> direct relations of subjection. They can arise and exist only when
> the development of the productive power of labour has not risen
> beyond a low stage, and when, therefore, the social relations within
> the sphere of material life, between man and man, and between man
> nature, are correspondingly narrow. This narrowness is reflected in
> the ancient worship of Nature, and in the other elements of the
> popular religions.[35]

The problem in Asia itself is that the revolutions in the ideas of
class, individual and labor as well as in those of nation, law and
citizenship were the result of recalcitrant and poorly assimilated
transfusions of the conceptual and ideological fruits of the genuine
revolutions that had taken place in the West, but without the
reproduction of their spiritual basis. And the fact remains that there
have not been indigenous religious bases in Asia itself for such
revolutions. It seems that one of the principles upon which Marx

would have seen eye to eye with sociologists of another persuasion, chiefly Weber and Tawney, is precisely this: the types of religious belief embodied in Christianity during the period in question, in cooperation with bourgeois capitalism, did play an indispensable role in the revolutionary transformation from earlier, narrower social forms of life and values to more complex and sophisticated ones. For Marx's dictum, "The religious world is but the reflex of the real world,"[36] meaning of course the world of social reality, ought to be true in its observe too; that is to say, the real world of social existence must have a reflex in the forms of religious belief and cultus. It is necessary, then, that the original and the image must exist together.

The turmoil in Asia is compounded by the fact that, not only in the contemporary Marxist revolution, but in the late eighteenth and nineteenth century liberal ones, the reflex and the original social reality which had generated the new Western ideologies (or the new *forms* of the Western ideology) have been absent. The ideology or ideologies produced in another context have had to be imported to Asia chiefly via intellectual vehicles and then superimposed with the aid of artificial, improvised supports, upon an alien social soil. This situation in turn has also adversely affected the intellectual vitality and originality of revolutionary ideologies in the East, in which the absence of these elements is conspicuous. To compensate for the lack there has been a tendency to introduce, on the one hand, truncated and denatured versions of liberalism and, on the other, exaggerated absurdities like the recent Chinese cultural revolution. The fact that there has been no truly effective and religious link in the chain of socio-economic processes has indeed been a great disadvantage. Until this situation is introspectively comprehended, ideology-based revolutionary activities will continue to run on parallel lines with realities of the context in which they take place, intensifying the tragic self-alienation which is so deep a malady in Asian societies today.

III. *The Intertwining of Western Ideology with the Quest for Universal Humanity and Human Unity*

It would be incorrect to say that the quest for universal humanity and human unity so characteristic of modern times is separable from the multifarious quests of Western ideology. This concept of unity first appeared in the modern world as one of the essential goals of man's Western quest, generalized as a world-wide human enterprize, into the machinery of which have been absorbed elements from all cultures and religions of the world. Christianity undoubtedly has been the spiritual inspiration behind this quest, but for Christianity itself it has been neither the supreme object of faith nor the highest ideal to be pursued, but one among several to be realized only in consonance with all the other purposes of God. Even for an idealistic philosophical system like Hegel's, whose Christian inspiration is unmistakeable,[37] it was not in itself an independent or even the principal goal. But the consummation devoutly wished for in the greatest of all idealistic systems of the nineteenth century, the universal presence of the Spirit, lent a rather sacramental aspect, as an outward and visible sign, to the *idea* of human unity, which became one of its auxiliaries.[38]

However, the Romantics of the late eighteenth and early nineteenth centuries had put the quest for the unity of man in a different light. The Romantic movement itself is not by any means to be divorced from the currents of Western ideology, as conversely some of the great articulations of that ideology have themselves a strong Romantic flavor. It was by and large an unrestrained expression, almost an outburst, of the Unconscious, amounting to what one writer describes, aptly, as "nothing less than the recuperation of man's past wisdom, entailing a colossal broadening of man's collective memory."[39]

Much of the work of the Romantics turned outward, away from Europe's traditional boundaries. Lessing's *Die Erziehung des Menschengeschlechts*,[40] 1780; J. G. Herder's *Aelteste Urkunde des Menschengeschlechts* (The Oldest Documents of Mankind), 1774-6; and Schelling's *Philosophie der Mythologie* (Philosophy of Mythology), 1842, are the most celebrated works that bear witness to this phase of Europe's outward looking to a larger humanity, whereby she found a new release from confinement. The scientific undergirding to this new Romantic expansion came mainly from comparative philology, which Max Müller dates from the foundation of the Asiatic Society of Calcutta in 1784,[41] from the labors of Frederick Schlegel, Bopp and Grimm. The Asia-centered romanticism found its most exuberant expression in the work of Johann Joseph von Görres, who located primordial humanity on the banks of the Ganges and the Indus.[42] In the eighteenth century China was the principal center of attraction. Panikkar writes effusively of the influence of Chinese literature on Voltaire and the French Encyclopaedists.[43] A shift occurred. "What Europe discovered with amazement in the nineteenth century was the profound thought of India, no longer the urbane humanism of an enduring China, and this at the time that German philosophic thought was becoming paramount in the West."[44] The Germans had a peculiar advantage in their work on Oriental studies, for, on the one hand, it coincided with their great Romantic, speculative outreaches to the world, and on the other, they were free from colonial involvement. This moved the poet, Heinrich Heine, to declare, "The Portuguese, the Dutch, and the English have been for a long time, year after year, shipping home the treasures of India...Today, Schlegel, Bopp, Humboldt, etc., are our East Indian sailors. Bonn and Munich will be good factories."[45]

This Romantic outreach, immensely significant as it is, might also be regarded as an elliptical movement of Europe's consciousness. The discovery she made is an awakening to her own hidden depth, to an insistent inner need for unity and universality. But in process of that both halves of the world have benefitted.

But the great Romantic interlocking of humanity in the nineteenth century, conceived mainly in East-West terms, has been the result of the work of scholars of both halves of the world. There was interest in mutual discovery as well as in self-discovery on either side. But it must always be borne in mind that mutual discovery is an element of self-knowledge of societies, and, that, to use the Hegelian scheme, self-knowing and self-making constitute a double-process that go back to the origins. If these truths, so powerfully enunciated in the nineteenth century itself, are apprehended, *misunderstanding* itself can be used as a stepping-stone to understanding.

The European expansions had a tremendous effect upon Asian thinking in terms not only of religious and social reform but also in terms of awakening and activating latent universalisms in her great religio-philosophical traditions. The Bengali-speaking part of India is undoubtedly the classic parcel of the whole Asia where Western impact can be most fruitfully studied. The giant figures of Raja Ram Mohun Roy (1772-1833) and Ramakrishna Paramahamsa (1836-1886) would stand out not only in India but in the whole world for the breadth and universality of their visions. Raja Ram Mohun Roy's famous letter to the French Minister of Foreign Affairs contains the following great statement:

Unbiased commonsense as well as the accurate deductions of scientific research lead to the conclusions that all mankind are one great
family of which numerous nations and tribes existing are only
various branches. Hence enlightened men in all countries feel a wish
to encourage and facilitate human intercourse in every manner by
removing as far as possible all impediments to it in order to promote
the reciprocal advantage and enjoyment of the whole human race.[46]

Rabindranath Tagore paid the highest compliment to the Raja,
observing that he was the only man in the whole world who understood the complete signifiance of the modern age.[47] Roy according to his own declaration was much influenced by Christianity.
In this letter he goes on to elaborate his concept of human oneness.
As has been universally acknowledged by his contemporaries and
biographers, he was a giant both of heart and mind, and above all, a
mighty renaissance figure whose love of freedom enabled him to
seek insights wherever he could find them, without making apology
or refusing to acknowledge his sources of inspiration. He searched
fearlessly the scriptures of mankind, particularly his own Vedas, as
well as the Bible and the Qur'an. His work, the *Precepts of Jesus:
Guide to Peace and Happiness*, is a landmark in the struggle of
Oriental religions to come to grips with the unique essence of
Christianity. Here was a line of intellectual and spiritual quest which
culminated in that outstanding but now nearly forgotten book,
The Oriental Christ, by Pratap Chandra Mazumdar, a later leader in
the Brahmo Samaj movement founded by Roy himself. Considering
his courageous openness to every form of spiritual aspirations it is
no coincidence that the statement quoted above bears such remarkable resumblance to St. Paul's declaration to the Athenians:
"God who...hath made of one blood all nations of men to dwell on
the face of the earth..." (Acts 17:24-27). But he did not obviously
share St. Paul's teleological vision that men should "seek the Lord
(Christ), if haply they might feel after him, and find him." On the
contrary, he moved towards comparative religion, of which inquiry
he is one of the acknowledged founders. He believed in the fundamental identity of all religions which will become manifest when
all of them, moving along the paths of their own historic traditions,
will have completed their journey. Roy was thinking less in theological and more in cultural-spiritual terms, which to him comprehended unhindered intercourse among the nations, peoples and
religions so that the dimly perceived grand design for all mankind
implicit in the universe itself will be progressively realized. And as

the letter to the French minister further shows, he was not only a visionary, but also a practical man profoundly aware of the need for calm, political negotiation on a global scale to settle the emergent differences between nations. He suggested an international congress to that end, the first time perhaps that we hear of such a thing.

But Ramakrishna was a different kind of man, who sought to ground the idea of human unity and universality, theoretically as well as experimentally, in Brahman doctrine.[48] To one and all the saint of Dakshineswar said, "Are you seeking God? Then seek Him in man. The divinity is manifest in man more than in any other object."[49] Undoubtedly, there is a tremendous implication of universalism to be drawn from this doctrine of Brahman-Atman, but it was not drawn in the past in the way it has been done in modern times. Vivekananda, (1863-1902) the chief disciple of Ramakrishna adopted lofty tones about the ideas of unity and universality of man embedded in Hinduism while chiding Hindus at the same time for not living up to them.[50] Although these noble ideas of universality and unity of man were latent in Asian religious and philosophical thought, the nineteenth century impact of the West surely activated them and set them on an entirely new path.

Much encouraged by admiration of Western savants, Eastern thinkers of the present century are also idealistically committed to promoting world community based on principles adapted from Hindu, Buddhist and Confucian religions. Tagore was perhaps the most outstanding spokesman of this point of view in this century. "The individual man," he wrote, "must exist for Man the Great and must express him in disinterested works, in science and philosophy, in literature and arts, in service and worship."[51] This was one of Gandhi's great dreams also. Radhakrishnan declared, "There are no fundamental differences among the people of the world. They are all working for a religion which teaches the possibility and necessity of man's union with himself, with nature and with his fellowmen, and with the Eternal Spirit..."[52] All these liberal, idealistic presuppositions would appear totally out of context today, in the light of the Marxist ideological revolution and nationalistic counter-revolutions that are rending the countries of the East. Taking Bengal as a specific case in point, the question may be asked if in some way the religious thinkers of the past, of the liberal and orthodox persuasions,

have failed to grasp the real thrust of modernity. This also applies ot
non-religious thinkers of the East, like Mr. Nehru, fired by the same
dream.

IV. *The Philosophic Idea of the Unity of Mankind and its Practical
    Dimensions*

It must be clear that, although the quest for human unity came to
the fore during the last three centuries as an expression of Western
ideology and connected with Western expansion, there has also
taken place a convergence of civilizations which gave body and
substance to this quest. Some men have been more powerfully
moved by this idea than others; yet let there be no mistake about it;
neither in the great religious movements nor in the political expansions has unity of mankind itself been a directly sought after
goal. Not many philosophers would have been willing to treat it as
an end in itself, but rather as a dimension of human destiny, which
must transcend the mere realization of unity. It is also an in-
trinsically valuable attribute in itself, a fact which the Romantics
have realized more deeply than the pragmatically inclined. Since
some nineteenth century Eastern thinkers have responded more
deeply to Romanticism than to any other movement, they and
their intellectual heirs have tended to feel for human unity with
idealistic sincerity and often in a utopian manner. They have not
taken sufficiently into account the obstinate resistances of history
in the path leading to that goal. The paradoxical nature of man
must be fully recognized. As Reinhold Niebuhr writes:

> He [man] stands at the juncture of nature and spirit. The freedom
> of his spirit causes him to break the harmonies of nature and the
> pride of his spirit prevents him from establishing a new harmony.
> The freedom of his spirit enables him to use the forces and processes
> of nature creatively; but his failure to observe the limits of his finite
> existence causes him to defy the forms and restraints of both nature
> and reason. Human self-consciousness is a high tower looking upon a
> large and inclusive world. It vainly imagines that it is the large
> world which it beholds and not a narrow tower insecurely erected
> amidst the shifting sands of the world.[53]

Such warnings as this may be profitably heeded at this juncture of
history when, anomalously enough, with so little concrete basis for
hope, there is a rising tide of Utopianism and Romanticism.

The notion of unity of mankind must be cherished even though it is only an idea. The feeling for it is symptomatic of what man needs, not assurance of what he will obtain. As Hegel writes, "The truth of independent consciousness is [accordingly] the consciousness of the bondsman."[54] This is exactly true also of the consciousness of unity, but it must move us, and the more urgently today than ever before.

But the idea of unity of mankind must also be regarded as a symbol. Symbol is that which releases us from the tyranny of the ideal and of the actual, and releases us also from the polarities of the possible and the impossible, and from pessimism and optimism at once. Symbols indeed speak to the human condition, particularly today. To use Paul Tillich's words, "The Symbol represents something which is not itself, for which it stands and in the power and meaning of which it participates...And now we come to something which is perhaps the main function of the symbol—namely, the opening up of levels of reality which otherwise are hidden and cannot be grasped in any other way."[55]

It is fair to say that the symbol of the unity of mankind, although today mainly a quasi-spiritual and essentially secular one, was one of the great ideas produced by Christianity. That the books of the New Testament, particularly the Pauline epistles, are shot through and through with this revolutionary idea is a point that needs no laboring. It is clear in the light of the literature of comparative religion that nowhere else do we find this idea so clearly and passionately expressed. The fundamental revolutionary aspect of the New Testament, in fact the Bible as a whole, is that in theologically delimiting the realm of intelligent beings to the human race—a questionable philosophical supposition, to be sure, if primarily approached as a biological notion—it succeeded in concretizing the universal. This is the only way in which the universal can hold specific content. Eastern religions, on the contrary, refused to bound the universal so that there did not arise a philosophical concept of man as such, man being just one instance of individualized selfhood, to be described as *jīva* (individual phenomenal being), *purusa* (spiritual entity), etc., and qualitatively continuous with every other possible being. This has its virtues, no doubt. However, because they did not arrive at a philosophic concept of man as distinct from the phenomenal world (*sarvam idam*) in its virtually limitless aspect, in the practical, perceptual order of life all kinds of boundaries between man and man, between groups of men, had to be permitted. As there has been no concept of man, there has been no concept of unity of man. This has had to be derived today in response to the Western challenge, purely deductively, from the concept of unity as such, as well as that of the unity of Being (*Brahman*). But the decisive operating principle even here is an inductive one, philosophically determined by modern modes of perception, according to which 'man' and 'humanity' are axiomatic.

Now, although as a theological notion and as a religious leitmotif the unity of man has been one of the great symbols of Christianity, it will be necessary to see that Christianity's contribution to the actualization of this has been somewhat contradictory. On the one hand, it has increased the 'reality' and 'content' of this symbol; and on the other, it has driven deeper the divisions of mankind. It has been the most potent force for the increase of self-consciousness in the world. It has been deeply self-conscious itself and has also made other religions and non-religions equally self-conscious. By consciously trying to overcome the 'natural' divisions of man—as between Jew and Gentile, for instance—it has internalized and conduced to the exacerbation of these. But this kind of contradictory result is inevitable and was foreseen from the beginning. Despite this, the work for realizing the goal of unity must be undertaken with redoubled vigour and truthfulness. That is the nature of the game.

NOTES

[1] Donald F. Lach, *Asia in the Making of Europe* (Chicago, 1965), I, xv.

[2] *Twelfth Night*, Act III, Scene 2.

[3] Quoted by K. M. Panikkar in *Asia and Western Dominance* (London, 1959), p. 47.

[4] "It is perhaps a little difficult for us to understand the importance of spices to the Elizabethans. It was dictated by a hunger more elemental than that of salvation, or the love of God, or even of gold...Spices were also part of the superiority of aristocrat over peasant." Michael Edwardes, *Asia in the European Age* (New York, 1962), pp. 21-22.

[5] A. J. Tudisco, *Asia Emerges* (Berkeley and San Francisco, 1964), p. 75.

[6] Hendrik Kraemer uses this apt metaphor in *World Cultures and World Religions* (London, 1960), p. 171.

[7] Panikkar, *op. cit.*, p. 313.

[8] *Ibid.*

[9] *Ibid.*, p. 314.

[10] Max Weber, *The Protestant Ethic and the Spirit of Capitalism*, trans. Talcott Parsons (New York, London, 1952), p. 27.

[11] *Ibid.*

[12] R. H. Tawney, *Religion and the Rise of Capitalism* (New York, 1926), p. 188.

[13] Quoted from Sir George Sansom, *The Western World and Japan* (New York, 1956), p. 56.

[14] See Thomas J. M. Burke, S.J. (Editor), *Beyond All Horizons* (New York, 1957).

[15] "Ideology" has been defined in several ways but it is simplest to define it as "a system of general ideas, by which men's outlook is conditioned, and by which at least in part, their actions are defined." Stephen C. Neill, *Christian Faith and Other Faiths* (London, 1961), p. 157.

[16] Karl Marx speaks for the whole Western ideology, although he actually inveighs against the bourgeoisie (having not been aware of religious forms of complete individualism available in the East) when he writes:"If a man is social by nature, he will develop his true nature only in society, and the power of his nature must be proved not by the power of separate individuals but by the power of society." *Die Heilige Familie*, quoted by Morris Stockhammer, *Karl Marx Dictionary* (New York, 1965), p. 235.

[17] In view of the fact that Christianity produced ideology in concert with other factors, there is little point in describing Christianity itself along with other Semitic religions, as R. C. Zaehner does, as ideological, (*The Comparison of Religions* [Boston, 1962], p. 120) for ideology is a product of Christianity, not one of its attributes.

[18] Kraemer, *op. cit.*, p. 298.

[19] Panikkar, *op. cit.*, p. 323.

[20] Panikkar puts it graphically thus: "If by an act of God, the relations of Europe with Asia had ceased all of a sudden in 1748, little would have been left to show for two and a half centuries of furious activity." *Ibid.*, p. 315.

[21] Tawney, *op. cit.*, p. 189.

[22] *Ibid.*, p. 191.

[23] Panikkar, *op. cit.*, p. 320.

[24] This is the sort of rationalization that Marx condemned as "ideology," a word, which, ironically enough, has come to be used as the most universally employed apellation for his system of "scientific" principles.

[25] Panikkar, *op. cit.*, p. 322.

[26] See F. Max Müller, *Chips from a German Workshop*, Vol. IV (New York, 1881), pp. 1-43. The question that Père Coerdoux put to the French Academy in a letter (1767), "How is it that Sanskrit has so many words in common with Greek and Latin?" (p. 14) indeed reflects the metaphysical sense of freedom over time and space as well as the spirit of exploration mentioned earlier.

[27] Panikkar, *op. cit.*, p. 324.

[28] Weber, *op. cit.*, p. 25.

[29] Panikkar, *op. cit.*, p. 324, quoted from his *A Survey of Indian History*, p. 257.

However, "In law it is impossible to conceive of a Hindu without a caste system." J. Duncan M. Derrett, *Introduction to Modern Hindu Law* (Oxford, 1922, 1963), pp. 27-28. Refer to P. V. Kane, *History of Dharmasāstra*, 5 vols (Poona, 1930-62).

[30] S. K. Datta, *Asiatic Asia* (London, 1932), p. 129.

[31] See *Ibid.*, pp. 136-8, and Panikkar, *op. cit.*, pp. 315, 316.

[32] Panikkar, *op. cit.*, p. 326.

[33] Weber, *op. cit.*, p. 23.

[34] *Capital* (English translation, copyright, 1906) (New York, 1932), p. 91.

[35] *Ibid.*

[36] *Ibid.*

[37] "Hegel flatly asserts that the Christian religion is *the* presupposition in life of his philosophic thought, and that it already contains—in principle— in non-philosophic form its essential content." Emil L. Fackenheim, *The*

Religious Dimension in Hegel's Thought (Bloomington and London, 1967), p. 71.

[38] "For it is the essence of Hegel's argument that the Absolute Spirit takes upon itself and makes its own the stupendous labour of the world's history: that in so doing it infuses the component parts with spiritual significance, embodies itself in human form, and in the process, at once eternal and in time, reconciles the world to itself and itself to the world." J. B. Baillie (trans.) *Phenomenology of Mind* (London, sixth impression, 1964), p. 54.

[39] Amaury de Riencourt, *The Soul of India* (New York, 1960), p. 264.

[40] Cf. *Education of the Human Race*, trans. by F. W. Robertson, Harvard Classics, XXXII, 1910.

[41] Cf. *op. cit.*, pp. 13-14.

[42] Cf. *Mythengeschichte der Asiatischen Welt* (Heidelberg, 1810), pp. 18-19; also George Bürke, *Vom Mythos zur Mystik* (Einsiedeln, 1958), p. 21.

[43] Cf. Panikkar, *op. cit.*, pp. 307-12.

[44] A. de Riencourt, *op. cit.*, p. 264.

[45] Quoted from S. Radhakrishnan, *Eastern Religions and Western Thought* (Oxford, 1939), p. 247.

[46] Quoted by Atulchandra Gupta, (ed.), *Studies in the Bengal Renaissance* Jadavpur, W. Bengal, 1958), p. 12.

[47] Cf. *ibid.*, pp. 11-12.

[48] Cf. M. Monier-Williams, *Brahmanism and Hinduism* (New York, 1889), p. 481.

[49] Romain Rolland, *The Life Ramakrishna* (Almora, 1931), p. 198.

[50] Romain Rolland, *The Life of Vivekananda* (Almora, 1953), pp. 70-74.

[51] *The Religion of Man* (London, 1961), p. 11.

[52] "Fragments of a Confession," Paul A. Schilpp, *The Philosophy of Sarvepalli Radhakrishnan* (New York, 1952), p. 81.

[53] *The Nature and Destiny of Man* (New York, 1941), I, 17.

[54] *Phenomenology of Mind*, trans. J. B. Baillie, *op. cit.*, p. 237.

[55] *Theology of Culture* (London, 1968), p. 56.

CHAPTER SEVEN

RELIGIOUS PLURALISM AND THE QUEST FOR HUMAN COMMUNITY

S. J. Samartha

Religious pluralism today is not just an academic issue to be discussed but a fact of experience to be acknowledged. Recognizing that traditionally religions have been moats of separation rather than bridges of understanding between people, how can men and women, committed to different faiths, live together in multi-religious societies? In a world that is becoming a smaller and smaller neighborhood, what are the alternatives between shallow friendliness and intolerant fanaticism? What is the Christian obligation in the quest for human community in pluralistic situations? These are some of the questions which will be briefly discussed in this chapter.

Some observations on the limitations of this discussion must be made at the outset. First, while it is recognized that pluralism in the world today is both religious and ideological, the latter is outside the scope of this essay. This is partly because some of the ideologies are considered elsewhere in this volume and partly because it is necessary to focus on fewer issues in a smaller area for the sake of some depth. Even the category of 'religions' is far too wide; therefore, the reference here will be only to certain religions, particularly in their renascent phases, which have an outreach beyond their geographic frontiers.

It should be kept in mind, secondly, that neither 'religious pluralism' nor 'human community' can be discussed as concepts that can be detached from the throbbings of surrounding life and held up for intellectual examination as hardened crystals under the microscope. They are part of the texture of human life, touching the conscience and emotions of people very deeply. The tentative paths to human community, too often marked by conflicting signposts, are furrowed with ambiguities and conflicts, tragedies and expectations. Therefore, different experiences, in the context of living together with people of different faiths, will inevitably influence the intellectual detachment one hopes to bring to the discussion.

This leads to a third observation which is more personal. This writer's experience of teaching in India for many years and of living together with men of other faiths, particularly with Hindus, inevitably forms the background of this discussion. This means that quite a few of the examples given will come from the multi-religious context of Indian life. However, the fact that the writer is at present trying to be essentially Indian and Christian in an ecumenical context, which is very much alive with the cross-currents of thinking from different parts of the world, will, it is hoped, widen the scope without deflecting the direction of this discussion.

I. *Religions Sacred and Secular*

Pluralism describes a situation "in which various religions, philosophies and ideological conceptions live side by side and in which none of them holds a privileged status."[1] Religious pluralism is, of course, not a new phenomenon in the history of mankind. Whether in the Roman Empire or later on, when dispersed in other countries, Christians have always had to live with people of other religious traditions. Recently, various factors have contributed to an increased recognition of this fact and its implications to Christian life and witness. The resurgence of national cultures with a strong religious content, both in the colonial and the post-colonial era; the emphasis on human rights and liberty of conscience; the rapid means of travel bringing people closer together; the growing use of mass media and audio-visual techniques—these are among the more important factors that have contributed to the sharper emergence of religious pluralism in the world today. To these must be added the important fact that today there are communities of people of many faiths—workers, students, teachers and migrants—living in countries of Europe and North America. "It is only in our days," writes Visser 't Hooft, "that the churches have come to face the issue of pluralism in its sharper form, namely, as the appearance on their own doorstep of a multitude of other conceptions of life, religious positions and ideologies which claim the same rights as the churches."[2]

When people of differing faiths try to live together in peace and harmony, does not the religious factor make their quest for community more difficult? Also, with the increasing influence of secularization, is it justifiable to look to religions for resources to build true community? Will not the 'secular' provide better possibilities of convergence of interests and, therefore, of co-operation? The answer to these questions has become more complicated partly because of the tendency to oversimplify the relation between secularization and religions, and partly because of the fact that the history of religions is not clear in this respect.

Historically it is true that the gap between profession and practice in any religion has been almost unbridgeable and that religious fanaticism has caused untold harm to responsible human community. One need not go so far back as the Crusades to prove this point. The examples in recent years are obvious. Without the tensions between Hindus and Muslims would the tragic division of India have come about with its unhappy consequences? Does the Hindu teaching on *ahimsa* and the Muslim emphasis on 'brotherhood' prevent the horrible occurrence of Hindu-Muslim riots with resultant loss of life and property and more lasting consequences of suspicion, mistrust, hatred and revenge that last for generations? Other examples are the Catholic-Protestant strife in Northern Ireland, the tensions between Christians and Muslims in Cyprus, and the continuing conflict in the Middle East where Islam and Judaism contribute to the complexity of the situation. When the heretics of one group within the same religion are regarded as martyrs of the other, there seems to be little chance of traditional religions providing any basis for harmony and peace. It would be unwise to presume that 'the religious' is the only factor in such situations because obviously political, social and economic factors tend to aggravate tensions. But the point remains that in spite of the peace potential of traditional religions, organised or institutionalised religions have not often been able to prevent human conflicts or to control religious passions once they have been aroused.

There is a further factor which, in recent years, has been perhaps more influential in shaping the tendency to dismiss religions almost completely from relevant areas of human life. This seems to have been brought about by an alliance between two strange bedfellows: on the one hand, some Christian theologians have dismissed religions as 'human attempts,' having no theological significance whatsoever;[3] and on the other hand, the prophets of secularization, in their enthusiasm for the 'secular,' have dismissed all religions from the meaning of modern life. The long debate on 'continuity-discontinuity' has been mostly sterile, mainly because it has been moving in a narrow circle of ideas unrelated to actual pluralistic living in the midst of people of different faiths. In societies where Christians live in daily contact with their neighbors belonging to other faiths, the harsh insistence on 'discontinuity' has been hopelessly unhelpful in the fostering of community living. It has tended to separate the Christians from their brethren of other faiths and is one of the reasons why the present stance of 'dialogue' is seriously suspect in certain quarters.

The prophets of secularization, in their judgment on religions, have not been able or willing to make a distinction between the traditional *forms* of religions on the one hand and their enduring *values* on the other. This is rather curious because in their consideration of Christianity they have been careful to distinguish between 'Biblical insights' on the one hand and the structures of historic Christianity on the other. Why this attitude should fall short when other religions in their particular situation are encountered is far from clear. They have lumped all of them together and assumed that it is only a matter of time before the onward march of secularization, with its geographic center in Europe and America and its spiritual center in the reinterpreted 'religionless' Judeo-Christian tradition, will sweep away all religions from relevant areas of life. Also, it seems to be taken for granted that the pattern of relationship between the march of secularization and the traditional religions in Asia and Africa will follow the same pattern as the relation between Christianity in the West and the rise of modern science, industrialization, and technology.

There is no point in trying to defend the other religions over against Christianity or to line them up against the process of secularization. It would also be foolish to ignore the influence of secularization in different parts of the world or the freedom it brings in liberating the human spirit from the thraldom of backword-looking religious systems. Neither should it be taken for granted that 'the mysterious East' has something subtle up its spiritual sleeve which the scientific eyes of the West have failed to discern. The question is not one of the East or of the West; these distinctions tend to become blurred in the world context of pluralism. But certain observations must be made here which should in some ways affect the approach to and the understanding of the 'sacred' and the 'secular' in the world context of religious pluralism.

It is difficult to understand the word 'religion' and what it means in the lives of people in the East or in the West. The content of the word is variously understood, causing a good deal of confusion. There is almost no equivalent of the English word 'religion' in the Indian languages. When one tries to translate it in some languages, it comes out as 'opinion,' which is, of course, hopelessly inadequate. The word usually used in this connection is the Sanskrit *dharma*, coming from the root *dhr*, to support, to sustain.[4] The earth is *dharani* because it supports all things, man and nature. *Dharma* (in Pali *dhamma*) in its narrow sense also means duty, for example, *rāja dharma* (the duty of the king) or *varna dharma* (caste duty), but in its fulness and totality, pervading the whole life of man, it includes both a view of life and a way of life inextricably mingled together. Even for one who rejects traditional dogmas and ritual it should not be difficult to be within the *dharma*. In its comprehensiveness, therefore, it indicates a religiosity which, without any difficulty or tension, *includes* the secular. Therefore, when Hinduism is described by Christians from a particular theological position, formed within a particular cultural context, as one of the 'human attempts' to reach God, or when unqualified observations are made that Hinduism as 'a religion' is being swept away by the flood of secularization, one must ask what these statements mean in the actual context of Hindu life. Hindu *dharma*, in its enduring values and renascent expressions, continues to provide meaning and direction to the lives of millions of people. The same observation applies also to Buddhism as it seeks to provide resources for the life of people in various countries. These ancient religions are also responding to the forces of modern life. Their essential attitudes and teachings, while maintaining a continuity with the past, are in some cases radically different from the 'Hinduism' and 'Buddhism' expounded in some books of the recent past.

We must ask, moreover, whether the church in the West has seriously encountered the Hindu and Buddhist *dharmas* or Islam and other faiths. This is not just a matter of 'scientific' knowledge but of sensitive understanding of what they mean in the actual life of the people.[5] It may seem presumptuous even to raise this question; but judging from the attitudes one encounters, the question is by no means irrelevant. In the early centuries the real struggle of the Church was not so much with the 'religions' of the Roman Empire as with Greek philosophy. It was only through coming to grips with the essentials of Greek philosophy that Christian theology could become relevant and intellectually cogent. In comparison with this struggle, in which some of the great church fathers actively participated, the church's encounter with the 'religions' can only be described as of minor importance. It is disquieting to see this attitude, namely, that of regarding the encounter with other religions as of minor importance, still persisting in certain quarters. In the nineteenth century the church's struggle was mainly with the method, presuppositions and discoveries of modern science, and in the twentieth with the promise of technology and the fruits of secularization. It is true that the church had a good deal to do with Islam during the Crusades and also in the later centuries, but it is doubtful whether Christianity and Islam seriously attempted to have a genuine *understanding* of each other. They were rivals battling with each other for conquest and victory, with pen or sword, not friends seeking comradeship and love. In the era of missionary expansion there was a tremendous explosion of knowledge *about* other religions but again, with certain exceptions, few serious attempts were made to *understand* other religions going beyond words, ideas, and ritual to their sources of power and depth. Also, the dubious alliance of Christianity with colonialism—a fact which it is unnecessary to deny or qualify in the post-colonial era—did not make it easy for men of other faiths to have a genuine understanding of the message of Christ because, more often than not, colonial Christianity obscured the luminous face of Jesus Christ. Moreover, if the world perspective of religious pluralism is really taken seriously, it is necessary to point out that the priorities of the church in the West should not be made universal and applied to all other situations. Whether or not the Jews are absolved of the 'guilt' in connection with the death of Jesus may be a matter of importance in a particular context—although two thousand years seem to be quite a long period to wait for the pronouncement. But in the perspective of six continents in which the church finds itself now, the implications of religious pluralism are far wider and much more complex than just the Christian-Jewish or sometimes the Christian-Jewish-Muslim relationships.

The question of the relationship between the sacred and the secular is much more complex than it is sometimes taken to be, particularly when the religions in Asia and Africa are taken into account. Does man's interest in the sacred decrease with the increasing influence of secularization? It has already been pointed out that the usual distinction made between the sacred and the secular does not hold true in those situations where the complex experience of life are integrated in a unity. Whether in classical Hinduism or its renascent forms in India, or Buddhism and the new religions in Japan, or Islam coming to grips with modern problems in the Middle East, Pakistan or Indonesia, or even in the highly secularized societies of the West, it all looks as if more of the sacred persists in the hearts of people than meets the casual eye. Drawing attention to the African response to the mystery of existence, Harry Sawyyer warns that much care should be taken when the term 'secular' is applied to the African. Stating that "the sacred is still within him" in spite of the external trappings of the secular, he goes on to say: "Religious pluralism therefore calls for an appraisal of the use of the term *secular* in relation to the educated African in particular. Does he in fact truly divorce God from everyday factors of his life, or have Christian teachers and ministers failed to give him a true nexus of life?"[6]

Should the secular at all periods of human history and in all cultures be considered as an *alternative* to the sacred? One of the striking features of life in Asia and Africa today is the co-existence of the sacred and the secular within the same society and sometimes within the same person. Questions about the tensions within a society are often raised by people from outside who have theoretically come to the conclusion that such tensions *must* exist; but they are unwilling to accept the denial of such tensions by the individuals concerned. The situation in Japan is a significant example of the complexity of this whole question. What is happening in China is unfortunately not known to us. Whether the cultural revolution has totally swept away the hold of classical religions on the hearts and minds of people, or whether the sacred still persists within the revolution in different forms is a question to which the answer should at least be left open at present. The same observation may be made about life in Tibet today. Japan is, by commonly accepted standards, the most highly literate and industrially advanced country in Asia, now leaping to the forefront in the race for technological advance in the world. But have scientific concern and technological advance become an alternative to the sacred in Japan? One should not forget that Japanese religions had to share the suffering and agony of national defeat as illustrated by the fact that 1,374 Shinto shrines, 2,540 Shinto temples, 4,609 Buddhist temples, and 446

Christian churches were demolished or damaged by war.[7] Thousands of priests were killed or wounded during the war. And yet, neither the damage suffered by traditional religions nor the advance of science and technology has prevented the emergence of hundreds of 'new religions' since the war. According to an official report published in 1963, 'the new religions' constitute about half the total of 379 religious juridical persons and the number of their adherents is estimated conservatively as well over ten millions.[8] This should at least indicate that the sacred is not necessarily related to the secular as a rival or as an alternative. To these must be added another bit of evidence, this time from countries where secularization has perhaps gone the farthest. Is the rejection of traditional Christianity in the West, particularly by the youth, just a symptom of the dominance of the secular or a sign of the deeper search for what may be more authentically regarded as sacred in those areas of human experience which touch the mysterious and the incomprehensible? Analyzing the situation in the United States, Huston Smith writes:

> With their Be-ins (not Do-ins), their going to where action isn't, they evidence what Tillich calls the ontological as against prophetic faith, celebrating the holiness of the "is" rather than the "ought," the present rather than the future. For the first time since the Renaissance and the Reformation, Western society is hearing through them the suggestion that perhaps the contemplative life is the equal of the active one.[9]

In view of these factors, the relationship between the sacred and the secular and, therefore, between the process of secularization and the resurgence of religions needs to be examined afresh *in the larger perspective of the six continents*, taking into account the implications of cultural and religious pluralism. We do not justify religions in their traditional immobility nor minimize the positive influence of secularization. Surely, petrified traditions, outmoded dogmas, meaningless ritual and cumbersome ecclesiastical machinery do not constitute the essence of any living religion. The dangers of a false religiosity looking backward and defending itself against new expressions of authentic freedom are ever present both in the East and in the West. If secularization or any other movement should sweep away irrelevant structures from contemporary life, the road to human community would surely be less cluttered up then it is today by the débris of fallen idols. One should, therefore, seek those *perspectives of faith* that will enable men everywhere to become more sensitive to the emergence of more reverence before the mysterious and more humility in the presence of the incomprehensible. Sharing with each other the insights gained through different responses to the mystery of human existence should be a natural activity of people seeking true community life in multi-religious societies.

II. *Syncretism a Danger to Faith?*

In all situations where people of different faiths live together the need is to relax the tensions that divide people and to foster those conditions under which co-operation becomes both desirable and possible. Although one way of doing this is to emphasize those common human concerns in which all share and those practical projects in which all can cooperate, at some point or other, the perspectives of faith which inspire and direct people have to be taken into account. The fact that these are not articulated and do not always come to the surface does not mean that they *are* there at deeper levels of consciousness. But the very need for human community and the desire for harmonious living together might create a tendency to avoid discussion on the implications of religious pluralism and lead to several temptations. Of these, *relativism* and *syncretism* are usually pointed as being more dangerous: the former because it tends to make people withdraw from the spiritual struggle to make fundamental decisions; the latter because it tends to use religion for 'human purposes' and results in divided loyalties. These points must be examined a little more carefully in respect to religious pluralism.

Many warnings have been sounded for the churches to be careful and cautious as they face situations of pluralism that are ideological or religious. These warnings, coming from responsible Christian leaders, deeply concerned with the integrity and the witness of the church in the world, should certainly be heeded. The situation does present the church with severe temptations. In the West, Christians are becoming disillusioned with institutionalized Christianity. Being confronted with Hindus, Buddhists, Muslims and others, along with their own 'mission centers' in countries that have been traditionally the home of Christianity, there is the serious danger of accepting uncritical mixtures as integrated faiths. The relativist is likely to argue that pluralism is the natural corollary of religious liberty. There must be recognition of the right of human conscience to hold whatever religious convictions one is disposed to accept without seeking to persuade others to accept any other conviction than those they hold already. This, however, would be a very shallow approach to questions of fundamental importance in human life. It is very doubtful whether it can provide a genuine basis for true human community. Visser 't Hooft is therefore right in pointing out that such a relativism "would breed a race of spiritually spineless human beings who would live in the sort of night in which all cats are grey. No one would any longer have to face the ultimate questions of life."[10] This is true; but it should still be possible for people in multi-religious societies to accept religious pluralism without necessarily becoming intolerant fanatics or uncritical relativists. It is possible if pluralism is accepted as a truly open situation in which people are ready and willing to accept not only the right to hold on to their respective convictions but also the right to speak about them to others in a climate of freedom, confidence and mutual trust. Whether such discussions should take place in a formal manner through organized 'dialogues,' through naturzl conversations in dail living together, or through co-operation in common concerns is immaterial. What is important is the recognition of such possibilities which should become natural once the suspicions are removed. But to be indifferent to these deeper concerns in the name of religious liberty or freedom of conscience or communal harmony would amount to an abdication of spiritual responsibility at a time when it is most needed. The twilight world in which all cats are grey would hardly provide conditions for growth in responsible freedom and community, because it would remove the necessity for inner struggle, for choice, decision and commitment. Without theological backbones people are likely to remian spiritual jellyfishes floating in the shallow waters of relativism.

Is syncretism, then, the answer to the problems created by religious pluralism? In some countries the very fact of religious pluralism appears to provide the conditions for syncretism. When the tensions created by different religions seriously disturb community life, the call is made very often for people of different persuasions to come together and make an attempt to understand the essential beliefs of each other. It has been remarked that "nowhere else has syncretism flourished as much as in India."[11] Visser 't Hooft adds, "The old Oriental syncretism was a religous phenomenon, a product of religious creativity. The modern Oriental

syncretism is in alliance with a secular indifferentism and agnosti-
cism. And it is in the last resort dangerously superficial."[12] In this
context the Asian churches are called upon to demonstrate their
essential freedom in Christ. "They must urge that the ecumenical
movement becomes increasingly a movement of liberation...that it
breaks down more and more all entangling alliances in which the
churches have become involved."[13] The freedom which Christ
brings is not the freedom to do as we please but "to be totally available for the work of Christ in the world." Therefore, drawing pointed
attention to the temptation of syncretism, Visser 't Hooft remarks:

> Are we therefore not driven to demand that the present pluralistic
> pattern be overcome as soon as possible and that a world religion be
> established? And since there is not the slightest change in the present
> circumstances that one of the existing religions or philosophies will
> be accepted by all as the one normative world faith for the world
> community, are we not forced to the conclusion that we must
> synthesise the existing religions and ideologies and thus create a
> genuine world faith? Or to put the matter more shortly: Should true
> world-citizens today become syncretists?[14]

Three reasons are advanced to show that syncretism is a dangerous
temptation and a misleading answer to the problem of religious
pluralism in the world: first, because a universal, synthetic religion
cannot be fabricated; second, because the creation of a world faith
is not an alternative to religious conflict; and, third, because any
prophetic religion will defend its spiritual integrity against the
attempts to use it for human purposes, however good these purposes
may be.

The meaning and implications of syncretism have been disputed
so much that it is now almost impossible to discuss the matter with
clarity or without danger of being misunderstood. The focus of this
present discussion is not the theological feasibility of syncretism but
the integrity of particular faiths and their help or hindrance to
growth in human community. It is very doubtful whether talk
about 'a world faith' to support an emerging 'world community' is
realistic at the present moment in human history in spite of certain
enthusiastic expectations in this direction. Technology and industrialization continue to produce a certain outward similarity in
the lives of people in different parts of the world, depending partly
upon the kind of consumer goods available and the degree of influence of mass media. But it is far from clear whether there is
deeper similarity in the thoughts, attitudes and values of people in

different cultures. All airports look alike, but they do not lead to identical societies in different countries. Contemporary signs point instead to cultural and religious pluralism than a monolithic world culture. The attempt to create a world faith, either by advancing one particular religion or by trying to mix up selected elements from different faiths—in a fruit-salad approach to the problem of religious pluralism—is doomed to failure. Such hypothetical religion would lack the throb of natural life and the spontaneity of spiritual creativity. "Even the merging of world-civilization (which in any case will not be Western, Latin or Roman in character) will not simply eradicate racial, or religious peculiarities, but will in some respects even re-inforce them. The closer drawing together of cultural areas promotes the awareness of differences."[15] Moreover, it is legitimate to acknowledge that there are universal elements in a particular faith which may be of value in other cultural situations; but it is questionable to suggest that these elements can be put together to form a world faith within the structure of which the differences and tensions between religions may be softened. It is more important today to focus on those particular areas of the world where religious pluralism has created tensions in the past and continues to intensify strife today. The church is in danger of being considered as the débris left behind by the receding tide of colonialism, if in its fears of syncretism it tends to keep itself separate from its neighbors.

The problem for India is how, in a multi-religious, multi-lingual and multi-ethnic society, true community life can be fostered so that the nation can move forward. In Pakistan and Ceylon, in Malaysia and Indonesia, the problems are the same, although with differences in degree. In the Middle-East, with three Semitic faiths painfully sharing a long history of conflict and strife, the question is not so much of syncretism as how to bring in the resources of these faiths, which have so much in common, to tame political passions, to reduce tensions and direct the feet of men in the ways of peace. In Africa the problem is threefold: to transcend the limitations of tribalism, which disrupts true community; to overcome those artificial boundaries drawn by the colonial powers in carving out the continent to themselves; and to look for the contours of a larger community within which people can grow with a reasonable measure of understanding and co-operation. In the West the fears of a disintegrating Christendom should not lead to an uncritical acceptance of Eastern mysticism and *yoga*, but to a deeper search for those enduring values of faith which may be of some help to men who seem to be caught in the cyclical movement of the wheels of technology.

Part of the difficulty of discussing syncretism in pluralistic situations is due to the different ways in which it is understood. At the risk of oversimplification one may distinguish between at least two kinds of syncretism. First, there is the syncretism which is simply an indiscriminate patching up of incompatible beliefs. It is the result of a lack of spiritual maturity, of commitment, of an inability to accept the open situation of religious pluralism. Second, there is the syncretism which has a center around which certain elements in the cultural situation are integrated naturally and consistently. This may probably be described as 'indigenization' and is the natural consequence of freedom and creativity. In this sense Christianity itself is a 'syncretistic' religion, because various elements have gone into its making. "Christianity, is sociologically speaking, certainly one religion; it is ancient paganism, or, to be more precise, the complex Hebrew-Hellenic-Graeco-Latin-Celtic-Gothic-modern religion *converted* to Christ with more or less success."[16] What is important is the centrality of the figure of Jesus Christ, the crucified and risen Lord, who holds together and transforms the various elements that are brought into the situation. If the theological attempts of Western Christians to come to grips with philosophy, science, technology, and secularization are syncretistic, how can they accuse the Indian or African theologian if he tries to come to grips with elements in his own culture or states the Christian faith in his own cultural terms? Who decides whether such attempts are syncretistic or not? Why should the norms set up in other situations and different times be used to describe expressions of Christian faith in particular countries as 'dangerously syncretistic'? P. Chenchiah, a convert from Hinduism, whose commitment to Christ cannot be questioned and who never hesitated to bring the gifts of Hindu culture to the feet of Christ, remarks on this subject:

> At the outset, a syncretist is not a common creature of modern times. He rarely exists. When he exists he is a descendant of the old syncretist who has forgotten his ancestry. The Church is syncretic —having patched up paganism with Christianity. It has forgotten it and gets cross if reminded of the fact.[17]

Is syncretism in the first sense such a danger to the integrity of the Christian faith? India is, of course, the country where different religions have existed side by side for many centuries. There have been other attempts in history to build up artificial synthesis of religions, notably that of the Egyptian king Amenhotep IV in the fourteenth century B.C., or that of Caesar Augustus in the first. But these have not been particularly successful. The *din ilahi* (the Divine Faith) which the Moghul Emperor Akbar, a contemporary of Queen Elizabeth I, devised is usually regarded as a syncretistic religion. It is true that Akbar mixed elements from Islam, Christianity, Judaism, and Zoroastrianism in a religion designed to weld together his subjects. But it did not last long. It produced no martyrs and it is doubtful whether it was in any way a serious threat to the faith of the Hindus or Muslims or Jesuit priests in the Moghul court. Perhaps the Brahmo Samaj, founded by Raja Ram Mohun Roy, should be regarded as syncretistic because it deliberately attempted to combine in thought and practise those elements which are considered to be the best in Hinduism and Christianity. But its weakness was that it had no center and no theological framework and therefore served only as a half-way house between Hinduism and Christianity. It is today a spent force, living in the past, lacking the depth of inner resources to give it power and direction.

One striking fact emerges from study of the past: namely, that in the long centuries of India's history, during which religious pluralism was a part of daily life, one can find very few examples of syncretism in the sense of deliberate attempts to blend incompatible beliefs. Therefore the church in India, should constantly ask itself the question whether concern with syncretism is one of the serious priorities which should engage its attention at the present time. Chenchiah was essentially right when he wrote:

> My regret is, I don't see it [syncretism]...On the Christian side nobody at least says let us have Hinduism and Christianity, let us worship Christ and Krishna...Syncretism, I said, is a bogey. Let us not turn it into a bugbear. Let us not be lured into a pursuit of shadows when far more urgent and decisive realities challenge our faith.[18]

III. *A Broadening View of Mission*

The nature of the Christian's obligation in a religiously pluralistic world becomes more complex if not more urgent. Some of the important issues in this connection are the content and practice of mission, the nature of Christian universalism in situations of pluralism, and the purpose of dialogue between people of living faiths.

In many countries there are insistent demands that people of different religious persuasions should come together for tasks of social renewal and nationbuilding. It would be most unwise for Christians to stand aloof from these requests. Such interfaith collaboration has been well established in several lands already.[19] Not only churches in particular countries but also the World Council of Churches and the Vatican are receiving invitations from other world religious organizations for closer cooperation. It is agreed that the most helpful relationship between men of different faiths in the world today must be one of co-operation in pursuing common purposes like justice, peace and human rights.

Is such co-operation becoming a substitute for 'mission'? This question troubles many sensitive people, particularly those of faiths whose integrity would be seriously disturbed if 'mission' is eliminated from their practice. The dilemma facing such people is this. On the one hand, to give up 'mission' would be to spill out the oil from the lamp of Christianity: sharing the good news of God in Jesus Christ has been the justification for the church's existence in the world. On the other, a unilateral proclamation of 'a uniquely saving truth,' far from making a contribution towards true community, is more likely to be misunderstood as the arrogance born out of an apparent claim to monopolistic possession of truth. To avoid the dilemma would be irresponsible. Is it possible to go beyond it? One way of looking at the problem is to point out that surely in many situations the co-operation with others and the practice of 'mission' are not to be regarded as mutually exclusive alternatives. Therefore to put the alternatives so badly as 'mission' or cooperation is to put the right question in the wrong context. There are many areas of human concern in which genuine cooperation between men of living faiths should be possible without prior debates to settle the theological issues on the meaning of 'mission.' A Christian, who, on the basis of the Gospel, believes that every form of racial discrimination is evil can surely work together with Hindus, Buddhists, Muslims, Marxists or any others to attain the same objective.

But this is not enough; it is also necessary to ask a deeper and more disturbing question. Has the time not come to restate the meaning of 'mission' in multi-religious contexts, taking into account the integrity of other faiths also? Is the Christian 'mission' the *only* mission of God in all the world at all times? To claim that only Christians have 'mission' and that others only engage in 'proselytization' would indeed be nothing less than arrogance although it might wear the cloak of a deceptive Christian humility. It is difficult to get away from claims and counter-claims regarding this question. If one takes into account just the three Semitic faiths, Judaism, Christianity and Islam, each one holding on to a revelation, a book, a sense of the people of God and a 'mission,' it is obvious that each one of them has built up through the centuries its own claims against the others both as theological defense and as basis for advance. Arthur Cohen, discussing the temper of Jewish anti-Christianity, remarks that he does not believe in "a Judeo-Christian tradition" but regards it simply as "an ideologizing of a fundamental and irreconcilable disagreement." He goes on to say, "We wait patiently the return of Christendom to the Synagogue, as we wait patiently the coming of the Messianic herald of the End."[20] Amir Ali remarks.

> Muslims do not recognise that modern Christianity overladen with Greek philosophy and Pauline mysticism, represents the true religion Jesus taught. *They consider that Islam represents true Christianity.* They do not think that Jesus who prayed in the wilderness and on the hillside in the huts of peasants, in the humble abodes of fishermen, furnish any warrant for the gorgeousness of Christian worship, with all the accessories that beguile the mind, mystify the intellect, and thus divert the human heart from the worship of the great God towards a symbol and a type.[21]

It is unnecessary to quote any of the numerous Christian claims in this connection or to draw attention to the increasingly more articulate defenses of Hindu and Buddhist missions in the West. To claim that these are misunderstandings of Christianity does not help, because a similar observation may be made of the Christian statements about other faiths from *their* points of view. It is unlikely that in the near future 'Christendom' will return to the Synagogue nor is the statement that Islam represents true Christianity likely to result in a Christian exodus to Islam. But the important point is this: it would be foolish to expect that the Christian relationship to the Jews, Muslims, as well as to the Hindus, the Buddhists and others will improve merely by assuming a stance of openness and dialogue. There must be a serious revision of the theological understanding of 'mission' in the total context of human history and with regard to the persistent fact of religious pluralism. Asserting that the 'mission' of the Church, while being world-wide in scope, is not God's *only* mission, Wilfred Cantwell Smith writes as follows:

> Few of us Christians know much about God's mission in the Islamic venture; God's mission to India, and nowadays it would seem to the world, through the Hindu complex; God's mission to East Asia, and nowadays to the world, in the Buddhist movement. Few Christians have any appreciation of God's mighty mission to the world in the post-Biblical Jewish community. But we learn. We are learning. Especially, our youth are learning it. Only as we learn to see God's activity in other movements and other communities should we learn to serve Him well in and through our own.[22]

If it is recognized that real conversion is not from one religion to another but from unbelief to God, and that 'mission' is not the church's work but God's, then, its implications in the actual context of religious pluralism must be more openly acknowledged. Moreover, the inadequacy of the instruments shaped to express 'mission' in previous eras should also be recognised and conscious attempts be made to shape new forms, working now with those who are committed to participation in God's mission in the world today.

Talk about partnership of Christians with men of other faiths inevitably raises the question of dialogue as a means of spiritual renewal and a way of building up community life. It may be helpful to distinguish between two kinds of dialogue. First, there is the dialogue in which the main purpose is to investigate together certain questions with the intent of reaching agreement wherever it is possible. This is the way of science, where investigatory dialogues continue to take place all the time in different parts of the world, where errors are eliminated by common consent, and where a continuing body of knowledge is built up through intellectual agreement. Violence cannot enter into this dialogue because in the quest for truth many errors are discovered and eliminated through rational discussion, experimentation and the general acceptance of evidence. The second type of dialogue takes place in the area of beliefs and convictions, where spiritual commitments confront each other and where unanimity is unlikely to be reached. Where people of different beliefs live together, dialogue brings about an encounter of commitments. Although it is surely possible to eliminate doubts and misunderstandings, the question in such dialogues is not primarily one of truth and error but of respect for the freedom of people to hold on to their convictions without pressure. The question of truth is not entirely eliminated; but where commitments are concerned, the issues are far deeper than verbal misunderstandings or intellectual controversies. This is one of the reasons why religious liberty is such an important issue in multireligious societies. "The dialogue is a common quest for liberty, and, as a consequence of progress in the liberty of each, a common effort to advance in the direction of Truth."[23]

In both particular communities and now in the larger context of the world, where people of different persuasions need to live together in harmony, the question of truth can be an issue only when there is sincere recognition of the liberty of all to hold on to their convictions without pressure, but at the same time opening themselves freely to the risks and choices this freedom brings. Dialogue, of course, is not new; it is at least as old as the Buddha, Plato and the *Upanishads*. Within Hinduism, for example, the diversity of theistic and non-theistic traditions as well as systems of philosophy has necessitated such open exchange of ideas and beliefs. Also within Buddhism, which transformed itself in different cultural situations of Asia, an internal dialogue has been taking place. And within the Christian tradition itself multi-denominational differences have called for ecumenical dialogue. The question now is whether people are ready to extend this freedom into the larger and more exciting context of pluralism in the world as a whole.

The state of religious pluralism should not always be regarded negatively as one of dangers and temptations; it also carries the possibilities of fresh discoveries and mutual enrichment. Where respect for the freedom of people to hold on to their convictions does not mean indifference or relativism, and where there is willingness to work together in projects that touch the community as a whole, there is always the possibility of sharing new insights. The Hindu teaching on the unity of all life and the inwardness of true religion, the Buddhist emphasis on *ahimsa* and its combination of disciplined meditation with compassionate service, and the Islamic insistence that peace within the human heart and with man and nature can be the consequence only of man's total submission to the sovereignty of Allah—these are insights which can enrich the Christian. "An unseemly anxiety to preserve our heritage is to lose it and, at the same time, to attempt to limit God; but a willingness finally to risk even the loss of our heritage in the service of God and man is to find it. When there is a readiness to risk all, God may be trusted to be faithful in giving all back again in a renewed and enlarged perspective."[24]

Is it possible, then, to combine Christian universality with a recognition of religious pluralism? Christians are tempted to advocate pluralism and religious liberty as a policy of expediency in situations where they are minorities. This has been the temptation to which many religions and ideologies have succumbed. And sometimes minorities become majorities, only to suppress others in the name of a false universalism, monolithic and hardcrusted, in which there can hardly be the possibility for mutual enrichment or for the emergence of something new. On the other hand, there is a universality which is based on the least common denominator and on the minimum acceptable convictions. If the former is the danger in societies where one religion predominates, the latter is the danger in those countries where two or three different religions are equally balanced.

With a broadening awareness of the world perspective of religious pluralism today and with several world organizations seeking a greater measure of co-operation, the time has come to search for a new style of ecumenism encompassing the whole of humanity, but which recognizes within itself the creative particularities of pluralism.[25] Far from making it easier for particular religions to perpetuate themselves, it would be a challenge to them to be less introverted and concerned with their own particular problems but to be more involved in those concerns which touch people everywhere as human beings sharing the burden and mystery of existence. The church would be compelled to spend less of its time and energy on its own domestic issues but more on the larger issues of all persons and people. Visser 't Hooft has rightly observed: "The pluralistic world throws us all back on the primary source of our faith and forces us to take a new look at the world around us. Thus pluralism can provide a real opportunity for a new united witness of the whole Church of Christ in and to the whole world."[26]

NOTES

[1] W. A. Visser 't Hooft, "Pluralism—Temptation or Opportunity?," *The Ecumenical Review*, April 1966, No. 2, p. 129.

[2] *Ibid.*, p. 129.

[3] Karl Barth, *Church Dogmatics*, I:2 (Edinburgh, 1956), pp. 299-300: "We begin by stating that religion is unbelief. It is a concern, indeed, we must say that it is the one great concern, of godless men."

[4] "Upon *dharma* everything is founded. Therefore *dharma* is called the highest good." *Taittiriya Aranyaka*, 10:79. For more complete discussion see

Sources of Indian Tradition, edited by William Theodore de Bary (New York, 1958), pp. 216ff.

⁵ See Carl F. Hallencreutz, *New Approaches to Men of Other Faiths* (Geneva, 1970) with introductory essay by S. J. Samartha, pp. 7ff.

⁶ Harry Sawyyer, "The Witnessing Scene—Africa," *South East Asia Journal of Theology*, January 1967, No. 3, p. 81.

⁷ Figures from the Japanese Ministry of Education, quoted by Joseph M. Kitagawa, *Religion in Japanese History* (New York, 1966), p. 282.

⁸ *Ibid.* See also Huston Smith, "Secularization and the Sacred: the Contemporary Scene," in *The Religious Situation*, edited by Donald R. Cutler (Boston, 1968), chapter 16; and Joseph J. Spae, "Christ and Religions," *South East Asia Journal of Theology*, January 1967, No. 3, pp. 34ff.

⁹ Huston Smith, *op. cit.*, p. 597.

¹⁰ W. A. Visser 't Hooft, *op. cit.*, p. 140.

¹¹ W. A. Visser 't Hooft, "Asian Churches," *The Ecumenical Review*, January 1950, No. 3, p. 229.

¹² *Ibid.*, p. 234.

¹³ W. A. Visser 't Hooft, "Asian Churches in the Ecumenical Movement," in *The Decisive Hour for Christian Mission* (London, 1963), pp. 46-58.

¹⁴ *The Ecumenical Review*, April 1966, No. 2, p. 142.

¹⁵ Hans Küng, *Structures of the Church* (London, 1965), p. 39.

¹⁶ *Christian Revelation and World Religions*, edited by Joseph Neuner (London, 1967), chapter by Raymond Pannikar, p. 169.

¹⁷ P. Chenchiah, writing on Professor Kraemer and Syncretism in *The Guardian*, Madras, 1951, p. 180 and p. 200; quoted by D. A. Thangasamy, *The Theology of Chenchiah* (Bangalore, 1966), pp. 173ff.

¹⁸ D. A. Thangasamy, *op. cit.*, p. 181.

¹⁹ The Religious League of Japan, founded in 1943, includes the following groups: The Federation of Sectarian Shinto (13 groups), The Great Japan Buddhist Association (55 sects), Association of Shinto Shrines (90,000 shrines), The Union of New Religions in Japan (86), and the Japan Christian Federation. It is appropriate that in October 1970 the World Congress of Religions dealing with world peace met in Kyoto, including ranking leaders of many Christian churches, Judaism, and the major Asian religions.

²⁰ David W. McKain, editor, *Christianity : Some Non-Christian Appraisals* (New York, 1964), p. 222.

²¹ *Ibid*, p. 29. Italics added.

²² Wilfred Cantwell Smith, "The Mission of the Church and the Future of Missions," *The Church in the Modern World*, edited by George Johnston and Wolfgang Roth (Toronto, 1967), pp. 154-170.

²³ D. Dubarle, "Dialogue and Its Philosophy," *Concurrence*, Spring, 1969, pp. 3-12.

²⁴ James K. Mathews, *A Church Truly Catholic* (New York, 1969), p. 160.

²⁵ See Eugene Hillman, *The Wider Ecumenism* (London, 1968) and James K. Mathews, *op. cit.*, pp. 130ff.

²⁶ *The Ecumenical Review*, April 1966, No. 2, p. 149.

CHAPTER EIGHT

FROM CONFUCIAN GENTLEMAN TO THE NEW CHINESE 'POLITICAL' MAN

DAVID A. ROBINSON

After twenty-five centuries with the Confucian gentleman as the dominant model, new China since its revolution in 1949 has looked to a new concept of 'political man' as its guiding ideal. How does the Chinese nation and its faith in 'man as rebel' challenge the rest of the world? Has the time come when the oppressed peoples of Asia, Latin America, Africa, and the 'underdeveloped areas' within the affluent societies of the West must assume the role of teachers? The Confucian gentleman, who served as the legitimating model for thousands of years, held Chinese civilization together. What role will the new 'political man' of the People's Republic of China play in rallying together the poor, the powerless, the terrible meek of our generation?

I. *The Rise of the Confucian Model of Gentleman*

In the sixth century B.C., Confucius came to a China which faced social anarchy. With the collapse of the Chou Dynasty's ruling power, almost continuous warfare took place in Homeric fashion. Noble warriors made elaborate recognitions before battle, exchanged haughty compliments from their chariots, drank together, and traded weapons before battle. By the time of Confucius' mature years, however, the Warring States period brought mass slaughters: the beheading of men, women, and children, with the conquered being thrown into boiling cauldrons and their relatives forced to drink the human soup.[1] The central question facing Confucius has haunted mankind ever since: How can men learn to live together?

In his *The Soul of China*, Amaury de Riencourt suggests that "the urge toward a united world for all civilized mankind"[2] was the major Confucian contribution to the world beyond the Middle Kingdom. As we now compare the classical Chinese view of man with the post-1949 revolutionary model of 'political man,' the problem becomes:

Is there a good chance that man in the new China will provide a convincing model to unify the nation and offer to the rest of the world a re-incarnation of the maxim "within the four seas all men are brothers"? Or does revolutionary China offer a threat to destroy the values which unite men?

A. Moral Exemplar and Man with a Mission

Confucius, because he sought to bring order and unity to the anarchy of his time, was a man on a mission. He saw his vocation to be that of cultivating an inner, moral force so that the whole world might feel the radiant force of the true gentleman and follow his example. The *Analects* suggest that Confucius was a man called to a special task as moral exemplar:

> The master said:
> At fifteen I set my heart on learning. At thirty I had planted my feet firm upon the ground. At forty, I had no perplexities. At fifty, I heard the command of heaven. At sixty, I was obedient. At seventy, I could follow my heart's desire and yet not overstep the bounds of right conduct.[3]

Confucius taught that no outside force, but only cultivation of the moral power (*tê*) within man leads to goodness (*jên*). The harmony of man and the social order with heaven makes a balanced universe function. Thus music plays a crucial role in the Confucian scheme. The pentatonic scale allows neither soaring heights nor tragic depths, but an optimistic and soothing style of music. As we analyze three elements in the Confucian view: moral force (*tê*), goodness (*jên*), and the gentleman (*chun-tzu*), we are often reminded of parallels between the Chinese and Greek interpretation of the doctrine of the Mean, the Middle Way. In its optimism about the capacity of man to develop himself through self-cultivation and its stress on the Golden Mean, Confucian views on human nature have striking resemblances to Aristotelian concepts.

B. *Tê* (Moral Force)

The Confucian Gentleman (*chun-tzu*) has *tê*. Arthur Waley makes a strong case for the interpretation of *tê* as moral force or moral power.[4] The sense of the Latin *virtus* as a power latent in things is a better interpretation of *tê* than 'virtue' in common usage. Waley translates *tê* as 'moral force,' 'character,' or 'the power of moral example.' An excellent example of the breadth of *tê*'s meaning is found in the *Analects* II.1:

The Master said,
  He who rules by *tê* (moral force) is like the pole-star which remains
in its place while all the lesser stars do homage to it.

Two sentences later in the Analects II.3 we find further examples:

  The Master said, Govern the people by regulations, keep order among
  them by chastisements, and they will flee from you, and lose all self-
  respect. Govern them with *tê*, keep order among them by ritual, and.
  they will keep their self-respect and come to you of their own accord.

Confucius is disquieted only by the thought that: "I have left my
tê untended, my learning unperfected, that I have heard of righteous men, but been unable to go to them; have heard of evil men, but
have been unable to reform them." In a more realistic mood, Confucius longed for the day when *tê* would have as much drive to it as
other natural forces, like sexual instincts:

  The Master said, I have never yet seen anyone whose desire to build
  up his *tê* was as strong as sexual desire.   (*Analects* IX.17)

A fascinating supplemental power is found when the two words
chung and *tê* are combined to mean: 'the piling up of moral forces,'
'loyalty,' or 'good faith' in the new word *chung-tê*.

  Tê must never be confused with physical force. The abhorrence
of violence is central to Confucian ethics. But the irony of a non-
violent Confucian ideology serving for centuries as the legitimating
power behind suppression of individual rights of the poor and ignorant Chinese masses has not been wasted on contemporary
Chinese scholars. It comes as no great surprise, then, to discover a
strand of elitism in the Master:

  The Master said, Where gentlemen (*chun-tzu*) set their hearts upon
  tê, the commoners set theirs upon the soil.   (*Analects* IV.11)
  The Master said, How transcendent is the *tê* of the Middle Way. That
  it is but rarely found among the common people is a fact long admitted.   (*Analects* VI.27)

The phrase "common people" (*an t'u*) is thus associated with those
peasants who must till the soil for a livelihood, ordinary folk who
will use force if necessary to defend their land from greedy landlords.

  The legendary Duke of Chou was an exemplar for Confucius, who
equated this Golden Age Ruler with all the power of *tê*:

  The moral power (*tê*) of Chou may indeed be called an absolutely
  perfect moral power.   (*Analects* VIII.20)

Tê is to be equated with the commanding moral example of the
chun-tzu whose actions speak louder than his words:

> The Master said, One who has accumulated *tê* will certainly also possess eloquence: but he who has eloquence does not necessarily posses *tê*. (*Analects* XIV.5)

In summary, then, we must understand how *tê* provides a central core to a man, and radiating from the man to all of society. When the wind of the *chun-tzu's tê* blows across the land, all are swayed by it, as grass bends before the wind. At this point the concept of *jên* joins *tê* in the Confucian understanding of man.

C. *Jên* (Goodness)

The simple Chinese character for man combined with the character for two forms the character *jên*. The Confucian gentleman tries to realize *jên* in everything he does and thinks. Arthur Waley has suggested the linkage between *jên* and lineage as follows:

> *Jên* refers to freemen, men of the tribe, as opposed to *min*, subjects, 'the common people.' The same word, written with a slight modification, means 'good' in the most general sense of the word, that is to say, 'possessing the qualities of one's tribe.' For no more sweeping form of praise can be given by the men of a tribe than to say that someone is a 'true member' of that tribe.[5]

Jên is that quality shown to all other members of the in-group, but not to outsiders. As the Latin *gens* (clan) gave rise to the 'gentle' in 'gentleman,' so *jên* comes to be translated as 'kind,' 'gentle' or 'humane.' A few centuries after Confucius the distinction between *min* (the subservient common folk) and the *jên* of the *chun-tzu* was dropped and *jên* came to mean 'a human being' as opposed to animals.

Waley argues that "*Jên* in the *Analects* means 'good' in an extremely wide and general sense...but that it cannot be said that *jên* in the *Analects* simply means 'good.' It is on the contrary the name of a quality so rare and peculiar...a sublime moral attitude, a transcendental perfection attained to by legendary heroes, but not by any living person...Confucius can point the way to *jên*, can tell the workman how to sharpen his tools, can speak even of things that are near to goodness...but the Master rarely discoursed on *jên*."[6]

The self-sacrificing nature of *jên* enriches our understanding of both the gentleman-knight (*shih*) and the wider view of man:

> Neither the resolute knight (*shih*) nor the humane person will ever seek life at the expense of *jên*. On occasion they will sacrifice their lives to preserve humanity. (*Analects* XV.8)

The true *shih* of the Way (*Tao*) must perforce be both broadshouldered and stout of heart; his burden is heavy and he has far to go. For *jên* is the burden he has taken upon himself; and must we not grant that it is a heavy one to bear? Only with death does his journey end; then must we not that he has far to go?   (*Analects* VIII.7)

The Master said, Be of unwavering good faith, love learning, if attacked be ready to die for the *jên*.   (*Analects* VIII.13)

The Confucian gentleman (*chun-tzu*) balances the inner (*nei*) and the outer (*wai*) with a unifying principle of *jên*. This goodness (*jên*) at the very heart of man, developed through inner self-cultivation, spreads from the inner (*nei*) to the outer (*wai*) in bringing harmony to the whole social order. "Is *jên* far away?" the Master asks. "If we really wanted goodness, we should find it has already arrived!" (*Analects* VII.29)

D. *Chun-tzu* (Gentleman)

Throughout the *Analects* Confucius uses the word *chun-tzu* to define the model man. We start with the derivation of the word in Chinese to avoid prejudging the meaning of the word. *Chun* is the character for "ruler," *tzu* means "son"—giving us *chun-tzu*: "son of a ruler." Originally *chun-tzu* was applied to descendants of the aristocracy, and so came to mean either a member of the upper classes or a 'gentleman.' Thus the *jên* is a common class trait shared by all gentlemen. The aristocratic side often lies just beneath the surface of statements like "within the four seas all men are brothers," meaning—if they share the same noble ideals of *jên* and are themselves *chun-tzu*.

But the *chun-tzu* is more than a man of superior birth. He is a moral aristocrat, one of superior moral power (*tê*). Confucius transforms the code of morals and manners for the aristocrat into a deeper Way (*tao*) of the gentleman. The Confucian *chun-tzu* is a member of a club. He refuses the friendship of all who are not like him lest he lower his standards. Yet this exclusiveness is held in tension with a universalizing principle that holds every man who follows the Way of the *chun-tzu* to be a *chun-tzu*, while every man who follows the 'small' or 'mean' way is a commoner.

The tragedy of the Confucian gentleman is that he is made for public office. He achieves his full self-realization only in his political vocation, but he is typically 'Gentleman out of Office.' Benjamin Schwartz has pointed out the tragedy of "innumerable idealistic Chinese Confucian gentleman down through the centuries" who could not use their *tê* (moral power and shared the fate of Confucius himself:

> The superior man can only achieve complete self-realization in his public vocation...Conversely, society can be harmonized and set in order only when men who have approached the ideal of self-realization are in public office...The central tragedy of the Master's own life was his failure to find any opportunity to fulfill his public vocation... The *Chun-tzu* is not always blessed with *Shih* (auspicious times) for the public employment of his talents.[7]

Contemporary Chinese man is the revolutionary seeking power eagerly, while the gentleman is waiting on the sidelines for a time when his *tê* can bring order again:

> The times will remain out of joint so long as *chun-tzu* are not in positions of responsibility, but such positions are not to be attained when the times are out of joint.[8]

Schwartz sees the essence of Confucian character, then, as the dignified withdrawal of the *chun-tzu* to as high a degree of self-cultivation as is possible, and thus to the role of teacher-prophet.

And yet, for over 2,000 years the Confucian gentleman has been the controlling model for Chinese society. Confucius put together the Chou traditions in a creative way and molded them into a cohesive system embracing Heaven, the Ruler, and the family-system. Max Weber is correct in calling Confucianism a Way that adjusts man to his world. The vast population crowded into small spaces, the exquisite perfection of social graces, in short the superb style of the adaptive transmitter of culture signal the *chun-tzu* as the exponent of harmony and smoothly functioning society. This is best symbolized by the Master's love of music, "the best way to improve manners and customs is to pay attention to music...and when one has mastered music completely and regulated his heart and mind accordingly, the natural, correct, gentle and sincere heart is easily developed and joy attends its development." (*Analects* II)

The *Chun-tzu* must be an all-round person. The Master says: "A *chun-tzu* is not an implement." (*Analects* II.12).

In other words, a gentleman is never a specialist, a tool used for a special purpose. He need have only general moral qualifications. And so his training is like that of the proper English gentleman: the classics and discipline in moral training. But to learn anything of actual utility, to soil his hands like a peasant, is unheard of! Around this phrase has raged many a controversy in recent China, with one side maintaining the cadre should resemble the *chun-tzu* and be more 'Red' than expert—an omnicompetent moral leader. But the other side has only scorn for the useless Confucian gentleman, with no special skills.

Confucian man is at the center of a harmonious world. His chief goal: self-cultivation around *tê*, leading to *jên* which radiates into all the world. An aristocrat, the *chun-tzu* calls all men to brotherhood—so long as they are 'gentle-men' of his own kind.

II. *The Contemporary Chinese 'Political' Man*

In sharp contrast to his predecessor, the Confucian *chun-tzu*, revolutionary man in modern China seeks a spiritual transformation of his own nature through a process of 'conscientization,'[9] political struggle against all those things which enslaved him in the old society. Like his Latin American peasant brother, Chinese man goes through *fan shen*, an overturning of his total previous existence very similar to conversion in religious circles. For a preliminary definition we use the analysis of Franz Schurmann in his recent studies of China:

> In traditional China, the trinity of ethos, status group, and modal personality was represented by Confucianism, the gentry, and the *pater familias (chia chang)*.
> By 1949 the revolution had destroyed all three...The modal personality in Communist China today is the CADRE, the revolutionary leader in organization. He is young, not old; he is a leader, not a conciliator; he operates in the public realm, not in the private.[10]

A striking parallel to the new Chinese political man is described by Michael Walzer in his study of the seventeenth-century English Puritan revolutionaries:

> The revolutionary saint not only repudiates the routine procedures and customary beliefs of the old order...but confronts the existing order as if at war. These men are marked off from their fellows by an extraordinary self-assurance and daring...It is the saints who lead the final attack upon the old order, and their destructiveness is all the more total *because they have a total view of the new world*. They set the stage of history for the new order.[11]

We cannot understand the radical break between old and new Chinese man unless we see some of the many facets suggested by the above comparisons. For clarification of the overall term contemporary 'political man' the following four sub-themes will be used:

'Man of the Masses.' 'Guerrilla Rebel.' 'Revolutionary Cadre.'
'Conscientized Man,' i.e. the spiritually transformed new political
being.

A. Man of the Masses

The achievement of 'liberation' of Chinese man—a process begun
long before the actual Communist victory of 1949, and still continuing in a neverending Cultural Revolution—is based squarely
on the development of people's power, the unfolding of human will
and spirit among the ordinary men and women and youth of China.
Mao Tse-tung gave prophetic voice to this mass participation of
Chinese man in his own liberation in the 1927 report on the Hunanese Agrarian Movement:

> The force of the peasantry is like that of the raging winds and driving
> rain. It is rapidly increasing in violence. No force can stand in its
> way. The peasantry will tear apart all nets which bind it, and hasten
> along the road to liberation. They will bury beneath them all forces
> of imperialism, militarism, corrupt officialdom, village bosses and
> evil gentry. Every revolutionary comrade will be subjected to their
> scrutiny and be accepted or rejected by them. Shall we stand in the
> vanguard and lead them, or behind them and oppose them?[12]

A more recent example of the massive participation of the ordinary people in their own transformation is given by an eyewitness
account of the 1966-67 Great Proletarian Cultural Revolution:[13]

> Much of Mao's prestige stems from his faith in the "rank and file"
> people... Students, workers, and peasants enjoyed a degree of power
> that would scarcely be tolerable even in democratic countries. In
> Shanghai, the whole administration was roundly criticized, and top
> Party and government jobs were up for grabs. Red Guard slogans
> at this time were: "Rebellion is justified!" and, "If we don't take
> power, who will?"

The people are to be trusted. The new Chinese man is as much a
part of the common people as Mao Tse-tung, who still loves hot
Hunanese food, favors the simple peasant garb, and reveals his non-
mandarinate background every time he speaks in his thick Hunanese accent. Mao profoundly believes in the power of the awakened
revolutionary consciousness of the peasant, and offers countless
examples of ordinary men who transform themselves from victims
of the old society to new men through struggle.[14]

B. Guerrilla Rebel

A second essential ingredient in the contemporary Chinese view of man is the deep identification with the struggle, heroism, and victory over the forces of nature and the enemy, symbolized by the guerrilla model. Mao Tse-tung sets forth this heroic dimension in his classic statement about the Long March:

> We say that the Long March is the first of its kind ever recorded in history, that it is a manifesto, an agitation corps, and a seeding-machine... We encountered untold difficulties and great obstacles on the way, but by keeping our two feet going we swept across a distance of more than 20,000 *li* through the length and breadth of eleven provinces. Well, has there ever been in history a long march like ours? It proclaims to the world that the Red Army is an army of heroes.[15]

Never before in Chinese history had the popular base of such a resistance movement educated the ordinary man in his new found dignity and freedom. After the Long March the Chinese Communist Party established itself in Yenan (1935-45), where it led a Robin Hood existence, built its power base in opposition to the Japanese, and produced legendary documents like Mao's "on Contradiction," "On the New Democracy," and "On Practice." As was the case with the Puritan saints in the seventeenth century, the Chinese guerrilla hero developed many new characteristics which effectively shattered the old traditions of Confucian man: harmony was replaced with *struggle*; self-cultivation yielded to *risk-taking* and total *involvement*; *jên* and non-violent obedience to social norms is replaced by *active rebellion* against all the old hierarchies; and a social order with emphasis on social control through scholarly education was ripped apart by the force of the angry guerrilla seeking redress for injustices perpetrated by the order and elitism of the traditional Confucian society.

Residents of China before 1949 still find it difficult to believe that the ordinary people of China have stood up. But the passive, silent, longsuffering masses of China have been transformed by their participation in the guerrilla struggle. Chalmers Johnson has made a convincing case for the crucial importance of the anti-Japanese struggle in this very matter:

> The Chinese masses, the peasants, were unified and politicized as a concomitant of the drastic restructuring of Chinese life that accompanied the Japanese conquest of North and East China. Participation in the popular guerrilla base governments, together with the

numerous other projects for national mobilization undertaken by guerrilla leadership, gave an entirely new political perspective to the Chinese peasantry.[16]

No longer is Chinese man one who seeks adjustment to the world—as Max Weber described it[17]—but he has become a world-transformer who tries to master the hostile environment (Long March) and achieves a new dignity and political awareness in the process of his involvement.

C. Revolutionary Cadre

The revolutionary cadre replaces Confucian *chun-tzu* as the modal personality in contemporary China. With neither wealth nor power, often picked up from one of many alienated groups in pre-revolutionary China—like the robber bands, secret societies, or drifting migrant labor forces—how did the cadre develop into a crucial exemplar? Franz Schurmann suggests two elements of crucial importance:[18]

> Critical self-analysis (*fenhsi fenhsi*), and a new
> moral authority and power.

1. *Fen-hsi fenhsi*

This Chinese compound word signifies the constant thinking and rethinking, the self-analysis and mutual self-criticism which lies at the heart of the transformation of illiterate peasants into dignified participants in the changing of the history of a vast nation like China. All who have been privileged to meet refugees from new China, despite their external appearance of ragged, often depressed conditions, notice their amazing capacity to discuss, analyze, and make very sophisticated socio-political observations. Schurmann comments on the reason they have this power:

> Members of the Communist Party analyze everything (*fenhsi fenhsi*)... If a minor industrial accident occurs, meetings will be held in which every human and material factor in the accident is discussed... Party life is mostly talk, discussion, group interaction, criticism and self-criticism. [This] gives him individual norms, rational tools for action.[19]

William Hinton presents similar evidence in his book, *Fan Shen*, that this self-conscious analytical capacity can be, and is, developed in modern China, providing the key element in 'conscientization.'[20]

2. *A New Moral Authority*

Recent theological inquiry into the meaning of 'rebellion'[21] suggests that the revolutionary cadre may be the new saint. Is he not squarely in the succession from Jesus to Paul to Martin Luther to modern rebels *with* a cause, such as Gandhi, Martin Luther King, the hero of Camus' novel, Malcolm X, black militant heroes, and countless others.? Where does the authority of the revolutionary cadre come from? How does this transformation take place from a blank passivity to moral force? We trust Schurmann's analysis at this point:

> It is more difficult to conceive of a fundamental moral and psychological transformation of the individual. The values of Chinese Communist ideology diverge sharply from traditional Chinese values. Thus, struggle differs from harmony, the stress on public life differs from the earlier Chinese love of privacy... If the ideology of the Chinese Communists is an instrument of value transformation, it is not easy to see how such a transformation could be successful in the face of such a traditional cultural heritage.[22]

And yet the evidence of numerous observers and many studies (emerging from Myrdal,[23] Nee,[24] Hinton,[25] *et al.*) of value transformation on the basis of increasing support from the effects of the continuing Cultural Revolution indicate that just such a moral transformation is taking place! Schurmann goes on:

> [The individual's] moral transformation can only take place if the ideology also imparts moral force. Chinese Communist ideology has such moral force... The CCP speaks of the forces of world history which are universal and cosmic... it bears certain similarities to the Taoist belief in Heaven as a real force... It is significant, in this respect, that Chinese rebellions in past centuries have often had religious ideologies, notably Taoist/Buddhist.[26]

The revolutionary cadre, then, provides a whole new set of values for the ordinary people of China. In place of despair, crushing poverty, ignorance, and hopelessness, the active participation of the cadre in political struggle to achieve a new society brings a syndrome of courage, a modest but fair livelihood, the chance to educate oneself, and a view of personal and social hope. It is increasingly clear that this is not just the experience of a limited part of humanity, located in the People's Republic of China since 1949; rather it is a growing experience and hope of groups in Latin America, Africa, and Asia, where men are beginning to take their own destiny into hand and act to change it.

D. The New 'Political' Man

A very brief summary of the previous themes of mass man, guerrilla rebel, and revolutionary cadre would be the single word:
'conscientization': i.e. the new political being who emerges as the
result of (1) his identification with suffering humanity, (2) rebellion
against nature and the enemy, and (3) participation in *fenhsi fenhsi*
leading to a new moral power.

The new political man in China can be observed best in the experience now emerging from the Great Proletarian Cultural Revolution (1965-67), especially its liberation of students and intellectuals. In a pioneering study,[27] Victor Nee and Don Layman have
used the impact of the Cultural Revolution on Peking University
in the era of 1965-67 as a laboratory experiment to test out the
effectiveness of the new era developing in China and the new model
of man which motivated it. We can supplement these data with the
earlier work of Hinton and Myrdal in two classic studies of Chinese
village life in the new China. Here is an account of recent events in
Shanghai during the Cultural Revolution, as an example of the
process of 'conscientization':

> It is quite untrue that Chinese education turns out docile and
> stereotyped cogs for the Party wheel. From my own experience as a
> teacher in Shanghai (1965-66), it was evident that flexibility was the
> order of the day. Most of the texts we used did not issue from the
> Ministry of Education; on the contrary, both Chinese and foreign
> teachers wrote most of their own material!
> The Cultural Revolution was an education in itself. Students argued
> out their differences on crucial subjects and challenged the Party
> bureaucrats either to accept reforms or to step down.
> This was the point of the Red Guard movement. In our Institute,
> a group of radical students sparked off protracted debate by charg-
> ing that the Party authorities had mismanaged the educational
> system. Instead of catering to the children of peasants and workers,
> our college had favored the Shanghai middleclass, whose children
> made up over 50% of the enrollment. The radicals demanded the
> abolition of entrance examinations, and called for the establishment
> of a system that would produce politically conscious and morally
> responsible graduates, not just "experts" who considered themselves
> part of an elite.[28]

As the work of Paulo Friere has shown with many oppressed
groups in Latin America, the spiritual transformation ('conscientization') of man will take place only when man himself participates
completely in his own liberation. No one can really transform anoth-

er person or manipulate another's freedom. The massive evidence of 800,000,000 people on their way to self-liberation must be the beginning and the end of our brief essay on the shift from Confucian gentleman to a 'new political being.' Let us hope that the world will watch what they do!

NOTES

[1] Huston Smith, *The Religions of Man* (New York, 1958), pp. 156ff.

[2] Amaury de Riencourt, *The Soul of China* (New York, 1965), pp. 260-261.

[3] Arthur Waley, *The Analects of Confucius* (London, 1938), II. 4.

[4] *Ibid.*, pp. 27-34.

[5] *Ibid.*, pp. 27-29.

[6] *Ibid.*, p. 28.

[7] Arthur Wright, editor, *Confucianism and Chinese Civilization*, Chapter I, "Some Polarities in Confucian Thought" (New York, 1964) pp. 5-6.

[8] *Ibid.*

[9] Conscientization' is a term used in reference to the Latin American experience of social change, used by Paulo Friere, *Pedagogy of the Oppressed* (New York, 1970).

[10] Franz Schurmann, *Ideology and Organization in Communist China* (Berkeley, 1966), pp. 7-8.

[11] Michael Walzer, *The Revolution of the Saints* (Cambridge, 1965), pp. 317-319.

[12] Mao Tse-tung, *Selected Works* (Peking, 1951-60), I, 19.

[13] Neale Hunter in *Social Action*, Jan. 1970, p. 7. Hunter taught in a high school in Shanghai from 1965 to 1967.

[14] Mao Tse-tung, *op. cit.*, III.

[15] Jerome Ch'en, *Mao and the Chinese Revolution* (London, 1965), pp. 199f.

[16] Chalmers Johnson, *Peasant Nationalism and Communist Power* (Stanford, 1962), p. ix.

[17] Max Weber, *The Religion of China* (New York, 1951).

[18] Franz Schurmann, *op. cit.*, pp. 48f.

[19] *Ibid.*

[20] William Hinton, *Fan Shen: A Documentary of Revolution in a Chinese Village* (New York, 1966).

[21] Harvey Cox, *On Not Leaving It to the Snake* (New York, 1967).

[22] Franz Schurmann, *op. cit.*, pp. 49f.

[23] Jan Myrdal, *Report from a Chinese Village* (London, 1965).

[24] Victor Nee, *The Cultural Revolution at Peking University* (1969).

[25] William Hinton, *op. cit.*

[26] Franz Schurmann, *op. cit.*, p. 50.

[27] Victor Nee, *op. cit.*

[28] Neale Hunter, *op. cit.*, pp. 8-11.

CHAPTER NINE

THE SCIENTIFIC REVOLUTION AND THE UNITY OF MAN

BERNARD TOWERS

I. *The Heritage and Promise of Science*

Science will one day prove to be the strongest and most effective force ever known for promoting the concept of the unity of man. Like all powerful forces it can be used both constructively and destructively. Like all human activities—and modern science is now a human activity on the grandest scale—it not only has positive and negative aspects, but it also includes in its makeup both conscious and unconscious elements. There are always, in practice, unconscious elements present in the first formulations of new scientific hypotheses. More particularly it is in the scientific *Zeitgeist* that one sees unexpressed and unacknowledged motivation at work. In this chapter we shall consider some aspects of the history of science and technology so as to see, if possible, what is to be learned from past mistakes in attitude, and also in order to extrapolate long-term discernible trends into the future. We shall hope that by seeing what choices lie open to us we might be prompted to move more firmly and with greater confidence into a future which currently both tempts and terrifies, one that could possibly be either a heaven-on-earth or a veritable hell-on-earth: more likely, it will prove to be a continuation of the peculiarly human mixture of both. But such a mixture, it should be noted, is never, in a scientific *milieu,* 'the mixture as before': change is built into, is theoretically anticipated in, the world of science. And although, as we shall see, great scientific advances, like great advances in any other field of human endeavour, always meet with opposition initially from within the discipline itself, yet it is true to say that every valid scientific insight does finally receive serious and sympathetic attention in the world of professional learning. Then, if it is true to the phenomena, true to *what is the case,* it will be bound eventually to take its place in the general corpus of accepted knowledge. After a period of relative stability within the system, any such insight will later come to serve either as a stepping stone or (especially if it once represented a great step forward itself) as a stumbling block to further advance.

A. The Scientific Revolution

It is important at the start to clarify the concept of 'the scientific revolution.' The term is generally used to express the impact, in the late sixteenth and seventeenth centuries, of the new discoveries in mathematical astronomy and physics, and to indicate the 'new' Baconian philosophy of induction that is generally thought to have formed the basis for those discoveries. It is not surprising then, in view of our empirical tradition, that phrases such as 'the scientific revolution' or 'the dawn of the modern age,' to express this seventeenth century phenomenon, should come easily to modern western man, moving as they do down well-worn paths in his mental make-up. One finds, amongst one's scientific colleagues, a degree of naiveté about these matters amounting almost to the creation of a mythology. The present writer has pointed out elsewhere[1] how difficult it is for many scientists to take the study of history seriously. Many practical scientists and technologists would argue, and with passion, that scientific truths become incorporated into the general consensus of scientific knowledge not merely eventually, as we have argued above, but *automatically*. Just how this comes about, they would say, is not important. So that ignorance of historical developments, far from being intellectually reprehensible, becomes for them almost virtuous. By not burdening one's mind with 'useless' exercises from the past, that is with 'historical lumber,' one frees it for exploration into new areas, for the solving of new problems, and for the development of those new techniques of enquiry on which scientific advance is ever dependent. Scientists tend naturally to be future-oriented, and there is much to be said in favor of such an attitude. But if science is to act as a unifying force for mankind (as we suggest); and if specialist scientists are to be able to communicate both with colleagues from other scientific fields and with those from 'the humanities'; if they are to help produce a unified and coherent system for man, then they must give up their often philistine attitude to the past, and learn how to incorporate scientific history into scientific practice.

Ignorance of the development of science is very widespread. So, for instance, the very notion of 'the scientific revolution of the seventeenth century' has all too often acted as an excuse for ignoring all that went before it. Judging from comments made by laboratory colleagues when such topics come up in conversation, it is almost as if they imagined that modern science sprang up fully matured, solely as the result of the courage of a single age's overthrow (as they see it) of 'authority,' and its attempt to look objectively, for the first time in history, at natural phenomena. In the minds of many this new objectivity, which produced the 'revolution', appears to be linked, in some dimly-discerned way, with both the Renaissance and with the Reformation, all three springing, like a great 'liberation,' out of the oppression of 'the Dark Ages.' To many, this last term appears to mean a time when clerical authority dominated the minds of men and suppressed independent thinking of any kind, up to at least the end of the thirteenth century. Now although one is deliberately exaggerating this very garbled version of history, nevertheless, the depths of the ignorance that is to be met in the scientific community about historical developments should not be underestimated. Although there are many scientists (including, as always, a greater proportion of the most distinguished ones) who are deeply aware of, and sensitive to, the values of the particular cultural heritage within which science was nurtured, yet in our present-day scientific and technological ('technetronic') society, there can be no doubt that many commonly-used expressions such as, on the one hand, 'scientifically proved' and, on the other, 'positively mediaeval,' contain such value-judgment overtones that the possibility of balanced assessment is altogether eliminated.

The counterpart to this kind of historical ignorance is the similar attitude not only of ignorance about, but also of proud disdain of, practical science, that one all too often meets amongst colleagues from 'the humanities.' For anyone who has tried to live within, and to experience in some real sense, what C. P. Snow called the 'two cultures' of modern society, it is distressing to hear wholesale condemnations of science by self-styled intellectuals from various fields of humanistic learning. The unity of mankind cannot be achieved, no more than can any other form of true human unity, except on the basis of mutual compassion and concern. The infighting and backbiting so prevalent in our intellectual and academic communities is wholly destructive of understanding. And yet 'understanding' is surely the primary aim of all scholarly endeavour.

The commonly-accepted view that science is essentially revo-lutionary (a 'once and for all revolution') was, for instance, stated directly in the title of a book by A. R. Hall.[2] Indeed it is such a commonplace view that it would be tedious to give a list of examples of its expression. Its effects are to be seen today in all the media of mass-communication; commentators are always talking in terms of 'scientific breakthroughs' or 'revolutionary new developments' in this or that. In all the clamour and glamour of this kind of expo-sition, it is not easy to obtain a hearing for the quiet voice of com-passionate reasoning. And yet, if man is ever to discover the unity which compassionate scientific reasoning tells us he possesses (not only within himself as an individual but also within himself as a species, a part of that greater physical unity in which and out of which he has evolved), then he surely must give himself time to re-flect on these things in an atmosphere of composure rather than of near hysteria. Commentators surely have an obligation not to play for sensationalism all the time, but rather to try to help man to understand his place in nature. This can only be done through a serious and sustained effort to see the scientific endeavour in true perspective, that is, to see how it 'co-inheres' with other valid ap-proaches to human understanding.

Many authors have tried to express the history of science in terms of developmental continuity, while at the same time giving full weight to the discontinuities that are part of the story. In this, as in all fields of history, what we are dealing with is 'descent with modifi-cation.' At times the modifications may be profound, and one is tempted to speak of 'revolution.' And yet modifications, however profound, are inevitably linked with descent, and in that case we are dealing not with 'revolution' but with 'evolution.' Sir William Dampier, in his influential study,[3] was thoroughly imbued with the idea of the evolution of scientific learning. So, too, is Sir Herbert Butterfield,[4] who starts his history at the year 1300, thereby ex-tending by some three centuries the usual time-span for the origin and development of modern science. More than any other author, Crombie[5] has shown how inadequate is the common view that science 'came about' in the seventeenth century because men be-came bold enough to rebel against authority and to start to think for themselves. The volumes of the *Journal of the History of Ideas* have clearly demonstrated how foolish it is to imagine that any-thing significant ever emerges in human history without a long period of gestation. We recognize the truth of this so far as the individual thinker is concerned, but do not sufficiently recognize it for the culture in which the individual is nurtured. Two chief editors of the above-mentioned Journal published, in 1957, a splendid collection of essays devoted to this topic.[6] Its forty chapters were divided into four main sections to specify the stages of scientific development: "The Classical Heritage," "From Rationalism to Experimentalism," "The Scientific Revolution," and "From the World-Machine to Cosmic Evolution." We see in this volume what ideas and methods had to be developed before the seventeenth-century-revolution, that led to the concept of the 'world machine,' could take place. Seen in context, that century marks a very important stage in the psycho-social evolution of man.

A good many ordinary scientists, together with most lay commentators, dazzled by the marvels of our technological age, still think of the world and everything in it in terms of 'machines.' Such a concept has long since ceased to attract the minds of more penetrating thinkers. Simple, mechanical cause-effect analysis is essential in any enquiry about the natural world. But anyone today who stops short at that seventeenth-century level of thinking shows himself to be in a state of arrested development.

B. Why in the Christian Milieu?

The most interesting question about the relation of science, faith, and human unity is why it should have been in Western Europe, and particularly in a Christian setting, that modern science did in fact arise. Instead of 'arise,' perhaps one should say 'take root and flourish,' because it is clear, for instance, that Arabic science (especially in the medical field) was making great progress at a time when Europe was still suffering the 'Dark Ages,' overrun by barbarians and broken by disease. It is also evident, from the monumental work of Joseph Needham,[7] that the kind of exact observation of nature, and development of technology, that are characteristic of modern science, had a long and fruitful history in the Far East long before Western Europe began to take the lead in these fields. Nevertheless, it remains true that science, as we now know it on a world-wide basis, stems directly from the culture of the Christian West. Even if many scientists of today are neglectful of the history of their disciplines, and are ignorant of the philosophical presuppositions that underlie their work, the fact remains that

without these presuppositions the scientific revolution of the seventeenth century would never have occurred.

What seems to have paved the way for the discovery of the
scientific method (controlled observation, and the devising of experiments to test hypotheses that are inherently falsifiable) was the
rediscovery of classical learning, itself preserved if not understood
in Christian monasteries after the collapse of the Roman Empire.
Apart from the appeal of the rational in the works of the Greek
philosophers and scientists, the motivation to start research into
the workings of the natural world appears to have sprung during
this period from a deep-seated conviction, biblical in origin, that
"God saw the world and saw that it was good." The history of
Christianity contains so many instances of powerful groups who
have looked upon the world and seen it to be bad rather than good,
that one is astonished at the integrity with which the original and
authentic message of God's love for the world has been preserved
in the Judaeo-Christian religion. It has always been the case that
the world-haters—the Manichees, the Albigensians, the Jansenists
and Puritans—have been condemned for distorting the Gospel
message. It is easy to see why a doctrine of world-abnegation, which
concentrates on a spiritual life divorced from a 'base material world,'
should make constant appeal to those Christians who find themselves
caught between the pincers of dualistic thinking. If we think of
ourselves as living in a state of constant tension between matter
and spirit, caught in anguish between body and soul, between the
things of this world and those of the next; if we are convinced that
life on earth is life in a vale of tears, a testingtime wherein our only
or principal obligation is to prepare for the life beyond, then we shall
not be highly motivated—indeed not motivated at all—to 'waste
time' in study of the natural sciences. If such an outlook had represented the traditional Christianity of the Middle Ages, as so
many appear to believe, then modern science could not have arisen
in the West. Or, if it had arisen in such a climate of thought, it
would have done so only through the efforts of real revolutionaries,
determined to overthrow their religion in the development of the
new philosophy. The record tells otherwise. For all that there have
been, and still are, martyrs of science, pioneers whose work puts in
question the authenticity of the particular sacred cows (or secular
cows) held in veneration by the authorities of church, or state, or
even by the high-priests of science itself, yet history shows us that

science developed within, and not in opposition to, a Christian culture that gave birth to and nurtured it. The mutual suspicion and recrimination between science and the Christian religion have been not only unnecessary, but have resulted from both a betrayal by Christians of their own tradition, and an ignorance on the part of many scientists of what that tradition really has to say about the world and our responsibilities to it.

We proceed to understanding only by degrees. This is as true of the development of Christian doctrine as it is of the development of modern scientific insights into the nature of reality. False steps or a wrong turning can hold back progress in any field of learning or understanding. For all its call to excellence, the puritan ethic (that 'indestructible philosophy' as it has been called) has proved to be a two-edged weapon, destructive in both directions. On the one hand it has tried to concentrate on other-worldly things to the detriment of science. And on the other, since it is obvious that in order to survive at all we have to learn to live in the world, the ethic has to find a way somehow to justify worldly endeavour. It does so, then, in a joyless way, through an ethic of hard work endured for the sake of a benefit outside itself and wholly divorced from it. A schizophrenia is thus produced, which allows development to take place in two distinct worlds, and which encourages hypocrisy in each. This is what lies behind that curious psychotic state so prevalent in the West today. This is where, as Holbrook puts it,[8] hate is dressed as love, where the members of the 'permissive society' wear 'masks of hate,' pretending to love those aspects of life which in fact are most feared and hated. It need not have been so. It need not continue to be so. It could not have been so in the thirteenth and fourteenth centuries, when an age of faith was busy preparing the ground for the birth of science.

C. Premises of Scientists

Before any scientist sets out on a piece of research into some natural phenomenon, whether it be a phenomenon on an interplanetary scale, or on a subatomic scale, or one on that most fascinating scale of complexity-in-organization which is displayed by living matter, he must have certain premises or presuppositions behind him. He may not animadvert to them, certainly not continually, and perhaps never at all, but he cannot escape them. The two fundamental ones are, first, the felt certainty that the matter or stuff that he is studying is not evil of itself, as so many religious sects have made it out to be; and, second, the unquestioned belief that somewhere within the problem that he faces there is an order to be discerned, an order which, once he finds, it can be tested for again and again either by himself or any other competent scientist. The testing allows for a continuous refining of concepts and a deepening of the understanding of the order disclosed. Another aspect of scientific work which is fundamental to the whole endeavour is the relation of one scientist to other scientists. Each one recognizes that the only way to ensure that he is not being misled in his observations by his own desires or needs, having already been as rigorous as he can be in trying to disprove his own most reasonable hypothesis, is to make known not simply his 'conclusions' (which might represent no more than opinion) but to publish his total 'findings,' including a full and accurate report on his techniques of investigation. Other scientists can then submit the hypothesis to independent testing. This is why science has been so correctly called 'Public Knowledge,'[9] and why it was asserted at the start of this essay that science is bound ultimately to act as an integrating force, promoting not merely the *concept* of the unity of man but also its *percept* or living reality.

The premises we have listed as coming prior to any scientific investigation are characteristically Christian in nature and also in origin: they suggest good reasons as to why science in its modern sense took root in the later Middle Ages, when the doctrine of the Incarnation was a part of the daily life of Europeans. Other vital ingredients were provided in the brilliant philosophical analyses of some of the early Schoolmen. Without the intellectual training in logic that had gone before in the universities, modern science would never have been born. Nor could it have grown in the way that it did, including the part played by rebellion against its parents, after the manner of any healthy offspring. Aristotle's metaphysics followed the physics, as the name implies, and not vice-versa, as we are suggesting is the case in modern science. Aristotle's approach is logical enough if by physics we mean only the apprehension and simple analysis of primary sense data. Such an attitude is common enough even in science today, where it is sometimes held that the simple collection of 'data' is the only necessary, and quite the most important, step for the objective analysis of reality. And yet, as Koestler has shown in a distinguished series of books,[10] such a

simple Baconian philosophy is quite inadequate to account for the
major successes of science. Although we must start with simple
observation, real success comes in science when subsequent appeal
to observable data is consequent to a metaphysical analysis, or an
intuitional insight, which tells one which data to look for. Charles
Darwin is often held up as an example of a scientist who pursued
his studies by the patient, unemotional, wholly 'objective' collecting
of data. But, as he acknowledged in his autobiography and letters,
it is, strictly speaking, impossible to make an observation which is
independent of a prior hypothesis. Every observation necessarily
carries with it some kind of interpretation.

It seems likely, then, that the scientific revolution came about as
much as a result of the training in logic and mathematics that was
encouraged in the mediaeval universities of Europe as it did as a
result of Galileo's simply applying his eye to his telescope. Galileo
doubtless was stimulated to look more closely and more carefully,
when his colleagues in science and mathematics refused to allow
themselves to repeat his observations. Opposition is the lot of all
pioneers, and sometimes it stimulates further developments. Galileo
is but one of a great multitude of new leaders in many fields of
human endeavour who have had to suffer for their forward looking
enterprises.

There was no single 'scientific revolution.' During the past millen-
nium, the intellectual life of Europe passed through a whole series
of 'revolutions,' many of them so closely intermeshed with each
other, particularly where the exploration of the natural world is
concerned, that it is more fitting to speak of a natural evolution than
of revolution. This has been particularly true in science. The last
hundred years have seen two major mutations quite as 'revolutionary' as the one we associate with Copernicus and Galileo.
Classical physics is now seen as only part of the truth: it represents
one aspect, at the macro-level, of what can be adequately accounted
for only on the basis of relativity theory and the indeterminacies of
subatomic particle physics. Another major break with traditional
science came with the advent and development of evolutionary
theory as the most reasonable interpretation of the origin of all of
the enormously varied natural objects that currently exist. It is on
evolution, and the significance of the theory for concepts relating
to the unity of man, that we wish to spend the remainder of the
space here available.

II. *The New Eminence of Biology*

How does the scientific endeavour in general affect our ideas on unity? There is no gathering in the world (not excluding the greatest of the Christian ecumenical meetings) that is currently so capable of generating the spirit of unity-in-diversity than is a large international scientific meeting. No matter from which country the participants come, no matter where they were trained, or with which scientific group they have pursued their research (and laboratory groups are often remarkably international in character), they create, in exposition and discussion, an atmosphere of mutual understanding and social tolerance which is a harbinger of the kind of society that ought to be possible for mankind as a whole if we are prepared to organize ourselves on the basis of an honest scientific ethic.

One of the greatest of the many 'revolutions' in thinking that have taken place in recent centuries has been the emergence of a general theory of biological evolution. Apart from occasional attacks from biblical fundamentalists there is abundant evidence that, amongst Christians generally, there is now at least a notional assent given to the idea that all living forms now extant on the earth are the products by descent of earlier and simpler forms, and that man himself is both a part and a product of the evolutionary process. But although we seem readily to give notional assent to evolutionary theory, most of us have hardly begun to feel its reality, or to understand its true nature and its significance. One has to develop a 'feeling' for this new dimension of scientific thought before one can give to it a real rather than a notional assent. As Pierre Teilhard de Chardin has put it:[11] "What makes and classifies a 'modern' man (and a whole host of our contemporaries is not yet 'modern' in this sense) is having become capable of seeing in terms not of space and time alone, but also of duration, or—it comes to the same thing—of biological space-time; and above all having become incapable of seeing anything otherwise—anything—*not even himself*." It requires a prodigious mental effort to begin to be able to think (or to *see* rather) in terms of biological space-time. The difficulties are evident on reading an important recent volume devoted precisely to consideration of the nature of time.[12] The task becomes virtually impossible for anyone who has the uneasy feeling that modern scientific knowledge of the dimensions of both space and time, when taken together with some currently-popular theories about how man is conditioned and constrained by biochemical and psychological

factors outside his control, all contrive to diminish man. Pascal's
fear in face of the "silence of those infinite spaces" was under-
standable enough. How small an object is man in comparison with
the dimensions of interplanetary space! How small and insignificant
an object is the planet earth in comparison with what we now know
of the dimensions of the universe! Both astronomy, 'the science of
the infinitely large,' and nuclear physics, 'the science of the infinitely small' (where a built-in indeterminacy principle appears at
first sight to rob us of our very basis of structural reality in 'solid
matter') have contributed to that modern 'existential vacuum'
about which Frankl has written so well.[13] Two other areas of
popular scientific teaching have also contributed at a profound level
to the conviction shared by many people today that life is in fact a
meaningless charade to which the only appropriate or possible responses are either a philosophy of despair or one of hedonism—both
of them desperate remedies for a truly fatal disease. These teachings
are, first, the theory of evolution itself when interpreted, as it has
been so often in the past and is still, as the result of 'nothing but'
a process of natural selection of meaningless chance mutations.
Second has been the teaching of some of the most influential schools
of psychotherapy, in which the most noble and apparently praise-
worthy of human acts are explained away as being 'nothing but'
the consequences of unresolved conflicts at the unconscious level.
Frankl starts his paper on "Reductionism and Nihilism" with the
following: "It is an inherent tendency in man to reach out for
meanings to fulfil and for values to actualise. But, alas, we are
offered by two outstanding American scholars in the field of value-
psychology the following definitions: 'Values and meanings are
nothing but defence mechanisms and reaction formations.' Well, as
for myself, I am not willing to live for the sake of my reaction formations, even less to die for the sake of my defence mechanisms.
And I would say that reductionism today is a mask for nihilism."[14]
Many students of depth-psychology consider conflict between unconscious drives and instincts to be the dominating forces that push
and pull a human being like a puppet, until he finds for himself a
formula for action which is successful in reducing tension and pro-
ducing the internal 'homeostasis' which is supposed to bring con-
tentment and happiness. In such a thought-system man is bound
again to feel himself diminished, and if he dares to think seriously
about his state and condition he is likely to feel an existential *Angst*,

a feeling of being adrift in a totally meaningless universe. Most people, of course, are not prepared to allow themselves to think so deeply: like children with a candybar, they will settle for the immediate rewards that pursuit of the pleasure-principle can bring.

A. Man's Present Stage in the Evolving World

As yet we are only at the beginning of the scientific exploration of the meaning to be attached to man's place in an evolving world-system. It would be disastrous if those who have a genuine feeling for, a love and respect for, their fellow human beings, were to dismiss or neglect the scientific approach to the study of man because of the evident shortcomings of these early and inadequate theories of evolution. More than any other branch of human knowledge, it is science that contains within itself, as we said earlier, automatic correction-factors for the elimination of error. Error persists unchecked if its formulation and expression is no more than 'opinion.' On the other hand, error that is formulated and expressed as scientific 'fact' or hypothesis will, if it is tested by the techniques of science, inevitably be discovered for what it is. Then it will be either discarded, eliminated, or else will be incorporated into some wider and more comprehensive theory of which it might form an important part. Now the primary criterion for survival, according to evolutionary theory, is simply 'fitness.' The concept of fitness has been grossly misinterpreted in the past even at the biological level, where it has been equated with the power of the individual animal to survive the attacks of others in competitive, aggressive situations. The real meaning of biological fitness is the capacity to reproduce offspring, to give rise to generations of members of the species which are 'fit' to survive. Fitness is meaningful, in evolutionary terms, only at the species level. And aggressive competition often has no significant contribution to make to this kind of survival. At the psychosocial level of evolution characteristic of man, the concept of 'fitness' is best interpreted as meaning 'coherence' or 'truth.' Error is bound to be self-defeating in the long run, even though the run may be very, very long. To back off from scientific exploration, simply because its past shortcomings have had some harmful and divisive effects for and on man, would be foolish in the extreme. The scientific method is one of those human inventions which, once discovered (like the wheel, for instance, as a means of locomotion), are never discarded but only improved. More and more it will be through science that man comes to know and understand himself. It is essential that men of the highest integrity and greatest sensitivity, men of vision and human compassion, should involve themselves in the actual construction and testing of hypotheses. The reductionist philosophy that has dominated biology for so long is now coming under considerable attack from within the science of biology itself.[15] Scientists are beginning to take seriously the possibility that their own valid discoveries in small areas (which is where the techniques of science are most commonly applied) might have very harmful effects for man unless they are integrated with other questions of human concern. Scientific theory needs to be interpreted in the light of man's constant search for meaning both in his own life-experience, and now also in an evolutionary process in which he has so recently discovered himself to be participating.

B. The Attraction of Elusive Meaning

The search for meaning is the essential factor in Frankl's interpretation of human psychodynamics. In his system the 'noetic dimension' (that is, of 'mind') transcends the 'psychic dimension' (of drives and instincts, which is what most psychotherapists alone concern themselves with) which man shares with other advanced species in the biosphere. Frankl follows most psychotherapists, and the existential philosophers whose thinking he incorporates into his system, in concentrating on the development of the individual in his search for meaning. If, however, one cannot understand man except in the evolutionary setting of *duration* or *biological space-time*, as Teilhard puts it, then we must enlarge our horizons and move into a new way of thinking, where the almost unimaginable period of a million years represents only one part in thousands of the total period of time during which the world we know has been in process of 'becoming.' One cannot overemphasize how very recent, in the history of man, is this insight into the nature of things. Of course, there were evolutionary theories, though on a different time-scale, in classical times. But our modern understanding goes so far beyond the knowledge that can possibly be acquired through a life-time's experience of the here-and-now (which is the dimension in which most people live), that it is not surprising that "a whole host of our contemporaries is not yet modern" in the sense that Teilhard uses that word.

It is ten thousand million years since the universe went through that 'period of singular time,' which is how modern astrophysicists describe the start of the expansion-phase in which it has ever since existed. Somewhere between four and five thousand million years have elapsed since the formation of our planet earth and the solar system—that minute part of the expanding universe. There followed a long, long phase of evolution at the organic level: the chemical elements were already in existence, but now they combined and recombined as molecules of infinite variety and ever-increasing complexity in internal organization. How extraordinarily complex these molecules had to become before they could assume the characteristics that we call 'living'! Today, in laboratories of biochemistry and microbiology all over the technological world, the keenest minds and most advanced apparatus combine in attempts to reproduce what at one stage, in the evolutionary history of the planet, came about naturally as part of the process we seek to understand. That was perhaps some two to three thousand million years ago. When that happened, when complex chemical molecules acquired the power to extract energy from the environment and use it for further development and self-duplication, it was the start of the 'biosphere.' Twenty years ago, such a word as biosphere would have been employed only by professional scientists. Today it has become commonplace: any newspaper article on problems of pollution (one of the biggest topics, probably, for the decade ahead) is likely to use the word biosphere as readily and as frequently as atmosphere. That fact represents an astonishing leap in understanding to have occurred in a single generation.

We ourselves, individual men and women, are obviously part of the biosphere. From the earliest beginnings of living matter, those many hundreds of millions of years ago, to the unbelievable diversity and complexity of the living creatures that today fill the globe in such profusion, there has been only one continuous process. Descent with modification: true descent, in that each one of us has a direct lineage right back through biosphere and inorganic hydrosphere and atmosphere, to the primordial energies of subatomic particles; but descent with what profound modifications! We are made of atoms. We are dependent for our physical survival on the constant supply of atoms in both simple and complex forms. And yet what *ordering* we structure for them in our bodies, so that they come to share in our lives, and contribute, as they must, to our very thought-processes! "To think, we must eat," says Teilhard. It really is as simple as that. "But," he goes on, "what a variety of thoughts can be got from a single slice of bread!" Bread, too, is a part of the biosphere, as also is wine. Symbols such as these assume wholly new significance in the perspective of 'duration,' of 'biological space-time.' Can anyone who has once 'seen' this ever want to revoke his modernity and return to a static, or cyclical, specialcreationist view of the world? In this new perspective it is not simply the concept of the unity of mankind that springs to mind. It is the concept of the fundamental unity of all of those uncountable billions of creatures of all kinds that contribute to the evolving system.

In total contrast to such a coherent, or coinherent, interpretation of the evolutionary process, it has often been said or implied by evolutionists of great distinction that the system itself is fundamentally random and chaotic. Species come and species go. Now one group is in the ascendancy, now another. There is no way to predict what will happen in the future, because genetic mutations and recombinations, which provide the basis on which the force of natural selection selects, are essentially random in nature. All we can be sure of, in the light of nineteenth-century or classical physics, is that in the end chaos, randomness, 'mixed-upness,' entropy will prevail: all differentiated energy-levels, all complex forms, will dissipate or disappear. Man will not escape this plunge back into the void from which he came. Indeed it may well be, they might say, that he will accelerate the catastrophic end, at least on the local level of this planet, by continuing with those exploitative and aggressive pursuits that seem to characterize this curious primate. It is a matter for astonishment that views such as these should be not merely accepted by, but should be actively pursued and promulgated by biological scientists of international repute. It is they who bear the heaviest load of responsibility for the sense of emptiness, meaninglessness and alienation that has characterized so much of the twentieth century, Perhaps the nineteenth-century theologians who fought so many rearguard actions against the theory of evolution saw with singular clarity what the end-results must be of a theory that seemed to assume that the universe not only began in chaos, but operates by chance, and is destined to end in chaos again. This outlook was vividly expressed in 1876 by the great scientist, Emil du Bois Reymond: "The possibility, ever so distant, of banishing from nature its seeming purpose, and putting a blind necessity everywhere in the place of final causes, appears, therefore, as one of the greatest advances in the world of thought, from which a new era will be dated in the treatment of these problems. To have somewhat eased the torture of the intellect which ponders over the world-problem will, as long as philosophical naturalists exist, be Charles Darwin's greatest title to glory."[16]

Many biologists still live in the atmosphere of the nineteenth century, from which this quotation comes. The Second Law of Thermodynamics (which states correctly that in any closed thermo-dynamic system entropy inevitably increases to the point of maxi-mum randomness) was invalidly held to apply to the universe as a whole, and in that context has exercised a profound effect on think-ing during the last hundred years. Although astrophysicists have long since ceased to consider it to be applicable to 'the universe,' yet many biologists seem still to assume that it is. If it *is* valid in that sense, then they hold as a logical consequence that the whole concept of 'progress' in evolution is nonsense. As the writer has sug-gested elsewhere[17] these are conclusions based not on science but on philosophical predilections. If, on the other hand, we are prepared to examine the facts of evolution objectively, and to think clearly about them, then we see that, whatever may be the mechanisms or forces at work, physical matter, when viewed in terms of 'dura-tion,' does have built into it a natural tendency to evolve into more highly organized forms. In an insight similar to that of Newton when he developed his general theory of gravitation (and incidentally met with opposition and ridicule from scientific colleagues as a result— another example of the trials of all genuine pioneers in thinking), Teilhard de Chardin has defined this tendency of matter-in-duration to become more complex and at the same time more aware of, or reactive to, its environment, in terms of what he has called the "law of complexity-consciousness." This 'law' refers simply to what is now known actually to have happened throughout the process of evolution. According to twentieth century physics, matter and energy are interchangeable, being two different aspects, or faces, that the 'stuff of the universe' manifests according to the technique we are using to investigate it. Out of this primordial 'stuff,' subject as it is to the Uncertainty Principle, and operating in regular, order-ly fashion only because of statistical laws, there has emerged, in the course of time, a most remarkable ecological system of interrelated component parts of the utmost complexity. As part of this system, a part that represents the most advanced shoot of it, we find man.

Here is a creature that not only *knows*, in the sense in which all
conscious creatures do, but who also *knows that he knows*. This is
consciousness 'raised to the power of two' as has been said, a self-
reflecting consciousness that allows man to emerge from the psychic
dimension and into the noetic dimension, to use again the terminology of Frankl. This great leap in the evolutionary process gives
man an awesome power. One can look at the process of evolution,
the trend towards increasing complexity-consciousness, as one
which permits organisms to assume ever-increasing degrees of freedom from the constraints of the environment. Man has now reached
a point where, by virtue of the knowledge that he has acquired
about himself and about the world, he can choose to modify the
environment as he will. Such enormous freedom must carry with it
tremendous responsibility. Only now, in the last third of the twentieth century, is man gradually becoming aware of the responsibility
he carries for himself, for the species to which he belongs, and also
for the whole ecological system which has produced us and on which
we depend for our very survival.

There can be little doubt that it is because of scientific and technological achievements, in both positive and negative aspects, that
there has recently arisen amongst so many young people an upsurge
of genuine concern for studies in ecology. This compassionate concern involves not only concern for mankind itself, but also for the
earth and everything in it. Television makes the world into a
'global village,' as Marshall McLuhan put it in one of his less
opaque passages. When one can be in contact, at the touch of a
button, with events all over the globe, instantaneously and as they
are actually happening, then the world begins to assume domestic
proportions. It has been observed that, amongst the intelligent,
politically-minded young people of today, there is no such thing as
domestic, national policy as distinct from international or foreign
policy. The world has become too small and too obviously fragile
for us to continue with ancient policies based on nationalism and
greed, on aggression, spite and envy. Common sense alone is enough
to teach such a basic lesson. At this level of 'gut-reaction' young
people no longer need, or have much time for, sets of moralistic
principles or ethical systems imposed from outside. They simply
see that the world is too fragile for hydrogen bombs. When the earth
is seen from a new perspective, as when the astronauts see it from
the moon, or as they circle in orbit (an experience which again,

through the medium of television, we can all share with them), then it begins to look small and vulnerable. One cannot then help but care about it, if one troubles to think. The numbers of those who do so may be small as yet, infinitesimal even, in some of the places where the greatest power is wielded. Yet the numbers are growing, and a new spirit is abroad. We seem to be living just now in a period of the greatest of all scientific revolutions, or rather, in a period when the evolutionary process is taking yet another great step forward. If, however, we misuse our freedom, and deny our responsibilities, then we may well defeat the process itself, and this when it is at last just beginning, through us, to become aware of its own nature and even of its goal. If, on the other hand, things go well, and we recognize our freedom to choose responsibly, then we may be destined for a future where compassion will be regarded not merely as desirable, but as the social norm.

Science is sometimes referred to as 'the art of the soluble.' That is to say, the traditional technique of science is to investigate problems which one can see in advance are inherently soluble. This means that, whatever the nature of the particular solution that is destined to emerge from the enquiry, its general form is predetermined since the scientist has chosen to operate only within the framework of some particular 'paradigm.' This is why the majority of scientists, despite their future-oriented attitudes, are strictly conservative at a deeper level. It is for this reason, as we have stressed earlier, that genuine pioneers of science have a hard time initially in obtaining a hearing for what will be regarded by the majority of their colleagues as heretical views. The traditional, safe, orthodox approach in science—and one should never underestimate the extent to which orthodoxy dominates the world of the professional scientist, as it does that of law, or politics, or theology—carries advantages as well as disadvantages. It has led to the establishment of firm, soundlybased scientific understanding, but it has done so at the expense of creating an essentially divisive system. All the specialisms of science, with all their harmful effects in terms of noncommunication and the mutual suspicion that ignorance so readily creates, are inherent in the concept of science as the 'art of the soluble.' Despite the power that is wielded by the official establishment of science, it may be that we are now entering a period when specialisms will become reintegrated, and will do it without sacrifice of the intellectual rigor which is the greatest benefit that specialism introduced into the system. The advent of computer-analysis will allow us to correlate and compute vastly more complex data-systems than we had ever conceived to be possible. It is true that no individual can be all things to all men. The day of the polymath is long since over. But there is no intrinsic reason why, with proper use of the new scientific tools, the essential aim of the polymath of former times (which was, to correlate all knowledge into a meaning-ful or coherent system) should not now be attempted.

C. Science and Man's Creative Community

"No man is an island," said Donne. The cult of the individual in recent centuries has tended to obscure that profoundly human and Christian viewpoint. In some ways science has contributed more than some other fields of endeavour hitherto, to the cult of the individual. The way we reward scientists with individual honors, with prizes and suchlike, is characteristic of the individualistic ethic. And yet, as we have seen, true science is above all a shared ex-perience. It is 'public knowledge.' In some laboratories today the individual members are refusing to allow their names to be publish-ed as authors or co-authors of papers emanating from the laboratory. This is because they recognize that the development of complex knowledge expressed in highly sophisticated theories and hypo-theses demands a style of cooperative endeavour that altogether supercedes the concept of the isolated, brilliant contribution of one man: they recognize that *many* brilliant contributions may have gone into the new insight, and that often it is quite impossible to say whose idea is whose. If this is a new development in the world of science and technology, historians will recognize that it is no new outlook so far as the history of civilization is concerned. If today one simply cannot point to any individual as 'the' author or creator of a complex artifact such as a space-satellite, a hydro-electric plant, or a nuclear reactor, the same was surely true of some of those monuments bequeathed by other civilizations, monuments that embody the spirit of the age as much as do our technical wonders. Who knows the architects of the mediaeval cathedrals, or of Roman amphitheaters, Egyptian pyramids, or of a monument such as Stonehenge? Science will represent the spirit of our present age, and it is important that we should ensure that it is a worthy monu-ment. We should encourage its development on a global scale, because the more that science assumes its public dimension on that scale, the more unified is mankind likely to become.

The arguments for such a development of the future have been put most clearly and forcefully by Teilhard. He was able to achieve this synthesis only because of his double commitment, carried out with complete integrity on both sides, namely his commitment to the things of this world as well as to those of the next. We may recall his concept of Alpha-Omega as the force that operates throughout the time-span of cosmogenesis; his law of complexity-consciousness indicating the fundamental 'drive' of matter in the four-dimensional system demanded by the theory of evolution; his concept of the noosphere as the principal uniting force at work in the process of anthropogenesis; his theory of Christogenesis as the movement within which "all of nature groans and travails" until the consummation, when finally "God shall be all in all"; and above all the depth of his insight into the meaning of the Incarnation in the light of modern scientific knowledge. All of these elements in Teilhard's thinking, expanded and explored in the way that an open system such as his demands, will in time canalize and crystallize those yearnings for union and harmony amongst men that can be detected even in the midst of all the bloodshed and horror of recent years. They are currently acting as powerful currents, moving the minds and hearts of contemporary men. As Einstein once said, "religion without science is blind; and science without religion is lame." In Teilhard's modern synthesis we see how it is possible, provided one always keeps in one's hands 'both ends of the chain' with courage and integrity, to construct a coherent and meaningful account of experience. To search for meaning is man's privilege and his responsibility. In the context of a comprehensive theory of evolution we can find the kind of meaning that satisfies both mind and heart, and that allows us to integrate all races of men and all forms of human striving. Ecumenism means, literally, a homemaking. Home today can be anywhere on earth. Home today can be found, if we let it, amongst men of all races, languages, philosophies and religions. This is the message of science. It is also the message of the ecumenical movement. It is the responsibility and privilege of us all to help to make it a living reality.

NOTES

[1] Bernard Towers, "Medical Scientists and the View that History is Bunk," in *Concerning Teilhard, and Other Writings on Science and Religion* (London, 1969).

[2] *The Scientific Revolution 1500-1800 : The Formation of the Modern Scientific Attitude* (London, 1954).

[3] W. A. Dampier, *History of Science and its Relations with Philosophy and Religion* (Cambridge, third edition revised and enlarged, 1942).

[4] Herbert Butterfield, *The Origins of Modern Science 1300-1800* (London, 1949, 1957).

[5] A. C. Crombie, *Augustine to Galileo : The History of Science AD 400-1600* (London, 1952), and *Robert Grosseteste and the Origins of Experimental Science, 1100-1700* (Oxford, 1953).

[6] P. O. Wiener and A. Noland, eds., *Roots of Scientific Thought : A Cultural Perspective* (New York, 1957).

[7] Joseph Needham, *Science and Civilization in China*, 7 vols. (Cambridge, 1954).

[8] David Holbrook, "Hate Dressed as Love," *Frontier*, XII (1969), 197-202.

[9] John Ziman, *Public Knowledge : The Social Dimension of Science* (Cambridge, 1968).

[10] Arthur Koestler, *The Sleepwalkers : A History of Man's Changing Vision of the Universe* (New York, 1959); *The Act of Creation* (New York, 1964); *The Ghost in the Machine* (New York, 1968). Arthur Koestler and J. R. Smythies, eds., *Beyond Reductionism : New Perspectives in the Life Sciences* (London, 1969).

[11] Pierre Teilhard de Chardin, *The Phenomenon of Man*, translated by Bernard Wall (New York, 1959), p. 219.

[12] J. T. Fraser, ed., *The Voices of Time : A Cooperative Survey of Man's Views of Time as Expressed in the Sciences and by the Humanities* (New York, 1966).

[13] Viktor E. Frankl, *Psychotherapy and Existentialism* (New York, 1968); *The Will to Meaning : Foundations and Applications of Logotherapy* (New York, 1969); "Reductionism and Nihilism" in *Beyond Reductionism : New Perspectives in the Life Sciences*, edited by Arthur Koestler and J. R. Smythies (London, 1969).

[14] *Ibid.*

[15] See, for instance, the volume of essays cited above (*Beyond Reductionism*) and *Naked Ape or Homo Sapiens?* by John Lewis and Bernard Towers (London, 1969).

[16] E. Du Bois-Reymond, *Darwin versus Galiani* (Berlin, 1876).

[17] Bernard Towers, "The Impact of Darwin's *Origin of Species* on Medicine and Biology" in *Concerning Teilhard*.(vide sup. ref 1)

CHAPTER TEN

LANGUAGE AND COMMUNICATION

Eugene A. Nida

Perhaps there is no more crucial problem in today's world than a correct understanding of the role of language in communication. This seems to be especially true in the realm of religion, for it is so easy to be mesmerized by words and to imagine that traditional words mean orthodox beliefs. The meanings of words, however, are constantly subject to change, and hence a majority of worshipers misunderstand such creedal phrases as "the holy catholic church" and "the quick and the dead." In our day many traditional beliefs have passed away, but for many people the charm of the words remains. They rest content with the verbal hull, only to discover in a time of stress, when spiritual nourishment is so greatly needed, that the kernel of truth has dried up and disappeared. We may, in fact, be enslaved by words, as happened in one instance when a missionary admitted that the New Testament he had translated badly needed revision, but he felt that he could not afford to introduce the necessary changes, since "the people have already memorized the Word of God."

I. *Misconceptions about Language*

Many of the most serious problems in the use of language stem from certain fundamental misconceptions about the role of language in communication. For instance, some persons contend that a person's language almost completely determines what and how he thinks, as in the adage, "we think the way we think because we speak the language that we speak."[1] Such persons regard language not merely as a reflection of the culture and a *Weltanschauung* of the people, but as a deterministic 'filter' by which alone one can conceive of the world around him. Some persons have even argued that since the Indo-European languages of Western Europe have tense in the verbs, we are obviously more time-oriented than the Ancient Hebrews, whose verbs showed completive and incompletive aspects.[2] If this type of reasoning were valid, then it ought to follow that some of the Congolese, who speak languages with four past tenses and two future tenses, should be even more aware of time than people in the western world, but this is just not true. On the other hand, the Japanese language is essentially as aspectual in its verb structure as is Hebrew,[3] but there are perhaps no people in the world who are more "clock-oriented" than the Japanese.

Some theologians have tended to see in the roots of Hebrew words practically all the essential elements in Jewish religion, as though the religion arose as a natural outgrowth of philological or semantic developments. But these same roots existed in other ancient Semitic languages, and yet no such distinctive ideas as characterized ancient Jewish religion evolved in these other cultures.

While it would be quite wrong to think that language in no way reflects the cultural context of which it is a part, it is equally erroneous to conclude that language is deterministic. In fact, as we shall see in a subsequent section, it is the basic freedom of language from a particular cultural milieu which allows it to be used creatively within the culture and permits it to be employed in saying things that people have not heard before.

Another fundamental misconception about language is the popular belief that so-called primitive languages are quite inadequate to express complex ideas. Some persons contend, though they usually hesitate to express such ideas openly, that one simply cannot expect intellectual maturity from persons who speak these languages. As a result they insist that all teaching, especially of theology, must be done in European languages, for no other medium, so they insist, is adequate to communicate the rich heritage of theological discussion and controversy. Unfortunately, many persons imagine that the languages used by tribal peoples consist of only a few hundred words with a clumsily inadequate grammar. This is, of course, nonsense. All so-called primitive languages which have been seriously investigated by linguists have been found to have tens of thousands of words and lexical units (i.e. tightly knit phrases which function essentially as word units). For example, the Kung Bushman language of South West Africa and southern Angola is spoken by perhaps only 10,000 persons whose material culture is extremely restricted. Nevertheless, there is an almost incredible wealth of vocabulary, with names for all the plants, animals, and birds of the region, and with an oral literature which is rich both in quantity and quality.[4] The syntactic and discourse structure of the language is equally amazing. the subtle use of the suffix -*a* clearly marks distinctions between such expressions as 'the peace of God' and 'the God of peace.' Different types of rhetorical questions are especially well developed, with four different grades of likelihood that the audience will know the answer. A question with the particle *re* indicates neutrality as to whether the answer should be known to the hearers. The particle *xae*, however, suggests that the answer is not at all evident, possibly in fact obscure. On the other hand, the particle *kai* suggests that the audience should know the answer, and the particle *ba* assumes that the audience in fact must know the answer. Such a set of particles presents a number of very subtle problems for the translator of the Scriptures. Equational sentences in Kung Bushman are particularly intricate in their semantic structures, with the possibilities of placing the interrogative either on the subject or on the predicate portion. Hence, an expression such as "What is it?" merely requests one to identify the object in question—the interrogation applied to the subject element. However, the Bushman question "It is what?" asks for information as to the function, significance, or value of something presumably already identified. In English both of these logically quite different relationships are communicated by the ambivalent question "What is it?"

The usual objection raised against so-called primitive languages is that they do not have the high-level generic vocabulary (often called 'abstract'), which is required to talk about philosophical and theological matters. It is quite true that many languages do not have the specialized vocabulary which has grown up with philosophical and theological speculation—nor do they, for that matter, have the technical vocabulary of present-day atomic physics. But it is not true that these so-called primitive languages have little or no generic vocabulary. In fact, an analysis of the lexical resources of languages indicates that for the non-specialist all languages have about the same proportion of specific and generic vocabulary. Languages are, however, much more alike in terms of the specific vocabulary for particular objects or events, since in this domain the meanings of terms depend largely upon perception. It is only when one uses highly generic vocabulary, e.g. *matter*, *object*, *movement*, *event*, etc., that languages tend to differ so appreciably, since these words depend upon conceptual categories, not upon perceptual ones.[5] Nevertheless, all languages are basically open systems and they all have the potentiality for the creation and use of generic vocabulary. The real problem is that for the most part missionaries and theologians from the West simply have not mastered these non-European languages sufficiently so as to be able to use them effectively in communication. They have rightly objected that such languages do not have the necessary textbooks, that schools would have to provide for several different language groups, and that advanced training abroad always requires students to be adequately instructed in a European language. These are all legitimate reasons, but they do not go to the heart of the problem—the serious linguistic void which is created. In the first place, the student is rarely able to think creatively in a foreign language and, second, he is linguistically cut off from the very people whom he is supposed to reach, since he is rarely given a clue as to how he can transpose his thoughts from the foreign language (and culture) into his own tongue and for his own people.

For many persons a 'primitive language' is defined not merely as one spoken by people with a primitive material culture—in reality, of course, there is no such thing as a primitive language—but as any language which does not have a long literary tradition. This only makes matters worse, for it suggests a kind of linguistic superiority complex that is a real deterrent to effective communication. The tendency to look down upon non-Indo-European languages is sometimes an unconscious (or even conscious) reflection of various evolutionary theories about language. One popular theory held that languages began as monosyllabic languages, such as Chinese, and then evolved through the stage of agglutinative languages, e.g. Turkish, until finally the inflectional type of languages, such as those in Western Europe, developed. Another theory simply reversed the presumed process, starting with highly elaborate linguistic structures, and through several stages of simplification was supposed to end up with English. Of course, all such theories as to the evolution of present-day languages are mere speculations, but they still seem to provide persons with subtle excuses for their own lack of linguistic identification.

Regardless of the reasons for failure to communicate theology meaningfully within the context of local languages, the results of this process have been nothing short of tragic. In the first place, students have often concluded that they cannot express profound theological insights by means of their own languages. Second, many have regarded Christian theology as primarily a 'foreign system of thought.' Third, they have tended to be linguistically alienated from their own people. Some missionaries have insisted that this is all changing now, in view of the fact that so many professors of theology are nationals. But in a number of institutions these national professors insist on using the languages of western theology, or they depend so much on unassimilated foreign terms that their communications are seriously lacking in cultural depth.

An even more serious misconception about language, and especially about religious language, is that such language is really not supposed to be understood. That is to say, it is not subject to the same techniques of analysis as other discourse. People who hold this position insist that religion is essentially a mystery and that it must rest upon mysterious language, in which not the cognitive content but the emotive atmosphere is of primary importance. Such an attitude toward religion and religious language exists among many people. For example, a Guatemalan Indian objected strongly to a missionary's explaining a particularly difficult but highly important expression in the Scriptures, since, as he said, "If I can understand it, then it will not be religion any longer."

There is a tendency in all religions to aestheticize language in ritual until it is scarcely intelligible. In many religions this means preserving archaic forms. In other religions priests may intentionally alter religious language in order to make it seem to be 'the language of the gods.' This practice of aestheticizing religious language usually takes place when the prophetic period in a religion is past. When the religionists have nothing to say, they like to say it as beautifully as they can. They are no longer concerned primarily with a message, only with a mood. Under these circumstances many people prefer translations of the Scriptures which they do not understand, for then the words sound so beautiful but the people sense no urgency to respond.[6]

Religious language obviously must deal with 'mysteries'—those events which are not readily analyzable by the quantitative measurements of scientific observation. Such events are not amenable to controlled experiments. The mystery of faith should not rest in mysterious verbal symbols, but in the reality for which they stand: the mystery of holiness, the mystery of the God in Christ, the mystery of the Holy Spirit in the the life of believer. These are the mysteries of Christian faith, not the inscrutable language of ancient creeds or the obsolescent renderings of century-old translations.

A further misunderstanding about language is that words themselves imply a reality. If there is a name for something, most people conclude that there must be some objective feature to correspond to the word. Some people even insist that at one time there must have been unicorns, for people would not have invented a word for something which did not exist. Many people are certain that the human personality must have three parts: body, soul, and spirit, largely because there are three different words. This feeling about the relationship between symbols and reality has been responsible for the endless disputes between the trichotomists and the dichotomists throughout the centuries. Similarly, because Freud used such terms as *id, ego,* and *superego,* many people imagine that these are really three quite different parts of the human personality, rather than representing a descriptive mechanism by which some psychiatrists attempt to explain certain behavioral traits.

People are so credulous about traditional words and sayings that they continue to cite them as justifications for beliefs, even in contexts in which they make no sense. For example, the adage "the exception proves the rule" is cited as a means of dismissing contrary evidence, while in reality the expression "the exception proves the rule" was originally employed when the word *proves* had the meaning of testing, not of confirming. As first used this saying is true, but in its present-day application it is completely false.

When faced by some of the difficult problems associated with the doctrine of the Incarnation, some people cite the phrase "eternally begotten by the Father" as proof that in some way or other (usually unexplained) the difficulties can be made to evaporate. Such expressions, hallowed by time and preserved from scrutiny, may provide a sense of religious security to those within the fold, but they are relatively empty phrases if used in trying to explain doctrinal subtleties to those who are not already convinced.

This tendency to find in words something more than may actually be involved explains why words can so readily become the stuff of which verbal idols are made. While primitive people may carve their gods out of wood, more sophisticated pagans tend to carve him out of words. By imposing upon God the limitations which are derived from our human finite systems of thought, we feel so much more secure, since God is then more predictable and more tractable.

He fits so much more neatly within our system and within our world view. There is nothing so frightening to man as an uncontrollable God.

II. *The Nature of Language*

Having discussed some of the fundamental misconceptions which prevent the meaningful use of language in communication, we must now turn to the positive aspect of this problem and describe briefly the basic nature of language as a part of the communication structure which people possess. Language is, of course, only one of the signaling systems which people employ. They may use gestures, screams, whistling, semaphore signals, and even spatial relations (degrees of closeness) to signal many subtle attitudes and circumstances. But language is by far the most elaborately organized, the most widely employed, and culturally the most significant of all the communication systems.

Language is fundamentally a code, consisting, as all codes do, of symbols and arrangements. The symbols are primarily the words (or the lexical units) and the arrangements are the grammatical structures in which these words may occur. The phonological shape of the symbols is essentially arbitrary. For example, there is nothing in the sounds of the words *Pferd* (German), *cheval* (French), *caballo* (Spanish), and *horse* to suggest that this is an equine animal used primarily for hauling and riding. In order to possess the necessary creativity required of a language, the verbal forms cannot be tied directly to fixed forms in the culture.

The symbols of a language cannot, however, be thrown together in any order. They must be systematically ordered so as to be fully efficient in interpersonal communication. At the same time, they cannot be rigidly confined merely to set expressions. If this were the case, then a person could never say anything that he had not heard from others. Language is not parrot talk. What is amazing about language is that with some 25,000 to 50,000 words, which represent the words and lexical units of the average language (as spoken by the non-technician), people can talk about literally millions of different objects, events, and features of these objects and events. In order to do this, language must be essentially arbitrary and open.[7]

Though we must say that language is essentially an arbitrary system, we are obliged also to indicate that at two points language must touch nonlinguistic reality. In the first place, the potentialities of language are influenced by the possibilities of the vocal apparatus. There are quite naturally an amazing variety of sounds which the vocal apparatus can utter, but nevertheless these are limited. Moreover, all languages employ exclusively vocal means as a basic part of the communication system. For example, no language has incorporated the clapping of the hands as a regular part of the verbal system, e.g. using certain claps as consonants.

In the second place, language touches nonlinguistic reality in the referents of the words. That is to say, the meanings of the words reflect the world in which the people live and the way in which they view this world. People who know only about the terrain of flat atolls in the Pacific have no word for a mountain. People living in tropical areas may have no word for snow, and indigenous languages of Africa have no word for kangaroo. But what is of interest in the semantic structures of languages is not what they lack, but what they have in common. In fact, there is an amazing similarity in the ways in which people perceive and talk about the real world. All languages, for example, make semantic distinctions (reflected in various ways in the language structure) between objects, e.g. *man, boy, dog, tree, canoe*; events, e.g. *run, walk, talk, see*; abstracts, e.g. *good, tall, old, this, ten*; and relationals, which mark in various ways (e.g. by prepositions, conjunctions, order of words, etc.) the diverse relations between the objects, events, and the abstracts. Moreover, all languages employ time and space as features of the 'setting' of objects and events. These fundamental semantic categories are language universals and seem to be based upon the categories of perception common to mankind. In this aspect at least one may speak of a psychological unity of all mankind.

In addition to the basic semantic categories of language, there is also the need for all languages to employ a number of grammatical classes of symbols, the so-called word classes, since without these communication cannot be efficient. If each term had a unique structural relationship to all other terms, the human mental processes would simply be overloaded. The ways in which words are grouped according to various categories differ, however, rather strikingly. In some languages the distinction between countable, e.g. 'tree,' 'house,' and 'man' vs. noncountable (or mass), e.g. 'sand,' 'water,' and 'air,' is fundamental. Many languages make a primary distinction between animates and inanimates. Many languages classify events in terms of active participation and nonactive participation. For example, "listen" is active and "hear" is nonactive. Many classifications of symbols, however, are related to relatively minor features. Kung Bushman has one class of nouns which specify primarily objects with legs, so that people, animals (but not snakes), chairs, tables, and toadstools all get into the same class. Cherokee has a special class of plurals which refer to animals which are born in litters, e.g. dogs, cats, pigs, and snakes, but not horses, cows, sheep, or goats.

Within the various classifications there are always arbitrary 'exceptions.' For example, English singular and plural contrasts are arbitrary in such words as *oats*, which is always plural, and *salmon*, which may be singular or plural. Sometimes, however, the assignment of words to particular categories appears to reflect some measure of conscious categorizing. For example, some languages classify spirits in the human class, while in other languages the spirits are in the animal class. One must not, however, be deceived by a 'fossilized syntactic structure,' which may have been consciously evolved at an earlier time but which is at present completely arbitrary. One cannot, for example, insist that French-speaking peoples are more sex conscious than English-speaking peoples simply because French preserves a gender distinction in the nouns and English has largely lost it. One cannot derive psychological theories about Germans from the fact that *Frau* is feminine in gender and *Weib* is neuter, when both may be regularly used in speaking of one's own wife. One must not attempt psychological explanations for such gender distinctions as *der Weg*, *die Richtung*, and *das Mittel*, all of which overlap in certain domains of meaning with the English word *way*.[8]

Since language does touch the reality of the cultural context, as perceived by people, there are ways in which languages mirror, though often rather imperfectly, a people's view of their world. For example, the density of vocabulary may reflect a cultural focus. By 'density' we mean the number of words which are used in relation to the area covered and the depth with which it is covered by means of generic vocabulary of a classificatory kind. The Ponapeans, for instance, have hundreds of words relating to yams and their cultivation. The Anuaks employ scores of words for different shapes, sizes, and types of cattle. The Hanunoo have hundreds of terms for the various plants in their part of the Philippines. In fact, they make more distinctions than professional botanists have found it necessary to make in classifying the plants of the area.

The structure of figurative extensions of meaning may also reflect conscious cultural viewpoints. The Venda people in the Northern Transvaal classify birds as being uncles, fathers, cousins, brothers of each other, but in these classifications they are quite unconcerned about the shape, size, and biological characteristics. Rather, they put together those birds which are normally associated in nesting and feeding. What counts is whether the birds in question are consistently seen together; biological resemblances are fundamentally unimportant. This classification of birds does, however, reflect something important about Venda cultural patterns, for the kinship terms as applied to persons are not primarily related to biological descent. The fact of being the biological father of a child is not as important as being the person who has paid the bride price. In fact, a financially independent woman, who is herself married to a man, can 'marry' another woman, arrange for her to be impregnated by some man, and become the 'father' of the child. That is to say, the child belongs to her, rather than to her husband.

The use of a number of substitute terms for a particular object or phenomenon may also indicate a cultural attitude or belief. For example, the numerous names for 'bear' in the various Indo-European languages seem to reflect early taboos on the use of the name. This same situation is to be found in words for 'lightning' within the diverse dialects and languages of Quechua in South America. Many persons have contended that the multiplicity of titles and names for God in the Old Testament represents something of the same situation.

The changes which take place in the meanings of words may also indicate developments in cultural beliefs. For example, the fact that *atom*, which originally meant 'uncuttable,' is now employed for something which is continually being 'split' and 'smashed,' shows something about what has happened within the culture. It is important to note, however, that people tend to preserve the words, even though they radically alter the concepts signaled by the words. For example, in Biblical language one talks about 'anoint,' though in the western world anointing is not a normal procedure for commissioning or appointing a person. This tendency for the retention of symbols while changing the contents should warn people against attempting to discover 'the true meanings' of words by historical, etymological processes. Such etymologies can tell us what words do not mean today, but they cannot tell us what they do, or should, mean. Only an examination of actual usage can reveal this aspect of language function.

Certain classifications involving hierarchical substitutes in language may be significant in mirroring the world view of people. For example, the fact that in English one may speak of man as an animal, using the term *animal* in this generic sense to include all animate beings of a certain type, is culturally significant, since it reflects certain beliefs about biological relationships which are widespread in our western culture. In some other societies, for example among some of the tribes in South America, one could never speak of man as an animal. He is regarded as completely distinct, and the very thought of some biological connection is regarded as unthinkable.

While pointing out some of these aspects of language which do touch reality and which may be said to mirror the world view, it is essential that we guard against two very common errors related to these types of inferences. In the first place, there is a tendency for people to think that for every word with several meanings there must exist some common core of significance which all the meanings of this term share. What is sought is a common denominator of meaning, and by means of this some persons believe they can detect the 'cultural heritage.' In some instances the different meanings of a term may have one or two common semantic components (the minimal units of distinctiveness in meaning), but in many instances the various meanings of a word have only attenuated 'chains' of such components. Compare, for example, the different meanings of *charge* in such expressions as *charge the enemy, charge the gun, charge the bill, he is in charge,* and *a charge of murder*. In the case of Greek *charis*, usually translated as 'grace.' the series of meanings include 'beauty,' 'attractiveness,' 'kindness,' 'favor,' 'gift,' and 'thankfulness.' There is no semantically useful common denominator of meaning in this series, only a chain of related meanings held together by interlocking shared components of meaning.

In the second place, one can too readily forget that words are not limited to a referential function. That is to say, words not only 'point' to something; they also acquire from associations with certain speakers, particular contexts, and typical settings certain connotative values of their own. Some words tend to have favorable values, e.g. *mother, love, holiday, delicious,* and *democracy.* Others have generally unfavorable connotations, e.g. *dungeon, slavery,* and *native.* The changes in connotations may also tell us something about what is happening in our world, e.g. *imperialism, colonialism,* and *exploitation.* Or note the radically different attitudes of different people toward certain words, e.g. *communism, revolution, strike, revolt, rightist, liberal, dialectical materialism.*

Religious vocabulary is especially susceptible to connotative associations and many times the connotative values of words clearly mark ecclesiastical affiliations and theological outlooks. Compare, for example, the different connotative values in the following two sets of expressions: (a) *saved by the blood, in the heavenlies, filled with the Spirit, by his grace,* and (b) *confrontation, dialogue, existential,* and *ecumenical.* Because of these associative values words often become labels of belonging. A man may be denounced as unorthodox, not because of what he says, but because of the words which he uses. Similarly, a person may be thought of as quite orthodox, if only he uses the good old words.

III. *The Bases of Interlingual and Intercultural Communication*

Having described a number of the misconceptions about language, and having analyzed some of the fundamental features of language, we must now consider the essential bases of interlingual and intercultural communication. These are naturally of two types: linguistic and cultural. As far as the linguistic bases of communication are concerned, we have noted that even though a language may in some respects mirror a people's view of reality, each language is essentially an arbitrary system of symbolization which is not specifically and irrevocably tied to a particular culture. In fact, it is primarily an open system, with the capacity for an unlimited amount of modification and change, to cope with constantly new circumstances and concepts. Furthermore, we have seen that, with regard to the semantic structures, the similarities between languages are such as to provide a solid basis for effective communication. The perceptual and classificatory categories of languages are sufficiently similar as to permit meaningful translation.

The anthropological bases for interlingual and intercultural communication are even more important than the linguistic ones. In the first place, the various cultures have much more in common than some people may have been led to believe. The major areas of culture are universals, e.g. material, social, religious, and esthetic. The details may not be the same, but the fundamental motivations which give rise to these developments are certainly universal, e.g. thirst, hunger, sex, need for belonging, physical activity, mental activity, and aesthetic activity. Moreover, all peoples exhibit a desire for 'meaning' either in the ultimate sense (as provided by some philosophical system) or in the supernatural sense (as provided by religion).

In the second place, all peoples have the capacity for adaptation. There are certainly no biological deterrents to complete cultural assimilation. A child of whatever biological background can become a completely natural participant in any culture, provided, of course, the society is not prejudiced against him. Even after upper puberty, when so many of the unconsciously acquired patterns of behavior seem to be 'frozen,' there are no completely insurmountable obstacles to adjustment. The so-called primitive Bushman make excellent auto mechanics and show much greater manual dexterity than most people. The 'stone-age' people of the highlands of New Guinea can become qualified drivers of trucks and bulldozers in a very short time. In fact, only twenty-two years ago people in the Baiyer River area of Eastern New Guinea were still living in protected villages along the steep ridges of tropical mountains, from which they raided their enemies from time to time to carry off human heads needed in religious ceremonies. Now there are schools and hospitals in the area, rapidly expanding cooperatives (for coffee and timber), and a flourishing agriculture. More than fifty percent of the people are associated with the Christian church.

Not only do all peoples have the capacity for change, but they also have the ability to put themselves in other people's shoes. All peoples seem to possess a kind of grid which they can apply so as to interpret more or less accurately the behavior of others. The use of such an adjustive grid does, however, presuppose goodwill on the part of the users, for without such goodwill all interpretations are subject to severe distortion and skewing.

The basic failures in communication do not arise primarily from a failure in the use of language, even though inability to use a language properly may be a severe stumbling block to comprehension. Far more fundamental to the problems of intercultural communication are the diverse presuppositions about values which exist in different cultures and which are often so fundamental to the culture as not to be overtly specified or talked about. In fact, the most basic values and attitudes of any society are largely covert— they are regarded as being so essentially right and correct as not to require specification. They are the presuppositions about life and values which all societies take for granted as being merely human. It never dawns on such people that their values are not universal.

In many cultures of the world, for example, there is an important dichotomy between politeness and truth. In fact, politeness may be much more valued than truth. When one is called upon to choose between telling the truth, which may hurt someone, or giving a polite reply (usually what is presumably wanted), the polite response will almost inevitably be chosen. This does not mean that the people of such a culture are confirmed liars. It is only that in certain circumstances politeness, that is, responding as one thinks he is expected to respond, is more highly valued. Furthermore, all societies have their culturally acceptable ways of doing this. In the western world misrepresentation is generally expected in political promises, advertising, introductions of guest speakers, requests for resignations, and funeral eulogies. All societies tend to make a difference between truth and nontruth in communications, but they simply draw the line at a different place. For one living in a foreign society it is not always easy to discover just where this line is drawn.

For many people in the western world work is at least theoretically regarded as good in and of itself. In fact, people take vacations in order to be able to work more effectively, and they recreate in order to be able to work harder. To people in many cultures this is quite incredible. Work exists only for the sake of enjoying nonwork. Hence if, as in Thailand, a fertilizer is introduced so as to double the yield of rice, many of the farmers simply cut in half the amount of land under cultivation. The fertilizer was interpreted as a means of reducing labor, not as a means of increasing production.

One of the most subtle differences in a people's attitude toward their environment involves the distinction between adjustment and change. In the western world the dominant concept is to change the environment so as to accommodate it to the needs of people—even weather control is being advocated as the next important field for man to undertake. Such an attitude is almost irreligious in some areas. Most Indians of Guatemala strive to adapt to nature, not to change the surroundings. Hence, one does not plow too deeply, for this would "cut the belly of Mother Earth"; and one does not dig out springs, for this would transgress upon the spirits which dwell there. This close relationship to the environment may also influence one's timing of events. The Kung Bushman, for example, seem completely oblivious of western time: hours, weeks, calendar months, and especially of obligations for certain types of farm work to be done at specific times. On the other hand, they are extremely sensitive to the time of their environment: the maturation of beetle grubs for making poison arrows, the ripening of various edible nuts, the migrations of certain animals and birds, and the nesting of ostriches.

The fundamental differences in world view and value systems which most directly influence the communication of religious concepts are of three rather distinct, but related, types: (1) the concept of limited good, (2) the view of the world as basically hostile or good, and (3) the concept of history.

A high percentage of peoples in the world possess a concept of 'the limited good.' That is to say, they regard the world as possessing just so much wealth and good. Accordingly, if one person has a disproportionate share, it must be at the expense of others.[9] In contrast with the attitude of so many in the western world, where "the sky is the limit," these people are reluctant to rise too high, for they prize group identification more than excessive material gain. Moreover, they fear that if they do rise too high, their own people will "cut them down to size," either as the result of jealousy or because they are afraid that too much wealth or power in a few people's hands can upset the balance of life. People who are influenced by this view of the limited good tend to be basically pessimistic about possible improvement and slow to change. It may not be that they fear getting more than their share, but they assume that the chances of rising very high are so slim as not to be worth the effort. This concept of the limited good is not, however, a belief usually shared by all the members of a particular society. A rapidly rising segment of a society may have an expansionist view of total resources, while the poor may be seriously crippled by their adherence to a view of life which tends to thwart whatever initiative they might have.

Views of the world as basically hostile or benign can have a very powerful influence upon people—influences which the people themselves are usually not aware of. In many parts of Asia, matter is regarded as essentially evil. This means that salvation exists only in an escape from this essentially hostile environment. Among many peoples of Africa, the world is not inherently evil, but the creator God (who is basically good in so many respects) has simply gone off. Effective supernatural control of the world has been left to the ever-present demons or ancestor spirits, who at best may be neutral, but who in general are malevolent, especially when they are not properly remembered or honored. Such an attitude toward the physical environment and the future usually proves a severe deterrent to long-range planning, to conservation of natural resources, and to the kind of confidence in interpersonal relations which is necessary for large-scale undertakings.

For many Christians there is considerable ambivalence about the nature of the world. For some the earth is God's gift to man, for him to dominate and exploit—often with cruel consequences resulting from man's ignorance and greed. For others, however, the world, including even nature itself, is in the "hands of the Evil One," the "Prince and Power" of this world. Therefore, both the physical world and the forms of human society are suspect as being essentially evil; man cannot and should not expect to change or reform them. He can only find salvation in isolation from the world and in the hope of the millenial kingdom. Many Christians regard the 'flesh' as basically evil, so that man is sinful simply by virtue of his human nature; while others insist that the plight of man is not his being flesh, but his having a rebellious spirit, which defies God. With such contrary views concerning man's environment and his nature it is not strange that Christianity has spawned a number of quite different social attitudes, e.g. the social isolation of so many Mennonites, the political involvement of traditional Roman Catholicism, the other-worldliness of most premillenialists, and the social concern of Protestant liberalism.

For many Christians, however, the underlying beliefs which give rise to these varied reactions to the world are usually entirely covert, that is to say, they are simply taken for granted. Some of the more articulate members of these groups may provide philosophical and theological justifications for one or another form of social concern or involvement, but for the most part the members of such groups take for granted the basic presuppositions on which their distinctive forms of behavior are based. It is for this reason that meaningful discussion of such differences is often quite difficult, since people are rarely inclined to discuss or to question the unconscious motivations for their behavior. To do so is usually interpreted as a sign of social heresy or of religious apostasy.

Almost as important as a people's view of the world is their concept of history. For those who regard history as symbolized by the unending motion of the wheel, as it moves through such cycles as spring, summer, fall, and winter; birth, youth, adulthood, old age, and death; morning, noon, evening, and night—only to be repeated again and again in endless succession—there is no real improvement in history, only seeming ameliorations, to be followed later by disintegration and ruin. It is scarcely any wonder, therefore, that so many Asians, who consciously or unconsciously view history as mere cycles of recurring events, respond only very slowly to the dynamic concepts of the western world which involve such optimistic claims for material progress and such utopian schemes for social betterment. For most Buddhists and Hindus real salvation consists essentially in escaping from this world of illusion, into either the eternal bliss of Nirvana or the world soul of Brahman.

For many primitive peoples history can be likened to the 'beaten path.' The ancestors have always lived in a particular manner and so their descendants have chosen a similar manner of life. Such a view of history results in a very static view of the world and of social relations, and produces an inertia which is very difficult to overcome, especially if the people have been threatened by the outside world and have retreated into traditional ways of life in order to protect themselves from both real and imagined threats.

Another view of history which is almost as stultifying is the concept of 'the Golden Age.' People who are always looking back to a previous imperial glory, are chained to their history, not helped by it. They take pride in something merely because it is tradition, rather than being able to judge objectively its merits in terms of the present and the future. A backward look can constitute a ball-and-chain to progress. Unfortunately, it would seem that almost the only thing we learn from history is that people do not learn from history.

A fourth view of history, namely, the concept of a future 'kingdom of heaven' is distinctly Biblical in origin, but it has been taken over in many forms by many persons: by anarchists, who are so convinced of the essential goodness of at least some men that they are willing to destroy all social structures and restraints; by Communists, who are convinced that out of the recurring conflicts of thesis and antithesis in society a new synthesis of peace and fulfillment will emerge; by the social reformers, who seek to transform society and mankind by constructive improvements in social structures; and by premillenialists, who see no hope in human institutions and therefore look forward to the personal rule of Christ on earth for one thousand years.

Such concepts of history, as fulfillments of hope for an abundant future, are the dynamic elements in the world today. Leaders in the emerging countries are determined to chart a new course for their lagging societies, and youth in the so-called 'tired countries' of the western world are determined to light revolutionary fires which will burn up the social dross and provide a foundation for 'a new life style.' However, few persons, even among those who are deeply involved in social action in various movements, are fully aware of the presuppositions upon which their programs are based. Such fundamental issues as human perfectability, ultimate values, ecological support, and the role of the personal fallibility lie at such a low level of awareness—that is, they are so much a part of the unconscious presuppositions about life—that even to raise such an issue seems impertinent in the mad rush to 'get things done.' However, if the church is going to prepare itself to speak meaningfully to the world in which it lives, it must study the presuppositions of others and become aware of its own underlying motivations. Only in this way can it speak with relevance.

IV. *Relevant Communication*

In order to understand something of the principles underlying relevant communication, it is important for us to note briefly what is happening among those groups which are communicating effectively. Since World War II the major increases in adherence to Christianity have occurred in the so-called 'independent churches,' which have no formal ties with traditional churches, but which in so many places are growing with incredible rapidity. One may estimate that perhaps 15 million persons have become associated with these independent movements since World War II. The members of these churches may be accused of being theologically naive, but they do take God and the Bible seriously. Moreover, they also take seriously the condition and beliefs of their neighbors. For them demon possession is real, and not merely some form of mental disorder. In fact, their fear of demons is much greater than the European's fear of hell ever was. And it is freedom from the domination of demons that the local prophet promises his followers. Furthermore, these religious leaders also take seriously 'divine healing'; they insist that God's power can extend to human disease. They not only pray for the sick; they expect and experience unbelievable healings. Most of these same movements are also deeply committed to the social and economic improvement of their members. They do not expect to be able to change their governments, but they are determined to find jobs for their people, organize cooperative buying and marketing enterprises, provide loans for housing, and foster communal farming and industrial enterprises. Because of their theological differences or social isolation from 'mainline denominations' such groups as the Iglesia na Christo in the Philippines, the Kimbanguists in Congo, the Cherubim and Seraphim Church in West Africa, the Pentecostals in Chile, and the Portales Church in Mexico City are rarely studied in terms of their communication principles. Of course, the content of their communication cannot be exported to another context, but the principles of communication which these groups employ, and the relevance of their message in terms of the cultural context in which they communicate, is extraordinary and could be very instructive.

Unfortunately too many persons have thought that in order to communicate one must of necessity have certain agreed premises in common. Therefore, some people are always looking for those ideological compromises which can form a presumed basis for dialogue. In reality, however, all that is required is a common humanity, openness to listen, and willingness to take the other person's viewpoint seriously, even though it may be wrong. For fear of seeming to be controversial, we actually talk past one another And out of an ignorance of one another's basic presuppositions about life we fail to touch upon the crucial elements of life and hope. It is not accommodation of ideas which is needed, but mutual comprehension. To accomplish this we must understand the real role of language and appreciate the significance of anthropological insights into the world views of others.

NOTES

[1] For an important discussion of these problems see Fritz Güttinger, *Zielsprache* (Zürich, 1963), pp. 7-48.

[2] A number of problems relating to wrong implications from linguistic evidence of Biblical languages is treated by James Barr, *The Semantics of Biblical Language* (Oxford, 1961).

[3] See Bernard Block, "Studies in colloquial Japanese," *Journal of the American Oriental Society*, LXVI (1946), pp. 98-100.

[4] For help in the procurement and analysis of the following data from Kung Bushman I am indebted to Ds Ferdie Weich.

[5] These basic semantic categories are more fully treated in Eugene A. Nida and Charles R. Taber, *The Theory and Practice of Translation* (Leiden, 1969), pp. 33-47.

[6] For a detailed analysis of various aspects of religious language in communication see Eugene A. Nida, *Message and Mission* (New York, 1960), and *Religion Across Cultures* (New York, 1968).

[7] For an introduction to the nature of language and certain linguistic approaches to its study see Émile Benveniste, *Problèmes de linguistique générale* (Paris, 1966).

[8] There is unfortunately a tendency for some persons to read into language a number of quite wrong implications. See, for example, Leo Weisgerber, *Grundzüge der inhaltbezogenen Grammatik* (Düsseldorf, 1962).

[9] For a very important analysis of this basic concept see G. M. Foster, "Peasant society and the image of the limited good," *American Anthropologist*, LXVII (1965), pp. 293-315.

CHAPTER ELEVEN

MAN AND THE SON OF MAN

Jürgen Moltmann

I. Analysis of a Dream

On August 28, 1963, Martin Luther King stood before the Lincoln Memorial in Washington and announced his unforgettable dream of peace, freedom, and humanity in a divided world:

> I have a dream that one day this nation will rise up and live out the true meaning of its creed: "We hold the truths to be self-evident that all men are created equal..."
> I have a dream that my four little children will one day live in a nation where they will not be judged by the color of their skin but by the content of their character...
> I have a dream that one day every valley shall be exalted and every hill and mountain shall be made low, the rough places will be made plain and the crooked places will be made straight and the glory of the Lord shall be revealed and all flesh shall see it together.[1]

In this dream two traditions of humanity are impressively joined. The first is the *Stoic idea of man*, contained in the American constitution. All men are equal and free—this is the core of universal human nature. To live in accordance with nature means to live a life in conformity with the divinity. Stoic humanism rests on two pillars: the postulate of a life in accordance with nature/God, and the concept of the universal idea (*Konai ennoiai, innatae notiones*). In this tradition, the truth of equal and universal human rights is self-evident. It is not a product of history and therefore is not passed on in history; it is inborn to every man in the universal ideas of reason, and is therefore self-evident.

The American Constitution is the Enlightenment's child, and it made this Stoic concept of humanity a part of its law. Yet it is Christian in replacing the idea of divine human nature with the Biblical concept of God creating all men equal. Not only did Martin Luther King dream his dream into the future; he gave it immediate and practical political relevance by appropriating and attaching to it the tradition of the revolutionary Enlightenment rights of man.

The goal of his dream is far more than the Stoic view of man, however; he replaces the Stoic ontology of human nature with *prophetic eschatology*. For Second Isaiah, whom King quotes, the commonality of all men lies in God's future. With the coming of the glory of the Lord, all the distinctions which men have devised to differentiate themselves from one another will be destroyed. When the glory of God comes, the mighty will be humbled and the powerless exalted so that "all flesh" can participate together and communally in the glory of His kingdom. Contained within this eschatology of the coming God is an eschatology of the free human community. The commonality of all men does not lie behind their concrete historical differences and conflicts, in the hidden core of their being; it is to be found in their concrete and common historical future in the coming God. What brings them together is not the universal reason inborn in all men, but that prophetic hope proclaimed to all men. This prophetic eschatology of the future new man and the coming human community is superior to the Stoic ontology of the new man: it does not ignore historical differences and conflicts; it takes them seriously in responsible hope, expecting that they will be overcome in the judgment of the mighty and the exaltation of the lowly which is beginning, here and now, to anticipate the possible. In one respect it is inferior to the Stoic ontology, however: it cannot appeal to reason in all men, but must rely on awakening hope in history and must depend on faith and consent. God's omnipresence in nature and the self-evident character of his truth in the inborn ideas of reason, which Stoic humanism considers to be eternal and present, prophetic eschatology expects only in the future new world where "God will be all in all" (I Cor. 15:28) and "None will have to teach another because they will all see him face to face."

Today Stoic humanism is in a crisis of relevancy, because it can no longer remain indifferent—*nec metu, nec spe*—to historical differences within humanity. The prophetic eschatology of humanity's common future in the coming God also has lost much of its power. First of all, Jews and Christians have not witnessed to it radically enough in their practices, and secondly, the effect of the Bible is always limited for, as Lessing and Kant said, "All have reason." Nevertheless, Stoic and prophetic humanity are a 'dangerous remembrance'; they question the present and threaten it with a 're-volution of rising expectations' by exhorting us toward an unfulfilled future.

Remembrance of the past may give rise to dangerous insights, and the established society seems to be apprehensive of the subversive contents of memory. Remembrance is a mode of dissociation from the given facts, a mode of 'mediation' which breaks, for short moments, the omnipresent power of the given facts. Memory recalls the terror and the hope that passed.[2]

In this sense, 'man' is a subversive remembrance today: man does not yet exist; man is betrayed everywhere. 'Man' is a revolutionary hope because the remembrance of man is irradicably engraved on the human spirit. There are societies in which even the word 'humanism,' as in 'humanistic' Marxism, is condemned and 'Communism with a human countenance' suppressed whenever it shows itself. There are societies in which humanism, even though a constitutional cornerstone, is used as a cover for racial division, class conflict, and colonialism. Yet the Stoic view of a universal human nature and the prophetic hope in the "son of man" continue to work beneath the surface.

II. Analysis of the "Divided World"

We live in a divided world, a world in which peace is maintained only by an endless process of dividing countries, peoples, and cities. One division follows another, paradoxically, at the same rate that the world's population increases and people, cultures, and religions enter into a common world history. World War II left behind the ideological conflict between East and West. The post-war period revealed the far more dangerous economic conflict between North and South. Wherever racial, religious, ideological, and social conflicts erupt today, political peace is achieved through division, apartheid, ghettos, walls, and barbed-wire barricades. Divided nations (Korea, Germany, Vietnam, Palestine, etc.), divided cities (Berlin, Belfast, etc.), populations divided by race, class, and caste characterize the world's countenance. The motto of all rulers who spread bondage is *divide et impera*, divide and conquer. Through division, the powers of inhumanity are now dominating men. Rulers play with the emotions of human fear and draw out of its bottomless depths endless new aggressions against other men. This deep fear in man can affix itself to race or religion or any other prerogative which gives men status and identity. By causing men to identify their selfhood with property, set ideas, and possessions, fear drives men to the idolization of existing realities. This idolatry then prevents men from affirming with their own lives the other life of other men. Only when this internal and external, psychic and both politically and economically institutionalized idolatry is destroyed and men are freed from it, can hope in 'man' and 'the kingdom of the Son of Man' become a concrete utopia. Needed as witnesses in the midst of a divided, fearful, and idolatrous world are 'men' who—like the Stoic wisemen and the Christian martyrs—"walk free," who no longer are driven by fear, its monstrosities and its exploitation. These are the men who "walk straight" (Ernst Bloch) and with "head held high," "because their liberation is near" (Lk. 21:28). They are the men who glimpse the future of a habitable earth and a kingdom of freedom and in whose faces is reflected even now, however imperfectly, the glory of the coming God and His freedom.

A clear tendency toward unification of the world, toward universalization, synchronization, and singularization of its history exists alongside this trend toward further division and fragmentation of humanity. For the first time in history, something approaching 'one world' is coming into being. The military threat has become universal, although it still emanates from only two or three nations. Were the 'balance of terror' to be destroyed, mankind would completely annihilate himself. In this situation man can survive only within a new political community in which military power is brought under international legal control. The same is true of the present and coming hunger catastrophe. Hunger is becoming a universal human problem that can be solved only by the united effort of all men. Nowhere on earth is the future any longer simply a continuation of the past; today for every nation it is something new. There was in fact no 'world history' before. There were only the histories of various peoples and cultures in their separate worlds. Only now are we entering a future in which we will be able to talk about one world history. In the past, men had histories only in the plural. Therefore our pasts are plural today. Every people, every culture, every religion has its own history and its particular traditions. Because from now on we will either be destroyed together or survive in a new community, our future is only singular. Through the technologies of military threat and mass communications, a universal world history is being created for man today. History is becoming universal and singular; the times in which we live are being synchronized to a single present. Humanity today is leaving behind the quantities of plural histories and is standing on the brink of a new quality of a single, universal history. The actual course of history is beginning to unfold within the universal horizon of eschatology. Unfortunately, our understanding of this one world's responsibilities in politics, ethics, and faith in its possible future is constricted in the provincial, national, and confessional thought forms of an epoch already past.

There are two spiritual ways to face the technical pressure unifying the world, to grasp the situation, and to deal with the future. One is the idea of a *unifying religion* and of ideological internationalism. The other is the idea of democratizing the various traditions and standpoints toward the ideal of a pilgrim community open to the future. How can we best represent humanity's common cause?

The basic concept of the religions of unity is: one God, one religion, one society. In religion, different men integrate themselves into a single society with the help of symbols and rites. This is the basic concept of the civil religion, even when Rousseau presented it. Conflicts of interest between various men and groups are transcended in the civil religion of a country in which they have to get along. Symbols of community are created and honored in such a nation as the means by which the people can identify with one another. The religious symbolism of the 'nation' has proven particularly powerful in an age of class struggles, conflict between economic interests, and racial strife. It symbolizes a 'folk community' which does not actually exist in the midst of the social and political conflict. "I no longer recognize any parties; I see only Germans," was the slogan Wilhelm II used in 1914 to bring the German people out of their internal differences "to the front" and into the war. The growth of nationalism in East, West, and South uses symbols in a similar way and with seemingly analogous success. To achieve a single human community, religions of unity, whether Christian, nationalistic, or Shinto, operate with a reference point that transcends conflict; it may be God or the Kaiser or the nation. Could a single world religion, which might integrate humanity, arise one day out of the various national religions and their integrative symbolisms? Is such an integral world religion desirable from the perspective of Christian faith?

Compared to the idea of religions of unity, today's tendency toward an *ideology of unity* seems far more effective in conquering common problems. While the religions of unity symbolize a unifying, transcendent reference point, the ideologies of unity formulate a common cause; for example, the creation of socialism or the establishment of a communist society. The unifying point here is in the future which is to be created, in a concrete utopia. What is truly unifying, however, is the past which is to be overcome, the solidarity in the class struggle and in the anti-colonial fight for freedom. The synchronization of world history in a common present has brought many Europeans closer to Mao and Ho than to their own fathers Marx and Engels. The communications media have engendered a new secular piety of solidarity with those farthest away. Newspaper and television reports replace morning prayer. As formulated by the ideology of unity, this solidarity is the common fight for freedom. Typically, however, this solidarity can only be negatively formulated and maintained beyond one's own borders. As soon as socialism is effected "in one country"—and not everywhere at the same time—it falls victim to national self-interest and strivings for hegemony, and international socialism is betrayed to national self-interest. Once established, socialism dissolves into a pluralism of interests. Unified socialism exists today only in opposition to capitalism; it is not to be found within the socialist world proper.

This leads us to the question about common roads in the midst of conflicting interests. Mankind does not have a single, universal nature which can be formulated in natural law, symbolized in religion, or realized in socialist society. Man is not a generic being. While animals have their generic character and can be understood as examples of their genus, man has only history, and at that an open-ended history in which he can squander or realize his humanity. 'Human nature,' or that which makes men men, is not given at the beginning of their history and does not exist as idea behind the multiplicity of man's appearances. If it exist at all, it stands at the goal and end of his history and its conflicts. "Man has no nature; he has only history" (Ortega y Gasset). "Man learns what he is through history, not through self-contemplation" (Dilthey). To the depths of his 'innermost being,' man is ambiguous, changeable and open. He does not rest on his nature, but is a creator and creation of his culture. Because he himself is an 'open question,' and often an 'open wound,' he must continually seek to answer the question and heal the wound through the history of his culture. One who imputes to man 'generic essence' or 'nature' or 'basic needs' does not recognize him as a free, open being, but is attempting to control him. The decisive question is not whether man has a nature or whether there will be a fulfilled, completed, good humanity; today's question is who has the right, in an open history, to tell men how they should define their common nature or their destiny. The use which churches, parties, and élites have made of these terms in the past shows that we are dealing here with ideologies of domination. They produce inhumanity and are always in conflict with other ideologies of authority. Instead of looking for religions and ideologies of unity, it is more in keeping with man's open history that we seek to deal rationally with conflict and to democratize competing viewpoints.

Our first observation at this point is that the world's population must enter into an open process society if it is to survive. An open process society is a pluralistic society which demonstrates its vitality by bearing the contradictions within it without falling apart. It is a dynamic society which rejects total ideologies and total planning and lives on the basis of the pragmatic changeableness of ideas. It is a society oriented on the future, in which all participate in working out and building the common future in which they will then all share. It considers its future open in principle, in order that absolute and total claims are banned from present ideas and programs. In this way it keeps its own historical process and democratic formation of policy permanently open to further revision and growth. It relativizes all religious and ideological views. But it does not relativize them with reference to a new absolute which makes any view arbitrary and ultimately absolute; its sets each viewpoint in perspective by its insight into the relationship of relativity. All views and positions are relative because they are related to each other, not because an absolute is to be found beyond them. In this society one can confidently present his views so long as he relates them to all other views and perspectives and enters into communication and dialogue. In summary of these ideas about the coming world society we would say: what we want is a *societas viae*, not a *societas patriae*, a *societas imperfecta*, not a *societas perfecta*. The solidarity of man from various nations, religions, and ideologies and the democratization of their political, social, and cultural common life are not visions of a sanctified and finished world. They are practical ideas for the way of a common history. Only when the paths of common life are humanized can common formulation of particular goals occur in a human way.

The discernment of the relationality of social relativity makes it possible for Christian faith to be integrated in this *societas viae* without fear for its destruction. It can disseminate its view of man's true and real future, and others need not fear the dictatorship of the church or the West.

III. *The Remembrance of the Image of God in a Not-yet Human World*

'Man' is not capable of empirical proof. To be sure, characteristics of *homo sapiens* can be listed. But new archaeological discoveries are constantly being made which fuzz out the boundary between man and the primates, and new forms of life and new characteristics constantly arise in history. Historical research and the historical future dissolve every assumed type of 'man.' When we speak of 'man,' we mean less the 'manness' (*hominitas*) of this being than the humanity (*humanitas*) which is not given to this creature as a fact but as a task. A cow is always a cow, but man both *is* and *must be* man. He is a task set for himself. Therefore he can become 'human' or 'inhuman,' but no cow can be an 'un-cow.' "Basically we *are* not true men, but must always *become* such".[3] There is no self-evident Biblical anthropology; there is only a Biblical theology of history which witnesses to that history which God conducts with man; in this history, man's destiny is to be 'man'; he fails his destiny and is brought home and freed from it in order that he might finally come into his glory. Biblical theology of history speaks about 'man' when it speaks of God's creation, action, suffering, and victory. It also speaks about man in an indirect way when it talks of a Wholly Other. It can speak of 'man' in universal terms because its starting point is not certain qualities which all men share. It does not begin with certain prerogatives which distinguish some men more than others. The Biblical universalism in the language about 'man' is based on the history of a Wholly Other God and the eschatology of His coming. It is turned polemically against every national polytheism and all international pantheisms. The witnesses to God's history in the Bible are anthropologically 'dangerous' in every human society, because that history attacks man's self-deification both in his nation and in his dreams of humanity. Man is not 'man' so long as he is the image of his nation or of his generic idea. He only becomes man, a free man, when he becomes the image of the Wholly Other God in a non-divine world.

Man is both God's creature and His image, according to the first

recollections of God's history with him. Man is God's creature. This
is an eminently critical definition of man. Like all other living things,
he was called into being out of chaos and nothing. Neither man nor
nature is divine. This de-mystifies both the old pantheism and the
new. Nature is neither numinous nor demonic. It is nothing other
than a creation of the transcendent God. In itself it has nothing
divine, yet it is God's good creation. In itself it contains nothing
demonic for it is not void, not anti-God, not anti-human. Man is
also a creature of God. He is neither a demon, an aberration of
nature, nor a demi-god. Man is God's creature; that also means that
he stands in solidarity with God's other creatures. Like them he has
been called into life. Like them he is threatened by annihilation.
Nevertheless, the remembrance that man is God's creature says
nothing about his particular definition. As God's creature, he is as
little similar or bound to God as any other creature. All creatures
are shapes of God's will, not his being, of his creative command, not
himself. Man's particular definition lies in his being the image of
God. In a world which does not correspond to his essence but is a
good work of his hands, God creates a being which corresponds to
him, with whom he deals, which represents him. To reiterate, this
conception is intended to be eminently critical. In the general understanding of the heathen idol religions, nature is everywhere capable
of being the image of the divine being. Everywhere and at any time,
a piece of creation may be penetrated by God and may serve as a
medium or window between God and men. But in Israel the creation
faith led to a prohibition of idols. Israel was so declared profane.
The creation is 'good,' but it is capable of being neither a likeness
nor an image of God. Only man, for whom there is no substitute, is
designated as God's image on earth. Tacitus was right to charge the
Jews with lack of piety: "To them all things are profane which we
hold sacred" (*Profana illis omnia quae apud nos sacra*). The old awe
of nature here yields to respect for the image of God in every man.
From the beginning, Israel had an anthropocentric 'world view';
everything was created for man's sake, and man is God's representative on earth. Wherein does man's being God's image lie? The
theological-humanistic tradition long sought to find the answer in
one human characteristic, in reason, freedom of will, or language.
What general philosophical anthropology calls man's special place
in the cosmos, religion has called the *Imago Dei*. This is nothing but
a re-mystification of a piece of the creation. Other traditions have

conceived of the image of God as man's original perfection which
was obscured or lost in the Fall. But neither the Old Testament nor
the New speaks of a 'loss' of God's image. Recent exegesis has shown
that the 'image of God' does not aim at one characteristic of man
but at a relationship involving the whole man and in which he is to
realize himself. Thus *Imago Dei* means not the essence of created
man, but his vocation and definition: to represent God in His
creation. This understanding of *Imago Dei* as relationship was present in ancient times in the various ideologies of kingship. The
priestly source probably took this idea over from Egyptian royal
ideology.[4] The king was God's representative and deputy on earth.
Divinity is present where the king appears and renders judgments.
Israel transferred this theology of kingship to 'man,' and thereby
humanized and democratized it. Every man is created as God's
representative, deputy, and viceroy on earth. "He is God's image
in that he is man' (Barth III, 1, 206f.). When 'man,' both the individual man and mankind in general, assumes authority over the
earth and spreads God's blessing in peace, he participates as deputy
and representative in God's world dominion and in the blessing of
creation. When man lives in fellowship with other men, he lives in
fellowship with God. As an individual and as a whole, man has the
vocation to be God's counterpart. At one and the same time, 'man'
is a creature like all the rest of creation and the image of God like
none other of God's creatures. He *is* a creature; at the same time,
he *has* the whole creation as the realm in which he represents God.
He stands in solidarity with creation, yet is set over against it
through his relationship as God's counterpart. Man is thus placed
in an eccentric position. It is a double relationship which might be
expressed in this way: man's vocation is to be God's representative
to creation and at the same time to represent the creation before
God. As God's image he is the 'crown of creation'—when he is
really 'man.'

  Man is both the image of God and an idolater, the second re-
collection of God's history with him says. Real man does not conform to his creation and vocation; he contradicts them. He is not
"man," but *Unmensch*, un-man, a monster. We will attempt to
avoid the traditional misunderstandings of what tradition has
called 'sin' by identifying it here as the compulsion to idolatry. Man's
inhuman reality is dominated by his perversion of his vocation to
be the image of God. The un-man does not face away from God, re-

presenting Him to creation. Instead he faces the other way, for he mistrusts the God whom he can properly only have behind him and trusts the things that he properly can only keep before him. He thus inverts the dialectic of trust and control. In trusting things or his own works, although they are not trustworthy but only controllable, he mistrusts God whom he cannot control but only trust. He perverts trust in God and his vocation into trust in the world. Instead of a living image of God, he becomes the image of an idolized creation or a reflection of his own celebrated accomplishments. The creation which he is to use and rule becomes the object of his trust. God becomes the object of his mistrust and his exercise of control. Trust of that which should be controlled blocks him off from the God who cannot be controlled, only trusted. That is superstition, idolatry, fetishism, personality cult, works righteousness, and anxiety about performance. What tradition has called 'sin' is not just unbelief; it is an inversion of faith into superstition. All further mistakes which are called sins have their basis in this worship of idols. Thus, as Paul says, the truth is changed into lies, the glory of the invisible God is changed into an image of mortal man, and the creation is served more than is the Creator. Other men, the creation, one's own works do not provide an adequate basis for such trust; therefore, idol worship spreads an atmosphere of anxiety. "Where you hang your heart, there is your God," Luther said in the Greater Catechism. For that on which one hangs his heart also influences, rules, and regulates him. The un-man is an image of his idols; his works righteousness makes him the image of his accomplishments; his apotheosis of nature makes him the image of this ambiguous nature. The inner structure of superstition clearly shows the structure of being the image of God, but in a perverted form. One cannot speak of a loss of the image of God, only of its perversion. One cannot speak of a loss of faith in sin, only of its perversion into superstition. The sinner is not a rebel against God (E. Brunner), but a man who forsakes his vocation. He no longer wants to be like God, nor even His image on earth. Instead he wants to be like all other creatures or only like a picture he makes himself. The un-man becomes godless, but he is not freed of his vocation to be the image of God.

The remembrance of man's vocation as the image of God on earth reminds the un-man of a freedom which he perverted into anxiety and a faith which he transformed into superstition, whether

the personality cult of the ancient ruler or the modern economic
material fetishism of the capitalistic world. Today, this remembrance
can only be a provocation to the self-righteous and superstitious
man.

*IV. Hope in the 'Kingdom of the Son of Man' in the Struggle for
World Domination*

Now we shall jump from Israel's earliest recollections—in which
Israel did not yet appear, only 'man'—to the prophetic vision in
which Israel no longer appears, only 'the Son of Man.' The major
prophets conceived of the salvation future which God will institute
after the judgment of Israel in a strongly Israel-centric way; Zion
will be re-established as the center of a world from which peace and
justice will go forth to the nations. In Daniel, however, we meet a
turn from prophecy to apocalyptic with a horizon of universal
history. The prophecy of the Son of Man begins with Daniel and is
found in IV Esdras, in the Ethiopian Enoch, and other apocalyptic
writings. They arose in the hour when Israel's political autonomy
was coming to an end and her particular political history stopped.
"Enduring world history becomes a threatening and destructive
power which one could not seriously oppose outwardly and with
which one could cope inwardly only if one conquered it spiritually."[5] Therefore, messianic hopes give way to universal hope in the
kingdom of the Son of Man. And this hope in the coming of the Son
of Man no longer refers only to the suffering of Israel, but to the
whole painful history of humanity in which Israel participates.

In the vision of the empires in chapter 7, Daniel sees world history
in a dream: one after another, four animals rise from the sea, rule
for a time, and are then condemned by the succeeding animal. The
lion with eagle wings represents the Babylonian Empire. He is
followed by a ravenous bear with long teeth, the Empire of the
Medes. Then comes the leopard with wings; he represents the
Persian Empire. Finally comes the kingdom of an indescribable,
dreadful monster which crushes all the kingdoms and people.
Certainly the Macedonian Empire is intended. All of these empires,
symbolized by beasts of prey, arise from the deluge, from the chaos
out of which the Creator had once created and ordered the world and
entrusted it to his image, 'man.' Against the background of ancient

Oriental symbolism, these four empires must be understood as powers of destruction and annihilation. According to Daniel's vision, the world's fate is determined by the succession of great kingdoms with differing focal points. Any authority which had been granted to 'man' is occupied and exercised by usurpers in inhuman, beastly form. According to the ancient concept of representation, a kingdom and its symbols determine not only external order, but also the internal, spiritual life of its subjects. If world empires are bestial, human life is objectively impossible within them. Therefore, Daniel says that in these four world empires, the judgment will continue until "rebellion shall be stopped, sin brought to an end" (9:24; cf. 8:12). The future of these world empires is the judgment of God. In the night of judgment when they pass away, the Son of Man will appear.

> I was still watching in visions of the night and I saw one like a man coming with the clouds of heaven; he approached the Ancient in Years and was presented to him. Sovereignty and glory and kingly power were given to him, so that all people and nations of every language should serve him; his sovereignty was to be an everlasting sovereignty which should not pass away, and kingly power such as should never be impaired.   (7:13ff.)

Who is this 'Son of Man'? "The Aramaic *bar änach* actually means the single example of the species man; thus it points emphatically to an individual, but at the same time manifests the whole in the idea of *pars pro toto*."[6] Adam is understood in precisely this way. The Son of Man does not emerge from the chaos like the bestial world rulers. He comes from heaven, the sphere of the Creator. That means that the kingdom of men does not develop out of the inhuman kingdoms; rather it comes as something new in the world's history of suffering. The Son of Man brings about this eschatological change which frees men for their actual vocation, to be 'man,' for he brings men into their own and their creator's justice.

Daniel's thinking about world history begins with the particular history of Israel, but his horizon expands to humanity's history of suffering under the yoke of tyrannical world rulers. Therefore the future of the Son of Man and his 'human kingdom' becomes the hope of all men. In the Priestly document, the idea of man as the image of God is a pointed allusion to the royal ideology. In Daniel, the tyrannical world empires are perversions of 'man's' world authority. The coming kingdom of the Son of Man thus fulfills in an eminently

political sense the vocation of man and of mankind to be the image
of God.

Daniel's vision has been called the first outline of universal history in the religious and intellectual history of the world. In fact,
this vision influenced the consciousness of history up to the nineteenth century. In universal historical terms, the 'kingdom of man'
appears only as the goal of the world empires. I would therefore
prefer to call the 'history of the world's suffering' the only appropriate category of universal history, as does W. Benjamin. The
universe is in one history, not through positive total planning, but
through common suffering. Understood in this way, the 'kingdom of
man' is not the goal of world history, but its end. It does not arise
from a development of the world, but enters man's history of
suffering as something new in order to free man for eternal justice.

Daniel has been charged with ahistorical speculation, unrelated
to present praxis. Certainly he anticipated the kingdom of man
only as an open future and expressed it only as a distant final hope.
For him the practical consequence lay in persevering resistance by
the holy and the just. Israel had its own politics no longer; now the
true Israelite, the just, would show himself in passive resistance in
faith and in perseverance in persecution.

The bestial world empires are superstition and forced idolatry.
They do not bring justice, but increase rebellion. The remembrance
of the creation and of man's vocation to be God's image on earth
becomes for Daniel hope for the end of the unjust history of tyrannical world rulers through the coming of the kingdom 'of man.' It
is an anti-tyrannical vision. The hope in the kingdom of man is a
politically relevant hope for the unity of the human race in the
kingdom 'of man.' The remembrance of this hope breaks through
the forces of oppression and injustice, makes the saints dissatisfied
and resistant, gives them a troubled heart and a critical spirit. There
can be no peace between hope in the kingdom of man and tyrannical
world rulers and empires. The God-question is the same as the
political-eschatological question: To whom does authority over the
world belong?

V. *The Belief that the Son of Man Has Appeared in Jesus of Nazareth*

The post-Easter church very early identified Jesus of Nazareth
with the promised Son of man. It connected the memory of Jesus'

works, suffering, and death with the coming 'of man.' Whether Jesus considered himself to be the Son of Man is exegetically disputed and need not be discussed here. Our interest here is with the nature of this identification. What does Jesus' concrete history do to the expectation of the Son of Man? What does the expectation of the Son of Man make of the remembered history of Jesus?

The figure of the crucified one is not aesthetically attractive; in him there was 'no form nor beauty.' Humanism, both ancient and modern, has considered the crucified one unaesthetic and the veneration of him improper and inhuman. Ancient love was *eros* of the good, the true and the beautiful. Humanism has always projected its ideal of the good, true, and beautiful man into the future because humanity is painfully absent in the here and now. Christian faith, however, confesses that the suffering, dying Jesus is 'the man': *Ecce Homo*, behold the crucified one! But how is what is human revealed in Jesus?

First of all, Jesus' public ministry from beginning to end is marked by the presence of men with all possible illnesses, obsessions, and deformities. They forced their way into the light of his presence out of the darkness into which decent society had banned them to get them out of sight. These men, as the gospel writers describe them are not good, strong, beautiful, and normal; it is rather the hidden suffering and secret sins of men which are revealed to Jesus in the gospel writers' story. The piteous figures who appear around Jesus are those without a place in society, those who have been driven out and exploited. Those who come forward are hopeless; they are not those with a will to live. They are accepted by Jesus as they really are for they cannot appear otherwise. Appearance and essence are the same for those who live on the edge of death. For 'normal men' appearance and essence are not the same in their social roles and acknowledgement of others; that is what makes 'decent' society inhuman.

Jesus' path has a definitely downward direction. His deeds and proclamation are valid for all men precisely because he sided with the weak, the sick, the poor, the rejected, those for whom the inhumanity of men and their good society is undisguised. Jesus is a friend of man, and what is most extraordinary, he lays hold of human society at its lowest point with the miserable, the despised, the lowly (Chr. Blumhardt).

Jesus helps all those whose humanity has been robbed or denied;

he acts not as a humanistic hero and aide of humanity; rather he shares their fate, enters into their suffering, and stands in solidarity with them in order to promise them the kingdom of God in this solidarity and to provide a symbol of physical and spiritual freedom. In the final analysis, Jesus helps not through his superior power, but "through his anguish and pain" (P. Gerhardt). By his wounds the wounded are healed. He understands himself in their sins by taking these sins upon himself. He understands himself in their sickness by burdening himself with their illnesses. He understands himself in their shame by taking upon himself the shame of the cross. He reveals himself as the Son of Man by taking the inhumanity of man as his fate. He understands himself in the other. Later Christian hymns quite properly sang of this path of the Son of Man as the Incarnation of the Son of God in the form of the servant. Jesus' claim is to represent the coming kingdom of God. His claim goes beyond the authority of Moses and the figures of hope, the Messiah and even the Son of Man. But Jesus' path does not go from below to above and from history through anticipation into a better future; instead it goes the other way, downward into mankind's history of suffering. By actualizing his claim among the sick, the guilty, the exiles, among those not welcome in any 'human' society, he causes them to become the vanguard and heirs of the kingdom of man. Thus the critical negation that any 'human' society is actually an inhuman society. The poor have no part in any kingdom, great or small, in the world. In a negative way, the ostracized, the disenfranchised, and the dying are "neither Jew nor Gentile, neither Greek nor barbarian, neither master nor slave, neither man nor woman." By addressing them rather than others, by calling them blessed and giving them signs of the new creation in the miracles, Jesus reveals himself as the Son of Man and his works as the preview of the human kingdom of man. It is not through the integration of the kingdoms of the world into one kingdom and of the various societies into one society that a mankind will be formed which deserves the name 'man.' It happens quite the other way, through the elevation of the lowly. This distinguishes Jesus, the Son of Man, from the pictures of man drawn by ancient and modern humanism.

As the history of Jesus shows, Christian faith did not simply adopt the apocalyptic expectation of the Son of Man in seeing its fulfillment in the history of Jesus. It also revised this expectation in the light of its experience of Jesus' history. This does not mean that the expected Son of Man is Jesus; rather Jesus is the Son of Man. It is not the predicate which molds the subject; the subject and his history shape the predicate.

What is new in Christian faith is that it no longer awaits the Son of Man and his kingdom at the end of humanity's history of suffering. Instead, in the suffering of the victorious Christ, it sees this distant future now present in the midst of this history of suffering. Thus the practical application of Christian faith in Jesus, the Son of Man, is no longer patient perseverance until the end. It is in following the self-giving Son of Man in his world-changing love of alienated men. The perspective of hope in faith has thereby shifted. Christian faith no longer looks longingly from the suffering of this time into a glorious future. Quite the contrary. With this future at his back, the Christian looks into the suffering of the present in order to incarnate himself and that future here. Christian humanism is no longer *eros* of a distant, beautiful vision of the true man, but creative love of the banished, ineffectual, worthless, and ugly un-men. Christian love makes their suffering unbearable; one cannot look at it. But neither can one look the other way. Through the power of Jesus' messianic possibilities it can be changed. For the sake of the hopeless, hope is given to the faithful.

Early Christianity was deeply concerned with the apocalyptic-political question: To whom does world authority belong? When will God establish his kingdom and carry out his justice and finally prove his divinity? Paradoxically, it found the answer in the suffering, dying Jesus and saw in him the God who is God and the man who becomes true man, that is, God's image. Therefore it did not set its hope in world empires, neither in the *Pax Romana* nor the re-establishment of Zion. It placed its hope only in the living fellowship with the crucified one. The faithful practiced their fellowship with the Son of Man through solidarity with the poor and the victims of world empires. "The Savior finds his disciples and first believers among the ostracized, not among the pillars of the old order. He untiringly offers his word to the wretched and the oppressed, to the blind and the lame, to the poor and the sick."[7]

VI. The New Humanity in Fellowship with Jesus the Son of Man

"There is no such thing as Jew and Greek, slave and freeman, male and female; for you are all one person in Christ Jesus" (Gal.

3:28). Thus proclaimed the Corinthian church in the exuberance of the Spirit, and Paul took up the message. In the fellowship with Jesus, the true man, those distinctions un-men create to set themselves off from others and to justify themselves lose their power. Abolished are the prerogatives from Israel's election over the Gentiles, the prerogatives of education and civilization of the Greeks over against the barbarians, the master's deed of ownership over the slave, and men's arrogance over women. When one identifies with Christ, the true man, in faith, all previous identifications with religion, race, property, and sex fall away. One who lives in Christ is called a new creation. "The old order has gone, and a new order has already begun" (II Cor. 5:17). Just as the law, sin, and death have lost their right to those who are reborn to a living hope in the fellowship of Jesus, so the old social expectations and obligations have lost their claim on the new man. In the fellowship with Christ, the new man is already living on the basis of the future of the human kingdom of the Son of Man.

In contrast to the enthusiasts in Corinth, Paul knew very well that earthly relationships and social distinctions are not so easily overcome and forgotten in a burst of enthusiasm. The Lord is not the Spirit, but he who was crucified by the powers and rulers of this world. Therefore Paul reminds this congregation that God does not make all men brothers through religious enthusiasm and ecstasy. Instead, he makes partisan, critical choices and rejections in the inhuman world of the cross. "Yet to shame the wise, God has chosen what the world counts folly and to shame what is strong, God has chosen what the world counts weakness. He has chosen things low and contemptible, mere nothings, to overthrow the existing order" (I Cor. 1:26-31). Here for once Paul agrees with James: "Has not God chosen those who are poor in the eyes of the world to be rich in faith and to inherit the kingdom he has promised to those who love him?" (James 2:5).

The idea of anticipation is much in the forefront today because of the new eschatological understanding of the Biblical message and the new historical understanding of the church as the 'pilgrim people of God.' This idea was taken up at Uppsala in 1968. *Christus Antici-pator* became the theme of a future-oriented Christology. This recognizes a main feature of the honorific titles in the New Testament: all of these titles state not only who Jesus was and is for believers, but primarily who he will be and what his vocation is. He is 'the one who comes,' and in his coming is announced the kingdom in which God is true God and man will be true man. Thus Jesus can be understood as the *anticipator* of the coming of God in a god-forsaken world, as the witness and beginning not only of faith, but of the new creation, the new humanity, new obedience, and the new time. Anticipation is thus the essence of the gospel as the incarnation of Christ's future epiphany in the word of promise. In the Gospel, the future is present in the Word because this Word liberates from the bonds of the present situation and allows men to live today on the basis of Christ's future. Anticipation also provides the way to a new understanding of the sacraments as road-signs of the Christian fellowship. As Thomas Aquinas said, they are *signa commemorativa* of Christ's suffering and also *signa prognostica* of the future glory, and in the coincidence of these two times, they are *signa demonstrativa* of God's grace today. In Word and Sacrament is concentrated the Christian consciousness of history; they are not a religious flight from the world into eternity. In addition, anticipation leads to an understanding of Christian fellowship in its significance for humanity. This fellowship arises not from separation from the evil world, but through anticipation of the new creation and through substitution for the unredeemed world. The message of the Fourth Assembly of the World Council of Churches in Uppsala drew the right consequences for Christian life and action in the world:

> We ask you, trusting in God's renewing power, to join in these anticipations of God's Kingdom, showing now something of the newness which Christ will complete.[8]

This idea of anticipation is left hanging in the air, as among the enthusiasts at Corinth, and leads to optimistic illusions and disappointments if equal emphasis is not given to the place where this anticipation of the future of the kingdom of God has occurred and should occur. That place is history in the crucified Christ. The liberating future of God has no other foothold on this earth of blood and tears than the cross of Golgotha. God's future does not appear in dreams of the future, but confronts us in the face of him who was crucified. The resurrected one 'who goes before us' is present as he who was crucified 'for us.' There are no good photos of the new humanity of the resurrected one and of the new mankind. The crucified Christ is the visible picture of the still invisible future of God and of man. Therefore "the power of the resurrection," as Paul

called faith, exists only in the "fellowship of the suffering of Christ,"
as he emphasized. As the reconciling, new future of man comes into
the world through Jesus' cross, so preaching and the service of reconciliation stand in the sign of the cross. Jesus preached the Gospel
of the kingdom of God to the poor. This message is joyous only for
the poor. For the rich it is painful. Paul proclaimed the Gospel of the
justification of sinners and godless people, and of them only. He
thus brings judgment on the self-righteous and religious of the world.
Thus the Gospel is the literal anticipation of Christ's future for those
whose brother the crucified one became. In the Christian fellowship, believers and the poor come together. Only then does this
fellowship stand as a sign of the crucified Son of Man. The idea of
anticipation can certainly arouse an avant-garde feeling; it becomes
Christian only when the glorification of Jesus and the justification
of the godless become social reality here and now.

Human communities naturally are always based on the homogeneity of their members. "Like attracts like," Aristotle said. And
therefore, "One crow will not pick out another crow's eyes." The
law of life in human societies is the homogeneity of their members.
The *phila politikē* which Aristotle saw as the bond of human community is rooted in shared participation in a being that transcends
society. Therefore the homogeneity and self-confirmation of such
societies usually lie in the civil religion; the integration of disparate
members occurs in common symbols, memories, and hopes. But it
is precisely not the similarity of its members and sympathy with
those of like mind which comprise the law of life of the Christian
community. It is the 'recognition of others' and creative love which
binds together those who are not alike—Jews and pagans, Greeks
and barbarians, masters and slaves. The ghetto walls and fences
which men erect against each other in order to stay with their own
kind, to justify themselves, and to degrade others are destroyed in
the Christian community. Churches which consist only of people
who are alike are heretical in their social structure. They are only
partially Christianized religious clubs. Only when the Christian
community is based on the recognition of others in their otherness
and on the social reality of justification by grace can it become a
sign of the human kingdom of the Son of Man. Practically this
means that the Christian community does not emulate the idealistic and humanistic dream so that it can become the world religion
of a unifying human society. Rather it practices the humanity of

the crucified Son of Man in its fellowship with the poor, the ostracized, and the supposed enemies of every human society, which the law of homogeneity demands must be exclusive. Only through concrete fellowship with 'the others' in a particular society does the church dissolve its alliance with the rulers and the dominant religious feelings. The messianic idea of anticipation is a good one, but we must know where and with whom God's future is to be anticipated. This social place was designated once and for all by the crucified Christ's fellowship with those brought under the shadow of the cross by the dominant society. The idea of a universal society says nothing about its humaneness. The prognosis of a necessarily totally administrated world is not optimistic. It is therefore even more important today for the Christian community to be working to build a new humanity of men. This humanity lies in the fellowship of believers with the poor and the recognition of others through creative love. From the perspective of Christian faith, the 'unity of the human race' does not come through sharing mastery of the world; it comes when man leaves behind his idols and his self-justification and, in free recognition of God, begins to live with other men through the power of this recognition. The Christian fellowship cannot be willing to provide a coming world society with the idols a certainly coming world religion will need. For the sake of the Son of Man, who was himself a victim of world history, it will ally itself with the victims of the history of the world empire. Only there is there any hope for liberation from the world's history of suffering at the hands of successive ruling systems. Christian faith in the crucified Son of Man is not optimistic. Historical success is not promised to it. Yet it is hopeful because it trusts in the coming God whose presence is in the history of the Crucified One.

NOTES

[1] *The Great March on Washington*, Phonograph Record (Gordy, Detroit, 1963).

[2] Herbert Marcuse, *One-Dimensional Man* (Boston, 1964), p. 98.

[3] M. Landmann, *Philosophische Anthropologie*, (Berlin 1964), p. 35.

[4] Werner J. Schmidt, *Die Schöpfungsgeschichte der Priesterschrift*, Wissenschaftliche Monographien zum Alten und Neuen Testament 17 (Neukirchen 1967), p. 135.

[5] A. Alt, "Die Deutung der Weltgeschichte im Alten Testament" in *Zeitschrift für Theologie und Kirche*, LVI (1959) p. 129.

⁶ Klaus Koch, "Spätisraelitisches Geschichtsdenken am Beispiel des Buches Daniel," *Historische Zeitschrift* (1961) p. 23.

⁷ Edgar Salin, *Civitas Dei* (Tübingen 1926) p. 25.

⁸ *Uppsala Speaks* (Geneva, 1968) p. 5.

CHAPTER TWELVE

THE POTENTIALITY OF CONCILIARITY:
COMMUNION, CONSCIENCE, COUNCIL

WM. BARNETT BLAKEMORE

I. *From World Council to Universal Council?*

At New Delhi in 1961, the Assembly of the World Council of Churches affirmed that Christian unity means the unity of "all Christians in *each* place," and then described how that unity is made visible. At Uppsala in 1968, the Assembly affirmed that Christian unity means equally the unity of "all Christians in *all* places," and further declared that "In a time when human interdependence is so evident, it is the more imperative to make visible the bonds which unite Christians in universal fellowship." There is, however, a real contrast between the two statements. With great confidence the New Delhi statement gives a detailed affirmation that the unity in each place is made visible by one fully committed fellowship, holding one apostolic faith, preaching one gospel, breaking one bread, joining in common prayer, and reaching out in corporate witness and service.[1] The Uppsala statement hesitates. After declaring that it is imperative to make visible the bond of universal fellowship, it says, "But there are hindrances," and identifies as "the clearest obstacle to manifestation of the churches' universality...their inability to understand the measure in which they already belong together in one body." Then, in what is a most remarkable leap forward in time, the Uppsala document speaks of a possible future event whose occurrence would be a visible expression of the unity of all Christians in all places—a genuinely universal council. "The members of the World Council of Churches, committed to each other, should work for the time when a genuinely universal council may once more speak for all Christians and lead the way into the future." With such an end in view, the World Council of Churches and regional councils are "a transitory opportunity for eventually actualizing a truly universal, ecumenical, conciliar form of common life and witness.[2]

No man is alien

15

The identification in 1968 of such a 'council' as the goal toward which the ecumenical movement should work is dramatic. Is such an objective to be understood eschatologically, as an ideal or norm to which the dialogue and assemblies of the Church may approximate, or is it to be understood as a proximate goal, achievable at some future point in history, following which there will be more future? It is the latter understanding which informs the Uppsala statement. The declaration is the more dramatic when it is realized that as recently as 1959, the 'ecumenical councils' belonged to past history. The first four councils, or the first seven, acknowledged as authoritative by some Protestants and by the Orthodox, were all held more than a thousand years ago. Rome, since the Reformation, had held only two general councils: Trent in the sixteenth century and a Vatican Council in the nineteenth century. In 1870, by promulgating a decree popularly known as 'the infallibility of the Pope,' frequently interpreted even by Roman Catholics to mean that no council need ever be called again, the Vatican Council had seemingly confirmed the 'historic' nature of such councils, in the sense that they were archaic and obsolete. 'The Conciliar Controversy' was a chapter in late medieval church history.

The announcement by John XXIII on January 25, 1959 that a general council of the Church was to be called suddenly made the question of a 'true ecumenical council' central to ecumenical discussion. At the same time "it became apparent that in ecumenical discussion the question of an ecumenical council had hardly been touched upon."[3] Immediately, the question of the meaning of the word "ecumenical" as it was employed both by the World Council of Churches and by the Roman Catholic Church became important. Inevitably there were questions regarding the 'ecumenical' character of both the forthcoming New Delhi Assembly of the World Council of Churches and the forthcoming Roman Catholic assembly which came to be named Vatican Council II.

The idea of a 'genuinely universal council' moved from virtual neglect in 1959 to become by 1968 the practical objective of the ecumenical movement. While many factors were involved in this resurgence of hope for a truly ecumenical council, studies carried on by the Commission on Faith and Order have been the most important. Decisive in those studies has been the identification of the process of 'conciliarity.'

II. *Varieties of Conciliarity*

At New Delhi in 1961 the World Council of Churches recommended a study of the significance of the historic ecumenical councils. The study became the responsibility of the Commission on Faith and Order which organized its work at its Aarhus meeting in 1964. The study group appointed to the project made a report to the Commission at its meeting in Bristol in 1967. Its report was published in 1968 as *Councils and the Ecumenical Movement* (World Council Studies, No. 5.)

The Report begins with a definition of the general notion of 'conciliarity.' By means of this concept, the attention of the study group was released from preoccupation with the 'councils' as events to a consideration of a process which was eventually to be identified as belonging to 'the nature of the church.' "By conciliarity we mean the fact that the Church in all times needs assemblies to represent it and has in fact felt this need. These assemblies may differ greatly from one another; however, conciliarity, the necessity *that* they take place, is a constant structure of the church, a dimension which belongs to its nature."[4]

Once the general notion of conciliarity has been clarified, it becomes obvious that conciliarity occurs at many different levels of church life. It is not only that churches must be able to come together to deliberate upon and make decisions concerning important questions; they do come together, and with amazing frequency. Furthermore, conciliarity takes place at every level of church life. In most Protestant communions the local congregation meets in ordinary session annually for the finalization of program and business for the year ahead. Local congregations may meet in extraordinary sessions as needed for the selection of a new pastor, or to decide with regard to some other matter which concerns the congregation as a whole. These are instances of conciliarity, as are synods, assemblies, associations, boards, conventions and a great variety of convocations which have responsibilities for deliberation and decision. So frequent and so wide-spread through all the denominations of Christianity is the process of conciliarity that Lukas Vischer states that "it can be counted among the marks of the Church."[5]

If there can come about among the churches a wide-spread recognition that they are already involved at many levels in conciliar procedures, there can come about a readiness for further involvement. The recognition of a common process at the heart of very

diverse bodies suddenly overcomes the sense of strangeness caused
by the diversity. What seem like extreme differences can be understood as expressions of the same process. A session of Vatican Council II in the Petrine basilica and the annual meeting of a Congregational church in a country town in Australia may seem to have
little enough in common, at first glance. Yet both are instances of
representative bodies moving toward authoritative decisions. Once
their common character as instances of conciliarity is recognized,
certain questions can be put—and are being put. The Roman Catholic can be asked, "You acknowledge authority in the general council
of the church; what authority do you grant to a parish council?"
The congregationalist, particularly if he is strictly congregationalist,
must be asked, "Why do you accord authority to a congregational
meeting, but grant no authority to any more widely-representative
body?" Indeed, the situation in the post-Vatican II, post-Uppsala
era is that more and more of the churches are seeking to determine
the authority to be granted to various levels of association, not only
within the communions, but between them. More and more this
inquiry takes place, not by the method of comparative ecclesiologies, but by seeking to understand what it means to "submit ourselves together with other churches to the judgment of Christ. This
change of outlook was achieved at the Lund Conference (1952), and
has since marked the work of Faith and Order."[6]

The change from dependence upon comparative ecclesiologies to
seeking to design structures adequate to fulfill Christ's mission and
ministry to the world can be seen in the progress made in the United
States of America between the 1953 *Plan for a United Church in the
United States* proposed by the Greenwich Conference on Church
Union, and the 1970 *Plan of Union for the Church of Christ Uniting*,
proposed by the Consultation on Church Union (COCU). The change
of outlook which has characterized Faith and Order since 1952, and
which characterizes the Consultation on Church Union in contrast
to the earlier Greenwich Conference, involves the recognition that
the churches are already one in Christ who judges them and whose
ministry they must carry out. If this unity, this belonging together
already, can increasingly characterize the people of God, there is
ground for hope in a rapid release of the potential that lies in conciliarity. But the full power of conciliarity, no matter at which level
of church life it takes place, is the binding, the authority, that is
implicit in it. In order to understand that potential it is necessary

to identify more precisely the meanings which attach to 'council' and 'conciliarity.'

In Latin there are two similar words which nonetheless have a clear difference in meaning: *concilium* and *consilium*. From *concilium* derive such English words as 'council' and 'conciliarity,' the French word *concile* and the somewhat archaic German word *Konzil*. From *consilium* derive the English word 'counsel' and the French word *conseil*. While either *concilium* or *consilium* can refer to a body of men in deliberation, the special force of *concilium* is that it implies actual union, expressive of the fundamental condition of the body deliberating, whereas *consilium* shades off rather in the direction of 'advice,' or 'suggestion,' or 'plan.' *Concilium* therefore carries a connotation of 'binding,' whereas *consilium* carries rather a connotation of 'advisory.' Furthermore, the binding power of *concilium* is there because of an original or fundamental unity which has simply come to expression in what has been declared by the *concilium*. The original unity is not unlike the primordial unity of an entity not made up of separate parts which could be denoted by the word *concilio*. It is significant that it is the word *concilium* by which the church through the centuries has identified its ecumenical councils. In the Roman Catholic doctrine of an ecumenical council it is obvious that it is the calling together of what already belongs together, and the purpose of the council is to give expression to that unity. Therefore the council deliberates upon any issue until that unity can be expressed in virtual unanimity. If unanimity upon some issue is not possible, there is no resort to a majority opinion and a minority opinion. The council declares that discussion on the issue is "immature," removes it from the council agenda, and suggests that theologians and *periti* continue study and discussion in the expectation that someday there will be found a way of stating the case adequate to express the unity of the Church on the matter. The Pope in council promulgates only such decrees as manifest unity. Such promulgations protect and enhance the unity of the church which existed prior to the meeting of the council, though the unity may have become obscured by some crisis in the life of the church. The council was called to rid the church of that obscurity by deliberating together until there could be a statement acceptable to all. Such unanimity is binding in the sense that it is expressive of a bond already existing.

It is interesting to notice in this regard that the German *Konzil* and the French *concile* have, until recent times, referred only to the ecclesiastical councils of the Roman Catholic Church. In the last century the German *Konzil* was occasionally used to denote certain other churchly associations, but such usage seems now to be archaic. In French, the usage of *concile* for various deliberative bodies has developed in this century. When, what is known in English as the 'World Council of Churches' was formed, the name chosen in French was *Conseil Oecuménique des Églises*; the name in German is *Ökumenischer Rat der Kirchen*. These two latter names may have tended to sharpen the distinction between the *Conseil* and *Rat* on the one hand and, on the other hand, *les conciles* and *die Konzile* by which would be meant only the historic 'ecumenical councils.' On the other hand, the French *Oecuménique* and the German *Ökumenischer* carry overtones which tend to associate with the historic 'ecumenical councils' more than does the English 'World' in the name of the World Council of Churches. What is not clear is the extent to which the binding character that is connotable by the term 'council' is weakened by the terms *conseil* and *Rat*.

In view of the meaning of *concilium* as an actual binding, it can be asked whether the concept of 'conciliarity' should be used only with reference to meetings in which the bond of unity is already experienced, or whether it may also indicate a process of growth toward unity. Certainly, when Uppsala spoke of a 'genuinely universal council' it was speaking of *concilium, concile, Konzil*.[7] What is clear is that in identifying conciliarity as a widespread process in the churches, the Faith and Order study group was indicating a process in which there is present a factor of union—either an existing union, or a union that is to come about. What should not happen is that 'council' and 'conciliarity' be allowed to slip off in the direction of meaning only consultation, mutual advice, prudence or prudential planning between units which, in a spirit of pluralism, intend only to work out procedures of co-existence which will allow the maintenance of their several autonomies. Such meaning can apply to *consilium* but not to *concilium*. Conciliarity should at the very least imply an intention to get unification under way.

It may therefore be questioned whether the term 'conciliar' ought to be generally applied, as is now the case, to the hundreds of local, regional and national federations or 'councils' of churches which have appeared in this century. In those instances where such associations are recognized as stages on the road to the unity of the church, or where they are recognized as "transitional opportunities" toward church unifications, they are part of a 'conciliar' movement in the original sense of *concilium*. But wherever these federations are put forward as being enough, where they do not challenge the divisions of the churches, particularly their divisiveness demonstrated at the Lord's Table, such federations are at best forums for mutual counsel, inheriting rather only the advisory role implied for the *consilium*. The World Council of Churches itself was pushed dangerously close to this latter definition of itself when it adopted the Toronto 1950 statement regarding its own ecclesiological significance. Fortunately, while denying as its purpose the negotiation of unions between the churches, the Council did affirm for itself the role of bringing the churches into living contact with each other, and of promoting the study and discussion of the issues of Christian unity. The Toronto statement clearly says, "The Council stands for Church Unity," and by that assertion remained in the 'conciliar' movement, when 'conciliar' is understood to mean both expressing unity and being committed to working toward unity. At Uppsala, by recognizing itself as a "transitional opportunity for eventually actualizing a truly universal, ecumenical, conciliar form of common life and witness," the World Council further underlined its right to share in the kind of authority implicit in *concilium*.

III. *Unity in Council*

Concilium, and therefore 'council' owe something to the Latin verb *conciliare*, meaning 'to unite,' and from which derives the English word 'reconcile,' and the French *réconcilier*. It is not strange that the Uppsala Report which sets as the ecumenical objective a genuinely universal council should have opened with a paragraph which speaks of the work of the Holy Spirit in transforming the relationships between separated Christian communities "so that we now speak to each other with greater mutual trust and with more hope of reconciliation than ever before."[8] The achievement of full reconciliation will be accompanied by the emergence of a truly universal council. A major criterion for the judgment of all present-day 'conciliar' involvement is whether it enhances the reconciliation of those who are involved. But what can 'reconciliation' here mean? The reconciliation which culminates in council means more than the abandonment of hostile attitudes, more than the closing of a chasm of separation by the emergence of mutual good-will. It means the acceptance of each other as sharing in the authority to which we submit. It means that my fellow Christian is someone with whom there is something more than cooperation on mutually planned projects. My fellow Christian is a brother to whom I must accord a place in an authority which I must obey.

In this ecumenical twentieth century, Protestantism is gradually becoming aware that the authority which should govern and guide the whole people of God is a very live authority to be embodied and given its voice now, in a now that moves forward as fast as time, and faster in so far as it looks eschatalogically forward to the achievement of the Kingdom of God. Protestantism certainly still accords to the Scriptures a place in relation to this living authority, but the Scriptures can no longer be understood as a sufficient rule and guide for Christian faith and conduct. The only sufficient guide for Christian faith and conduct today is the voice of the whole people of God, the Body of Christ speaking now. Certainly the people of God are not the Body of Christ unless their minds and spirits are constantly nurtured by the Holy Scriptures, and unless they are guided by the Holy Spirit. It is as biblically nurtured, representative bodies under the guidance of the Holy Spirit that the historic ecumenical councils have commended themselves to the churches. Is it not in 'council' that the Body of Christ finds voice? The rediscovery of the authoritative role of council and conciliarity releases Protestant and Catholic alike. It releases the Protestant from the dead hand of that fundamentalist biblicism which has been the perverse sequel of the Reformation cry of *Scriptura sola*. It releases the Roman Catholic from the oracularism which was the perverse sequel of the misinterpretation of Vatican I as promulgating a doctrine of infallibility in the Pope alone. In both instances the release is into the freedom of an authority, rooted in the apostolic experiences and faith, which nonetheless moves with the times, responsive to contemporary conditions, seeking to design an authentic ministry to the world today, calling all Christians to ceaseless effort to redeem society from its contemporary ills of racism, economic inequalities, international injustices and conflicts, and polluting exploitations of nature. At the same time, this living voice of the church, in communion with saints - past, present and future —will persist in its timeless mission of transmitting and enhancing the Christian tradition, of bringing individuals to a consciousness that they belong not only to local causes but to a universal people of God, nurturing them increasingly in biblical understandings, awakening them to faith and hope and upholding them throughout the course of personal existence, and providing for them participation in sacramental worship. To shape the words and devise the programs which now, this day and decade, carry out these ministries and missions, the churches must come together through representatives who can come to decision on behalf of the whole people of God. Since such 'council' does not yet take place, none of the existing churches, nor any other extant organization can claim to be *the* Church. This does not mean that a genuinely universal council can never take place. There have now been four general assemblies of the World Council of Churches, and Vatican II has been held. These are events of recent history which by their approximation to true ecumenical councils create a lively hope that a genuinely universal council can become a historic reality. As is true in many other realms, the contemporary world has achieved the solution to the technical problems involved. The speed of communication and travel make ecumenical council possible.

The achievement of the technical possibility of a genuinely universal council heightens the issue of unity at the Lord's Table.

The ecumenical councils of the past have all been councils around the table of the Lord. They have been the deliberations of a eucharistic fellowship. These historic councils have been meetings in which those with whom communion was shared in the opening hours of the sessions are those who are granted a place in the authoritative body. The Mass celebrated each morning of Vatican Council II was necessary to the council, to affirm at the outset of each session the already existent bond. The reality of that bond became especially clear during concelebrated masses. Then the kiss of peace was exchanged by the concelebrants, expressive of the fact that all division was fundamentally overcome, demonstrating an already existent unity prior to the 'debate' of the morning. That debate might reveal differences. While there could be disagreement, there would be no dissension as between those who do not sense themselves to belong together.

In other words, from the conciliar point of view, to share the Eucharist with another man is to acknowledge him as sharing in authority over one's self. To share in communion is therefore to accept bondage to those with whom one communes. It should mean being fully responsive and responsible to all those who are at the Table. Can any ceremony that involves anything less than such full responsiveness be a true Eucharist? Such full responsiveness acknowledges the Eucharistic *koinonia* as being not only a *koinonia* of redemption, but also a *koinonia* of authority, to use terms employed by Professor A. C. Outler.

> ... as never before and in ways still unfamiliar to most of us, Protestantism is being reoriented (by Vatican II and other ecumenical stimuli) toward *ecclesiology*. The twin problem of ecclesiology looks, on the one hand, toward a *koinonia* of *redemption* and, on the other, to a *koinonia* of *authority*. Protestantism, since the stabilization of fragmentation in the seventeenth century, has been loathe to join the two communities, preferring to locate *authority* in Scripture alone, and then to relate *redemption* to the Church conceived chiefly in metahistorical terms (*ecclesia invisibilis*). But where *is* the authority of Scripture ...
> ... hermeneutics has long since passed from its locus in Scripture alone and has become ecclesiological in the strict sense.[9]

When it is recognized that table fellowship is also a fellowship of authority, questions arise regarding the appropriateness of speaking of the Eucharist in terms of 'invitation.' Even the idea that the Table is the Lord's, and that communicants are present at his 'invitation' must be questioned. Christian communion is not properly understood when it is thought of as an instance of 'table hospitality,' as to one outside the family circle. The Eucharist is rather to be thought of as the sitting down together at table of a family— with every member present not by invitation but by virtue of membership in the family. The children in one's home are not 'invited' for breakfast tomorrow morning, or for dinner tonight. They belong there. The fellowship of the Table is redemptive fellowship as is the fellowship of family, and its redemptive power is not apart from the fact that in this fellowship each one exercises authority over each of the others. When one rejoices, all rejoice; when one suffers, all suffer. This is not to sit down as a guest at a special meal when the closet doors are shut and family skeletons are out of sight. To share Eucharist is to share the scandal of the Cross and the joy of Resurrection; it is to hear the plaint and plea of the least member of the company of God's children with whom one shares as at the Father's table—and to know that the sorrows and dismays and disasters suffered by any one of the family will be authoritative in the sense that they will determine the style of life of all those who share the meal. Therefore, there can be no 'inter-communion,' but true communion only among those who have acknowledged the fellowship of authority and who have created those structures through which they can be responsible to each other. Perhaps there can be communion as a sign of intention to persevere in the discovery of such structural unities as will provide for the functioning of a fellowship of authority. A ceremony which only celebrates some of the common elements of our humanity, or one which makes no demand that we be truly responsible to each other after we leave the Table, is not a Eucharist in which we recall again the full sacrifice of His life which Christ made in response to our need.

The achievement of the technical possibility of a genuinely universal council, in heightening the issue of unity at the Lord's Table, deepens the poignancy felt by sensitive souls everywhere as they seek to give expression, not only to the solidarity of the Church with human need, but also to the fundamental unity of mankind. In the decade of the sixties, technology advanced to the point of landing men on the moon. There now exist photographs of the earth from space, earth-rise seen from the moon. At a time when the population is exploding, mankind is confronted with psychologically compelling evidence of the limited size of earth. He has looked at photographs of space-ship Earth, with blue oceans and brown continents lightly veiled in clouds of white mist. Suddenly there is wide-spread a vivid consciousness that the whole planet could quickly be polluted, that war could lead to the destruction of the human race, that mankind must find the way to a unitary view of the inhabitable earth. In other words, there is a new consciousness of the *ecumene*, and in that growing consciousness there is a new level of potentiality for the achievement of 'ecumenical' council.

Christian faith carries not only the ideal of universality, but the confidence that mankind can be blessed by political unity and economic equality. This confident hope has some of its basis in history. Christianity was born, and had its earliest growth at a time when the ancient world came nearest to the achievement of political and cultural unity. Furthermore, Christianity did not have its greatest growth among those Jews who were strongly particularistic and felt Roman rule as a tyrannous burden. Christianity received its greatest impetus from a Jew like Paul who prized his Roman citizenship. It grew rapidly among the Gentiles. While Christianity may have made an especial appeal to the depressed classes, by the third century it was winning converts from every level of society and throughout the Empire. In times of persecution, Christians may have identified Rome by symbols of bestiality and corruption, but the periods of persecution while intense were relatively short. Throughout the Empire the *Pax Romana* had allowed for the development of a very comfortable standard of living. Sir Winston Churchill in his *History of the English Speaking Peoples* writes that Britons in Roman times lived more comfortably than any of their successors until late Victorian times, and "a poll in the fourth century would have declared for an indefinite continuance of the Roman regime."[10] It was in such a world that Christianity prospered. From it, the Christian community borrowed many a form, not the least significant of which was 'council.'[11] Representative assemblies were widely used throughout the Empire, at municipal and provincial levels, to exercise conciliar decision. The churches adopted councils as the method by which they could gather to deliberate on and make decisions together concerning important questions. This is not to say that Christianity was nurtured on a dream of empire; it is to say that Christianity was nourished by the experience of unity in the *ecumene,* and when that unity was lost Christianity continued to feed upon the memory of what had been achieved. Even the New Testament reflects a consciousness of the classical *ecumene*. The account of Pentecost is 'ecumenical' in this realistic sense. The listing of those present is not haphazard. The mind's eye of the author of The Acts of the Apostles sweeps in orderly fashion east to west across the *ecumene*. He depicts the world as seen from Jerusalem in apostolic times. First mentioned are those people who lived farthest east, the Parthians and the Medes; next named are those nations closer to Jerusalem and immediately to its east, the Elamites and Mesopotamians. Next are listed areas contiguous to Jerusalem: Judaea and Cappadocia, Pontus and Asia, Phrygia and Pamphilia. The eye of the writer continues its westward bent, southwest first as he mentions Egypt and the parts of Libya belonging to Cyrene; then northwest to mention visitors from Rome and Crete. Finally his eye drops south and mentions the Arabians. It was this vision of a united *ecumene* that Christianity embraced. It was a unity constantly threatened by divisions between nations and cultures. Christianity was proposing in Christ a more sure ground of unity than could be found in

Ceasar or in military might. When Paul wrote, "here there cannot be Greek and Jew, circumcised and uncircumcised, barbarian, Scythian, slave, freeman, but Christ is all and in all," he was pointing to the sure ground of unity in the *ecumene*. The early Christians, it is said, boasted that they held the world together.

As Rome decayed, the Christian community sensed the tragedy of the loss of unity. It could be critical of many elements in the fading empire, but it never turned its back on the vision of universality to embrace parochialism. It clung to the vision of a united humanity because there had been the experience of approximation to it. Without that approximation the universalism of Christianity might never have taken hold of the minds and hearts of men as it did. It may very well be said that one element of the 'fulness of time' into which Christ was born was the achievement two thousand years ago of a remarkable degree of human unity and accord. It was an experience of the "goodness of the Lord in the land of the living" which since that time has lured men by its promise that an even better unity of the *ecumene* may be achieved.

In this generation, the need for such unity is increasingly recognized, and the idea of 'council' again moves to the fore. If the first three centuries may be looked upon as a time when the church sought those structures essential to the maintenance of unity, it must be acknowleged that 'council' and 'conciliarity' are among those structures. It is remarkable that to the quadrilateral of creed, canon, sacrament, and historic episcopate, 'council' was not added by Lambeth in 1896, nor to any other listing of essential and authoritative structures of the church. The omission underlines the degree to which, until the decade of the sixties, the councils were looked on as belonging only to past history. What is needed now is a widespread recognition of the full force of the declaration of the study group which reported to the 1967 Bristol meeting of the Commission on Faith and Order that "conciliarity is a constant structure of the Church, a dimension which belongs to its nature."

IV. *The Holy Spirit Makes Community*

Whatever technological advancements have been accomplished, the achievement of a genuinely universal council will depend ultimately upon the Holy Spirit, particularly as the Holy Spirit is recognized as that spirit which brings men within an understanding distance of each other. Here again the instinct of the ecumenical movement has been right in emphasizing Pentecost as the origin of the unity of the Church rather than the Jerusalem Conference. The latter brought about only the renewal of manifest unity which had originally become visible at Pentecost. Involvement in this century in ecumenical conference or dialogue repeats the essential experience of the Day of Pentecost. Now, as then, men who speak a variety of languages come together. Now, as then, there is the experience of psychic pain as men strive to cross the barrier of different languages in order to understand each other and to come to a common understanding. Under the stress of striving to understand others, especially when languages differ, there is inevitably fatigue and the constant temptation to relinquish the effort to understand. There is always the possibility of misunderstanding, of failing to communicate one's own position clearly, of taking umbrage or giving offense. When, despite these difficulties, men are possessed by a spirit which constrains them to persevere in the effort to understand each other, and which sustains their energies for such dialogue and encounter, it must be recognized that the spirit which possesses them is Holy Spirit. Thus, it is Holy Spirit which created the church originally, and continuously sustains it. It is within the congregation that the spirit of God is templed, as Paul indicated to the Corinthians in the third chapter of his first letter to them. It is Holy Spirit which makes community.

The community making character of the work of the Holy Spirit brings into question all doctrines of the Holy Spirit which seek to make Him the source of private knowledge given to individual persons. The community making character of the Holy Spirit brings to view the place of community in the achievement of understanding, and the role of holiness of spirit as, in discussion and dialogue, men are led forward from more restricted apprehensions of truth to ever more comprehensive apprehensions of truth. As a holiness of spirit holds men together in a community of discourse until new levels of understanding are achieved, the Holy Spirit certainly leads them into larger and larger truth. Holy Spirit is never private, but is the constitutive element of publics. The Holy Spirit 'descending into the midst of a group of men converts them from a conglomerate into a community—from a clump of individuals into 'a people.' The Holy Spirit converts men from the state in which they are set against each other to the state in which they are for one another.

When the Holy Spirit is recognized as the principle of community, there is no longer a tendency to think of Holy Spirit as a particular kind of emotion or as the provocation to enthusiasm. 'Spiritual feelings' may not accompany possession by the Holy Spirit at all. What possession by the Holy Spirit means is that one stays in creative inter-action with other men until an understanding distance is achieved. This may be a painful experience, but the fruit of such spiritual possession, the result of the attainment of understanding, is indeed "love, joy, peace, patience, kindness, goodness, faithfulness, gentleness and self-control." "If we live by the Spirit, let us also walk by the Spirit. Let us have no self-conceit, no provoking of one another, no envy of one another." (Gal. 5:25, 26)

When the Holy Spirit is understood as the principle of community it is evident that both the Assemblies of the World Council of Churches and Vatican Council II were indeed under the guidance of the Holy Spirit. To make such a claim does not mean that the promulgations of either the Assemblies or the Councils are without error. It does mean that the decrees published represent understandings which can properly be said to belong to the common mind of the respective assemblies. It is a mark of the power of the Holy Spirit that there could be agreement over such vast areas as are presented in the sixteen documents of Vatican Council II. Such a large amount of work could be done because of the length of time the Council Fathers were able to devote to their labors. The World Council has, as yet, no such single body of material. On the other hand, the World Council does have a wide-flung schedule of studies by groups of representative scholars. The totality of these studies provides an ever-growing body of materials to which the churches can respond. Through their responses the consensus of the people of God can gradually become clear. Study groups made up of representatives from the churches are a substantial element of contemporary conciliarity. It may be that structures which provide for a continuous process of study will be an important element of the future shape of a 'genuinely ecumenical council.' The older structures through which conciliarity was expressed had the great disadvantage of inevitably long delay in discovering what 'reception' the people of God gave the teachings of the councils. In two ways the modern world may provide for more speedy discovery: by the truly 'representative' character of those who deliberate within whatever new forms of conciliar structure are developed, and the rapidity with which teaching can be printed and disseminated. It could be known almost at once whether a council had truly identified the common mind of the whole people of God. The speed with which conciliar teachings can be made available in the contemporary world means that Christian conscience can be created with a rapidity which matches the dynamic of contemporary society.

The ultimate authority for the Christian is his own individual Christian conscience. To make this assertion is not to endorse individual*ism*, for it is not just conscience, but Christian conscience to which the Christian must harken. The problem for every Christian is the attainment of Christian conscience.

A conscience cannot be Christian apart from knowledge and understandings drawn from the Christian community. But where, today, can a man discover how issues are understood by the whole people of God? He can know the mind of part of the church, but he cannot know the mind of the whole church. It is possible to have a denominational conscience, but not yet possible to have a truly ecumenical conscience. How can a man have Christian conscience until he has listened very seriously to every claim that the whole Church makes upon his belief and conduct? Every Christian's conscience is today defective because there is yet no fully universal council which can promulgate teachings upon which the whole church is agreed. Until such a genuinely universal council comes, the consciences of individual Christians everywhere will fail to be informed by the fulness of knowledge, the catholicity of understanding, that only universal council can supply.

The indispensable function of Christian knowledge in the formation of Christian conscience is the final argument respecting the necessity of giving structurally visible expression to the universality of the Church. Lukas Vischer has pointed out that

> ... fellowship cannot be merely an idea. If it is to become effective it must assume form and structure. Hardly anyone will disagree with this, unless he happens to limit the reality of faith to the inner or even private sphere.[12]

But for even his most private actions the individual needs knowledge and understanding—and that he cannot have apart from a community, apart from a fellowship of authority which has devised the structures through which to give voice to the mind of the Christian community regarding the content of faith and the conduct of the individual and society.

It must be pointed out that even when a genuinely universal council has been achieved, even when there is a body of teaching which the whole people of God approves, the ultimate authority for the individual remains his own conscience. Having paid strict attention to the voice of the whole church, and given it prayerful consideration, an individual may still in conscience have to say, "I cannot agree. Here I stand. I can do no other." But such an action will be action in Christian conscience. It must be acknowledged that a council can err, and that some one individual may discern the error. Nonetheless, Protestantism still stands in great need of correction of the over-emphasis it has placed on the individual conscience whenever it has spoken as if the individual could be truly conscientious apart from taking into account what his fellow Christians believe. Much of Protestant thinking about individual conscience as the ultimate authority needs correction by the typical Roman Catholic attitude that the light of revelation belongs to the community as a whole. Gregory Baum expresses this attitude thus:

> It seems to me that it is a basic conviction of Roman Catholics that wisdom is given by God to a community. As the Christian depends upon his brothers for love, so he depends on his brothers for insight. A Roman Catholic never totally commits himself to his personal theological conclusions unless he has tested them with the brethren and finds confirmation among them.[13]

What Baum does not tell us is what the Roman Catholic does when, after the most serious searching of the mind of his brethren (and of the whole church so far as he can discover it) he finds himself still convinced of truth or rightfulness which they do not confirm. Nonetheless Protestant thinking about the authority of the Bible can profit from Baum's next sentence, which reads:

> In our traditional way we would say that we always read the Scriptures in the Church. The Spirit confirms the understanding of the Gospels through his witness in the Church.

Bible and Church do belong together. It is within the universal Church that we receive the light of Scripture. Whatever the future shape of a genuinely universal council may prove to be, it will be a council with the Bible in its midst. The 'fathers' of such a council will be able to discern the issues of their day in the light of Scripture only if they are themselves richly cultivated in biblical imagery and thought. Conciliarity necessarily implies reflection and decision regarding present issues in the light of the faith to which the apostolic

No man is alien

sources give witness. This was understood in the early ecumenical councils which followed the custom of enthroning the Scriptures in the center of the council. The custom may have been lost for a time in the Middle Ages, but at both Vatican I and Vatican II the Gospels were once again enthroned at the outset of every morning's meeting of the Council.[14] Perhaps World Council Assemblies have done better by making Bible study a normal part of each morning's schedule, but some ceremony of placing the Bible in the midst of the Assembly would be a helpful, additional reminder that the Bible and the Church belong together, that there is no Christian knowledge apart from Christian community, and therefore no Christian conscience apart from listening to the voice of the whole church with the Bible in its midst.

It is when we consider the nature of Christian conscience that both the necessity and the limits of even a genuinely universal council appear. The limit of conciliarity is found in that area of life which is personal, in the sense that each individual stands in a unique situation in relation to his fellowmen. His fellowmen include not only his peers, but his elders and his children. His neighbor's children, and those whom Paul, in I Corinthians 8, indicates by reference to the *weak* "brother for whom Christ died" are also among his fellowmen. Conscience is knowledge in the light of which we must act. Part of that knowledge is in the public domain, but part of it is personal. That personal part of conscience is the knowledge of what one's actions mean to his fellowmen. In writing to the Corinthians about the issue of eating meat that had been offered to idols, Paul pointed to the truth known to the Christian community —namely, that "an idol has no real existence, and there is no God but One. For though there may be so-called gods in heaven and on earth...yet for us there is one God, the Father, from whom are all things and for whom we exist." This theological truth is clearly and strongly known by many in the Corinthian Christian community. But what about those who do not possess this knowledge clearly? Their understanding is clouded; their consciences are weak. They may misunderstand the conduct and the faith of the man of strong conscience if they see him eating meat in an idol's temple. And they may be led astray.

The question that every Christian must constantly be asking is, "What does my conduct mean to those who witness it?" And this constitutes knowledge that can be gained only by each man personally in terms of his immediate relationships, knowledge in terms of which conduct must be guided. Therefore such personal knowledge is part of the knowledge that constitutes the Christian's conscience. Though it is intensely personal knowledge, it serves the unity of the church. The unconsidered behavior of the strongly Christian Corinthian might have led his weaker brethren into idolatry. The unconsidered behavior of the man of clear vision and knowledge in any age may lead his fellowmen into idolatries, splintering the Church. The unity of the Church is served not only by what all Christians together can discover in council. It is served by what each Christian in each place in conscience knows that he must do. At New Delhi it was declared that the unity God intends is made visible by the faith and action of "all in each place." At Uppsala it was declared that unity must be visible also among "all in all places." The unity of the people of God will be visible also in the faith and conduct of "each in each place," in the personal lives of saintly and sensitive folk who seek always to behave in ways that strengthen Christian understanding in their fellowmen, creating in them strong conscience.

The Christian community is still sadly divided in many ways. But the twentieth century is an "ecumenical" century in which many kinds of divisions between Christians have been overcome. Christians of many different names and signs have, in this century, been possessed by a spirit which has brought them into deliberation with each other. This spirit has held them together until they have begun to understand each other. This understanding has been increasingly expressed in words and pronouncements regarding an ever wider range of topics. As the common mind of Christians becomes manifest, they recognize more and more that they belong together—not because they bind each other's minds and consciences, but because their minds and hearts are already bound to the same truth about Christ. This process initiated by the Holy Spirit is conciliarity, more and more wide-spread, and more and more understood and appreciated among the churches. The potential in conciliarity is that it can lead us to that genuinely universal council "for which all Christendom yearns when it prays for the unity of the church."

NOTES

[1] *The New Delhi Report* (New York, 1962), p. 116.

[2] *The Uppsala Report 1968* (Geneva, 1968), p. 17.

[3] Hans J. Margull (ed.), *The Councils of the Church* (Philadelphia, 1966), p.v.

[4] "The Report of the Study Group," *Councils and the Ecumenical Movement* (World Council of Churches Study, No. 5) (Geneva, 1968), p. 10.

[5] Lukas Vischer "The Church—One People in Many Places," *What Unity Implies* (World Council of Churches Study, No. 7) (Geneva, 1969), p. 93.

[6] Edmund Schlink, "The Unity and Diversity of the Church," *What Unity Implies*, p. 36.

[7] Lukas Vischer, "A Genuinely Universal Council...?," *Minutes and Reports of the Twenty-third Meeting, Central Committee* (Geneva, 1969), Appendix VII, p. 183. We do not agree with Vischer's footnote statement that "the English language has no possibility of distinguishing between council in the sense of *concilium* and council in the sense of *consilium*." The distinction is present in the difference between 'council' as a deliberative body with powers of decision, and 'counsel' as advice or suggestion received in counselling.

[8] *The Uppsala Report*, p. 11.

[9] A. C. Outler, "Vatican II and Protestant Theology in America" in J. H. Miller (ed.), *Vatican II : An Interfaith Appraisal*. (Notre Dame, 1966), p. 632.

[10] Winston S. Churchill, *A History of the English Speaking Peoples*, Vol I (*The Birth of Britain*) (New York, 1956), pp. 35, 37.

[11] Edwin Hatch, *The Organization of the Early Christian Churches* (New York, 1909), Lecture VII, "Councils and the Unity of the Church," pp. 169ff.

[12] *What Unity Implies*, p. 75f.

[13] Gregory Baum, "How I Am Making Up My Mind" *The Christian Century*, LXXXIII (1966), 428.

[14] Romeo de Maio, *The Book of the Gospels at the Oecumenical Councils*. (Vatican, 1963), Chapter 1, "The Gospels Enthroned", pp. 9-20.

CHAPTER THIRTEEN

ONENESS MUST MEAN WHOLENESS

J. ROBERT NELSON

I. *Abuses of 'Catholicity' Corrected*

This is a time when many people are discarding old words and seeking new ones to express their main ideas. Words are like automobile tires. They roll smoothly at first, gripping the mental surface and conveying the load of meaning. Eventually and inevitably, however, excessive use wears them down to the point where they are uncertain and unsafe in the traffic of verbal communication. Then a decision has to be made, whether to reject and replace them, or to have them re-treaded.

'Catholicity' is a term which some Christian thinkers have by now abandoned. During centuries of both use and abuse it has become a victim of distasteful connotation and ambiguous reference. From the second century, we know, the Christian church has been designated catholic (Ignatius: *ad Smyrnaeans* 8.2). The Apostles' and Nicene Creeds both declare catholicity to be an irreducible mark of the one, holy and apostolic church. So important to Western Latin Christianity was this word of Greek origin that Christians came to be known simply as Catholics. Perhaps this was the initial factor in the long and melancholy history of contention over the word, especially during the four centuries since the Reformation.

A stern *defensiveness* has been the first of the unfortunate usages. Not only Roman Catholics, but Orthodox and Anglo-Catholics have felt it to be their obligation to protect the Catholic faith as once delivered to the saints (Jude 3), defined by the ecumenical councils and fathers of the church, and handed on by catechetical teaching and doctrinal formulation. Having acquired the doctrinal pearl of great value, so to speak, they have kept it under an armed ecclesiastical guard, constantly defending it against the questionings or challenges which smack of heresy. St. Paul's perennially useful metaphor reminds us that we have the treasure of the Gospel in earthen vessels (II Cor. 4:7). However important it is to keep the contents free from corruption, the purpose of the vessels is to convey the news of God's love; they are not intended for perpetual storage. So a mainly defensive employment of the concept of catholicity must be rejected.

The word has also been used *polemically* by many Protestants. Both in past and present they have attacked the alleged errors of Rome, and to a lesser extent of Constantinople, because they believed that, in the realm of faith, 'catholic' and 'evangelical' were antithetical names. The fact that Lutherans still recite the modified version of the Apostles' Creed—confession of 'the holy Christian church' instead of 'the holy Catholic church'—is an indication of the depth of mistrust and misunderstanding which date from the Reformation. To correct this misconception, some Protestants have sought to make a compromise by calling the church 'evangelical catholic.' This was the favored expression of the great ecumenical leader, Nathan Söderblom, Lutheran archbishop of the Church of Sweden.[1] He did not invent the term. It had a certain currency in seventeenth century Germany, and continues in the present one. The British theologian, P. Carnegie Simpson published in 1934 *The Evangelical Church Catholic*. And even Karl Barth, after many years in which he launched trenchant attacks against certain teachings of the Roman Catholic Church, made a post-conciliar pilgrimage to "the threshold of the apostles" in Rome; and there, in order to soften the familiar Protestant polemic as well as recognize the changes in Rome, he suggested the appropriateness of evangelical catholicity.[2]

In spite of the obvious mellowing of church relations today, there are many who persist in using 'catholic' and 'catholicity' in a virtually *sectarian* sense. They would deny the very name to any Christian or church which failed to meet the proper mark on their own doctrinal measuring rod.

These three kinds of misuse have caused the erosion of the cognate words of catholicity, rendering them almost otiose in contemporary religious discourse. Who can be sure today what catholicity means? When is a church truly catholic? Is it a restrictive, or a comprehensive, concept? Is catholicity a treasure to be hoarded, a banner to be waved, a threat to be opposed, or possibly a broad defintion of the being and task of the whole Christian community on earth in relation to all mankind?

One difficulty in understanding catholicity is our disposition to discuss it in abstractly theological and intellectualistic terms. But the issue separating the 'Catholic' and 'Protestant' church-types and theological styles cannot be settled merely by a redefining of the words. There must be enough candor in our thinking to admit that both types of Christianity, whatever their claims to revealed truth, are susceptible to the distortions and even perversions which threaten in this time of extensive secularism. A British newspaper recently described a local church which, by traditional standards, possessed the three indispensable elements of catholicity: namely, Catholic doctrine, the apostolic ministry, and the dominical sacraments. But due to the spiritual decay within and the almost total secularization without, this church's effectual membership was reduced to two men: a wearied organist and a frustrated priest. Likewise we do not have to search long to find communities of Protestant persuasion, which solemnly claim their catholicity in terms of being the pilgrim people of God; but in reality they consist of introverted, aging, dispirited parishioners, who have scarcely a trace of interest in extending the mission of the Gospel or serving the urgent needs of the estranged and the poor of human society. The dismal scenes created by the great film-maker of Sweden, Ingmar Bergman, of the faithless pastor in a dying congregation (*Winter Light*) are both a description of the present for some churches and a preview of the future for some others. Apparently neither the allegedly Catholic type nor the Protestant has advantage over the other in keeping out of the dock of accusation, where the ancient church of Sardis once stood: said the accusing Lord, "I know your works; you have the name of being alive, and you are dead" (Rev. 3:1).

If the idea of catholicity has only these ancestral meanings, weighted down by the arrogance and polemic of the past, then the word itself is of no further use. But there are some promising signs that the tire, though worn smooth, may still be retreaded for more use. For the first time history, the effort has been undertaken by representatives of the Orthodox, Roman Catholic and Protestant churches to discover through common inquiry a comprehensive and ecumenically satisfying understanding of catholicity. An early harvest, probably unripe but hopeful, was the report of Section I of the Fourth Assembly of the World Council of Churches at Uppsala, entitled "The Holy Spirit and the Catholicity of the Church."[3] Concurrent with this, and involving some of the same theologians, has been the common study on "Catholicity and Apostolicity" by

representatives of the World Council and of the Vatican.[4] Supporting the studies are the avowed intentions of the American Consultation on Church Union and similar union negotations to discover
together what a church 'truly Catholic' will be.

Some critics have insisted that such discussions are entirely irrelevant and useless: the ecumenical movement has already passed
through its catholicizing period, they claim, and is now concerned
properly and almost exclusively with engagement in the tough
issues of secular society: racism, poverty, freedom struggle, and
avoidance of warfare. But this strong criticism is levelled against
the idea of catholicity which is already regarded by theologians as
obsolete. If the words of the Uppsala report are taken seriously,
indeed, it will be seen that the emerging sense of catholicity is one
which firmly undergirds with expressions of faith the needed programs of social witness and radical reform to which the churches
ought to be committed. While catholicity usually carries the connotation of archaism and traditionalism, therefore, it is just possible
that the new ecumenical interest will provide both a definition and
an impetus to seek realization of a catholicity which has the greatest
practical meaning for the future of the church's service in the world,
and thus for wider dimensions of the human family.

In the past, catholicity has been burdened and thrown out of
balance by a *quantitative* meaning. It has often been equated with
the breadth of church membership and the geographical extension
of ecclesiastical institutions, as well as with a comprehensive body
of authoritative doctrine and the provision in all places for a
ministry of the sacraments. Any church which regarded its catholicity in a sectarian, exclusive manner (according to the judgment of
its critics) nevertheless held to the intent and hope of realizing this
universality.

The emerging concept of catholicity places more emphasis upon
the *qualitative* than the quantitative aspect of the church. The
nearest approach to a definition, however general, which was made
at Uppsala, declares it to be "the quality by which the Church expresses the fullness, the integrity and the totality of life in Christ."[5]
As a matter of faith and theological seriousness, the report denies
that catholicity is the sum of the best efforts of church members to
achieve an ideal goal. It must always be regarded first as the gift of
the Holy Spirit; but every gift of the Spirit implies also the concomitant gift of spiritual power to make use of it for God's purpose.

If this gift is such that it enables that broadly heterogeneous community known as the church to experience an approximation to the fullness, integrity and totality of the corporate expression of Christ's life, then catholicity is surely the attribute of the church which is primary and most variously pertinent to all its activities.

II. *Six Signs of Wholeness*

Unless these very general terms are to float away, like gas-filled balloons making a pretty spectacle but leaving no tangible substance, there must be described some concrete and specific components of catholicity. These are not lacking in either the Uppsala report or other ecumenical thinking on the matter. They can be delineated by several gerunds, which indicate the attitude and responses of the church.

A. *Receiving* the gift of catholicity comes first in both logic and experience. The gift without the giver may be bare, but the gift without the receiver is no longer a gift. Never have Christians ceased talking about the divine gifts, ever since St. Paul's original discussion of the *charismata* in I Cor. 12. In popular parlance the 'natural gifts' which make a 'charismatic' individual have been cut loose from the biblical meaning, since the secularized mind has no idea who or what the 'giver' might be. In Christian faith, however, the idea of gifts cannot be dissociated from the Holy Spirit. Thus the ecumenical discussion of the gift of catholicity is predicated upon faith in the reality and the activity of God the Spirit.

In actual practice, however, people are often most reluctant to receive. Receiving implies an attitude of dependence upon the Spirit which is by no means held by all. This applies especially to some who have responsibility for directing the affairs of the churches: internal pastoral care, administration of properties, planning of social action and programs of education or strategy for justice and welfare, and even the preparation of evangelistic mission. In every sphere of the church's existence there are responsible ones who tacitly, if not admittedly, assume that the church is their business and theirs alone. Without knowing it, they are transferring the sin of the autonomous man, who lives by and for himself, to the church. Unlike the Christians depicted on the walls of the Roman catacombs, the *orantes*, who pray with outstretched arms and open, receptive hands, these church leaders feel little need to offer supplications and petitions in a mood of expectant faith. As men can 'run' a bank, a business, a university, or a government, so they can run a church, whether it be a local congregation, a denominational institution, or a hierarchical system.

The point may seem contentious; but honesty requires that it be made. Evidences of such wilful exercise of autonomy are by no means rare. And they contradict both the theory of the Spirit's working as well as the catholicity, or wholeness of life for the church, which the Spirit does indeed offer and bestow.

Such ancient formulations as walking by the Spirit, being led by the Spirit, and heeding the inner testimony of the Spirit are designations of real experience, not of pious speculation. This is known to those who commit themselves in faith to God's guidance, and look for the power of it in the Scriptures, in study, communal deliberation done in corporate faith, and in worship. It is perhaps an anomalous thing, yet true, that the strongest emphases upon the reality of the Holy Spirit which are sounded in the ecumenical dialogue come from members of churches which, as ecclesiastical entities, seem farthest apart: the Orthodox and the Pentecostals. In their different ways they are testifying to the same basis of catholicity. They have learned in isolation from each other what all are due to learn together: what it means to receive the gifts of the Spirit.

In this regard there is a play upon German words, which is perhaps the most overworked cliché in the jargon-littered literature of that language. It is this: what the Spirit of God gives to the church is both *Gabe* and *Aufgabe*, both gift and task. To receive the elements of catholicity means to accept the task of re-employing them in service in the world. Resolute discipleship is thus the consequence of receiving the gifts by which the fullness and integrity of the life in Christ may be expressed. What are these gifts?

B. *Declaring* the contemporary meaning of the Gospel after men have received it in faith is directed by the Spirit. Many who struggle today with the theological question of mission and the acceptance of faith are convinced, as St. Paul was, that "no one can say 'Jesus is Lord' except by the Holy Spirit" (I Cor. 12:3). Both the psychological mystery of how someone comes to have faith, and the power which makes him want to declare and share this faith, are answered by reference to the Spirit, who bears witness with human spirits (Rom. 8:16).

Having affirmed this gift of declaring, sharing, teaching, and preaching the Gospel as a prominent ingredient of catholicity, however, we are driven again to the perplexing problem of how or whether the full range of doctrines which grow out of the Christian belief can be agreed upon. For many persons the essential Gospel is not just a simple message of salvation by faith in Jesus Christ. It is a complex body of beliefs on God, man, Christ and the world which, it is asserted, have been received by revelation and handed on from generation to generation in the church. Thus the message to be declared is justly called 'Catholic doctrine.' This component of catholicity is the gift of doctrine which carries with it the task of declaration. Declaring and interpreting to others is manifestly a more onerous task for the defender of Catholic doctrine than it is for the exponent of a simple, uncluttered expression of faith. The special need of the former kind of Christian is to preserve the quality of the faith elaborated in the articles or canons, without permitting them to be regarded as just a large quantity of propositions. The need of the latter, who finds in his simple Gospel the undoubted quality of life in Christ, is power to resist the temptation of minimizing the importance of the struggle to cope with many issues of faith and human existence, as the framers of elaborate systems of doctrine have done.

The whole enterprise of theological and ethical research, nurture and education of church members, preparing men and women for special ministries, and interpreting Christian faith through the many media of modern communication is an appropriate response to the Spirit's gift of catholicity in belief and doctrine.

Since one of the hallmarks of catholicity is integrity of life in Christ, it is mandatory that the declaring of Christian teaching and faith be done with the utmost honesty and sincerity. Sincerity does not guarantee certainty; nor does the intent of honesty always assure truthfulness. Dogmas of infallibility are usually challenged by Christians who hold them to be fallible. So the fervor and force of verbal assertion must be conjoined with the sincerity and honesty which effectively restrain the impulses of dogmatism. Dogmatism cannot be called catholic just because it is insistent. Conversely, the catholicity of speech about God's work in Christ can be demonstrated more honestly today by straightforward statements

in the milieu of man's myriad conversations than by the craven
equivocations and deliberate deceptions which Christians are usually tempted to express.

C. *Continuing* the existence of the church in history is an indispensable mark of catholicity. For Christian faith, the sense and
meaning of human history are epitomized in Jesus Christ, who once
lived and still lives; but he does not live in the world without his
body, the church. A churchless world is thus inconceivable for Christian faith, since the elimination of the church as the bearer of Christ's
message and ministering would evacuate human history of its
purpose. This does not imply that the church as such is the savior
of mankind; but it is the distinct instrument among others with
which the Spirit effects the continuing ministry of Christ for salvation.
Continuity may be called the replication of living cells in the body
of Christ. Given the condition of human mortality, it is utterly plain
to see that the church, if only as an instrument of God, must keep
adding members to the body. The church, it is said, is never more
than one generation away from extinction. Those who now assert,
in the name of the principle of toleration, that it is unimportant for
the church to be concerned about mission, conversion and new
members are thus willing a kind of ecclesial suicide. It is indeed
proper that the whole church, as community of Christians, should be
ready to forfeit its historical life as institution, if and when fidelity
to Christ clearly demands such death. But "losing life for the sake
of Christ" is not the same as suicidal disdain for sharing the faith
in mission. There are others who trust the Holy Spirit as the guar-
antor of the church's continuity, having confidence that the church
will survive in some form or other and by some means or other, however unconcerned they may be about the traditional call to mission.
This may seem to be an admirable expression of faith; but actually
it is so irresponsible as to be unfaith. The Christian community cannot be content to live by procreation within its own families.
Another means of continuity is the ministry of the apostolic Word
and Sacraments. Here we need not go into the vexed question of
what constitutes the apostolic ministry, although it is being shown
in the accelerated ecumenical discussions that a wider agreement
surmounting the ancestral barrier of the exclusive doctrine of
apostolic succession may be possible. Beyond dispute is the logical
implication of the belief in the priesthood of all believers. If this be

the category of service which comes between the primary ministry of the living Christ and the special ordained ministries, then the first human channel of continuity is the entire membership of the body, or the people of God.[6] Nor should this interpretation of ministerial continuity detract from the importance, indeed indispensability, of the ordained ministry. The ministry is justly called a gift of the Spirit. In both I Cor. 12:27-31 and Eph. 4:11-12 the diverse kinds of ministry are designated as charismatic, literally the gifts of the Spirit to the church for its service. The line from these special functions in the New Testament church to the settled offices of the second century church is admittedly obscure. But from the standpoint of one who evaluates them for the wellbeing and effective service of the church to God and mankind, the kinds of ministry which have prevailed in history, when not corrupted by human avarice and pretension, are acknowledged as gifts.

To regard the ministry as necessary for the continuity of the church does not require adherence to immutable forms of the ordained ministry, however. In the light of past stalemates of ecumenical argument over the meaning of the apostolic ministry, it is the more remarkable that the delegates to Uppsala, in their quest for understanding of catholicity, could agree on this statement: 'We are now called afresh to repentance and humility in the search for one ministry recognized by the whole Church, and for an understanding of ministry more adequate to the New Testament, to the Church, and to the needs of our own times."[7]

It is this candor which prevents the Christian mind from identifying continuity with the perpetuation of an unchanging past. Happily there is now a sharp decline in the attractiveness of archaism, which is the nostalgic appreciation of the past just because it is past. Part of this attitude towards continuity with the past requires a new dimension of honesty in the willingness of the present generation to assume the debts of the past. We cannot enjoy all the benefits of the best of the church's efforts to humanize our present civilization without also accepting certain indignities and paying the costs for the numerous infidelities and grave moral errors of the church in the past. Christians may indeed be forgiven by God, but their worst actions are not quickly forgiven or forgotten by other people, who rightly judge the mistakes and sins of the churches by the standard of Jesus Christ. So continuity with the past has the double effect of benefit and burden.

Continuity may also be called temporal catholicity, or the catholicity of history. Therefore it includes the future as well as the past. We look before and after, backward and forward, remembering where the church and mankind have been and anticipating the conditions into which they are going. The present enthusiasm for a theology of hope is to be welcomed, because its opposite is despair. But this preoccupation with the future is not an innovation into Christian thought. From the time it first spread in the Roman Empire, the message of the Gospel has been one of hopefulness. Breaking the sad cycle of eternal return to which the majority of people have always been resigned, in which history is just a rotating carousel, the Christians have taught men to think in terms of deliberate social change, development and evolution, both for the individual's life and the destiny of the race. The amelioration of living conditions may not be the full substance of the faith, but it is surely a valued consequence. Yet this is only one of the causes for hope which is stimulated by the concept of human life which we see in Jesus Christ. Beyond social improvement, beyond all the astonishing, prodigious achievements of men for the human uses of environment and resources (but leaving aside for the moment the notorious abuses), beyond such moral education of the human race as has been successful, there still lies ahead the beckoning vision of the fulfilment of history in the Kingly Rule of God.

The long perspective of history necessitates a reserved judgment about the church's realization of catholicity. However the elements of this gift may be designated as doctrine, continuity, community or mission, their present partiality and incompleteness must be acknowledged. In these and other respects, no church or denomination is truly catholic as now constituted. Not only is there an insufficiency of catholicity due to, let us say, temporal immaturity; but the quality of fullness and integrity is lacking precisely because of the brokenness of the church. This brokenness is shown not only in the existing unreconciled divisions within it, but also in the church's having contributed to the fracturing of the society of men and women in which it is supposed to act as a reconciling power. If in the long course of historical continuity the church is enabled to overcome the divisions, give priority to its ministrations to the needy, advance its mission, and exercise faithful stewardship of the patrimony of its traditional faith and structure, then it will be coming closer to that wholeness of corporate life under God's rule for which Christ has given reason to hope.

D. *Gathering* the people into one place for common life in worship and service is of the essence of the church catholic. This may not be so self-evident as a church member who is at home in his parish or congregation might think. An allusion in the New Testament indicates that even then there were Christians who were inclined to stay apart and go alone: "...let us consider how to stir up one another to love and good works, not neglecting to meet together, as is the habit of some, but encouraging one another..." (Hebrews 10:24-25). Today there are many Christians who are not merely careless about 'going to church' on Sunday, but who are fully convinced that they can live just as faithfully apart from a congregation as with it. That individuals in certain places or circumstances can remain apart from the communal or organizational life of a church without forfeiting their faith is beyond dispute. That the church, however, should ever consider this normal would violate its own identity and purpose.

Heretofore the discussions of catholicity have been confined to consideration of the church universal, the body of Christ in the world. This is the broad and undefinable image which is usually summoned to the mind by the word catholic, because it is still identified with the idea of terrestrial extension. There is, however, an intensity of catholicity in each local community of the church. And contrary to some popular notions, the local church is not to be regarded as a mere fragment of the whole church, or as one of the constitutive parts of the whole. Catholicity inheres in the local church as much as in the universal church. Both the local and the universal partake of the gift of catholicity, even as each is susceptible to the defects and insufficiences which prevent full catholic realization. The congregational polity exercised in modern church history by several Protestant denominations gives expression to a catholic principle which is actually quite ancient. In the Greek Orthodox tradition especially, the first and foremost instance of the church's existence has been the local community, conceived as 'the eucharistic center' of Christian life in that place. It was a relatively late development in Orthodoxy for a hierarchy of authority and power to take form; but this development has never gone so far as that of the hierarchical pyramid in the Roman Catholic Church.

Even though Roman ecclesiology has tended to scale the reality

of the church from the papacy downward to the local parish, it
appears to be returning to an appreciation of the catholicity of the
local church. In the normative teaching of St. Robert Bellarmine's
De Ecclesia Militante, for example, his theology of the church included no mention at all of the locality, or parish.[8] But in the first
of the documents adopted by the Second Vatican Council, the Constitution on the Sacred Liturgy, there is a halting acknowledgement of parishes: "in a certain way they represent the visible
Church as it is established throughout the world" (Para. 42). The
tentativeness of the words 'in a certain way' seem to indicate that
some Catholic theologians are not ready to accord authentic catholicity to the parish, except it be considered in relation to the bishop
of the diocese and the higher levels of the hierarchy.

It should not be assumed that all Protestant churches operate on
the principle of local catholicity and congregational autonomy.
Those which are absolutely congregational in their church theory,
such as the Churches of Christ and certain Baptists, accept such
polity *de jure divino*, but do not reflect on whether it is an expression
of catholicity. The lack of reflection would be true of other Protestant denominations by and large, since the issue of local and universal catholicity has not been an urgent one. However, the matter
is assuming greater importance thanks to the ecumenical encounter
with Orthodox and Catholic Christians, and especially due to the
efforts to realize church union. Where is the primary locus of the
church? In the congregation? The presbytery? In a district or
regional unit? Or in one of the highest judicatories of the denomination? Since this question has begged an ecumenical answer
without agreement so far, it is more than likely that the current
inquiry into the meaning of catholocity will be a great aid to finding
that answer.

If such theorizing can be done about the catholicity of the local
church, can it be extended to include the various spontaneous and
unregulated forms of local Christian community which have been
arising in growing numbers? They do not fit neatly into the tables
of organization of a large denomination, either as parish or local
congregation. This may be disconcerting to the bishop or the denominational executive secretary; but the groups have to be considered somehow as ecclesial communities. There is good, under-
standable reason why many Christians join them. They cannot find
any local congregation or parish in which they discover a style or

worship or a commitment to social justice or the kind of personal sensitivity which is sufficiently agreeable to their faith and conscience. They may be well instructed Christians, nominal Christians whose interest has been awakened, inquiring seekers who are on the periphery of the faith and community or even disaffected church members who are already on the way out of recognizable church life. For diverse reasons they choose to affiliate with so-called house churches, underground churches, voluntary task groups, and the like. If the prevailing standards and canons of well-established churches were applied to these *ad hoc* communities, they would almost certainly fail to be accorded recognition as local churches. But if these are places where the gathering of two or three in the name of Jesus Christ means that he is present among them, and if it continues to be true that ferment and motivation for healthy changes and reforms of the church are found in such voluntary groups, and if the contemporary emphasis upon the need for dispersed Christians in society is valid for mission in the new kinds of urban technological society, then a place must be found for them in the concept of the catholic church.

Finally, it is a sign of the catholicity of the local church when the invitation to membership is extended to all persons without consideration of race, nationality or social class. The fact that this formula of non-discrimination has been broadly adopted by a government, university, industry or social institution does not make it any less applicable and urgent for the churches. The case for openness and inclusive membership has been argued cogently and formally accepted by all but a few churches and church organizations. It is not the principle which is at stake in relating it to catholicity, but the practice. A local congregation of Christians, or a large church body, which deliberately shuts out all believers except those belonging to a certain race, nationality or class is thereby rejecting the very gift of the Spirit, which is the catholic inclusiveness of the Christian fellowship.

E. *Sending* forth the members who are gathered in a community is an inescapable implication of the church's catholic nature. Once again the false connotation of catholicity which recent history has bequeathed to European languages is evident. Even though it connotes a broad horizontal extension throughout the world, it seems to carry with it the idea of a static establishment. Churches which are catholic appear to the popular mind as closed societies, whether they be Roman, Orthodox, Anglican, Lutheran or another. The outsider, even the Christian outsider, is defined by the fact that he is outside. And when the attempt at mission is made by the particular church, it looks more like the making of a proselyte to be absorbed by the closed society than the offering of a new faith to affect one's understanding of himself and his relationships to God and to other persons.

Catholicity undergirds the impetus to send forth members of the church into the world about them precisely because it is concerned with the quality of life in Christ. Such life just cannot be self-contained, nor can its fullness and integrity be realized within the closed community. Not only does the authentic life in Christ stimulate Christians to mission, but it really depends upon the exercise of mission. The necessary rhythm of the church's life, therefore, is one of gathering and sending, arriving and departing, concentrating and dispersing, learning and teaching, studying and preaching, worshipping and serving, being loved and loving. To be sure, this is an idealized version of what a church does; but it is not beyond actual experiencing, if the members are very serious about receiving and employing the gift of catholicity.

At the level of verbal games, we can say that catholicity and apostolicity meet and coincide wherever mission is concerned. They become virtually identical and synonymous, since they both point to the declaring, sharing and transmitting of faith in Jesus Christ.

Yet the peril which is most insidious to mission is the lazy Christian attitude which leaves discussion of apostolic sending at the place of verbal commendation but never actually accepts the reality of being sent. It is ironical that the distinctively Christian word 'mission' has been appropriated for other purposes: a military mission, a jet bomber's mission, a diplomatic mission, or a commercial mission. By and large these secularized missions have become actions which are capable of commanding more serious and energetic participation than the church's mission can muster. Instead of looking upon the endless numbers of living human brethren as being the sphere of God's mission, there are millions of intimidated, lukewarm or dispirited Christians who see mankind as too overwhelmingly large for the church to address or serve in Christ's name. This lack of zealous faith is the minus sign which stands in front of all theological formulae for mission and all equations of strategy for sharing the knowledge of Christ.

How to change that minus sign for a plus is obviously a challenge of most critical significance for the church and mankind today. It is critical for mankind, that is, insofar as one shares the conviction of the church, that the Creator of the world and men has an ultimate purpose for them which is mediated by the church.

We are learning today that catholicity must be regarded both as a God-given possession of the church, giving the church its distinct character, and also as a powerful presence of the Holy Spirit, equipping the members for their increasingly difficult mission among men and women and children of the world. It is this gift, as the quality of life in Christ, which enables the church, despite all its limitations, to be used as God's medium of healing and reconciling mankind.

Is that not a boastful, ecclesiastical triumphalism? Must we not speak instead of the self-effacing, undependable, weak and suffering church? Rather than calling it God's primary medium in the world, would it not be more fitting to call it mankind's servant and let it go at that? Perhaps concern for defining and discussing catholicity tempts us away from the disposition of modesty and receptivity to criticism. Thus is the current crisis of credibility intensified, which already has been responsible for driving people out of the church— not because they are sent out for mission, but because they choose to depart in peace and not return.

To be sure, there is a subtle and devastating danger here. But opposite to triumphalism is the danger which is even more pernicious. It is the abject surrender of the church's claim to catholicity, the forfeiture of faith in the living Christ's embodiment in historical community, and the acknowledgement that the present and future well-being of man can be realized wholly by human invention and social planning.

The sending of the church, or the members, to mankind to serve others and invite them to share in the new life in Christ is an act which is vitiated by the church's assumption of grandeur and seizure of wealth and power. So triumphalism must be suppressed and rejected because it is the enemy of catholicity. It is this urgently important lesson which many church leaders are at last learning today. On the other hand, the repudiation by some Christians of the right and the mandate to share the faith by commending Christ to others or deliberately serving in his name is equally antagonistic to catholicity. It comes to proper expression instead, when Christians eschew both extremes and become modest but unrelenting advocates and personal exemplars of this ancient yet always contemporary and effectual message of reconciliation in Christ.

F. *Suffering*, then, is the last and most difficult indicator of the presence of the gift of catholicity. Again, in contrast to familiar usage, this seems to be a strange and strained idea, like substituting a lugubrious melodrama for a gala spectacle. There is no incongruity here, however. If we are seriously trying to understand catholicity in terms of the fullness and integrity of life in Christ, then we cannot avoid a major mark of Jesus' life, which was suffering, The splendors of a papal audience in St. Peter's Basilica, the fervor of a Billy Graham revival, or the well-tailored correctness of an upper-class urban church have little significance for the church's catholicity as compared to a priest's all-night vigil with a dying person, the imprisonment of a witness against apartheid in Johannesburg, or the accidental death of white pilots flying food to starving black Biafrans. Or, to change from these journalistic illustrations of contrast, it may be emphasized that the catholic character of the church's faith and life includes not only moral maxims of the Sermon on the Mount but also the injunctions to lose one's life in service and to bear one's cross as Jesus did at the deadly trash dump outside Jerusalem.

There is no lack of human suffering, of course. In acute hunger and disease, under political persecution, hindered from opportunity by racial hatred, subject to vocational frustrations, plodding dully through endless years of long tedious hours of routine work—so could begin a catalogue of human woes *ad dolorem*. The Christian faith is not a call to masochism, but a summons to realism. Virtually all segments of human society and civilization are scenes of sadness, pain and suffering. Despite the period of life when nothing out of the ordinary happens, or those shorter ones when real pleasure and success are enjoyed, no one can be exempt from some experience of bitterness, bereavement and desolation. Hedonism is one way to face these experiences; Stoic resignation, or even cynicism, is another. Yet neither of these is consonant with the Gospel's genius for interpreting the universally experienced ambiguity of suffering and joy. Just as the Christian faith has a singular source in neither the crucifixion of Jesus nor in his resurrection as such, but arises from reflection upon the meaning of both events, so the experiences of a bittersweet, *chiaroscuro* life are understood as a unity. Good Friday and Easter are inseparable. In the world there is always tribulation for men and women under the pressures of pain and adversity (*"in mundo pressuram habebitis"* is the Latin rendering of John 16:33); but be of good cheer! When Jesus told his disciples to be happy when men revile and persecute them and utter all manner of evil against them falsely, his words were not a specious antidote for a sense of despair. "Rejoice in that day, and leap for joy" (Matt. 5:1) is his counsel to them and to us, because there is scarcely anything better in life than the opportunity to be a witness to the righteousness of God and to suffer, if need be, on account of it. Suffering for righteousness' sake is vicarious, therefore. It is not accepted in the name of an abstract principle, but for the preferment and love of other persons, since righteousness is a personal quality involving human relations.

If the willingness to suffer may be considered an element of catholicity, it shows how far our thinking has moved from the traditional dogmatic, institutional sense of the term. Following the simple definition of Uppsala, we are considering whatever quality makes for the authentic life in Christ. St. Paul was not indifferent to the rectitude of belief and the sincerity of faith in Christ; neither was he cavalier about church organization, since he carried responsibility for all the churches. But when he wrote explicitly to the Christians at Philippi about their manner of life which was worthy of the Gospel of Christ—i.e. the living style of catholicity—he described it thus: "For it has been granted to you (*a gift!*) that for the sake of Christ you should not only believe in him (*doctrine*) but also suffer for his sake, engaged in the same conflict (*the struggle in mission*) which you saw and now hear to be mine (*the apostolic pattern of life*)" (Phil. 1:29-30).

III. *Catholicity and Mankind*

These six aspects of catholicity are not ideal counsels of perfection; they are essential requirements laid upon the Christian communities if these are to exhibit the authentic nature of the church. The mode and manner by which the many diverse communions, denominations, local congregations and individuals give expression to the elements of catholicity must inevitably differ according to the social and cultural conditions in which they live. But it is precisely this ability of the church to comprehend all the diversities of mankind which justifies its being called catholic. A confining, deadening uniformity is thus ruled out.

Then what has catholicity to do with the concept and the reality of mankind's unity? We can readily deny the erroneous notion of the Christian triumphalists, that the church will swallow up the whole race and thus achieve God's purpose of unifying it. The military analogy of 'the Christian soldiers' marching across the six continents to conquer all people for Christ was always a misleading idea; and in the present era of militarism it is especially abhorrent.

Neither can we place confidence in the naive hope that a revived Christianity will somehow mount a mighty movement of compassion and charity, in such wise that the whole of mankind will be persuaded to declare for Christ and become Christians. Both the military analogy and the progressivist illusion of universal moral persuasion lost their meaning in the nineteenth century; and even then they were distortions of understanding of the church's calling to mission to all peoples and nations.

If these must be denied, what can be affirmed in this generation of uneasy anxiety and epidemic dread of disaster?

The preceding essays of this book have shown that there can be no simplistic assurance of a utopian order of living on this planet. But they do not show any cause for dreary despair either. From its biblical origins to the present day, Christian faith has seen human history as a continuing drama of struggle and conflict, within which the leavening and reconciling power of faith, hope and love is constantly and in various ways having effect. What is this effect? Whenever members of Christ's church have not been betraying their vocation by lusting after arrogant power or retreating into selfish isolation, the church has been the embodiment and conveyor of the attitudes and convictions most requisite to the striving after human peace and unity. These attitudes are manifest: the resolute insistence upon righteousness and justice for all persons, the disposition to become responsibly engaged in the actions by which oppressed persons are liberated, the willingness to give oneself in service and suffering for others, the joyful persistence in the hope that the good and providential God will not abandon his creatures to destruction, and the proclaiming and teaching of Jesus Christ as the warrant for this hope. They are the practical expressions of what the Uppsala definition of catholicity means: the fullness, integrity and totality of life in Christ. In truth they are the ultimate needs of all human beings.

NOTES

[1] See Bengt Sundkler, *Nathan Söderblom* (Lund, 1968), pp. 262-267.

[2] Karl Barth, *Ad limina apostolorum* (Richmond, 1969).

[3] *The Uppsala Report* (Geneva, 1968), p. 11. Reports of Sections II, III and IV (Mission, World Development, and International Justice and Peace) also emphasize the wholeness of the church in service to total human reconciliation and unity.

[4] The reports and documents of this important study, which lasted from 1967 to 1970, are published in *One in Christ*, 3 (1970). The French version is in *Istina*, 1 (1969), and the German will appear in *Kerygma und Dogma*.

[5] *The Uppsala Report*, p. 13.

[6] Among the most significant declarations of the primacy of the priesthood of all members for one another and for all persons are those in the following documents: *Report of the Fourth World Conference on Faith and Order*, Montreal, 1963 (London, 1964), pp. 63-67; The *Pastoral Constitution on the Church* (*Lumen gentium*) in *Documents of the Second Vatican Council*, edited by Walter J. Abbott (New York, 1966), p. 57; and *A Plan of Union of the Consultation on Church Union* (Princeton, 1970), pp. 40ff.

[7] *The Uppsala Report*, p. 16.

[8] See the excellent discussion by Emmanuel Lanne, O.S.B., "The Local Church: its Catholicity and Apostolicity," *One in Christ*, 3 (1970), p. 291.

A BIBLIOGRAPHY OF THE WRITINGS OF
Dr. W. A. VISSER 't HOOFT
1918–1970

COMPILED BY

A. GUITTART
(Secretary to Dr. Visser 't Hooft 1946–....)

The following pages contain a first attempt at a comprehensive list of Dr. Visser 't Hooft's writings up to December 31st, 1970. They include all the books, pamphlets, articles in periodicals, stencilled documents, typescripts and manuscripts that we have been able to trace. All, that is, except:

i) unsigned items in the *World Council Diary*, a regular section of *The Ecumenical Review*, of which Dr. Visser 't Hooft was the editor from 1948-1966;

ii) a number of sermons and other addresses, mostly in manuscript and often in note form, but some also in typescript;

iii) Dr. Visser 't Hooft's numerous unpublished reports on European churches in war-time (1939-1945) which still await classification in the World Council of Churches archives.

The items are arranged as far as possible in chronological order. In tracing any particular item or the writings of any one period it may be helpful to bear in mind the successive professional positions held by Dr. Visser 't Hooft, i.e.:

1918-1924 Student at Leiden University

1924-1929 Secretary Boys Work Department of the Alliance of Young Men's Christian Associations

1929-1932 Secretary of Boys Work Department of the World Alliance of YMCA's (half time)

Secretary World's Student Christian Federation (half time)

1932-1938 General Secretary World's Student Christian Federation
(1929-1939 Editor of The Student World)
1938-1948 General Secretary of the World Council of Churches (in
              process of formation)
1948-1966 General Secretary of the World Council of Churches
1968   Honorary President of the World Council of Churches

One particular puzzle for the chronology is caused by the existence of so many translations, often made long after the original was published. We have tried throughout to provide the appropriate cross-references.

This bibliography, as we are all too well aware, is incomplete. Incomplete both because Dr. Visser 't Hooft is still an active and frequent writer and because it has been impossible to be sure that we have traced every single item that came from his pen during these 52 years. We are happy however to make it available to friends, colleagues and students of the writer, while yet leaving room for one or more dedicated bibliographers in later years to prove their industry by completing it.

BIBLIOGRAPHY

1918

1. Naar het bevrijde Brussel, in: Stads-Editie Oprechte Haarlemsche Courant, 27, 29, 30 Nov., 3 Dec. 1918.

1919

2. Uit Parijs, in: Stads-Editie, Oprechte Haarlemsche Courant, 6 Dec. 1919.
3. Het Reims van nu, in: Stadseditie, Oprechte Haarlemsche Courant, 20 December, 1919.

1920

4. Bernard Shaw, in: Virtus Concordia Fides, 4 Nov., 1920.
5. Het conflict van Pierre Abélard met de leer der Kerk, Lecture held at Theological society "Quisque", Leiden, 1920, 23 pp. ms.

1921

6. To the Young Friends, in: Friends Fellowship Papers, March 1921, pp. 56-58.
7. Oostenrijksch studentenleven, in: Haarlemsch Dagblad, 28 Dec. 1921.

1922

8. Groen van Prinsterer's "Ongeloof en Revolutie", 1922, 30 p. ms.

1923

9. Twee internationale Conferenties (YMCA, Pörtschach and European Student Relief, Parad Fürdo), in: Haagsche Post, 14 July 1923.
10. Het beroep der Staatsleer op Rom. 13, Lecture held at Theol. Soc. "Quisque", Leiden, 1923, 26 p. ms.
11. Kantiaansche en Schleiermacheriaansche elementen in het werk van Ernst Troeltsch, paper for examination for doctorate, Leiden, 1923, 34 p. ms.

1925

12. Een naklank van de Opiumconferentie, in: Algemeen Weekblad voor Christendom en Cultuur, 13 Mrt. 1925.
13. Travels of your secretaries, Impressions of W. A. Visser 't Hooft on a recent trip to Germany, in: The World's Youth, Vol. I no. 2, March 1925, p. 9.
14. Zur Vorbereitung der Helsingforser Konferenz, in: Der Ruf, Nov. 1925, pp. 337-340.
15. Forward to Christian Manliness, in: The World's Youth, Vol. 1 no. 4, May 1925, p. 7.
16. Report on visit to the United States of America and Canada, 1925 16 p. stencilled.
16a. Die Kunst, die Jugend und die Welt, Skizze einer Einführung in: Jugend in Aller Welt, 1. Jhrg. Nr. 2, Dezember, 1925, pp. 21-23.

1926

17. Die Fortsetzung von Stockholm und die Jugend, in: Jugend in Aller Welt, Feb. 1926, 2. Jhrg. nr 2, p. 18.
18. Who is the American boy? in: The World's Youth, Feb. 1926, Vol. II no. 2, p. 11.
19. Die CVJM-Arbeit für die Mittelschüler in den Vereinigten Staaten I und II, in: Jugend in Aller Welt, 2. Jhrg. 3 & 4, March-Apr. 1926, pp. 43-45 & 57-59.
20. Eindrücke vom Vereinsleben in den Vereinigten Staaten Nord-Amerikas, in: Die Sphere, April 1926, No. 2 pp. 77-84.
21. Helsingfors 1926, in: Jugend in Aller Welt, 2. Jhrg. Nr. 6, June 1926, p. 82.
21a. The Year of International Concentration of Youth, in: The World's Youth, vol. II nr. 6, June 1926, p. 2.
22. Coup d'œil sur les principaux mouvements internationaux de jeunesse, in: La Sphère, July 1926, No. 3, pp. 156-162.
23. Some impressions of American youth, in: The Congregationalist, August 5, 1926, p. 169.

1927

24. Youth Today and our Message to it, in: The World's Youth, Vol. III no. 5, May 1927, pp. 12-13.
    For translation see no. 25.
25. Die Jugend von heute und unsere Botschaft an sie, in: Jugend in Aller Welt, 3. Jhrg. Nr. 6, June 1927, pp. 82-84.
26. De YMCA en het Communisme in China, in: De Nederlander, 18 June, 1927.
27. *Christus im Schulleben*, Bericht über die erste internationale Konferenz für Arbeiter unter den Schülern höherer Lehranstalten abgehalten in Dassel, 15-24 June 1927, Herausgegeben von W. A. Visser 't Hooft, 120 p.
28. *Christ in School Life*, being the report of the first international conference of Christian workers among boys and girls of High Schools, held at Dassel, Germany, June 15-24, 1927, edited by W. A. Visser 't Hooft, 110 p.
28a. The Dassel Conference, in: The World's Youth, vol. III, no. 7, Sept. 1927, pp. 14-16.
29. Moderne Jugend und das internationale Ideal, in: Jugend in Aller Welt, 3. Jhrg. Nr. 7, Sept. 1927, pp. 98-99.
30. Report on visits to Holland and Denmark in the interest of work among High School Boys. Autumn 1927, 16 p. stencilled.
31. Additional report on activities apart from High School Work. autumn 1927, 10 p. stencilled.
32. Wereldbond (YMCA), 1927 or 1928, 8 p. printed.

1928

33. *The Background of the Social Gospel in America*, Proefschrift, Rijksuniversiteit te Leiden, Vrijdag 26 October, 1928, Haarlem, Tjeenk Willink, 1928, 187 p. (Reprinted in 1962, sponsored by the Committee on Reprinting of the American Theological Library at St. Louis, Missouri, Bethany Press).
34. Bringing boys to Christ, in: The World's Youth, Vol. IV no. 1, Jan. 1928, pp. 11-12.
34a. A New Type of Youth? in: The World's Youth, vol. IV no. 4, April 1928, pp. 51.
35. Observations on the Prague meeting of the Continuation Committee of the Stockholm Conference, 1928, 4 p. stencilled.
36. Report to the National Committee of the KFUM (Swedish initials for YMCA) of Sweden, May 1928, 11 p. stencilled.
37. Unter der gebildeten Jugend, in: Jugend und Kirche, Sept. 1928, pp. 50-71.
    French translation see no. 42.
    English translation see no. 64.
38. Report on two visits to Czechoslovakia in May and September 1928 in the interest of work for secondary school boys, 11 p. stencilled.

39. Le message de Karl Barth, in: Foi et Vie, no. 16, Oct. 1928, pp. 915-921.
    German translation see no. 43.

40. Kerk en C.J.M.V. in Tsjecho-Slovakije, in: Het Korenland, Kerstnummer 1928, pp. 183-189.

1929

41. Report on some aspects of the situation of the YMCA in Greece, Bulgaria, Yugoslavia and Turkey, April 1929, 9 p. stencilled.

42. L'Église et la jeunesse cultivée, in: Foi et Vie no. 4, 16 Feb. 1929, pp. 178-186 and no. 5, March 1, 1929, pp. 246-257.
    For the original see no. 37.

43. Die Botschaft Karl Barths, in: Der Wegweiser, March 17, 1929.
    For the original see no. 39.

44. A new start in Odysseus' Island, in: The World's Youth, Vol. V, no. 4, April 1929, p. 52.

45. Christianity in modern life, Religious psychology of the Adolescent and Secondary School Boys, Lectures held at First International Boys' Workers Institute, Geneva, April-May 1929; Appendices to: An adventure in International Training, (11, 16 and 16 p. stencilled).

46. Remarks on the present situation of the Orthodox Churches in the Balkan area, in: Association Papers of the World's YMCA nr. 8, May 1929, 15 p. stencilled.

47. Orthodox Youth in the Balkans, in: The World's Youth, Vol. V no. 5, May 1929, pp. 77-78.
    For translations see no. 48-51.

48. Griechisch-orthodoxe Jugend auf dem Balkan, in: Jugend in Aller Welt, 5. Jhrg. Nr. 7, September 1929, pp. 107-109.

49. La gioventù ortodossa dei Paesi Balcanici, in: Gioventu Christiana, June 1929, pp. 175-178.

50. De Griecksch-Orthodoxe Jeugd in de Balkan-Landen, in: Het Korrenland, June 1929, pp. 34-39.

51. Ungdommen og Kirken paa Balkan, in: Kristeligt Dagblad, 2 August 1929.

52. La jeunesse et l'Église dans les Balkans, in: Semeur Vaudois, 15 and 17 August 1929; in: Le Christianisme au XXe siècle, 15 août 1929; and in: Le Témoignage, 20 August 1929.
    For translation see no. 53.

53. Jugend im Osten, in: Das Evangelische Deutschland, August 18, 1929, Nr. 33, pp. 273-274.

55. The Inclusive and Exclusive Aspects of Christian Truth, in: The Student World XXII no. 4, October 1929, pp. 349-355 (also German translation pp. 356-361).

56. Das Christentum im modernen Leben, in: Jugend in Aller Welt, 5. Jhrg. Okt. 1929, pp. 116-118.

57. Richtingslijnen voor het CJMV werk in de groote stad, in: Orgaan voor leiders van knapenvereenigingen, 15 Oct. 1929, pp. 146-148.

58. "Youth in Orthodox countries", article in Greek, printed in: "Gregorios Palamas", Oct. 1929, pp. 390-400.

Christianity in Modern Life

59.   I. The battle before our boys, in: The World's Youth, Vol. V, No. 7, Sept. 1929, p. 110-111.
60.   II. The Humanitarian Cul de Sac, in: Vol. V no. 8, Oct. 1929, pp. 124-125.
61. III. Secularism in Moral Life, in Vol. V. no. 9, Nov. 1929, pp. 143-144.
62.   IV. The Christian and the World, in: No. 10, Dec. 1929, pp. 158-159.

63. De gevaarlijke positie van het Christendom, in: Het Korenland, November 1929 and December 1929, pp. 196-200, 227-234 (for the original see no. 59).
64. The Church and Educated Youth, Chapter V in: Youth and the Church, edited by Basil Mathews, London, Pilgrim Press, p. 69, (1929?) (for the original see no. 37).

1930

65. Who challenges whom?, Editorial in: The Student World XXIII, no. 1, Jan. 1930, pp. 1-3.
66. Qui jette le gant?, French translation of no. 65 in same issue of The Student World, pp. 4-6.
The Student World, pp. 4-6.
67. We believe in prayer, Edited by Sydney Strong, New York, Conard-McCann, 1930, pp. 89-91.
68. Report on a visit to Great Britain, Jan./Feb. 1930, 8 p. stencilled.
69. Our Christian Message to Boys, in: The World's Youth, Vol. VI no. 2, Feb. 1930, pp. 28-29.
70. Christianity and Modern thought, series of lectures at YMCA Training course 1930, 43 p. stencilled.
For translation see no. 71.
71. Het christendom in het moderne leven en andere onderwerpen, Sekularisme in het morele leven, in: Leidersblaadje NCSV, Apr. 1930 (and preceding issue).
72. Les Églises orthodoxes et les U.C.J.G., in: Le Journal de Genève, 27 March 1930.
For translation see no. 73.
73. The Orthodox Churches and the YMCA, in: The World's Youth, Vol. VI no. 4, Apr. 1930, pp. 52 and 58.
74. The Moral Responsibility of Intellectual Leaders—and Dr. John R. Mott, in: The Student World XXIII no. 2, Apr. 1930, pp. 93-95.
75. German translation of no. 74 in same issue of The Student World, pp. 95-97.
76. The Message of the World's Student Christian Federation, in: Message papers No. 1, WSCF, May 1930, 20 p.

77. En ekumenisk konferens a Balkan, in: Kristen Gemenskap, May 1930.
78. Er Kristendommen en Hindring for en fuld Livsudvikling? in: Maanedsblad K.F.U.M., Juni 1930.
79. Towards a Rehabilitation of Doctrine, 15 p. typescript.
    For translations see no. 80 and 81.
80. Signes d'un Renouveau doctrinal, in: Le Semeur, June 1930.
    For the original see no. 79.
81. Tecken till en troslivets förnyelse, in: Sveriges Unge Män, July, 1930.
    For the original see no. 79.
82. Do we believe in a personal God? editorial in: The Student World XXIII no. 3, July 1930, pp. 197-199.
83. German translation of no. 82, in the same issue of The Student World, pp. 200-202.
84. Impressions of a visit to North America, 1930, 15 p. stencilled.
    For translations see no. 85 and 97.
85. Indrukken van een bezoek aan Noord-Amerika (translation of part of no. 84) in: Eltheto, Oct. 1930, pp. 26-36.
    German translation see no. 97.
86. La Conférence de Salonique, in: Bulletin du Bureau de Pédagogie religieuse à Paris, No. 1, July 1930, pp. 4-5.
87. Réponse à Enquête: Pour un Humanisme Nouveau, in: Cahiers de Foi et Vie, 1930, p. 270.
88. Report on a Visit to Italy, September 1930, 4 p. stencilled.
89. Préface, in: Jeunesses Orthodoxes, (Report on Conference of youth leaders at Salonica), autumn 1930, pp. 3-7.
90. Het Christendom en de moderne moraal, in: Eltheto, Nov. 1930, pp. 51-63.
    For translation see no. 91.
91. Christianisme et Moralité Moderne (translated from Dutch) Address at Student Conference, 20 p. typescript (1930?).

1931

92. Religiöse Erziehung bei den östlichen Orthodoxen Völkern, in: Die Eiche, 19. Jhrg. Nr. 2, 1931, pp. 211-212.
93. Belangrijke tijden voor de Wereldfederatie, (1931?), 7 p. typescript.
94. An Introduction to the Theology of Karl Barth, Lecture at King's College, London (Jan. 1930), in: The Canadian Journal of Religious Thought, Jan./Feb. 1931, pp. 37-51.
95. Introduction à Karl Barth, in: Études théologiques et religieuses July/Aug. 1931. Edition "Je sers", Paris, 23 p.
    For translations see no. 95, 96 and 115.
96. Inleiding tot de theologie van Karl Barth, 16 p. typescript, n.d.
97. Eindrücke bei einem Besuch in Nordamerika, in: Führerdienst, Jan./Feb. 1931, pp. 12-18.
    For the original see no. 84.

98. A week in Scandinavia. March 1931, 6 p. stencilled.
99. Nationalism as a Religion, in: The Friend, Feb. 20, 1931 and in Friends Intelligencer, 3rd month 1931.
   For translation see no. 100.
100. Nationalisme als religie, in: Eltheto, June 1931, pp. 302-308.
101. The Student World looks at North America, Editorial in: The Student World vol. XXIV no. 1, 1931, pp. 1-2.
102. Europe looks at America, in: The Student World XXIV no. 1, 1st quarter 1931, pp. 72-78 (also in: The Friend, Apr. 17, 1931, pp. 330-331).
103. Nationalism contends with Christianity for the World's Youth, in: Federal Council Bulletin, Apr. 1931 (also in: The Friend, Feb. 1931).
104. Mobilizing for Disarmament, in: The Christian Century, 9 Dec., 1931, p. 1572.
105. Religious Tendencies in Facing a World Crisis, Report World Committee YMCA, 1931, pp. 62-72.
106. Dieu et les Dieux de l'Occident, in: Foi et Vie, 1er mai 1931, pp. 320-331.
   For translation see no. 107.
107. Der Gott und die Götter des Abendlandes, 13 p. typescript.
108. After a year of Message Study, Editorial in: The Student World vol. XXIV no. 2, 1931, pp. 101-103.
109. Currents and Cross-Currents among European Students, in: The Intercollegian, June 1931, pp. 288-290.
110. Introduction in: A traffic in Knowledge, an international symposium on the Christian message, London, SCM Press, 1931 (12 p.).
111. Knowing God. Helping boys to know and to respond to God, in: World's YMCA. World Conferences Study Outlines, Series C. Nr. XVI, 1931, pp. 3-16.
112. Preface or Epilogue, Editorial in The Student World XXIV no. 3, 3rd quarter 1931, p. 187-189.
113. The real challenge of Communism, in: The Student World XXIV no. 4, 4th quarter 1931, pp. 285-286.

1932

114. "Wishing peace but not the means of it", Editorial in: The Student World, vol. XXV, 1st quarter 1932, p. 1-4.
115. Bevezetés a Barth Karoly theologiajaba, in: Debreceni Protestans Lap, Jan./Aug. 1932.
   For the original see no. 95.
116. Modern Revivalism, 6 p. typescript.
117. Impressions sur un mouvement religieux de réveil, in: Foi et Vie, 33e année, no. 35, Feb. 1932, pp. 156-162.
   For translation see no. 118.
118. The Oxford Groups Movement—Appreciation and criticism, in: The Messenger, Nov. 11, 1932, p. 310.
119. The emergence of the Message Issue, in: World's Youth, April 1932 Vol. VIII no. 1, pp. 39-44.

120. Students and the Church, Editorial in: The Student World XXV no. 2, 2nd quarter 1932, pp. 91-92.
121. Secular Religion, book review on: Paul Schütz, Säkulare Religion, in: The Student World vol. XXV no. 2, 1932, pp. 172-173.
122. L'Allemagne missionnaire, l'Inquiétude, Du Nil au Caucase (Longer edition in French of no. 121), in: Le Monde non-chrétien no. 4, Cahiers de Foi et Vie, Dec. 1932, pp. 38-45.
123. Gandhi Startles Geneva Hearers, in: The Christian Century, 6 Jan. 1932, pp. 35-36.
124. Geneva Welcomes Arms Conference, in: The Christian Century, 17 Feb. 1932, pp. 231-232.
125. Hope Grows at Arms Conference, in: The Christian Century, 2 March, 1932, pp. 299-300.
126. Optimism Gains at Geneva Meet, in: The Christian Century, 9 March 1932, pp. 332-333.
127. Europe Belies Geneva's Hopes, in: The Christian Century, 23 March 1932, pp. 390-391.
128. China Appeals to Assembly, in: The Christian Century, 30 March 1932, pp. 421-422.
129. Churches Differ in Scandinavia, in: The Christian Century, 11 May 1932, p. 617.
130. Lack of Good Will Halts Conference, in: The Christian Century, 15 June 1932, pp. 774-775.
131. Henderson Sees Disarm Progress, in: The Christian Century, 6 July 1932, p. 869.
132. American Note Arouses Geneva, in: The Christian Century, 20 July 1932, pp. 914-915.
133. Geneva Results Held Meager, in: The Christian Century, 17 Aug. 1932, p. 1014.
134. Geneva's Hopes at a Low Ebb, in: The Christian Century, 12 Oct. 1932, pp. 1248-1249.
135. League Evades Many Problems, in: The Christian Century, 19 Oct. 1932, pp. 1279-1280.
136. Japan Isolated Before League, in: The Christian Century, 2 Nov. 1932, pp. 1353-1354 and 1358.
137. Geneva Ruled by Machine Guns, in: The Christian Century, 12 Dec. 1932, pp. 1551-1552.
138. Mission of the Younger Generation, book review, in: The Christian Century, 2 Nov. 1932, pp. 1341-1342.
139. Bookreview of : International Survey of the Young Men's and Young Women's Christian Associations, in: International Review of Missions, Vol. XXL, no. 83, July 1932, pp. 441-443.
140. The Pilgrimage of the Federation in Europe, in: The Student World XXV no. 3, 3rd quarter 1932, pp. 223-228.
141. Les étudiants en quête d'une foi, Address held at Foyer International, Paris, in: Le Semeur, 34e année no. 9, juillet 1932, pp. 525-545.
142. Die Jugend 1927 und 1932, (Address given in Dassel at Conference

of High School Boys), in: Arbeit und Stille, 14. Jhrg. Nr. 3, Juli-Sept. 1932 pp. 83-90. (Also in: Die Pflugschar, 14. Jhrg. Nr. 8 Aug. 1932 ,pp. 229-234, und Nr. 9, pp. 266-270; and in: Führerdienst im Bund Deutscher Bibelkreise, Aug. 1932, H.4, pp. 82-84).
    For translations see no. 143, 144, 185.

143. Jeunesse 1927 et jeunesse 1932, in: Foi et Vie, Sept. 1932, 33e année, no. 41, pp. 638-648.

144. The Youth of 1927 and the Youth of 1932, in: World's Youth, Oct. 1932, Vol. VIII no. 3, pp. 225-235.
    Dutch translation see no. 185.

145. Kommunismus, Jugend, Christentum, (Address at national meeting C.V.J.M., Apr. 1932), in: Jungschar XIII, Jhrg. Nr. 9, Sept. 1932, pp. 193-198.
    Swedish translation see no. 167.

146. Communisme—Jeugd—Christendom, in: Algemeen Weekblad voor Christendom en Cultuur, Sept. 1932 (for the original see no. 145).

147. The end of the Bourgeois, Editorial in: The Student World vol. XXV no. 4, 4th quarter 1932, pp. 281-282.

148. Notes on a visit to Italy, Nov. 1932, 4 p. stencilled.

149. Le Fascisme est-il une religion? Notes de voyage, in: Foi et Vie, Dec. 1932, pp. 818-824.
    For translation see no. 150.

1933

150. Is Fascism a Religion? in: The Christian Century, Dec. 28, 1932, pp. 1602-1604 and in The Student World XXVI No. 1, 1933, pp. 72-76.

151. *Anglo-Catholicism and Orthodoxy*, A Protestant View, London, Student Christian Movement Press, 1933 (175 p.).
    For translations see nos. 152, 153, 170, 950.

152. *Le Catholicisme non-romain*, Paris, 1933 (131 p.), Cahiers de Foi et Vie, March 1933, no. 1.
    Italian translation of first chapter see no. 170.

153. Ortodoxia Vazuta de un Protestant, Rumanian translation of chapter of no. 152 on Orthodoxy from "Le Catholicisme non-romain", in: Revista Teologica, Sibiu, 1933.
    German translation of chapter from no. 151 on Non-Roman Catholicism and Protestantism, see no. 950, B2, pp. 245-259.

154. Zichzelf zijn in de worsteling om de eenheid, address at Federatiedag NCSV, Holland about 1932, 30 p. ms.

155. Idealism Drops in League Circles, in: The Christian Century, 18 Jan., 1933, pp. 95-96.

156. Catholics Favor Military Service, in: The Christian Century, 15 March, 1933, p. 370.

157. Geneva's Tension Greatly Eased, in: The Christian Century, 14 June, 1933.

158. Christ or Ceasar in Germany?, in: The Christian Century, 3 May, 1933, pp. 589-590.
159. Special Correspondence from Java: "Java Is Host to Eastern Students", in: The Christian Century, 6 Dec. 1933, p. 1554.

Book Reviews in: The Student World, Volume XXVI, 1933; on:
160. The Other Spanish Christ, by John A. Mackay, in no. 1, pp. 82-83.
161. Nouvelle Revue Française, Cahier de Revendications; Esprit and Hic et Nunc, in no. 1, pp. 92-93.
162. Rethinking Missions (Laymen's Foreign Missions Inquiry), in: no. 3, pp. 270-273.
163. Moral Man and Immoral Society, by Reinhold Niebuhr. in: no. 3. pp. 275-276.
164. The Plain Man Seeks for God, by Henry P. Van Dusen in: no. 4, pp. 371-372.
165. Today, editorial in: The Student World XXVI no. 1, 1st quarter 1933, pp. 1-3.
166. The Editor's Travel Diary, in: The Student World XXVI no. 2, 3 and 4, 1933, pp. 175-178, 266-269, 357-362.
167. Kommunismen, Ungdommen og Kristendommen, in: Kirke og Kultur, Apr. 1933, pp. 214-220.
     For the original see no. 145.
168. The Significance of Jesus Christ, in: Christ and Students of the East (Java Conference of W.S.C.F.), 1933, pp. 79-82.
169. Het nieuwe Duitschland, in: Algemeen Weekblad voor Christendom en Cultuur, 12 mei 1933.
170. Il Cattolicismo nella Chiesa Anglicana, in: Fede e Vita, May/June 1933, pp. 246-260.
     For the original see no. 152.
171. German Protestantism at the Cross-Roads, in: The Student World XXVI no. 3, June 1933, pp. 256-259.
     For translation see no. 172.
172. Het Duitsche Protestantisme op den Tweesprong, in: Algemeen Weekblad voor Christendom en Cultuur, June 30, 1933, 9e jrg. no. 35.
173. Youth 1933, 8 p. typescript.
174. On the present situation of the German Student Christian Movement. June 1933, 5 p. stencilled.
175. Our amazing equilibrium, A European looks at American Campus, in: The Intercollegian, June 1933, pp. 243-244.
176. Has our movement *the* answer? Address WSCF Conference, La Chataignerie, 1933, 13 p. typescript.
177. Le trésor dans les vases d'argile. Text in English, 5 p. typescript.

1934
178. Le trésor dans les vases d'argile, (in French) in: "Hic et Nunc" 1933 or 1934.
179. Het Thema der Oecumenische Beweging, in: De Openbaring der Verborgenheid, Baarn, Bosch en Keuning, 1934, pp. 159-170.

180. The Editor's Travel Diary, in: The Student World XXVII, 1934, no. 1, 2, 3 and 4, pp. 82-85, 176-181, 256-259, 349-354.
181. Notes on Student Evangelism Old and New, in: The Student World XXVII no. 1, 1934, pp. 75-81.
182. Student en Evangelisatie, Address at Summer Conference N.C.S.V. Nunspeet, in: Eltheto, no. 4, January 1934, pp. 118-127.
183. Report on the latest developments in the German Church, Feb. 1934, 3 p. stencilled.
184. Christ and Nationalism, Study Course Papers, no. VI, World's YWCA, Address at Study Course, Geneva, 1934, 4 p. printed.
185. Vijf Jaar (translation of address at Conference Dassel, 1932), in: Leidersblaadje van de Jongenskampen der NCSV, Apr. 1934, pp. 1-7.
     For the original see no. 142.
186. The Bible a meeting place, in: The Student World XXVII no. 2, 1934, pp. 97-99.
187. Les Missions et le dernier paradis, in: Foi et Vie, 35e année, no. 57, jan. 1934, pp. 81-85.
188. The Church in Germany, in: The Student World XXVII, 1934, no. 2, p. 182-188.
189. The Idol of Young India, in: The Christian Century, May 23, 1934 pp. 695-697 and in: The Student World XXVII, 1934, no. 3, pp. 260-263.
190. Destin du siècle. Lecture at Semaine universitaire, Genève, 1934, 10 p. typescript.
191. Christians and other pagans, editorial in: The Student World XXVII, no. 4, 1934, p. 289-291.
192. We must choose, in: The Intercollegian and Far Horizons, Nov. 1934, pp. 31-33.
     Reprinted in no. 244.
193. The Christian Choice, in: The Intercollegian and Far Horizons, Dec. 1934, pp. 65-67.
     Reprinted in no. 244.

1935

194. Kiezen (translated from English) in: Leidersblaadje van de Jongenskampen der N.C.S.V., July 1935.
     For the original see no. 244.
195. Vocation dans l'Église, address at Conférence Nationale de la Fédération française des Associations Chrétiennes d'Étudiants, Marseille, Febr. 1935, 18 p. typescript.
196. L'Homme chrétien. De qui est-il parlé dans Romains 7? De Saul ou de Paul? In: Foi et Vie, janv. 1935, pp. 1-10.
197. God?—or Religion? in: The Intercollegian and Far Horizons, Jan.-Feb. 1935, pp. 103, 104 and 108.
198. "Totalitarian Christianity", in: The Student Movement, Jan. 1935, pp. 76-78.

199. Blessed are the Peace-makers, in: The Student World XXVII no. l, 1935, p. 1-3.
200. The Editor's Travel Diary, in: The Student World XXVIII no. 1, 2, 3 and 4, 1935, pp. 60-64, 150-154, 251-254 and 435-439.
201. Over de christelijke Jeugdbeweging onder jongens van Middelbare scholen in het buitenland, in: Jeugd en Kampwerk, 1935, 13 p.
202. Inleiding, in: Tor Andrae: Nathan Söderblom, Zutphen, N.V. C. J. A. Ruys, 1935, pp. 7-9.
203. Herleving van den Duitschen Kerkstrijd, in: De Groene Amsterdammer, 16 mrt 1935.
204. Catholics and Protestants, in: Sobornost No. 1, March 1935, pp. 12-18 and in: The Student World XXVIII no. 2, 1935, p. 155.
       Dutch translation see no. 232.
205. A note on books dealing with Eastern Orthodoxy in: The Student World XXVIII no. 2, 1935, pp. 170-171.
206. The Federation and the Eastern Orthodox, in: The Student World XXVIII no. 2, 1935, p. 93-96.
207. Let's be realistic, in: The Intercollegian and far Horizons, March 1935, pp. 131-132.
       Reprinted in no. 244.
208. The Stuff of Christian Life, in: The Intercollegian and Far Horizons, Apr. 1935, pp. 167-169.
       Reprinted in no. 244.
209. The Job of the Christian Community, in: The Intercollegian and Far Horizons, May 1935, pp. 187, 188 and 198.
       Reprinted in no. 244.
210. L'Église, in: Le Semeur, avr.-mai 1935, pp. 417-437.
211. Jesus Christ our Contemporary, Editorial in: The Student World XXVIII no. 3, 1935, p. 189-190.
212. Humanité de Jésus Christ, Address at Semaine universitaire, Jan. 1935, in: Foi et Vie, juin 1935, pp. 425-436.
       For translations see no. 213, 214.
213. The Humanity of Jesus Christ, in: The Student World XXVIII no. 3, 1935, pp. 231-240.
       For the original see no. 212.
214. Der Mensch Jesus Christus, in: Die Furche, vol. 21, Sept./Okt. 1935, pp. 376-385.
       For the original see no. 212.
215. De roepstem van Indië tot den Nederlandschen Student, in: Indië roept, uitgave van de Studenten Zendingscommissie 1935, pp. 1-8.
216. Das Bekenntnis zu der Einen Heiligen Christlichen Kirche, in: Evangelische Woche, Hannover, Sept. 1935, pp. 131-139.
       Reprinted in no. 950, B. 2, pp. 38-44.
217. Karl Barth en de oecumenische beweging, in: Nieuwe Rotterdamsche Courant, 5 Sept. 1935.
218. International Student Conference on Missions, Editorial in: The Student World XXVIII no. 4, 1935, p. 285.

219. Hoc vobis signum ... (Luc 2:10). Address at University, Geneva, Christmas 1935, in: In Extremis no. 7/8, 1935, pp. 150-153.
220. Le Protestantisme et le problème oecuménique, in: Foi et Vie, sept./oct. 1935, nos. 74-75, pp. 613-627.
221. Das Leben des Zeugen, in: Evang. Missionsmagazin, Nov. 1935, 79. Jhrg. Nr. 11, pp. 406-416.
   For translation see no. 222.
222. The Life of Witness, in: The Student World XXVIII no. 4, 1935, pp. 400-412.
   Dutch translation see no. 238 and no. 253.
223. *Students find the truth to serve*, The story of the World's Student Christian Federation 1931-1935. WSCF, Geneva, 1935, 84 p.
224. Der Christliche Studentenweltbund in 1934 und 1935, (1935?), 5 p. typescript.

1936

225. Statement of Faith, presented at Ordination in Église Nationale Protestante de Genève, 1936, 7 p. typescript.
226. The Editor's Travel Diary, in: The Student World XXIX no. 1, 2, 3 and 4, 1936, pp. 62-64, 147-152, 274-277 and 447-450.
227. Christian Social Task, Editorial in: The Student World XXIX no. 1, 1936, pp. 1-2.
228. Pacific Area Conference WSCF, Editorial in: The Student World XXIX, 1936, no. 4, pp. 293-294.
229. Message to Danish Christian Student Movement (in German), in: Danmarks Kristelige Studenterbevaegelse Nr. 6, p. 3, Jan. 1936.
230. None other Gods. Address at Friends' House, London, Feb. 7, 1936, in: The Friend, Vol. 94 no. 7, Feb. 14, 1936, pp. 133-135. Also in: The Lecture Recorder, July 1936.
231. Christliche Existenz an der Universität. Address at University, Basle, in: In Extremis No. 2, 1936, pp. 36-46.
   French translation see no. 272.
232. Katholieken en Protestanten, in: Algemeen Weekblad voor Christendom en Cultuur, 29 Mei en 5 juni 1936.
   For the original see no. 204.
233. Das "Hundertguldenblatt" als Spiegel unserer Zeit, in: Jungenwacht, Ein Blatt Evangel. Jugend, Heft 6, Juni 1936, pp. 132-134.
   For translation see no. 234.
234. La pièce aux cent florins, miroir de notre époque, in: Foi et Vie, juin/juillet 1936, nos. 83-84, pp. 349-355.
235. Lord, teach us to pray, in: The Student World XXIX no. 2, 1936, pp. 85-86.
236. De jeugd in de massabeweging der laatste jaren, in: Leidersblaadje van de jongenskampen der NCSV, Juli 1936, p. 1-8.
   For the original see no. 244.
237. The Christian situation today. Address given at Oberlin College, Ohio, Sept. 7, 1936, 5p. typescript.

238. Getuigen, in: De Stuurman, maandblad voor bestuurders der CJMV in het Nederl. Jongel. Verbond, Oct. 1936, pp. 177-181.
For the original see no. 222.

239. Address to H. M. Emperor Haile Selassié, Geneva, 1936, 1 p. typescript.

240. L'Église entre Dieu et le monde, 1936, 15 p. typescript.

241. Have you not read that He created them male and female? in: The Student World XXIX no. 3, 1936, pp. 181-182.

242. The Meaning of Sex, in: The Student World XXIX no. 3, pp. 192-203.
For translation see no. 243.

243. Le problème sexuel, in: Foi et Vie, nov.-déc. 1936, pp. 600-612.

1937

244. *None other Gods*, New York, Harpers & Brothers, and London, SCM Press, 1937, 185 p.
Chinese translation see no. 282.
Portuguese translation see no. 477.

245. *The Church and its Function in Society* by W. A. Visser 't Hooft and J. H. Oldham. London, G. Allen & Unwin, and New York, Willett, Clark & Co., 1937, 260 p.
For translations see nos. 246, 247.

246. *Die Kirche und ihr Dienst in der Welt*, eine ökumenische Kirchenkunde der Gegenwart von W. A. Visser 't Hooft und J. H. Oldham. Berlin, Furche-Verlag, 1937, 244 p. (Translation from English).

247. *La mission de l'Église dans le monde* par W. A. Visser 't Hooft et J. H. Oldham, Paris, Éditions "Je Sers", 1937, 253 pages.

248. The Miracle of the WSCF, in: The Intercollegian and Far Horizons Vol. 54, no. 3, Jan. 1937, p. 67-68.

249. An end and a beginning, Editorial in: The Student World XXX no. 1, 1937, pp. 1-2.

250. The Federation in this oecumenical year, Editorial in: The Student World XXX no. 2, 1937, p. 105-108.

251. The Editor's Travel Diary, in: The Student World XXX no. 1, 2, 3 and 4, 1937, pp. 70-74, 179-182, 268-270 and 346-353.

252. De Religie van het Leven, in: Eltheto, 91e jrg. No. 6, March 1937. pp. 165-177.
For the original see no. 244.

253. Leven als Getuige, in: Leidersblaadje van de Jongenskampen der NCSV, Juli 1937, p. 1-8.
For the original see no. 244.

254. La première prière des disciples après la Pentecôte, sermon sur Actes 4:24-30, in: Parole de vie, mai 1937, pp. 69-83.
English translation see no. 277.

255. Pourquoi Jésus-Christ? Il faut choisir, in: In Extremis No. 6, 1937, pp. 155-164.

256. Aufruhr um Gott in der Völkerwelt, Lecture at Evangelische

Woche, Darmstadt, in: Junge Kirche, 5. Jhrg. H.10, May 1937, pp. 381-388.

Also reprinted in no. 950, B.1, pp. 124-132.

257. Oxford en Edinburgh, address given at the Ned. Herv. Predikantenvergadering, Utrecht, Apr. 1937, in: Vox Theologica, 8e jr. no. 6, June 1937, pp. 162-169.

258. The Church as an oecumenical society, in: The Student World XXX no. 3, 1937, pp. 271-279.

259. Theologische Randbemerkungen zur ökumenischen Aufgabe der Kirche, in: Die Furche, Juli/Aug. 1937, pp. 310-319.

260. Pour l'Union des Églises, in: Semaine religieuse de Genève, 30 Oct. 1937.

261. The "Christian" West, in: God speaks to this generation, Birmingham, SCM Conference, London, SCM Press, 1937, pp. 41-57.

Also printed in no. 244.

German translation in no. 950, B.1, pp. 73–81.

262. We look at Great Britain, in: God speaks to this generation, Birmingham SCM Conference, London, SCM Press, 1937, pp. 58-63.

263. Weakness and Strength of the Christian Community, in: The Student World XXX no. 4, 1937, pp. 289-290.

264. "Goed Leven" of Geloof, Lecture at University, Utrecht, in: "Vier Tijdvragen", Nijkerk, G. F. Callenbach N.V., 1937.

265. What is the purpose of the University? 1) The Christian challenge; 2) The Christian answer, in: The Student Movement, Oct. and Nov. 1937.

266. Rembrandt et la Bible, Nov. 1937, 5 p. typescript.

267. Le secret messianique, Nov. 1937, 25 p. typescript.

For translation see no. 268.

1938

268. The Messianic secret, in: The Student World XXXI no. 3, 1938, pp. 209-216.

269. Die Predigt von Rembrandts Hundertguldenblatt, in: Der Heiland, Furche Verlag, Berlin, 1938, pp. 164-170.

270. The Editor's Travel Diary, in: The Student World XXXI no. 1, 2, 3 and 4, 1938, pp. 66-67, 167-170, 252-255 and 359-360.

271. A university in a university which is not a university, Editorial in: The Student World XXXI no. 1, 1938, p. 1.

272. La vocation chrétienne de l'étudiant, in: Le Semeur, jan. 1938, pp. 146-161.

For the original see no. 231.

273. Qu'est-ce que la vérité? in: Foi et Vie, no. 2, 1938, pp. 133-142.

For translation see no. 274.

274. Pilatus spricht: "Was ist Wahrheit?", in: In Extremis 1938, no. 2, pp. 43-52.

275. Christianity as its own Adversary, Editorial in: The Student World XXXI no. 2, 1938, p. 97 and in World's Youth, Spring 1938, pp. 162-170.

276. l'Ascension, sermon on Acts 1:4-11 (preached in 1937) in: Parole de Vie, mai 1938, pp. 69-80.
277. The First Prayer of the Disciples after Pentecost, sermon on Acts 4: 24-30, in: The open Bible no. 10, June 1938.
   For the original see no. 254.
278. Le Protestantisme de Rembrandt, in: La Vie intellectuelle, juin 1938.
279. Rembrandt als protestantischer Meister, in: Die Furche, 24. Jhrg. H.11, Nov. 1938, pp. 468-481.
   Dutch translation see no. 318.
   Czech translation see no. 319.
280. Notes sur la vie de Rembrandt, in: Le Semeur, July 1938; pp. 485-493.
   Spanish translation see no. 317.
   English translation see no. 316.
281. What youth is seeking—what youth is finding, in: The Council Fire, the International Girl Guide and Girl Scout Paper, Vol. XIII no. 4, Oct. 1938, pp. 81-84.
282. *None other Gods, Chinese translation*, Hongkong, The Association Press of China, 1938, 75 pages,
   For the original see no. 244.
283. Notes on a visit to Czechoslovakia and Germany, Nov. 16, 1938, 5 p. stencilled.
284. Questions, in: International Student Service-Bulletin, Nov. 1938, Vol. XV no. 2, pp. 11-13.
285. Jeunesse 1938. Address at Adelboden, in: Le trèfle, 18e année no. 2, Nov. 1938, pp. 1-7.
286. Introduction to: D. T. Niles, Sir, we would see Jesus. London, SCM Press, 1938, pp. 5-6.
287. l'Incognito de Dieu, Address at Vaumarcus, in: Les cahiers protestants, 22e année, no. 7, Nov. 1938, pp. 400-410.
288. A conversation with Rome, in: The Student World XXXI no. 3, 1938, pp. 256-263.
   For translation see no. 289.
289. Une conception catholique de l'unité de l'Église, in: Foi et Vie, no. 101-102, 39e année no. 3, 1938, pp. 299-308.
290. Glimpses into mysteries of the Kingdom, Editorial in: The Student World XXXI no. 3, 1938, p. 193.
291. Students and the Younger Churches, Editorial in: The Student World XXXI no. 4, 1938, pp. 289-290.
292. Rembrandt's Weihnachtspredigt, in: Evangelische Weihnacht, Tübingen, Furche Verlag, 1938, pp. 93-100. (Reprinted in 1948).
   For translation see no. 293.
293. Message de Noël de Rembrandt, in: La Vie Protestante, 23 déc. 1938.
294. *Report of the World's Student Christian Federation 1935-1938*, Geneva, WSCF, 72 p.

1939

295. An Impression of the World Missionary Conference at Madras, in: Internat. Christian Press and Information Service, Articles Series no. 4, Jan. 1939, 3 p. stencilled.

296. Order and Judgment, Editorial in: The Student World XXXII no. 1, 1939, pp. 1-4.

297. True Bread, Editorial in: The Student World XXXII no. 2, 1939, pp. 89-91.

298. Editorial in: The Student World XXXII no. 3, 1939, pp. 193-195.

299. Voorwoord in: Stemmen uit de wereldkerk, Vijf lezingen van de Wereldconferentie van Christen-jeugd, Amsterdam 1939, met een overzicht van de conferentie, Amsterdam, Ten Have, 1939, pp. 5-6.

300. La Mission et le Monde, address at Montpellier for Fédération franç. des Associations chrétiennes d'Étudiants, in: Le Semeur, 42e année, 1939, pp. 339-355.

301. Notes on the Church situation in Germany, April 1939, 5 p. stencilled.

302. The Ecumenical Task. The Church as an Ecumenical Society in time of war. A statement prepared by the Provisional Committee of the proposed WCC (written by V. 't H. and William Paton) printed by S.P.C.K., London, April 1939, 4 pages.

303. Die Gemeinde inmitten irdischer Gemeinschaften, address at Missions Studententagung, Halle, Apr. 1939, in: Sendende Gemeinde Nr. 58/59, Die Gemeinde Jesu Christi in der Völkerwelt II. Von dem Ort der Gemeinde, pp. 11-18.

304. l'Église et la situation internationale, lecture held at St. Germain, May 1939, 15 p. typescript.

305. Memorandum concerning relations between the Provisional Committee and the German Evangelical Church, June 1939, 7 p. stencilled.

306. La base chrétienne de notre action internationale, address at YWCA Leaders Course, Mont Pèlerin, July 1939, 13 p. typescript.

307. Bible study at YWCA Leaders Course, July 1939, 4 p. typescript.

308. Some considerations about the situation of the Church in the World, address at YWCA Leaders course, Mt. Pèlerin, July 1939, 9 p. typescript.

309. I have overcome the world, Address at World Youth Conference, Amsterdam 1939, in: Christus Victor, The Report of the World Conference of Christian Youth, Amsterdam 1939, pp. 230-235.
       For translations see no. 310, 311, 312.

310. Ich habe die Welt überwunden, in: Christus Victor, Bericht der Weltkonferenz Christlicher Jugend, Amsterdam 1939, pp. 259-265. Reprinted in no. 950 B. 1, pp. 239-243 with the title: Revolution wider die Trägheit.

311. J'ai vaincu le monde, in: Rapport de la Conférence mondiale de la Jeunesse chrétienne, Amsterdam 1939, pp. 273-279. Reprinted in: In Extremis, 1939 no. 4/5, pp. 120-126.

312. Ik heb de wereld overwonnen, in: Stemmen uit de Wereldkerk, vijf lezingen van de Wereld Conferentie van Christen Jeugd, Amsterdam, Ten Have, (1939) pp. 52-59.
313. Opening address at World Youth Conference, Amsterdam, in: Christus Victor, Report, pp. 146-149.
    For translations see nos. 314, 315.
314. Eröffnungsrede, in: Christus Victor, Bericht, pp. 167-170.
315. Discours d'ouverture, in: Rapport, pp. 175-179.
316. Notes on the life of Rembrandt, in: World's Youth, Special issue on the Netherlands, Summer 1939, pp. 217-222.
    For the original see no. 280.
317. Notas acerca de la vida de Rembrandt, in: La nueva democracia, Oct. 1939, pp. 21-23.
    For the original see no. 280.
318. Het Protestantisme van Rembrandt, in: Algemeen Weekblad voor Christendom en Cultuur, 15e jrg. No. 12 & 13, Jan. 20 & 27, 1939, Reprinted in: De Kroniek van de Vriendenkring van het Rembrandthuis, 31 dec. 1968, pp. 153-167.
319. Rembrandt Jako Protestantsky Mistr; Poznamky o Rembrandtove Zitové a Dile 22 p., in: Vydavatelské Oddeleni YmkY, Praha 1939.
    For the original see no. 279.
320. The work of the Provisional Committee in time of war, with Appendix: The Ministry to Prisoners of War and Interned Aliens, Sept. 1939, 6 and 5 p. stencilled.
321. Consolés. Sermon on II Cor. 1:3-7, in: Parole de Vie, Oct. 1939, pp. 129-141.
322. Notes on the attitudes of Christians to this war, Nov. 1939, 10 p. stencilled.
323. What is the World Council of Churches? In: Christendom Vol. IV, Winter 1939, pp. 21-31.
    For translation see no. 324.
324. Was ist der Oek. Rat der Kirchen? 5 p. typescript (translated from English).
325. Sermon on 2 Chron. 14:11 preached at service of intercession for Finland, Geneva, Dec. 1939, 3 p. typescript.
326. Le Magnificat, sermon on Luke 1: 46-55, Dec. 1939, 4 p. typescript.
327. Which Peace? in: World's YWCA Monthly, Dec. 1939, p. 2.
    For translations see nos. 328 and 329.

1940
328. Welke vrede? in: Op Weg, Feb. 1940, pp. 323-326.
329. Paix sur la terre! (abbreviated translation) in: In Extremis, 1940, No. 1, pp. 24-26.
330. De Ekumene in Oorlogstijd, in: Woord en Wereld, 2e jrg. No. 1, 15 February 1940, pp. 20-27.
331. Germany and the West. (Study Dept. Life and Work) March 1940,

13 p. stencilled. In: International Conciliation (Carnegie Foundation), Oct. 1940, no. 363. Reprinted in part by George Bell in: Christianity and World Order, London Penguin Special, 1940, pp. 92-95.

For translation see no. 332.

332. Deutschland und der Westen, 1940, 13 p. typescript.
333. Are there two Germanies? in: The Christian News Letter, Spring 1940, 5 p. typescript.
334. The Ecumenical Church and the International Situation. Memorandum, Apr., 1940, 12 p. stencilled.
335. l'Église à la Croisée des chemins, in: Cahiers Protestants, avril-mai 1940, pp. 135-150.
336. Is the Church the Church in war-time? May 1940, 8 p. stencilled.
337. Facteurs spirituels dans la faillite de la paix (1919-1939), in: Aperçus et rapports du Groupement Consultatif International pour la paix et le désarmement, May 1940, 12 p. stencilled.

For translations see nos. 338 and 339.

338. Geistige Ursachen des misslungenen Friedens (1919-1939) May 1940, 12 p. stencilled.
339. Spiritual Factors in the Peace Failure, in: Internat. Conciliation Oct. 1940, no. 363 pp. 358 ff.
340. Notes sur Introductions à l'eschatologie biblique, in: Le Semeur et Notre Revue réunis, May-June 1940, no. 7-8, pp. 268-276.
341. Report on the Work of the Provisional Committee, Jan. 1940-July 1940, 14 pages stencilled.
342. Bericht über die Arbeit des vorläufigen Ausschusses, Jan. 1940-July 1940, 14 p. stencilled.
343. l'Église devant les événements, in: Messager de l'Église évangélique libre de Genève, 1940, pp. 3-8.
344. The ethical reality and function of the Church, June 1940, 40 p. stencilled; with annex: A questionnaire (3 p.).

For translations see nos. 345 and 370.

345. La fonction éthique dans l'Église (translation from English), 29 p. typescript.
346. La foi qui triomphe du monde, 12 études bibliques (avec Mlle Suzanne de Diétrich) Genève 1940, 48 p. (Imprimerie La Concorde). For translations see nos. 347 and 348.
347. The faith which overcomes the world, Bible studies for Amsterdam World Christian Youth Conference (with Suzanne de Diétrich) SCM Press, 32 p.
348. Der Glaube die die Welt überwindet (translation from German), 1940, 40 p. stencilled.
349. L'Église et l'Europe, lecture at Vaumarcus, July 16, 1940, in: Cahiers protestants, Nov. 1940, pp. 1-16.

For translation see no 350 and 367.

350. The Church and Europe, in: The Student World XXXIII no. 3-4, July 1940, pp. 97-109.

Dutch translation see no. 367.

351. Le combat du chrétien, sermon on Phil. 1:27-30, In: Parole de Vie, July 1940, pp. 97-109.
352. The task of the Christian community in the world today, in: The Student World, XXXIII, 2nd quarter 1940, pp. 75-86.
353. Détresse et Espérance de l'Église, Dec. 1940, 6 p. typescript.

1941

354. Der Oekumenische Rat der Kirchen, Address held in Switzerland, 1940 or 1941, 8 p. typescript.
355. Notes on "Long Range Peace Objectives" (from a Continental European standpoint) 1941, 4 p. typescript.
356. Notes on the situation of the Church in Europe no. 1, Jan. 1941, 8 p. stencilled.
357. Notes on the situation of the Church in Europe no. 2, March 1941, 5 p. stencilled.
358. Tu ne prendras point le nom de l'Éternel ton Dieu en vainand
359. Souviens-toi du jour du repos pour le sanctifier, in: L'ordre de Dieu, Genève, Édit. du "Messager", 1941, pp. 29-46 and 47-62, reprinted: Neuchâtel-Paris, Delachaux & Niestlé, 1946.
360. Du sollst den Namen des Herrn, deines Gottes, nicht missbrauchen;
361. Gedenke des Sabbathtages, dass du ihn heilig haltest (translation from French by David Lerch), in: Der Heilige Wille Gottes, Zürich, Gotthelf Verlag, 1941, pp. 34-47 and 48-60.
362. Dire. Lecture given at Lausanne and Geneva, Jan. 1941, in: In Extremis, Feb. 1941, pp. 3-12.
363. Bericht über die Arbeit des vorläufigen Ausschusses, Juli 1940-Feb. 1941, Feb. 1941, 17 p. stencilled.
364. Report on the Work of the Provisional Committee, July 1940-Feb. 1941, stencilled.
365. Rapport concernant le travail du Comité provisoire, juillet 1940-février 1941, 16 p. stencilled.
366. Des églises qui deviennent l'Église. in: Semeur Vaudois, 22 mars, 1941.
367. De Kerk en Europa (translation of part of no. 349), in: Oecumenische Berichten, April 1941, 14e jrg. no. 4, pp. 53-56.
368. Some considerations concerning the post-war settlement, March 1941, 4 p. stencilled.
369. Notes on the situation in France, Apr. 1941, 5 p. stencilled.
370. Die ethische Wirklichkeit und Funktion der Kirche, Entwurf eines einleitenden Memorandums, Studienabteilung des ÖRK, Apr. 1941, 29 p. stencilled.
      For original see no. 344.
371. L'Église parle au Monde (Ecclesia Militans I), 1941, 75 p. stencilled. (Introduction and choice of texts by Dr. V. 't H.).
      German translation see no. 384 (enlarged)
372. Sermon on Math. 16:18b, preached at Pomeyrol, Apr. 20, 1941, 4 p. typescript.

373. Conditions in Holland, Apr. 1941, 2 p. stencilled.
374. Le travail oecuménique en temps de guerre, conférence pour la Fédération des Églises protestantes de la Suisse, Neuchâtel, Attinger, June 1941, 8 p.
    For translation see no. 375.
375. Die ökumenische Arbeit in der Kriegszeit, Basel, K.Werner, n.d. 12 p.
376. Report from the Geneva office of the Provisional Committee Jan. 1-July 1, 1941, 13 p. stencilled.
377. Les Églises en temps de guerre, lecture given in Switzerland in 1941, in: Suisse contemporaine, nov./déc. 1941, no. 10, pp. 837-852.
378. Mission als ökumenische Tat, Vortrag Jahresversammlung Basler Mission, 1941, in: Evang. Missions-Magazin Sept. 1941, pp. 134-143. (also in: Die Sammlung der Gemeinde).
    Reprinted in no. 908, pp. 9-19 and in no. 950, B.1, pp. 203-212.
    Dutch translation in no. 1024, pp. 124-134.
379. A letter from the chairman, in: The Student World XXXIV no. 4, 1941, pp. 280-284.
380. Notes on the situation of the Church in Europe No. 3, Nov. 1941, 8 p. stencilled.
381. Le service du Chrétien, Résumé in: Fédération franç. des Assoc. chrét. d'étudiants. Correspondance de la zone non-occupée. Supplément au Semeur, déc. 1941, pp. 110-117.
382. Le chrétien et le péché, in: Le péché, Dec. 1941, pp. 11-14, (stencilled).
383. Le message de Noël de Rembrandt, in: Lumière dans les ténèbres, brochure pour les prisonniers de guerre, Noël 1941, pp. 39-40.

1942

384. Die Kirche spricht zur Welt (Ecclesia Militans I) 1942 (enlarged edition of the French no. 371).
385. Notes on the situation of the Churches no. 4, Feb. 1942, 5 p. stencilled.
386. Notes on the situation of the Church in Europe, 1942, (on Germany) 2 p. stencilled.
387. Notes on the situation of the Church in Europe no. 5, July 1942, 6 p. typescript.
388. The Church is the nucleus. How shall the Christian Church prepare for the new world order? in: The Christian Century, March 4, 1942, pp. 277-280.
389. Easter. Meditation on Luke 24:13-15, in: Kingdom and Patience, published by Ecum. Comm. for the Chaplaincy Service to prisoners of war, 1942, pp. 29-32.
    For translation see no. 390.
390. Pâques, Méditation on Luke 24:13-35, in: Royauté et Patience, pp. 13-16.
391. Ascension, Meditation on Acts 1:4-11 and 2 Cor. 5:1-10, in: King-

dom and Patience, publ. by Ecum. Comm. for Chaplaincy Service
to prisoners of war, 1942, pp. 33-36.
   For translation see no. 392.

392. Ascension, Méditation sur Actes 1:4-11 et 2 Cor. 5:1-10, in: Royauté et Patience, pp. 17-20.

393. Die Not der Kirche und die Oekumene, address Wipkinger Conference, Zürich, Nov. 1941, in: In Extremis, Apr. 1942, pp. 33-56.

394. La situation des Églises Évangéliques en Espagne, June 1942, 5 p.
   stencilled.

395. Report on activities during the period July 1941-July 1942, Aug.
   1942, 18 p. stencilled.

396. Die Lage der Europäischen Kirchen in der Gegenwart, Address at
   Synod Berne, 11 Oct. 1942, 10 p. typescript.

397. Notes on the situation of the Eastern Orthodox Churches, Nov.
   1942, 6 p. typescript.

398. The Function of a Christian in the world, in: The Student World
   XXXV no. 4, 1942, pp. 254-260.

399. La Commission oecuménique, in: Églises de la Captivité, publ. par
   Comm. oecuménique pour l'Aide spirituelle aux Prisonniers de
   guerre, 1942 pp. 11-18.

400. Salutation oecuménique (with Olivier Béguin), in: Un Sauveur
   vous est né, brochure de la Comm. oecum. pour l'aide spirituelle
   aux Prisonniers de Guerre, Noël 1942, p. 66.

401. Foreword (with Olivier Béguin), in: Unto us a child is born, published by the Ecumenical Commission for the Chaplaincy Service
   to Prisoners of War, Christmas 1942.

                              1943

402. Misère et Grandeur de l'Église, Genève, Labor et Fides, 1943, 100 p.
403. Az Egyhaz Nyomorusaga és dicsösége, Budapest, Reformatus Trak-
   tatus Vallalat Kiadasa, with foreword of translator Dr Victor
   Janos, n.d. 68 p. (for the original see no. 402).
      English translation see no. 433.
      Dutch translation see no. 508.
      German translation see no. 446 and no. 509.

404. The Church and International Reconstruction, Jan. 1943, Study
   Department WCC Nr 3/E/43 An analysis of agreements and dis-
   agreements concerning the message of the Church about the creation of just and durable peace, 23 p. stencilled.
      For translation see no. 405.

405. Die Kirche und die Internationale Wiederaufbau. Nr. 3/G/43.
   (Eine Analyse der Übereinstimmungen und Meinungsverschieden-
   heiten hinsichtlich der Botschaft der Kirche über die Herbei-
   führung eines gerechten und dauerhaften Friedens), 22 p. stencilled

406. Perspectives oecuméniques, in: Témoins, brochure Prisonniers de
   guerre, Pâques 1943, pp. 67-70.

407. Droit naturel ou droit divin? in: La correspondance fédérative, Jan./Feb. 1943.

> For translation see no. 408.

408. Natural Law or Divine Law? In: The Student World XXXVI no. 4, 1943, pp. 261-270.

409. La reconstruction du monde considérée du point de vue chrétien, Semaine d'études oecum., March/Apr. 1943, 3 p. stencilled.

410. The People of God, in: The Student World XXXVI no. 2, 1943, pp. 90-102.

411. The Post-War Task of the World Council of Churches memorandum, May 1943, 39 p. stencilled.

412. Ascension, Sermon on Marc 16:19-20, in: Parole de Vie, juin 1943, pp. 81-93.

413. Report on Activities during the period July 1942-July 1943, 15 p. stencilled.

414. Het licht schijnt in de duisternis (Sermon on Matth. 2:1-12), Christmas 1943, Brochure published by the Ecumenical Commission for the Chaplaincy Service to Prisoners of War, 22 p.

415. Rembrandt's Kerstboodschap (in same brochure as no. 414).

416. The situation of the Protestant Church in Germany, 8 p. typescript, Dec. 1943.

417. Is de toekomst aan de jeugd? Dec. 1943, 2 p. typescript.

418. Die Kirche im besetzten Gebiet, lecture given in Switzerland, 10 p. typescript (1943 or 1944).

419. Notes on the European situation, in: Christianity and Crisis, Dec. 13, 1943, pp. 3-7.

1944

420. l'Église en marche, lecture given in Jura bernois, 1944? 6 p. typescript.

421. *Holländische Kirchendokumente* (1944), Evang. Verlag, Zollikon, 18 p.

> French translation see no. 445.
> English translation see no. 469.

422. Sermon on Phil. 4: 11b-13 in: Parole de Vie, March 1944, pp. 33-47.

423. Preface in: One Sole Lord, Easter 1944 (published by Ecumenical Commission for the Chaplaincy Service to Prisoners of War).

424. Dutch translation of no. 423: Er is maar één Heer, Paschen 1944.

425. Sermon on St. Luc 24:13-35 in Dutch in: Er is maar één Heer, (Brochure voor krijgsgevangenen), Paschen 1944, pp. 5-9.

426. Hemelvaart, sermon on Acts 1:1-11, in: Er is maar één Heer. Paschen 1944, pp. 10-16.

427. Pinksteren, sermon on Acts II: 16-17, in: Er is maar één Heer, 1944, pp. 17-21.

428. Whitsun, sermon on Acts II: 16-17 in: One Sole Lord, publ. by Ecumenical Commission for the Chaplaincy Service to prisoners of war, pp. 34-37.

429. Préface in: Ambassadeurs dans les chaînes, Commission oecuménique pour l'aide spirituelle aux prisonniers de guerre, Genève, 1944, pp. 3-4.
     German translation see. no. 455.

430. l'Église chrétienne et les forces de l'histoire, in: Correspondance, Lyon, avril-mai 1944, pp. 282-296.

431. Address at Funeral service for Dr Denzil G. M. Patrick, June 1944, 1 p. typescript.

432. Report on Activities during the period July 1943-July 1944, 14 p. stencilled.

433. *The Wretchedness and Greatness of the Church* (translated from French by D. Mackie and H. Martin) London, SCM Press, 1944, 88 p.
     For the original see no. 402.

434. Les besoins des Églises. July 1944, 6 p. typescript.

435. Kirchlicher Wiederaufbau, in: Mitteilungsblatt der Kreuzritter, Juni-Juli 1944, pp. 4-6.

436. Social and Political Forces of Tomorrow, a European critique, in: The Student World XXXVII no. 3, 1944, pp. 202-217.

437. Ons hoogste goed, in: Lucter et Emergo Auctore Deo Favente Regina, August 31, 1944, pp. 16-19.

438. Nederland herrijst, Broadcast for: Herrijzend Nederland, Oct. 1944, 4 p. typescript.

439. Berichten uit de Oecumene, Résumé of communications, Oct. 1944, 6 p. typescript.

440. La reconstruction des Églises en Europe, in: Cahiers protestants, oct./nov. 1944, pp. 3-13. Reprinted by La Concorde, Lausanne, 1944, 13 p.
     English translation see no. 443.

441. Souvenez-vous de ces premiers jours, Préface in: Le Don de Dieu, brochure published by the Ecumenical Commission for the Chaplaincy Service to Prisoners of War, Noël 1944.

1945

442. Reconstruction and Inter-Church Aid in Europe. Towards a pattern of united action for the constituent churches of the World Council (in process of Formation). Excerpts from 3 papers, compiled and introduced by Dr Henry Smith Leiper, published for the Church Cttee on Overseas Relief and Reconstruction by the American Office. 44 pages, n.d. (1945?).

443. The reconstruction of the Churches in Europe, in: International Review of Missions. Vol. 34, 1945, pp. 80-85.
     For the original see no. 440.

444. La crise contemporaine, ses aspects universitaires, in: Le Semeur No. 3-4, Jan./Feb. 1945.

445. *l'Église sentinelle*, Documents sur la lutte de l'Église aux Pays-Bas

réunis, 1945, introduits et commentés par W. A. Visser 't Hooft, Genève, Labor et Fides, 98 p.
For the original see no. 421.

446. Wiederaufbau der Kirche, translation of chapter from "Misère et Grandeur de l'Église", given as lecture, Basle 1945, 16 p. typescript.
For the original see no. 402.

447. l'Église et la mission actuelle de l'Europe, address given at St. Cloud, Feb. 1945, in: Les deux Cités, Cahiers des Associations Professionnelles Protestantes, no. 2, pp. 35-46.

448. Jugend im Krieg, ein Bericht über die gegenwärtige Lage der christlichen Jugend Europas, message for Feb. 11, 1945, in: Fürbittegottesdienst der evang. Schweizerjugend, pp. 5-7.
For translation see no. 449.

449. La jeunesse en temps de guerre. Translated from German. 2 p. typescript.

450. Notes on Ecumenical Developments during the war which have not been reported in the Annual Reports of the WCC, March 1945, 10 p. typescript.

451. Editorial (on Dutch Universities) in: Fonds Européen de Secours aux Étudiants, Apr. 1945.

452. Undergirding the Church's new power, message broadcast by Canadian Broadcasting Company, June 3, 1945, 5 p. typescript.

453. Report on Activities July 1944-July 1945, 22 p. stencilled.
For translation see no. 454.

454. Rapport Annuel (juillet 1944-juillet 1945), 20 p. stencilled.

455. Vorwort in: Sendboten hinter Stacheldraht, Oek. Kommission für die Pastoration der Kriegsgefangenen, 1945, pp. 3-4.
For the original see no. 429.

456. The Chairman sums up, in: The Student World XXXVIII no. 3, 1945, pp. 227-229.

457. Begegnung mit Dietrich Bonhoeffer, in: Das Zeugnis eines Boten, Oek. Kommission für Kriegsgefangene, 1945, pp. 6-11.

458. The Bible, the War and Europe, in: Bible Society Record, July 1945, pp. 84-87.

459. De Kerk na den oorlog, Dr Visser 't Hooft vertelt..., Interview in: De Nieuwe Nederlander, July 9, 1945.

460. The Place of the German Church in Post-War Reconstruction, in: Christianity and Crisis, June 1945, pp. 4-7 and in: Christian fellowship in War-Time, Oct. 1945, pp. 2-4.

461. Europe—Amérique—Russie, in: Réforme, 14 July 1945.

462. Les forces politiques et sociales en présence, vues par un Européen, in: Vocations, Revue protestante, no. 1, août 1945, pp. 17-39.

463. l'Éthique sociale de la Bible, series of lectures given at the Theological Faculty, Geneva, 1945, 71 p. typescript.

464. Tour d'horizon oecuménique, 1945, 22 p. typescript.

465. Not strangers, but ... brethren! Report on visit of the World

Council delegation to Germany, Oct. 1945. New York, WCC (1945) 12 p. (printed).

1946

466. Our way through ethical chaos. Address at Exec. Cttee WSCF, New York, in: The Student World XXXVIII no. 4, 1945, pp. 268-273.
   For translations see no. 467 and 468.

467. Nos responsabilités devant le désarroi éthique, in: Vocations, revue protestante, 1ère année no. 4, Feb. 1946, pp. 162-168.

468. Unser Weg durch das sittliche Chaos, in: Sehet, welch ein Mensch, Publ. Ecum Comm. for Prisoners of War, Easter 1946, pp. 61-69.

469. *The Struggle of the Dutch Church* for the maintenance of the commandments of God in the life of the State, 1946 (94 p.), Church documents collected and edited by W. A. V. 't H., New York, American Committee for the WCC (1945).
   For original see no. 421.

470. The outlook for the World Council of Churches, in: Current Religious Thought, Jan. 1946, Vol. VI no. 1, pp. 13-18.

471. The task of the World Council of Churches, report of the General Secretary to the Provisional Committee, Feb. 1946, in: The WCC Its Process of Formation, Minutes and Reports, pp. 74-90.

472. Les forces en présence (lecture given in Gwatt 1944), in: Le Semeur, 44e année no. 3, Jan. 1946, pp. 249-258.

473. The Witness of the World Council of Churches, in: Christendom, an Ecumenical Review. Vol. XI no. 3, summer 1946, pp. 289-302.

474. What are the churches doing? Talk for Home Service BBC, Aug. 1946, 4 p. typescript.

475. Le Conseil oecuménique des Églises: Sa nature—ses limites, in: Hommage et reconnaissance, 60ème anniversaire de Karl Barth, 1946, Neuchâtel et Paris, 1946; and in: l'Église universelle et le dessein de Dieu, Neuchâtel, Delachaux et Niestlé, 1949, pp. 263-289.
   English translation see no. 481.
   German translation see no. 489.
   Dutch translation see no. 1024, pp. 391-408.

476. Reaping with Joy. Sermon on Psalm 126:6 (preached in St. Bartholomew's Church, New York), in: Best sermons, New York, Harper, 1946.

1947

477. *Não Terás outros deuses*, Brasile, Unio cultural Editora, 1947 (104 p.) (translated from English by Hydio Burgos Lopes).
   For original see no. 244.

478. *Rembrandt et la Bible*, Neuchâtel et Paris, Delachaux & Niestlé, 1947, 160 p. (Les trois Mages).
   German translation (enlarged) no. 630.

Spanish translation see no. 631.
Dutch translation see no. 645.
English translation see no. 660.
Japanese translation see no. 758.
Danish translation of first chapter see no. 727.

479. *Het Koningschap van Christus* (Translation from English by N. Wessels), The Hague, Boekencentrum, 1947, 138 p.
For the original see no. 487.

480. Report by the Gen. Sec. to the Provisional Committee, in: Minutes and Reports of the meeting of the Prov. Comm., Buck Hill Falls Pa., Apr. 1947, pp. 43-58.

481. The World Council of Churches: Its nature—its limits. Paper written for Assembly Commission I on "The Universal Church in God's design", printed by Study Department, WCC, Geneva, 1947 (No. 47E/102 (A). Later published in the Assembly Series: Man's Disorder and God's Design, London, SCM Press and New York, Harper Bros, pp. 177-195 (1948) under the title: The significance of the World Council of Churches.
For the original see no. 475.

482. The Church's task and the University. July 1947, 8 p. typescript.

483. Opening address, World Conference of Christian Youth, Oslo 1947, in: The Report of the 2nd world conference of Christian youth, pp. 125-136.

484. Ten ecumenical questions. Notes of speech at Faith and Order meeting, Oct. 1947, 2 p. stencilled.

485. Over oecumenische vragen. Summary of address at Gereformeerd Studieverband, Baarn, Sept. 1947, in: In de Waagschaal, 10 oct. 1947.

486. Qu'est-ce que la liberté? Sermon on Gal. 5:1, in: Parole de Vie, 13e année no. 12, déc. 1947, pp. 179-191.

1948

487. *The Kingship of Christ*, Stone lectures, Princeton Theological Seminary, 1947, London, SCM Press, 1948, 112 p. New York, Harper (Cop. 1948) 158 p.
For translations see nos. 479, 488, 590, 712, 950.

488. *La Royauté de Jésus Christ*, Genève, Roulet, 1948, 169 p.
Japanese translation see no. 590.
Portuguese translation see no. 712.
German translation of parts in no. 950 B.1, pp. 109-123 and pp. 189-202.

489. Die Bedeutung des Oekumenischen Rates der Kirchen, in: Die Unordnung der Welt und Gottes Heilsplan, Band I: Die Kirche in Gottes Heilsplan IV, 4. 1948, pp. 196-217.
Reprinted in no. 950, B.2, pp. 184-200.

489a.The Programme and Policy of the World Council of Churches, in: Documents of the World Council of Churches (1948), pp. 33-73.

For translations see no. 489b and 489c.

489b.Grundsätze und Praktische Durchführung der Arbeit des Oekumenischen Rates der Kirchen, in: Dokumente des Oekumenischen Rates der Kirchen, 1948, pp. 37-84.
For the original see no. ...

489c. Programme d'activité future du Conseil oecuménique des Eglises. in: Documents concernant le Conseil oecuménique des Eglises, 1948, pp. 32-72.
For the original see no. ...

490. Transcript of talk at Conference on Theological Seminaries, Bossey, Dec. 1947-Jan. 1948, 7 p. stencilled.

491. Voorwoord in: Marc Boegner: De Eenheid der Christenen, Hoenderloo, Hoenderloo's Uitgeverij en Drukkerij, (1948).

492. The Christian in World Affairs, address at London Quadrennial SCM, Jan. 1948, in: The Student World, Second quarter 1948, pp. 108-125.

493. Amsterdam 1948, French talk for broadcast, (before Assembly), 4 p. typescript.

494. Amsterdam 1948, in: Federal Council Bulletin, Vol. XXXI No. 6, pp. 13-14.

495. The Amsterdam Assembly and the organization of the WCC, address at Conference of Secretaries at St Cergue, March 1948, in: Ecumenical Press Service, 10 March 1948, 10 p.
For translation see no. 496.

496. l'Assemblée d'Amsterdam et l'organisation du COE, in: Christianisme social, spring 1948, no. 5-6, pp. 255-265.
For the original see no. 495.

497. The Great Adventure into Unknown Territory, in: Missions, no. 7, June 7, 1948, pp. 409-411.

498. De kerken op weg naar Eenheid, in: De open deur, 9 juli 1948.

499. The task of the World Council of Churches. Report presented on behalf of the Provisional Committee at the First Assembly, Amsterdam, Aug.-Sept. 1948, 21 p. (printed).
For translations see no. 500 and 500a.

500. Bericht des vorläufigen Ausschusses, 17 p. stencilled.
Later printed see no. 908, pp. 41-56 and no. 950, B.2 pp. 98-113.
Dutch translation in no. 1024, pp. 303-318.

500a.Rapport du Comité Provisoire à la première Assemblée du COE, 15 p. stencilled.
For the original see no. 499.

501. Conférence sur l'Assemblée d'Amsterdam, Genève, 4 nov. 1948, 6 p. typescript.

502. l'Église catholique et la premiére Assemblée du Conseil oecuménique des Églises, in: Réforme, Déc. 1948.
English translation see no. 511.

503. Editorial, in: The Ecumenical Review Vol. I no. I, Autumn 1948, pp. 1-3.

504. Archbishop Söderblom, Forerunners of the World Council, in: The Ecumenical Review, Vol. 1, no. 1, Autumn 1948, pp. 84-86.

1949

505. *The First Assembly of the World Council of Churches*, The Official Report, edited by W. A. Visser 't Hooft, New York, Harpers and London, SCM Press, 1949, 271 p.
    For translations see no. 506 and 507.

506. *Die Erste Vollversammlung des Ökumenischen Rates der Kirchen*, Amsterdam 1948 (5. Band von: Die Unordnung der Welt und Gottes Heilsplan), herausgegeben von Dr. W. A. Visser 't Hooft, Zürich, Gotthelf Verlag 352 p. (n.d.)

507. *La première Assemblée du Conseil oecuménique des Églises*, Amsterdam 1948 Rapport officiel, (Volume V de: Désordre de l'Homme et Dessein de Dieu), Neuchâtel-Paris, Delachaux & Niestlé, 315 p.

508. *Droefenis en grootheid der Kerk*, (Translated from French by Mia Cramer) Nijkerk, G. F. Callenbach, 1949, 96 p.
    For the original see no. 402.

509. *Not und Grösse der Kirche*, (Beiträge zur Evangelische Theologie, Theologische Abhandlungen, Band 12) (translated from French by Otto Weber) München, Chr. Kaiser, 1949, 71 p.

510. Editorial, in: The Ecumenical Review, Vol. 1 no. 2, Winter 1949 pp. 129-130.

511. The Roman Catholic Church and the first Assembly of the WCC, in: The Ecumenical Review Vol. I no. 2, 1949 pp. 197-201.
    For the original see no. 502.

512. The Moscow Patriarchate and the first Assembly of the WCC, in: The Ecumenical Review, Vol. I no. 2, 1949, pp. 188-197.

513. Report of the General Secretary to the Executive Committee, Feb. 1949, 12 p. typescript.

514. The task of the YWCA in the World Church, address at Consultation at Presinge, Feb. 1949, 5 p. stencilled.

515. The raison d'être of the Federation within the Ecumenical Movement, notes on speech given at consultation, Feb. 12, 1949 5 p. stencilled.

516. Address given at Presbyterian Alliance meeting, March 1949, 4 p. typescript.

517. Editorial, in: The Ecumenical Review Vol. 1 no. 3, Spring 1949, pp. 249-250.

518. Réponses à des questions posées par des délégués français à propos de l'Assemblée d'Amsterdam, mars 1949, 2 p. typescript.

519. Broadcast interview with Dr. Gallagher, Canadian Council of Churches, May 1949, 4 p. stencilled.

520. Speech at Missionary Consultation WSCF, Rolle, 1949, 8 p. typescript.

521. Églises orientales et églises occidentales. Lecture given Apr. 1949, 15 p. typescript.

For translations see no. 522 and 523.

522. The World Council of Churches and the struggle between East and West, in: Christianity and Crisis Vol. IX no. 13 pp. 98-103, July, 1949.

523. De Oecumenische beweging en de spanningen tussen Oost en West, in: De Hervormde Kerk, 8 Oct. 1949.
For the original see no. 522.

524. An ecumenical approach to Soviet-Western tensions, in:Christian responsibility in world affairs, a symposium under the auspices of the CCIA. Apr. 1949, pp. 15-18. Later edition: The ecumenical approach to Soviet-Western tensions. Sept. 1949, 4 p. typescript.

525. Einheit und Erneuerung der Kirche (address at Swiss Church Federation, Basle, June 12, 1949) in: Kirchenblatt für die Reformierte Schweiz, 21. Juli 1949, 105. Jhrg. Nr. 15 pp. 226-229.

526. The Regeneration of Europe. (Address held at meeting of Reconstruction Department, Bex, March 1949), in: The Student World, July 1949, pp. 249-262.
German translation see no. 536.

527. Report of the General Secretary to the Central Committee, in: Minutes and Reports of the second meeting of the Central Committee, Chichester, July 9-15, 1949, pp. 63-73, also: in The Ecumenical Review, Vol. II no. 1, pp. 57-70.

528. Religious persecution in Europe. The Orthodox, Roman Catholics and the World Council of Churches, in: Church Times no. 4. 510 pp. 460, 453, July 15, 1949.

529. Wir rufen Europa. Der Christ zwischen den Nationen, in: Die Stimme der Gemeinde, Sept. 1949, pp. 1-5, also in: Die Zeichen der Zeit, Heft 9, 1949, pp. 305-312 and in no. 950, B.1, pp. 62-72.

530. Die Politik, (Lecture at Conference of German S.C.M.;) in: Der christliche Student, Sept./Okt. 1949, Nr. 16, pp. 18-27.

531. A pillar in the Temple, book review of: Margaret Sinclair, William Paton, in: The Ecumenical Review, Vol. II no. 1, pp. 103-104, Autumn 1949.

532. What the World Council of Churches is not. Paper for Istina meeting WCC-RC., Sept. 1949, 12 p. typescript.

533. The ecclesiological significance of the WCC, Oct. 1949, 11 p. stencilled.

534. Answers to questions from Mr. A. A. Ribicoff, Oct. 1949, 2 p. typescript.

535. Een jaar na Amsterdam, in: Gemeenschap der Kerken, Nov./Dec. 1949, no. 6-7, p. 3.

1950

536. Die Wiedergeburt Europas, in: Der Christliche Student, Jan. 1950, pp. 2-11, Reprinted in no. 908, pp. 57-66.
For the original see no. 526.

537. Enquête Commissie Regeringsbeleid 1940-1945, Deel 4 C.-I. De Nederlandse geheime diensten, etc. 1950, pp. 611-621.
538. The original confidence. Sermon on Hebr. 3:14, preached at Madras, Jan. 1950, in: The South India Churchman, Feb. 1950.
539. Interview at Radio-Genève (Me Suès), Feb. 1950, 5 p. typescript.
540. Statement on the Vatican, 1 p. typescript, March 1950.
541. Le christianisme ferment de liberté en Asie, address given in Geneva, March 1950, 10 p. typed notes.
   For translation see no. 542.
542. Kerken in Azië stellen ons vragen (address Predikantenvergadering, Utrecht, Apr. 1950), in: Wending, Juni 1950, no. 4, pp. 193-203.
543. Asian Churches, in: The Ecumenical Review, vol. II, no. 3, Apr. 1950, pp. 229-240.
   For translations see no. 544 and 545.
544. De Kerk in ontwakend Azië, in: Gemeenschap der Kerken, July 1950 (translation of summary of no. 543).
545. Asien erlebt die Freiheit, in: Der christliche Student, July 1950, Nr. 24, pp. 2-9.
   For the original see no. 543.
546. Was können die Kirchen für den Frieden tun? Address at Synod of EKD, East Berlin, Apr. 1950, in: Die Zeichen der Zeit, 1950 H.7, pp. 240-246. Also in Junge Kirche, in: Die Stimme der Gemeinde, etc.
   Reprinted in no. 908, pp. 67-77 and in no. 950, B.1, pp. 52-61.
   For translations see no. 547, 548 and 559.
547. What can the churches do for peace? (Translation from German), in: Christianity and Crisis, Vol. X no. 10, June 12, 1950, pp. 74-77.
548. Wat kunnen de kerken doen voor de vrede? (Translation from German), in: Wending, sept. 1950, pp. 361-370.
   Reprinted in no. 1024, pp. 54-64.
   Danish translation see no. 559.
549. Diversities of Gifts but one Spirit, address at Congregational Assembly, May 1950, 15 p. typescript.
550. Theology for Churches in times of struggle. Address at American Association of Theological Schools, Columbus, Ohio, June 1950, in: Bulletin of the 17th Biennial meeting of the American Assoc. of Theological Schools, no. 19, pp. 138-141.
551. Communism. Address given at National Council of Women's Organizations, Presb. Church in the USA, June 1950; in report of that meeting pp. 41-45.
552. The Church is a Beacon of Light in Europe. Notes of a journalist on address held at Pittsburg, July 1950, 3 p. typescript.
553. Report of the General Secretary to the Central Committee, in: Minutes and Reports, Toronto, July 1950, pp. 63-72. Also in: The Ecumenical Review, Vol. III no. 1, Oct. 1950, pp. 53-61 and in

Christianity and Crisis, Sept. 18, 1950, pp. 114-119 (title: The World Council looks forward).
For translation see no. 554.

554. Wereldraad van Kerken—Huidige situatie en uitzicht (Translation from English no. 553), in: Wending, 5e jrg. no. 8, Oct. 1950, 439-450.

555. The Church in the world of nations, address at NCCC/USA meeting at Cleveland, Dec. 1950, 8 p. typescript.

556. The World Council of Churches and the conflict between the East and the West, address given at Bossey, Dec. 16, 1950, 6 p. typescript.

1951

557. Misère et grandeur des Églises Minoritaires. (Rapport présenté à la Conférence des Églises protestantes des pays latins, sept. 1950), In: Foi et Vie, juillet 1951, pp. 293-303.
For translation see no. 558.

558. Miseria y Grandeza de las Iglesias Minoritarias. Spanish translation, in: El Predicador Evangélico, jan./mar. 1951, pp. 193-200.

559. Hvad gør kirkerne for freden? in: Kirkens Front Nr. 6, medio Apr. 1951.
For the original see no. 546.

560. Europe—Survival or Renewal? in: World Faith in Action, edited by Ch. Leber, Indianapolis, Bobbs-Merrill Company, 1951, pp. 73-96.

561. Cannon to right of them, Cannon to left of them, bookreviews of Oecuménisme, by René Pache; L'Oecuménisme au Carrefour, by André Bouvier and: Hernieuwde Bezinning by J. A. Diepenhorst, in: The Ecumenical Review Vol. III no. 3, Apr. 1951, pp. 310-311.

562. What is the Anglican attitude to Reunion? in: The Ecumenical Review, Vol. III no. 3, Apr. 1951, pp. 311-312.

563. The World Council of Churches and its work, in: Crossroads, Apr. 29, 1951, pp. 22-24.

564. The spiritual significance of Inter-Church Aid, address at American University, Beirut, May 1951, in: Report from Beirut, Report of Conference on Arab Refugee Problems, 1951, pp. 40-43.

565. Greek translation of no. 564, in: Ortodoksia, July/Sept. 1951, pp. 319-326.

566. From one cloud to another. Address at Refugee Field Staff meeting at Bad Homburg, June 1951 (report 4 p. typed).

567. The economy of the charismata and the Ecumenical Movement, in: Paulus-Hellas-Oikumene, Athens 1951, 5 p. (printed).

568. Word of recommendation for brochure of Stringfellow Barr, in: De Groene Amsterdammer, July 1951.

569. Greeting at Kirchentag, Berlin 1951. 1 p. typescript.

570. Spiritual adventures of wandering scholars, book review of Länder, Menschen, Üniversitäten. Edited by Paul Collmer; in: The

Ecumenical Review, Vol. III no. 4, July 1951, pp. 426-427.

571. The Role of the Layman in the World Council of Churches, summary of speech at European Layman's Conference, Bad-Boll July 1951, 3 p. stencilled.

For translations see nos. 572 and 573.

572. Was haben die Laien mit dem Oekumenishen Rat der Kirchen zu tun?, 4 p. stencilled.

For the original see no. 571.

573. Le rôle des laiques dans le Conseil oecuménique des Églises, 4 p. stencilled.

For the original see no. 571.

574. Report of the General Secretary to the Central Committee, in: Minutes and Reports, Rolle, Aug. 1951, pp. 56-63, also in: The Ecumenical Review Vol. IV no. 1, Oct. 1951, pp. 59-66.

575. De kerk tussen Oost en West, address at De Hervormde Jeugdraad, 3 Nov. 1951, in: Contact, Nov. 1951.

576. Ost-Westprobleme vom Gesichtspunkt der Ökumene aus. Berlin 1951. Abbreviated version, 4 p. typescript.

577. Wer nicht mit mir sammelt, der zerstreut, Sermon on Matth. 12:30, in: Die Zeichen der Zeit 1951, H.11, pp. 401-403.

1952

578. *La Renovacion de la Iglesia*, Buenos Aires, La Aurora, 1952, 223 p. (Translated from English typescript).

English edition see no. 643.
French translation see no. 644.
Norwegian translation see no. 661.
Dutch translation see no. 672.
Japanese translation see no. 713.
German translation of parts see no. 950, B.1, pp. 168-188 and no. 950, B.2, pp. 51-56 and in 908, pp. 78-86.

579. Foreword in: The Service and Status of Women in the Churches, report by Mrs. Kathleen Bliss, London, SCM Press, 1952.

580. Currents and undercurrents in the Ecumenical Movement, summary of address at Fraternal Workers retreat, Feb. 1952, 5 p. typescript.

581. Address at Lutheran World Federation meeting in Hanover, (in German) July 1952, 2 p. typescript.

582. *Visit to the South African Churches, A report to the Central Committee of the WCC on a visit to the South African Churches* in Apr. and May, 1952, Geneva and London, World Council of Churches, 1952, 24 p. Reprinted in: The Ecumenical Review, Vol. V no. 2, pp. 154-197.

583. *Christianity, Race and South African people, report on an ecumenical visit*, printed by Department of Racial and Cultural Relations of National Council of the Churches of Christ in the USA, Nov. 1952, 32 pages. (American edition).

For translations see nos. 584, 585, 591.

584. Visite aux Églises de l'Afrique du Sud, in: Le monde non-chrétien, juillet/sept. 1952, no. 23, p. 1-37.
585. Enkele aspecten van de Zuid-Afrikaanse situatie, in: Wending, jrg. 7 no. 10, Dec. 1952, pp. 514-532 (translation, abbreviated).
586. Renewal and wholeness, in: The Ecumenical Review, IV no. 4, July 1952, pp. 385-392.
    German translation in no. 908 pp. 78-86.
587. Make us joyful witnesses to thy promise (prayer), in: Presbyterian Life, Dec. 27, 1952, pl. 11.
588. Address at St. Thomas Celebration, Kottayam, Dec. 1952, (summary 2 p. typescript).
589. Thy Kingdom come, Address at World Christian Youth Conference, Kottayam, Dec. 19, 1952. in: NCC Review, Madras, March 1953, pp. 122-124.

1953

590. *Japanese translation of the Kingship of Christ*, an interpretation of recent European theology, S. Shuppansha Publ. Co., Tokyo, 1953, 156 p.
    For the original see no. 487.
591. Besuch bei den Südafrikanischen Kirchen, in: Kirche in der Zeit, Nr. 1 & 2, 1953.
    For the original see no. 583.
592. Faith and Order and the second Assembly of the World Council of Churches, address at F & O World Conference, Lund, Aug. 1952, in: Report Third World Conference on Faith and Order, London, SCM Press, 1953, pp. 128-138.
    For translation see no. 593.
593. Glauben und Kirchenverfassung und die zweite Vollversammlung des Oekumenischen Rates der Kirchen, in: Lund, Dritte Weltkonferenz der Kirchen für Glauben und Kirchenverfassung, Witten/Ruhr, Luther Verlag, 1954, pp. 94-101.
594. Report of the General Secretary to the Central Committee, in: Minutes and Reports of the 5th meeting of the Central Committee, Lucknow, Dec. 1952-Jan. 1953, pp. 71-75, also in: The Ecumenical Review, V, no. 3, April 1953, pp. 277-283.
    For translation see no. 595.
595. Wie steht es mit dem Ökumenischen Rat? (Translation from English of no. 594) in: Oekum. Rundschau, Sept. 1953, pp. 65-71; and in Zeichen der Zeit, Heft 2/54, pp. 64-68.
596. Défense de l'Europe, address given at University, Geneva, Nov. 1952, in: S'engager dans le monde présent. Cahier du Renouveau (suppl.), Genève, Labor et Fides, pp. 7-19, (1953).
    For translations see no. 597, 598, 599.
597. Can Europe be defended? in: Bulletin of the Ecumenical Commission on European Cooperation, Feb. 18, 1953, pp. 2-9.

598. Soll Europa verteidigt werden? in: Europäische Entscheidungs-
fragen (Informationsbrief der Oekumenischen Kommission für
Europäische Zusammenarbeit), 18 Feb. 1953 Nr. 1, pp. 2-10, Also:
in: Genossenschaft, March 1953, Nr. 13 and in: Mitteilungsblatt
der Schweizerischen Christl. Studenten-Vereinigung, Jan.-Feb.
1953.

599. Moet Europa verdedigd worden? in: Wending, Apr. 1953, pp. 70-
82, also in: Naar de wereld van morgen, Carillon-reeks Amsterdam
1961.

600. *The Meaning of Ecumenical*, London, SCM Press, 1953, 28 p. (The
Burge Memorial Lecture, Westminster, Nov. 10, 1953).
   German translation see no. 613.

601. Address to National Council of Churches, Washington D.C., 1953,
5 p. typescript.

602. Address at Plenary meeting of World's Committee of YMCAs
July 1953, 11 p. typescript.

603. To worship, live and work together regardless of race—these
truly human relationships are the only normal ones, in: UNESCO
Courier, Aug.-Sept. 1953.

604. The meaning of Evanston 1954, in: The Christian Century, Aug.
19, 1953.
   For translation see no. 605.

605. De betekenis van de Assemblée in Evanston, in: Wending, Oct.
1953 pp. 563-566.

606. A living hope, sermon on I Peter 1, 3, in: The Cambridge Review,
Nov. 1953; also in: The Pulpit, vol. XXV no. 4, Apr. 1954.
   For translation see no. 607.

1954

607. Een levende hoop, Sermon on I Peter 1, 3, broadcast by IKOR,
Apr. 1954, 2 p. stencilled.

608. *The Ecumenical Movement and the Racial Problem*. UNESCO,
Paris, 1954, 70 p.
   For translations see nos. 609, 610, 908 and 1024.

609. *Le mouvement oecuménique et la question raciale*, UNESCO, Paris
1954, 70 p.

610. *El movimento Ecuménico y el problema racial*, UNESCO, Paris,
1954, 70 p.
   Dutch translation of second part in no. 1024, pp. 80-93.
   German translation of second part in no. 950, pp. 96-108.

611. The first six years. Report to the Second Assembly of the World
Council of Churches, 1954. (General section by Visser 't Hooft, p.
4-19).

612. The Genesis of the WCC, in: A History of the Ecumenical Movement, London, SPCK, 1954, pp. 697-724.
   German translation see no. 678.

613. *Der Sinn des Wortes "Ökumenisch"*, Eine Vorlesung, Stuttgart,

Evang. Verlagswerk, 1954, 34 p. Reprinted in no. 950, B2, pp. 11-28.
For the original see no. 600.

614. Sozialprobleme der Rasse, Article in: Evangelisches Soziallexikon, Stuttgart, Kreuz-Verlag, 1954, pp. 828-831.

615. The issues to be faced at Evanston, in: The Chicago Theological Seminar Register, Jan. 1954, pp. 7-11.

616. Evanston 1954, in: The Student Movement, March 1954, pp. 4-7.

617. The relevance of the Gospel at the point of hope, book review of Das Ewige als Zukunft und Gegenwart, by Emil Brunner, and: The Christian Hope—The Presence and the Parousia, by J. E. Fison, in: The Ecumenical Review, Vol. VI, no. 3, Apr. 1954, pp. 332-333.

618. Yet One O'er all the Earth, a Preview of the World Council Assembly, in: Presbyterian Life, May 1, 1954.

619. The Ministry of the Bible Society today, Towards a common strategy on the part of the Churches and Bible Societies. Address at conference, Eastbourne, Apr./May 1954, in: Bulletin of the United Bible Societies, 4th quarter 1954, pp. 11-15.
Dutch translation (shortened) see no. 633.

620. Summary of address to General Assembly of the Presbyterian Church in USA, Detroit, May 1954, 9 p. typescript.

621. Prayer for Aug. 16, 1954 in: The Upper Room, July/Aug. 1954, p. 50.

622. Christ—the Hope of the World, in: NBC radio discussion with Manikam, Nichols and Niemöller, Aug. 1954, in: The University of Chicago Round Table, August 8, 1954, pp. 1-10.

623. What the World Council can and cannot do, in: British Weekly, August 26, 1954, pp. 1, 3 and 6.

624. Interview with Mr. Wagoner for NBC, Aug. 1954, 4 p. stencilled.

625. The General Secretary's statement to the Evanston Assembly, in: The Ecumenical Review Vol. VII no. 1, Oct. 1954, pp. 73-83.
German translation in: Evanston Dokumente, Witten/Ruhr, Luther Verl., 1954, pp. 165-174, and in no. 950, B.2, pp. 114-124.
Dutch translation in no. 1024, pp. 319-330.

628. Introduction à l'Assemblée, in: Foi et Vie, 52e année, no. 6, nov.-déc. 1954, pp. 465-479.

1955

630. *Rembrandt's Weg zum Evangelium* (translation from French by Hilde Laederach), Zürich, Zwingli Verlag, 1955, 161 p. (for the original see no. 478). One chapter reprinted in: Die Zeichen der Zeit, 1956, 10. Jhrg. Nr. 12, 442-445.

631. *Rembrandt y la Biblia*, Mexico D.F., Casa Unida de Publicaciones, and Buenos Aires, Editorial "La Aurora", 1955, 93 plus 34 p. (translated from the German edition no. 630).

632. Reply to Cardinal Stritch, in: The Ecumenical Review VII no. 2, Jan. 1955, pp. 169-171.

633. De taak van het Bijbelgenootschap vandaag, shortened and translated from English, in: De Heerbaan no. 1, Jan. 1955 (for the original see no. 619).

634. Ecumenical Institute; Ecumenical Movement; World Council of Churches, articles in: New Schaff-Herzog Encyclopedia of Religious Knowledge, Supplement volumes, Grand Rapids, Michigan, Baker Book House, 1955, pp. 362, 363, 1184-1186.

635. *Notre tâche oecuménique à la Lumière de l'Histoire*, address at John Knox House, Geneva, 6 June 1955, Lausanne, La Concorde, 1955, 16 p.
    For translations see nos. 636, 637, 638, 673, 1024.

636. *Our Ecumenical task in the light of History*, lecture John Knox House, Geneva, 1955, 15 p. Also in: The Ecumenical Review Vol. VII no. 4, pp. 309-320.

637. *Unsere Oekumenische Aufgabe im Lichte der Geschichte*, translation, John Knox Gesellschaft, Genf, 1955, 16 S. Also in: Reformatio IV H.10, Oct. 1955.
    Reprinted in no. 908, pp. 99-109 and no. 950, B.2, pp. 219-228.

638. Ökumenikus feladatunk a történelem megvilagitasaban, Hungarian translation, 7 pages typescript (1961).
    Polish translation see no. 673.
    Dutch translation in no. 1024, pp. 425-534.

639. Report of the General Secretary to the Central Committee, Davos, Aug., 1955, in: Minutes and reports of the meeting of the Central Committee of the WCC, pp. 14-18. Also in: The Ecumenical Review VIII no. 1, Oct. 1955, pp. 60-64.

640. Various meanings of Unity and the Unity which the WCC seeks to promote. Introduction of the General Secretary to the Central Committee, Davos, Aug. 1955 in: Minutes and Reports, pp. 86-92 and also in: The Ecumenical Review, VIII, no. 1, pp. 86-92.
    For translations see nos. 641, 642, 1024, pp. 425-435.

1956

641. Das verschiedene Verständnis der Einheit und die Einheit, für die sich der ORK einzusetzen sucht, in: Ökumenische Rundschau, März, 1956, pp. 2-12.
    Reprinted in no. 908, pp. 110-123.

642. Des différentes manières de concevoir l'Unité et l'Unité que le Conseil oecuménique des Églises cherche à promouvoir. Translation of no. 640, in: Istina 1956, no. 3, pp. 358-368.

643. *The Renewal of the Church*, London, SCM Press and Philadelphia, Westminster Press, 1956, 128 p. (Dale lectures, 1955).
    For translations see no. 578.

644. *Le Renouveau de l'Église*, Genève, Labor et Fides; Paris, Libr. protestante, 1956, 86 p.
    For the original see no. 643.

645. *Rembrandt's weg tot het Evangelie* (translated from French by A. Guittart), Amsterdam, Ten Have, 1956, 160 p. (enlarged no. 478).

646. The Bible in an ecumenical setting, in: The Student World XLIX no. 1, 1956, pp. 45-51.

647. Notes on R.C. writings concerning Ecumenism, in: The Ecumenical Review, vol. VIII no. 2, Jan. 1956, pp. 191-197.

648. The implications of the ecumenical movement for theological education. Address at Melbourne, Feb. 1956, 5 p. stencilled.

649. Speech at the 60th anniversary of the NCSV, Utrecht, Apr. 1956, 11 p. typescript. Shortened version in: Nieuwsblad voor de Oud-leden van de NCSV, no. 9, Juni 1956, pp. 3-6.

650. Ein Gruss aus der Oekumene, in: Antwort, Festschrift zum 70. Geburtstag von Karl Barth am 10. Mai 1956, Zürich, Evang. Verlag, 1956, pp. 14-15.
    For translation see no. 651.

651. Message oecuménique, in: Remède de cheval, textes publiés à l'occasion du 70e anniversaire de Karl Barth. Les cahiers du renouveau XIII, mai 1956.

652. Inter-Church Aid and Mission, address held at Consultation, Les Rasses, 1956, 4 p. stencilled.

653. Sa voix ne s'est pas tue, in: Foi et Vie, 54e année no. 3, mai/juin 1956, pp. 270-272 (on Pierre Maury).

654. Report of the General Secretary to the Central Committee, Galyatetö, 1956, in: Minutes and Reports, 1956, pp. 69-73. Also in: The Ecumenical Review, IX no. 1, Oct. 1956, pp. 40-46.

655. Visser 't Hooft and Charles W. Ranson: Introduction, in: The Ecumenical Review, VIII no. 4, July 1956, pp. 361-363 (on the tenth anniversary of the CCIA).

656. Die Sammlung der zerstreuten Kinder Gottes, in: Weltmission Heute, 1956 H.4. Also in: Evang. Missions Magazin, Sept. 1956. Reprinted in no. 950 B.1, pp. 148-157.
    English translation see no. 711.
    Dutch translation in no. 1024, pp. 101-112.

657. Rembrandt—a painter of the Bible, in: Bulletin of the United Bible Societies, 4th quarter 1956. Also in: The New Christian Advocate, May 1957.
    For translation see no. 658.

658. Rembrant 1606-1956, in: Evangelische Presse Dienst, June 29, 56.

659. *Rembrandt et nous*. Lecture given in Paris, Oct. 1956, in: Collection des conférences du Consistoire réformé de Paris, éd. Berger-Levrault, 1956, 30 p.
    German translation in no. 950, B.1, pp. 291-302.
    Dutch translation in no. 1024, pp. 232-245.

1957

660. *Rembrandt and the Gospel*, London, SCM Press, 1957 (193 p.) and Philadelphia, Westminster Press, 1958 (128 p.).

Reprint: New York, Meridian Books, 1960, 193 p. (Living Age books) (for the original see no. 478).

661. *Kirkens Fornyelse* (translated from English), Oslo, Forlaget Land og Kirke, 1957, 112 p.
    For the original see no. 643.

662. Jesus Christ the Reconciler. Address at WSCF meeting, Tutzing, in: The Student World vol. I no. 1, 1957, pp. 22-32 and in: The Student Movement no. 2, Dec. 1956, pp. 5-6.
    Portuguese translation see no. 714.
    German translation in no. 950, B.1, pp. 158-167.
    Dutch translation in no. 1024, pp. 113-123.

663. Über-nationale Kirche. Article in: Der Johanniter, Jan. 1957.

664. Zu Asmussens Äusserungen über die politische Bedeutung der ökumenischen Bewegung, in: Ökumenische Rundschau 6. Jhrg./ Apr. No. 2, 1957, pp. 88-91.
    For translation see no. 665.

665. Dr. Asmussen on the political significance of the ecumenical movement, 4 p. typescript.

666. Report of the General Secretary to the Central Committee, New Haven, Conn., July/Aug. 1957, in: Minutes and Reports pp. 81-85. Also in: The Ecumenical Review, Vol. X no. 1, Oct. 1957, pp. 60-67.
    For translation see no. 667.

667. Zehn Jahre Zentralausschuss, in: Ökumenische Rundschau, Heft 4, Nov. 1957, pp. 172-178.

668. The ground of our Unity, sermon on Hebr. 3:1, in: Report Oberlin Conference on Faith and Order 1957, Bethany Press p. 121. Also as: Do we really want unity? in: Motive, Nov. 1957, pp. 1-4.

669. De eenheid die wij zoeken, (shortened translation of no. 668), in: Gemeenschap der kerken, Dec. 1957, pp. 5-7. Reprinted in no. 1024, pp. 269-274.
    German translation in no. 950, B.2, pp. 45-50.

670. The Mission of the Church, address given at Bossey, Oct. 1957, in: The Student World no. 4, 1957, pp. 321-324.

1958

671. Bemühungen der Kirchen um den Frieden. Talk for Radio Bern, Dec. 1957, in: Die Friedens-Warte Bd. 54, Nr. 3, 1958, pp. 247-251.

672. *De Vernieuwing van de Kerk*, 's Gravenhage, Boekencentrum, 1958, 163 p. (translated from English by C. A. Elink-Schuurman).
    For the original see no. 643.

673. *Nasze Ekumeniczne Zadanie W Swietle Historii*, Wydawnictwo "Straznica Ewangeliczna", Warszawa, 1958 22 p.
    For the original see no. 635.

674. Préface in: Brève Histoire de l'Oecuménisme par Paul Conord, Paris, Les Bergers et les Mages, 1958, pp. 5-8.

675. Ecumenism, Article in: Handbook of Christian Theology, New York, Meridian Books, 1958, pp. 90-95.
676. De oecumenische beweging, Article in: Winkler Prins Encyclopedie, Amsterdam, Elsevier, 1958.
677. Introductory note, in: From missionfield to independent Church, Report on a decisive decade in the growth of indigenous churches in Indonesia by H. Kraemer, London, SCM Press, 1958.
678. Die Entstehung des ÖRK, in: Geschichte der Ökumenischen Bewegung II, pp. 385-433, Göttingen, Vandenhoeck & Ruprecht, 1958.
    For the original see no. 612

679. God is Spirit, (sermon) in: St Martin's Review no. 804, March 1958 pp. 77-80.
680. The Pre-War History of Schools Work and Present Tasks, Summary of speech at Consultation on High School Work, Basle, Feb. 1958, in: Schools Newsletter No. 4, March 1958, pp. 14-20.
681. Life through the Church, address at Edinburgh SCM Conference, in: The Student World LI no. 3, 1958, pp. 237-248, also in: Church of England Newspaper, May 2nd and 16th, 1958.
682. Kirken under Anklage, in: Universitas, Copenhagen, Sept./Okt. 1958.
    For the original see no. 681.

683. Rauschenbusch in Ecumenical Light. Address given at Colgate Rochester School, Sept. 1957, in: Colgate Rochester Bulletin XXX no. 2, May 1958.
684. Das Christentum als gestaltende Kraft Europas, address at Handelshochschule St. Gallen, 29 Apr. 1958, 9 p. typescript.
685. Slaves and Spokesmen, in: The Nature of the Ministry We Seek, 1958. Interseminary Movement Triennial; Oberlin, Ohio. Aug. 27-Sept. 1, 1957, pp. 2-4.
686. Renouveau et unité de l'Église, sermon on Rom. 12:1-5, Geneva 1958, in: Prédications romandes, June 1958, 9e année no. 95.
    English translation see no. 715.

687. Je ne suis pas venu apporter la paix, mais l'épé (Math. 10:34), in: l'Algérie protestante, June 1958, 20e année no. 205.
688. The Super-Church and the Ecumenical Movement, in: The Ecumenical Review, July 1958, Vol. X nr. 4, pp. 365-385.
    For translations see nos. 689, 690, 1024.

689. "Über-Kirche" und Oekumenische Bewegung, in: Ökumenische Rundschau Nr. 4/1958, p. 1-19 and in Zeichen der Zeit, 1959 H.1. Reprinted in no. 908, pp. 124-145 and in no. 950, B.2, pp. 157-172.
    Dutch translation in no. 1024, pp. 365-381.

690. El Ecumenismo y el Anticristo, Spanish translation. in: Testimonium, Vol. VI no. 4, Dec. 1958, pp. 15-35.
    For the original see no. 688.

691. Report of the General Secretary to the Central Committee, Nyborg

Strand, Aug. 1958, in: Minutes and Reports, pp. 75-79 also in: The Ecumenical Review vol. XI no. 1, Oct. 1958, pp. 72-78.

692. The Scope of the WCC programme, in: Minutes and Reports of the 11th meeting of The Central Committee, Nyborg Strand, Aug. 1958, pp. 91-95.

693. The World Council—Its first decade, sermon on Phil. 1:27 preached for BBC, London, Aug. 1958, in: The Christian-Evangelist, Oct. 20, 1958. Also with the title: "Where unity begins" in: Motive, Nov. 1958.
    German translation in no. 950, B.2, pp. 173-175.

694. Talk on Bishop G. K. A. Bell, BBC, Oct, 7, 1958, 2 p. typescript.

695. Bishop Bell's Life-work in the Ecumenical Movement, in: The Ecumenical Review XI no. 2, pp. 133-142, Jan. 1959. Also in: The Bridge, May 1959, pp. 3-11.
    German translation in no. 950, B.1, pp. 267-274.
    Dutch translation in no. 1024, pp. 217-225.

696. The YWCA's role in providing Christian Education for its members without trying to do the work of the Churches, summary of speech at YWCA Consultation, Glion, Nov. 1958, in: Report of that Consultation, pp. 5-6.

697. Commitment to Christian Unity in the YWCA as a Lay ecumenical movement, in the same report as no. 696, pp. 7-9.

1959

698. *The Pressure of our common calling*, London, SCM Press, and Garden City, New York, 1959, 91 pages.

699. *The Pressure of our common calling.* Finnish translation. Kutsu Kuuliaisuuteen; suomentanut Esko Rintala. Sisälähetysseura, Suomen Kirkon, 1959, 99 pages.
    Japanese translation see no. 724.
    German translation see no. 725.
    French translation see no. 726.
    Dutch translation see no. 756.
    Swedish translation see no. 757

700. Die Magier und die Mission, in: Festschrift für Freytag, Basel, Basileia; Stuttgart, Evang. Missionsverlag GmbH 1959, pp. 208-211.

701. Foreword, in: D. T. Niles: The Preacher's Calling to be Servant, London, Lutterworth Press, 1959, pp. 9-10.

702. Die Bedeutung der regionalen Kirchlichen Zusammenarbeit für die ökumenische Bewegung, address Nyborg, Jan. 1959, 5 p. typescript.

703. Active shame, in: Youth Department News Sheet No. 2, 1959, pp. 2-4.

704. Easter message, in English and in Welsh. Easter 1959.

705. Witnesses together. (Acts 2:32) Address given at Kuala Lumpur, EACC Assembly, May 1959, 3 p. typescript.
    German translation see no. 779.

706. The significance of the Asian Churches in the Ecumenical Move-
     ment (John R. Mott memorial lecture, Kuala Lumpur, May 1959),
     in: The Ecumenical Review vol. XI no. 4, July 1959, pp. 365-376.
     Also in: A decisive hour for the Christian Mission, London SCM
     Press, 1960, pp. 46-58.
        For translations see no. 707-709.

707. De betekenis van de Aziatische kerken voor de oecumenische be-
     weging, in: Wending jrg. 14 no. 7, sept. 1959, pp. 548-561.

708. Importance des Églises d'Asie dans le mouvement oecuménique,
     in: Église vivante, nov./dec. 1959, pp. 420-433.

709. Die Bedeutung der Kirchen Asiens in der Oekumene. in: Gott ist
     am Werk, Festschrift für Landesbischof D. Hanns Lilje, Ham-
     burg, Furche Verlag, 1959, pp. 85-89 (for the original see no. 706).
        Reprinted in no. 908, pp. 146-150 and in: no. 950, B.2, pp. 229-233.

710. Asian Issues in the ecumenical setting (2nd John R. Mott lecture)
     Kuala Lumpur, 1959, in: A decisive hour for the Christian Mission,
     London, SCM Press, 1960, pp. 59-71.
        German translation in no. 950, B.2, pp. 234-244.
        Dutch translation in no. 1024, pp. 443-455.

711. The gathering of the scattered children of God. To John Mackay
     who has consistently stood for the interrelation of "unity" and
     "mission", in: The Ecumenical Era in Church and Society, New
     York, MacMillan, 1959, pp. 21-35.
        For the original see no. 656.

712. *A Realeza de Jesus Cristo*, (Translated from French by J. M. Mota
     Sobrinho). Sao Paulo, Imprensa Metodista, 1959, 160 p.
        For the original see no. 487.

713. *The Renewal of the Church*. Japanese translation, Tokyo, Shinkyo
     Shuppansha Pub. Co., 1959 156 p.
        For the original see no. 643.

714. Jesus Christo, O Reconciliador, translation from English, in:
     Biblos, vol. XI no. 1, 1959, pp. 7-19.
        For the original see no. 662.

715. Reformed and Catholic. Sermon on: Romans 12:1-5, held at Pitts-
     burg, in: Communio Viatorum 1959/2-3, pp. 291-294.
        For the original see no. 686.

716. Le message de la Réforme et le monde, address Paris, May 1959,
     in: Actualité de la Réforme, Librairie protestante, Paris, 1959,
     pp. 41-53 (Second part also in: Réforme, 13 juin, 1959).

717. Our common Christian calling, address Tokyo, 1959, 3 p. type-
     script.

718. Brief over de Wereldraad van Kerken en de Gereformeerde Ker-
     ken, in: "Met al de heiligen", Kampen, J. H. Kok, 1959 (2e druk
     1966).

719. Rembrandt, painter of the Bible, in: Presbyterian Life, June 1,
     1959, pp. 19-21.

720. Foreword in: brochure on Kirchentag (in Engl.) 1 p. (June 1959).

721. Sermon on: Marc 7:32-37 for Süddeutscher Rundfunk, Stuttgart, Aug. 1959, in: Kirche im Rundfunk, München 1. Jhrg. Nr. 34, pp. 6-8.

722. Report of the General Secretary to the Central Committee, in: Minutes and Reports of the 12th meeting of the Centr. Cttee, Rhodes, Greece, Aug. 1959, pp. 95-99. Also in: The Ecumenical Review, XII no. 1, Oct. 1959, pp. 70-77.

723. French translation in: "Istina" no. 3, 1959, pp. 319-326.

1960

724. *New Life and Mission of the Church*, Japanese translation of: The Pressure of our Common Calling (Translation by William Enkichi Kan) Tokyo, Shinkyo Shuppansha Publ. Co., 1960, 149 p.
    For the original see no. 698.

725. *Unter dem einen Ruf* (mit fünf biblischen Studien von Françoise Florentin), Stuttgart. Evang. Verlagswerk, 1960, 149 p.
    For the original see no. 698.

726. *Les exigences de notre vocation commune*, (translation by Philippe Maury), Genève, Labor et Fides, 1960, 136 p.
    For the original see no. 698.

727. Rembrandts Pilgrimsvej, in: Kirkens Verden no. 11, 1960, pp. 328-335.
    For the original see no. 478.

728. Foreword in: Ein feste Burg ... Vom Werden und segensreichen Wirken der Evangelischen Kirchen in der Welt. Edition Volksbildung und Kultur, Wien, 1960.

729. Oekumenisch. Oekumenische Bewegung, in: Weltkirchenlexikon, Stuttgart, Kreuz-Verlag, 1950, pp. 1034-1035 and 1036-1039.

730. Oekumenisch & Oekumenische Bewegung, in: Die Religion in Geschichte und Gegenwart, Band IV, Tübingen, J. C. B. Mohr, 1960, pp. 1569-1770 and 1575-1581.

731. Letter to Otto Dibelius on his 80th birthday, in: Otto Dibelius, Leben und Wirken in der Evang. Kirche in Deutschland, Berlin, Wichern, 1960, p. 33.

732. Sermon on St Jean 11:51-52 (in French) St.-Pierre, Geneva, Jan. 1960, 4 p. typescript.

733. Beginning at Edinburgh, in: Anglican world, London, 1960, Vol. I, no. 1, pp. 33-36.

734. Fry's ecumenical leadership, in: Mr Protestant, informal biography Franklin Clark Fry, Board of Publication, United Lutheran Church of America, pp. 46-50 (1960).

735. De Hervormde Kerk in de Oecumene. Notes on speech made at 10th anniversary of Kerk en Wereld, in: Gemeenschap der Kerken, Utrecht, Feb. 1960, pp. 3-6.

736. Address in honour of Max Huber, 2 p. typescript in French.

737. English translation of no. 736 in: The Ecumenical Review XII no. 3, Apr. 1960, pp. 353-355.

738. Address at Sao Paulo Conference on Social responsibility of the Church, Feb. 1960, 10 p. typescript.
739. Sermon on 2 Cor. 5:1-10 at funeral service of Dr and Mrs van Beyma, Geneva, March 1960, 2 p. typescript (French and Dutch).
740. Speech at farewell dinner Moscow, dec. 1959, in: The Ecumenical Review, XII no. 3, Apr. 1960, pp. 348-350.
741. World Council tasks to-day, address at US Conference for the WCC, Buck Hill Falls, Apr. 1960, 6 p. stencilled.
742. Onze plaats in de Oecumene, in: Hervormd Nederland, 25 June 1960.
743. Fenêtres ouvertes. Address Tramelan, June 1960, 3 p. typeschript.
744. Opening address at Ecumenical Youth Conference, Lausanne, July 1960, 12 p. typescript.
745. Abbreviated translation in Dutch of no. 744, in: Gemeenschap der Kerken, Sept. 1960, pp. 3-6.
746. God's Son, God's People, God's World. Address at Study Conference of the WSCF at Strasbourg, July 1960, 11 p. typescript.
747. The Una Sancta and the Local Church. Address at Study Conference of the WSCF, Strasbourg, July 1960, in: The Ecumenical Review Oct. 1960, vol. XIII no. 1, pp. 2-13.
    German translation see no. 760.
748. Report of the General Secretary to the Central Committee 1960, in: Minutes and Reports of the 13th meeting of the Central Cttee, St Andrews, Aug, 1960, pp. 108-112.
    Also in: The Ecumenical Review XIII no. 1, Oct. 1960, pp. 51-59.
    For translations see nos. 749 and 750.
749. German translation of no. 748, in: Oekumenische Rundschau Okt. 1960, pp. 205-213 and partly in no. 905, pp. 105-106.
750. Dutch translation of extract of no. 748 in no. 953, pp. 115-117.
751. Syncretism as a world problem. Address Tokyo, Sept. 1960, in: Asian Cultural Studies no. 2, sept. 1960, pp. 11-17.
752. De Kerk moet deelnemen aan de maatschappelijke strijd, in: Vrij Nederland, 17 dec. 1960.
753. Christmas message 1960. 1 p. typescript (English).
754. La véritable lumière, in: Journal de Genève, 24 déc. 1960 (longer than English text).
755. Kerstmis 1960, in: Het Parool, 23 dec. 1960.
    For the original see no. 753.

1961

756. *Tot eenheid geroepen*, (translated from English by S. M. Holsteyn) Nijkerk, G. F. Callenbach N.V., 1961, 112 p.
    For the original see no. 698.
757. *Under kallelsens grepp*, (translated from English by Anne-Marie and Lars Thunberg), Stockholm, Gummessons Bokförlag, 1961, 109 p.
    For the original see no. 698.
758. *Rembrandt's Weg zum Evangelium. Japanese translation*, Tokyo, Shinkyo Shuppansha Pub. Co., 1961, 159 plus 16 p.
    For the original see no. 478.

759. The threefold Christian calling. Address at Study Conference WSCF Strasbourg, July 1960, in: The Student World, no. 1-2, 1961, pp. 24-39.
    German translation in no. 950, B.2, pp. 280-291.
    Dutch translation in no. 1024, pp. 474-487.

760. Die Una Sancta und die Ortsgemeinde, in: Die Zeichen der Zeit No. 4, 1961, pp. 84-91. Also in: Oekum. Rundschau H.1, 1961. Reprinted in no. 908, pp. 151-164 and in no. 950, B.2, pp. 57-66. For the original see no. 747.

761. La mission de l'Église, Address at Assemblée du Protestantisme français, Montbéliard, Oct./Nov. 1960, in: Foi et Vie, 60e année no. 1, janv. févr. 1961, pp. 115-124.

762. l'Année oecuménique 1961, in: Almanach protestant et annuaire des Églises romandes, Lausanne, 1961.

763. Foreword in: Churches and Immigrants by J. J. Mol, The Hague, Albani, 1961 (Research Group for European Migration Problems, vol. 9, suppl. 5, May 1961).

764. Foreword in: Pentecost and Missions by Harry R. Boer, London, Lutterworth, 1961.

765. Préface in: André Biéler: l'Humanisme social de Calvin, Genève, Labor et Fides, 1961.

766. Vorwort in: Kontinente wachsen zusammen, von Klaus von Bismarck und F. Karrenberg, Stuttgart, Kreuz-Verlag, 1961.

767. Jésus Christ, Espoir du monde. address at Rassemblement protestant, Strasbourg, May 1961, 5 p. typescript.

768. Die Stelle des Altkatholizismus in der Oekumene, in: De Oud Katholiek, June, 1961.

769. The world is too strong for a divided Church, August 1961 (earlier edition Apr. 1961) 6 p. typescript.
    German translation see no. 778.

770. The significance of the Graduate School for the Ecumenical move-ment, in: The Ecumenical Review XIV no. 1, Oct. 1961, pp. 1-3.

771. The Grace of the Lord Jesus be with all the saints, Rev. 22:21 Meditation, in: The Upper Room, 24 Nov. 1961 (with German translation).

772. Epilogue, in: From Evanston to New Delhi, World Council of Churches, Geneva, 1961, pp. 189-192.

1962

773. The Calling of the World Council of Churches, Report of the General Secretary to the Third Assembly, Nov. 1961, in: The Ecumenical Review XIV no. 2, Jan. 1962, pp. 216-226.
    For translations see nos. 774-776.

774. Rapport du Secrétaire Général à la troisième Assemblée, in: Foi et Vie, 61e année no. 3, May/June 1962.

775. Der Auftrag des Oekumenischen Rates der Kirchen, Bericht des Generalsekretärs an die dritte Vollversammlung in Neu Delhi 1961,

in: Neu Delhi 1961, Dokumentarbericht über die dritte Vollversammlung des OERK (1962), pp. 524-534.
Reprinted in no. 908, pp. 165-176 and in no. 950, B.2, pp. 125-135.

776. Dutch translation in no. 1024, pp. 331-342.

777. Regards vers Rome et vers Genève. Interview together with
Father Yves Congar, in: Le Lien, 25 jan. 1962.

778. Für eine geteilte Kirche ist die Welt zu stark, in: Bis an das Ende
der Erde, Ökum. Beiträge zum 70. Geburtstag von M. Niemöller,
München, Chr. Kaiser Verlag, 1962, pp. 91-97.
For the original see no. 769.

779. Sermon on Acts 2:32, preached at Berlin, July 2, 1962, Evang.
Studentengemeinde, pp. 5-10 in stencilled report.
For the original see no. 705.

780. Après l'Assemblée de la Nouvelle-Delhi. Lecture given in several
places in Switzerland, 1962, 9 p. typescript.

781. Nach der Vollversammlung von Neu-Delhi. address 1962, in:
Ökumenische Rundschau, 1962, pp. 137-146.

782. Unsere ökumenische Aufgabe im Lichte der Vollversammlung von
Neu-Delhi, in: Kirche im Gespräch, Vorträge der Evang. Woche
in Wien, März 1962, pp. 31-40.

783. Ökumene und Kirche, in: Zeichen der Zeit, Juni 1962. Also in:
Konfession und Ökumene, Berlin, Evang. Verlagsanstalt, 1965,
pp. 21-27.

784. Easter message (in German), in: Die Woche, Easter 1962.

785. Un seul pour tous et une seule fois pour toutes. Address at Rassemblement protestant romand, Lausanne, June 1962, 17 p. typescript.
For translation see no. 786.

786. Einer für alle und ein für Allemal, Stärke und Schwäche des Synkretismus (translated from French) 23 p. stencilled.

787. Christians in a divided world. Address at Youth Assembly,
Coventry, June, 1962, transcribed from tape 14 p.

788. Consecration of the Unity Chapel in Coventry Cathedral, Sermon
on Ephes 4: 3, June 1962, 3 p. printed, Dec. 1962.
German translation in no. 950, B.2, pp. 75-78.
Dutch translation in no. 1024, pp. 295-298.

789. Interview for Italian T.V. about Vatican Council, July 1962, 2 p.
typescript.

790. Report of the General Secretary to the Central Committee, in:
Minutes and Reports of the 16th meeting of the Central Cttee,
Paris, Aug. 1962, pp. 77-81 and in: The Ecumenical Review XV
no. 1, Oct. 1962, pp. 74-81.
For translations see nos. 791-793.

791. Bericht des Generalsekretärs, in: Protokoll und Berichte, 1962,
pp. 107-113 and reprinted in: no. 905, pp. 107-110.

792. Rapport du Secrétaire général, in: Procès-verbal et rapport, 1962,
pp. 97-103.

793. Extract in Dutch, in no. 953, pp. 117-120.
794. Interview for Dutch radio together with Mgr. Willebrands, 31 Aug. 1962, 8 p. stencilled.
795. Is oecumenisme syncretisme? Lecture in Holland, nov. 1962, 5 p. stencilled.
796. Oekumenischer Dialog mit Rom, Wünsche und Hoffnungen im Blick auf das 2. Vatikanische Konzil, in: Evang. Welt, Jhrg. 16 no. 16, Aug. 1962, pp. 465-469.
797. Talk at the occasion of the launching of "clinomobiles" for Algeria, Nov. 1962 (in French) 2 p. stencilled.
798. Talk for the radio on the death of Princess Wilhelmina, Nov. 29, 1962, 1 p. typescript.
799. Message given on Dec. 8 for the Dutch "Nationale Omroep" concerning the death of Princess Wilhelmina, in: Adieu van een volk, Amsterdam, Ten Have, 1963. Reprinted in no. 1024, pp. 226-228.
800. Interview with Fr. Placid Jordan on Vatican Council, in: National Catholic Welfare Conference News Service, Dec. 17, 1962.
801. Christmas is a fairy tale. Message for Christmas 1962, 1 p. stencilled. (Translations in French and Dutch.).

1963

802. *No other name.* The choice between syncretism and Christian universalism, London, SCM Press, 1963, 128 p.
American edition, Philadelphia, Westminster Press.
For translations see nos. 803, 804, 805, 839, 861, 901, 1024, 1044.

803. Redécouverte de l'Universalisme christocentrique dans le mouvement oecuménique (translation from English of one chapter of no. 802), in: Verbum Caro no. 66, 1963, Hommage à Schlink.
French translation of the whole book see no. 839.

804. Die Wiederentdeckung des Christozentrischen Universalismus in der Ökumenischen Bewegung, in: Oekum. Rundschau, Apr. 1963, pp. 165-172.
German translation of the whole book see no. 861.
Italian translation see no. 901.
Dutch translation (of part) in no. 1024, pp. 286-294.
Japanese translation see no. 1044.

805. Universaalia uskoa etsimässä (Finnish translation of last chapter on Syncretism from no. 802), in: Näköala no. 1 and 2, 1963.

806. La Division de l'Église et l'Unité que nous cherchons. Address at Assemblée de Jeunesse de la Conférence des Églises de toute l'Afrique, Nairobi, Jan. 1963, 6 pages stencilled.
For translation see no. 807.

807. The division of the Church and the unity we seek. Address at All Africa Christian Youth Assembly, Nairobi, Jan. 1963, in: Ministry, Apr. 1963, Nr. 3, pp. 119-122.
For the original see no. 806.

808. Interview with Jean Grootaers, in: De Maand, Feb. 1963, 6e jrg. no. 2, pp. 99-105.
809. Memorandum on statements by the WCC officers at times of international crisis. Exec. Cttee no. 3, Feb. 1963, 5 p. stencilled.
810. Preface in: The Soldier's Armoury, London, Hodder & Stoughton and the Salvation Army, 1963.
811. The Bible and the ecumenical movement. Address at Conference on Bible Reading Notes and Biblical theology, Bossey, March 1963, in: Bulletin of the United Bible Societies no. 56, 1963, pp. 165-171.
812. The significance of the new ecumenical situation for religious liberty, Apr. 1963, 2 p. typescript.
   For translation see no. 813.

813. Significación de la nueva situación ecumenica para la Libertad Religiosa, in: Cuadernos Theologicos, tomo XII no. 4, oct./dic. 1963, pp. 272-274.
814. Meditations for Holy Week for Board of Women's Work, Presbyterian Church U.S. in: "One for all", Easter 1963.
815. Sermon on 1 Peter 1:3 "A living hope". Preached at Kampala All Africa Christian Conference, Apr. 1963, in: Ministry, Theological Review, July 1963, pp. 149-150.
816. Second part of the sermon, (see no. 815), in French on Romans 5 and 6, 3 p. typescript.
817. Answer to question: What books did most to shape your vocational attitude and your philosophy of life? in: The Christian Century, vol. LXXX no. 18, p. 583, May 1, 1963.
818. Statement on Pope John XXIII, spoken for radio, June 1963 in French and English.
819. Sermon on Col. 3:15 at Closing service of Montreal Faith and Order Conference. 4 p. stencilled (in English).
820. German translation of no. 819, in: Reformierte Kirchenzeitung, Sept. 1, 1963, Nr. 17.
   Reprinted in no. 950, B.2, pp. 79-81.

821. A spiritual discovery, Address at Public meeting, Montreal, July 1963, in: Steps to Christian Unity, edited by John A. O'Brien, London, Collins-Fontana Books, 1964, pp. 298-299.
   French translation, 3 p. stencilled.
822. Report of the General Secretary to the Central Committee, Aug. 1963, in: Minutes and Reports of the 17th meeting of the Centr. Cttee, Rochester N.Y., pp. 64-69. Also in: The Ecumenical Review XVI no. 1, Oct. 1963, pp. 92-100.
   For translations see no. 823-826.

823. Bericht des Generalsekretärs, in: Protokoll und Berichte, 1963, pp. 104-113. Reprinted in no. 905, pp. 110-114.
824. Rapport du secrétaire général, in: Procès-verbal et rapports, 1963, pp. 75-82.
825. Dutch translation (extract), in no. 953, pp. 120-125.

826. Swedish translation, in: Kristen Gemenskap, 1963 H.4, s. 153-161.
827. The meaning of membership in the WCC, address at Centr. Cttee meeting, Rochester, 1963, in: Minutes 17th meeting Centr. Cttee, 1963, pp. 134-138. Also in: World Parish, vol. 11 no. 10 Nov. 1963, pp. 1-2.

For translation see no. 828, 828a.

828. Die Bedeutung der Mitgliedschaft im Oekumenischen Rat der Kirchen, in: Ökumenische Rundschau, Nr. 4/63, pp. 229-236.

Reprinted in no. 908, pp. 194-203 and in no. 950, B.2, pp. 148-156.

828a. Dutch translation in no. 1024, pp. 356-364.
829. Wo stehen wir heute? summary of address at Arnoldshain, Oct. 1963, in: Evangelische Welt, 1. Nov. 1963.
830. Word of thanks for Festschrift, Arnoldshain, Oct. 1963, in: Ein Festakt 25 Jahre Ökumenischer Rat, Berlin, Lettner Verlag, pp. 15-21.
831. Sermon on Ps. 142:2, 3, Memorial Service for President John F. Kennedy in St-Pierre Cathedral, Geneva, Nov. 1963, in: Christianity and Crisis, vol. XXIII no. 22, Dec. 23, 1963, p. 241-242.
832. French translation, 2 p. stencilled.

German translation in no. 950, B.1, pp. 288-290.
Dutch translation in no. 1024, pp. 229-231.

833. The Church's mission and service in the world, address at Philadelphia, Dec. 1963, in: Church of the Brethren Gospel Messenger, Feb. 15, 1964, pp. 14-15. Also in: National Christian Council Review (India) vol. LXXXIV no. 3, March 1964, pp. 107-111.
834. Address on relationships NCCC/USA and WCC, Philadelphia, Dec. 1963, 3 p. typescript.
835. The substance of the ecumenical encounter, the William Belden Noble lectures, held at Harvard University, Dec. 1963, 58 p. typescript.

German translation of two of the four lectures in no. 950, B.2, pp. 292-316.

1964

836. Missions as the test of Faith. Address at meeting of World Mission and Evangelism, Mexico, Dec.1963, In: The Ecumenical Review XVI no. 3, Apr. 1964, pp. 249-257. Also in: Ministry, a quarterly Theological Review for East and South Africa, Vol. 4 no. 4, July 1964; in: Go Ye, a publication of the inter-Orthodox missionary centre "Porefthendes" no. 21-22 vol. VI, 1964 and in: Witness in 6 continents, Edinburgh House Press 1964, pp. 20-28.

For translations see no. 837, 838, 838a.

837. Mission—Prüfung des Glaubens, in: In sechs Kontinenten, Dokumente der Weltmissionskonferenz Mexiko 1963, Stuttgart, Evang. Missionsverl., 1964, pp. 17-24.

Reprinted in no. 980, pp. 204-212 and in no. 950, B.1, pp. 213-220.

838. Zending als toetsteen van het geloof. (translated from English),

in: J. Verkuyl, Gods initiatief en ons mandaat, De betekenis v.d. wereldzendingsconferentie in Mexico City, Carillon reeks Nr. 36, 1964, pp. 82-95.

838ᵃ. Las misiones come una prueba de la fe. in: Ekklesia, Revista Luterana editada por la Facultad Luterana de Teologia, año 8 (1964) núm. 18, pp. 152-158 (José C. Paz, F.C.G.S.M., Prov. Buenos Aires, Argentina).
For the original see no. 836.

839. *l'Église face au syncrétisme*, Genève, Labor et Fides and Paris, Librairie protestante, 1964, 173 p.
For the original see no. 802.

840. "Oecumenische perspectieven" talk for the radio (NCRV), Jan. 1964, in: De strijdende Kerk, 18 Jan. 1964, pp. 4-5.

841. Die Ihr nun Gottes Volk seid, Sermon on 1 Petr. 2:10, for TV Eurovision, Jan. 1964 (parts in each language: French, German, English and Dutch) Printed by Evang. Presseverband für Bayern, München, 22 p.

842. Sermon on Rom. 10:12, preached in Moscow, Feb. 1964, 3 p. type-script. (Russian translation in: Journal Moscow Patriarchate, 1967, no. 10, pp. 66-67).

843. The Christian's role in transformation of society. Address at Southern Africa Christian Consultation on Race Relations, Min-dolo, May 1964, in: Conflict resolution and World Education, vol. III of the World Academy of Art and Science, chapter 11, part I, 1966, pp. 104-115 (The Hague, Dr. W. Junk Publishers) and in: Race Relations in Ecumenical perspective, no. 5, July 1964, pp. 3-13.
German translation in no. 950, B.1, pp. 82-95.
Dutch translation in no. 1024, pp. 65-79.

844. Genf zwischen Konstantinopel und Rom? talk for Norddeutscher Rundfunk, Whitsun 1964, in: Evangelische Welt, 1 Juni 1964, Jhrg. 18 Nr. 11. Also in: Die Zeichen der Zeit, 8-9, 1964, pp. 281-283, and in: Protestantische Texte, 1964, Kreuz-Verlag, pp. 66-72. Reprinted in no. 950, B.2, pp. 259-264.
For translations see no. 845 and 846.

845. Between Constantinople and Rome. (Translated from German), in: The Christian Century, Sept. 9, 1964, pp. 1106-1108.
Reprinted in: The Ceylon Churchman, Dec. 1967, pp. 43-47.

846. Genève tussen Constantinopel en Rome? in: Gemeenschap der Kerken, July/Aug. 1964, nr. 7-8, pp. 3-5 and 30-32.
Reprinted in no. 1024, pp. 436-442.

847. Ecclesiam suam, statement of the General Secretary of the WCC regarding the first encyclical of Pope Paul VI, in: The Ecumenist, V. 2 (1963/1964): 6, pp. 113.

848. Sermon on Acts 4:31 at General Council of World Alliance of Reformed Churches, Frankfurt, Aug. 1964, in: Report of Frank-furt meeting of W. P. A.; also in: Preaching on Pentecost and

Christian Unity, Philadelphia, Fortress Press, 1965, pp. 241-248.
For translations see nos. 849, 850, 1024.

849. Viens, Esprit créateur! in: Prédications romandes, Oct. 1964, no. 164, pp. 1-8.

850. Gebet um den Heiligen Geist, 6 p. stencilled. Reprinted in no. 950 B.1, pp. 229-234.
Dutch translation in no. 1024, pp. 144-150.

851. Address at Aarhus meeting of Commission on Faith and Order, Aug. 1964, 5 p. typescript.

852. Allocution de bienvenue à S.S. le Patriarche Alexis de Moscou, Sept. 1964, 2 p. stencilled.
For translation see no. 853.

853. German translation, 3 p. stencilled.

854. Die Einheit der Kirche Jesu Christi und die Uneinigkeit der Kirchen. Address at Schweizerische Reformierte Pfarrverein, Sept. 1964, in: Die Kirche Jesu Christi und die Kirchen, Verhandlungen des Schweiz. Reform. Pfarrvereins, Schaffhausen, Sept. 1964, pp. 18-30. Also in: Evang. Theologie, 25. Jhrg. nr. 9 Sept. 1965 (Title: Bilanz der ökumenischen Situation), pp. 455-466.
Reprinted in: no. 908, pp. 213-225 and in no. 950, B.2, pp. 204-215.

855. The Greatness and Wretchedness of the search for Church Union, Address at Faith and Order Conference, Nottingham, Sept. 1964, 8 p. typescript. (Not exactly the same as no. 854).
Spanish translation see no. 907.
Portuguese translation see no. 952.
Dutch translation in no. 1024, pp. 412-424.

856. Opening speech at Nyborg Conference of European Churches, Oct. 1964, 3 p. stencilled.
For translations see no. 857, 858.

857. Der Auftrag der Christen in der heutigen Welt. (translation from English), in: Kirchenblatt für die reformierte Schweiz, Jhrg. 120 nr. 24 pp. 370-372. Also in: Zeichen der Zeit, Jhrg. 18 (1964): 12, pp. 433-434 with the title: Es gibt keinen Weg zurück; and in: Amt und Gemeinde, Okt. 1964, 15. Jhrg. Folge 10 as: "Zusammen leben". Reprinted in no. 950, B.1, 11-17.

858. Dutch Translation in: Gemeenschap der Kerken, 18e jrg., dec. 1964, pp. 4-8. Reprinted in no. 1024, pp. 9-16.

859. Pas op: Mènsen. address for Jubilee meeting of NCRV (Dutch Christian Radio) Nov. 9, 1964, 3 p. typescript.

860. Christmas message 1964 (in English, German, French and Dutch).

1965

861. *Kein anderer Name*, Synkretismus oder christlicher Universalismus? (Translation from English), Basel, Basileia Verlag, 1965, 134 p.
For the original see no. 802.

862. Report from the General Secretary to the Central Cttee, Jan. 1965,

in: Minutes and Reports of the 18th meeting of the Centr. Cttee, Enugu, Jan. 1965, pp. 78-82 and in: The Ecumenical Review XVII no. 2, Apr. 1965, pp. 165-171.
>   For translations see nos. 863, 864, 953.

863. Bericht des Generalsekretärs, in: Protokoll und Berichte, 1965, pp. 121-127 and in: Die Zeichen der Zeit Nr. 4, 1965, pp. 143-146. Reprinted in no. 905, pp. 114-118.

864. Rapport du Secrétaire général, in: Procès-verbal et rapports, 1965, pp. 87-92.
>   Dutch translation in no. 953, pp. 125-129.

865. Welcome address (in French) at the reception of Cardinal Bea and Dr. Boegner, 18 Feb. 1965, in: Rencontre oecuménique à Genève, Labor & Fides, 1965.
>   For translations see nos. 866, 867, 953, 1024.

866. English translation in: The Ecumenical Review, Apr. 1965, pp. 127-130 and reprinted in no. 954, pp. 156-161.

867. German translation in Zeichen der Zeit Nr. 5, 1965, pp. 190-193 and reprinted in: no. 905, pp. 121-125 and in no. 950 B.2, pp. 276-279.
>   Dutch translation in no. 953, pp. 133-137 and in no. 1024, pp. 470-473.

868. Le fonctionnaire international et le monde d'aujourd'hui, address at yearly Conference John Knox House. Association du Foyer John Knox, Grand-Saconnex, Geneva, 1965, pp. 5-11.

869. Chancen einer Vereinigung der Kirchen? Address at Bossey for study week of Directors of Baden-Württembergische Ingenieur-schulen, March 1965, typed from tape (11 p.).

870. Bonhoeffer, Vraaggesprek voor IKOR, Apr. 1965, 2 p. stencilled.

871. Die vier Entscheidungen Dietrich Bonhoeffers. in: Die Zeichen der Zeit, H.7, 1965; in: Berliner Reden, Lettner Verlag and in Ökum. Rundschau 14. Jhrg. H.3 and (shortened) in: Begegnungen mit Dietrich Bonhoeffer, ein Almanach, München, Chr. Kaiser, 3. Aufl. 1965, pp. 172-174 (Ein Akt der Busse).
>   Reprinted in no. 950, B.1, pp. 275-281.

872. Dietrich Bonhoeffer 1945-1965, in: The Ecumenical Review XVII no. 3, July 1965, pp. 224-231.

873. Foreword in: Layman Extraordinary John R. Mott 1918-1955 by Robert C. Mackie and others, London, Hodder & Stoughton, 1965, pp. 5-6.

875. John R. Mott, Address on the occasion of the John R. Mott Centenary Celebrations, Geneva, in: The Student World no. 3, 1965, pp. 284-290 and in: Federation News no. 3, 1965.
>   German translation in no. 950, B.1, pp. 259-266.
>   Dutch translation in no. 1024, pp. 200-208.

876. Sermon on John 20:24-29 (Thomas), held in St. Pierre, Geneva, Apr. 1965, 5 p. typescript.

877. Summary of speech at British and Foreign Bible Society, May 1965 6. typescript.

878. Aux pasteurs des Églises réformées en Algérie, déc. 1956, in: Foi et Vie, 64e année no. 3, mai-juin 1965, pp. 222-226.
879. Dr. Alphons Koechlin, in: The Ecumenical Review XVII no. 3, July 1965, p. 265.
    For translation see no. 880.
880. German translation, 1 p. typescript.
881. Sermon on Matth. 7:12. Baccalaureate sermon at Brown's University, June 1965, 5 p. typescript.
882. Die Notwendigkeit der Mission, address given at 150-year jubilee of Basler Mission, June, 1965, in: Evang. Missions Magazin H.3 1965, pp. 152-160. Reprinted in no. 950, B.1, pp. 221-228.
    Dutch translation in no. 1024, pp. 135-143.

883. Treasure and Pearl, sermon on Matth. 13:44-46, Prague, John Huss 550th anniversary, July 1965, in: Communio viatorum VIII no. 2-3, summer 1965, pp. 93-94.
    For translation see no. 884.

884. German translation, 7 p. typescript.
885. Marche de l'Oecuménisme, in: Gazette de Lausanne, 8 juill. 1965.
886. Sermon on Col. 4:17 on the occasion of dedication of the Ecumical Centre, Geneva, July 1965, in: The Ecumenical Review XVII no. 4, Oct. 1965, pp. 382-384.
887. German translation of no. 886 in no. 950 B.2, pp. 201-203.
888. French translation, 3 p. stencilled.
    Dutch translation in no. 1024, pp. 409-411.

889. Predigt über Matth. 18:21-35, Kirchentag, Juli 1965, 4 p. typecript.
890. Schlusskundgebung, Aug. 1965, in: Erlebter Kirchentag Köln 1965. In der Freiheit bestehen, pp. 265-269.
    Reprinted in no. 950, B.2, pp. 235-238.
    Dutch translation in no. 1024, pp. 151-154.

891. Rapid change and slow motion in the ecumenical movement, address Annual luncheon of the Friends of the WCC, Dec. 7. 1965, 3 p. typescript.
892. Nach dem Konzil, Gespräch mit Dr. W. A. Visser 't Hooft. Interview for Süddeutsche Rundfunk, Stuttgart, 22 Dec. 1965, in: Protestantische Texte aus dem Jahre 1965, Stuttgart-Berlin, Kreuz Verlag, 1965, pp. 43-50.
893. Préface in: Hendrik Kraemer, Théologie du Laicat, Genève, Labor et Fides, 1965.
894. Licht aus der Finsternis. Rembrandt - Maler des Evangeliums, eine Dokumentation. Script for German TV, Dec. 1965, 24 p.
895. Dr. W. A. Visser 't Hooft, 's werelds eerste oecumenische vakman. Interview with Hans Kessens, in: Brabants Dagblad, 24 dec. 1965.
896. Christmas message 1965 in English, German, French and Dutch.
    Portuguese translation see no. 942.

1966

897. The future of Evangelism: Is the concept still valid? in: Christianity Today, Vol. X no. 7, Jan. 7, 1966, p. 44.

898. Pluralism—Temptation or Opportunity, lectures at Cornell University, Dec. 1965, Abbreviated in: The Ecumenical Review, vol. XVIII no. 2, Apr. 1966, pp. 129-149.
      Reprinted in no. 954, pp. 205-234.
      For translations see nos. 899, 900, 1024.

899. Pluralismus—Versuchung oder Chance, in: Oekumenische Rundschau, Juli 1966 Jhrg. 15 H.3, pp. 221-241, in: Süddeutscher Rundfunk Sendung 31. 7. 66, in: Zeichen der Zeit Nr. 8-9, 1966, pp. 289-301 and in: Oekumenische Rundschau, July 1966, H.3 Jhrg. 15, pp. 221-241.
      Reprinted in: no. 905, pp. 142-169 and in no. 908, pp. 226-248 and in no. 950, B.1, pp. 18-38.

900. Le Pluralisme—Tentation ou occasion? 24 p. typescript.
      Dutch translation in no. 953, pp. 156-186 and in no. 1024, pp. 17-39

901. *La fede cristiana dinanzi al sincretismo.* (Verso l'unione di tutte le religioni?) Torino, Claudiana editrice, 1966, 141 pages.
      For the original see no. 802.

902. Ökumene. Talk for Süddeutsche Rundfunk, Nov. 1964, in: Theologie für Nichttheologen, Stuttgart, Kreuz Verlag 1966, pp. 268-273.
      For translation see no. 903.

903. Oecumene, in: Theologie voor niet-theologen, Utrecht, Amboboeken, 1966, pp. 79-84.

904. The dimensions of this story, Foreword in: Flee the Captor (life of Jean Weidner) by Herbert Ford, Nashville, Tenn., Southern Publishing Association, 1966, pp. 7-9.

905. *Friede zwischen Christen,* Augustin Kardinal Bea and W. A. Visser 't Hooft, Freiburg im Breisgau, Herder Verlag, 1966, 172 p.
      English translation see no. 954.
      Dutch translation see no. 953.
      Swedish translation see no. 982.
      Spanish translation see no. 000.

906. Dankrede bei der Verleihung des Friedenspreises des Deutschen Buchhandels, in: *Augustin Kardinal Bea—W. A. Visser 't Hooft,* 1966 (Börsenverein des Deutschen Buchhandels E.V., Frankfurt am Main) pp. 51-56.
      Also in: Protestantische Texte 1966, Stuttgart-Berlin, Kreuz-Verlag, pp. 57-61, reprinted in no. 950 B.1, pp. 48-51.
      Dutch translation in no. 1024, pp. 50-53.

907. La situacion ecuménica actual, in: Orientaciones, Feb. 1966, pp. 1-13.
      For the original see no. 855.

908. *Oekumenische Bilanz, Reden und Aufsatze aus 2 Jahrzehnten,* Stuttgart, Evangelischer Missionsverlag GmbH, 1966, 268 p.

909. Lesslie Newbigin, in: International Review of Missions, vol. LV no. 217, Jan. 1966, pp. 96-97.

910. Introduction in: I knew Dietrich Bonhoeffer (English translation of Begegnungen mit Dietrich Bonhoeffer), London, Collins, 1966.
For the original see no. 871.

911. In memoriam Hendrik Kraemer. in: The Ecumenical Review, XVIII no. 1, Jan. 1966, p. 100.

912. Herdenking van Dr. Hendrik Kraemer (1888-1965), in: Jaarboek der Kon. Nederlandse Academie van Wetenschappen 1965-1966, pp. 404-408.

913. Nathan Söderblom was born 100 years ago, in: The Ecumenical Review, Vol. XVIII no. 1, Jan. 1966, p. 101.
German translation in: no. 950 B.1, pp. 247-248. Dutch translation in no. 1024, pp. 186-199.

914. Letter to the Friends of the WCC, New Year 1966, WCC, New York.

915. Les tâches des Églises dans la situation oecuménique nouvelle, lecture at Brussels, in: Irénikon 1966, no. 2, pp. 163-176.
For translations see nos. 916, 917, 918, 946.

916. I compiti delle Chiese nella nuova situazione ecumenica nel mondo. (Translation from French) in: Il regno, documentazione cattolica, 3/113, pp. 98-102, Feb. 1966. And in: La Chiese provocata dal mondo, Theologia publica no. 9, 1968, pp. 77-92.

917. De taken der kerken, nu. (Translation from French) in: De Maand no. 3, 1966, pp. 141-152. And in: Christendom en Wereld, Roermond, Maaseik, 1966, pp. 82-100.
Reprinted in no. 953, pp. 138-155 and in no. 1024, pp. 456-469.

918. Die Aufgaben der Kirchen in der neuen ökumenischen Situation, in no. 905, pp. 126-141; in no. 908, pp. 249-261; in no. 950 B.2, pp. 265-275 and in: Christentum im Spannungsfeld von Konfessionen, Gesellschaft und Staaten, Herder, 1966, pp. 59-64.
English translation see no. 946.

919. Niet meedoen aan zelfbedrog, in: Apartheid. Feiten en commentaren, Amsterdam, H. J. Paris, 1966, pp. 173-174.

920. Report of the General Secretary to the Central Committee, Feb. 1966, in Minutes and Reports of the 19th meeting of the Central Committee and in: The Ecumenical Review, Apr. 1966, vol. XVIII no. 2, pp. 129-149.
For translations see nos. 921, 922 and 1024.

921. Bericht des Generalsekretärs, in: Protokoll and Berichte, 1966, pp. 110-116; in: Zeichen der Zeit 1966, H.5, pp. 194-198 and in: Integritas, Tübingen 1966, pp. 559-569. Reprinted in no. 905, pp. 118-120 and in no. 950, B.2, pp. 176-183.

922. Rapport du Secrétaire général, in: Procès-verbal et rapports, 1966, pp. 110-116.
Dutch translation in no. 953, pp. 129-132 and in no. 1024, pp. 382-390.

923. Een leven in dienst van de Oecumene, interview in: Haarlems Dagblad, 5 Feb. 1966 (Kees Maas).
924. Statement on Mixed Marriage Instruction, in: The Ecumenist, July-Aug. 1966, pp. 85-86.
    For translations see nos. 925, 926.
925. Commentaire sur l'instruction "Matrimonii Sacramentum" (translated from English), in: Tribune de Genève, 12 Apr. 1966.
926. Stellungnahme zu Römisch-katholische Instruktion über die Mischehen, in: Protestantische Texte aus dem Jahre 1966, pp. 38-40.
927. De kerk van de toekomst is een zendingskerk. Interview (with Mr Phaff), in: De Haagse Post, 16 apr. 1966.
928. The shape of things to come in the Ecumenical Movement. Address at Buck Hill Falls, Apr. 1966, In: The Episcopalian, June 1966, pp. 6-9; also in: The United Church Observer, Jan. 1, 1967, pp. 61-63.
929. Forme des événements futurs au sein du mouvement oecuménique. Talk given at Toronto, Apr. 1966, in: Credo, juin-juill. 1966, pp. 8, 9, 15.
930. Karl Barth. Address at 80th birthday (in German) 2 p. typescript.
931. Die ökumenische Bewegung—Woher? Wohin? Address at Wiesbaden, June 5, 1966. 9 p. typescript.
932. The ecumenical movement from Amsterdam to Geneva (1948-1966) Address held at University, Athens, June 1966, 9 p. typescript.
933. Greek translation in: Epistemoi Logoi, University Athens (1965-1966) Athens, 1966, pp. 359-367.
934. Remarks at dinner given by Under-Secretary for Foreign Affairs, Athens, June 1966, (in English and in Greek) in: Reception in the University of Athens and Addresses by Dr. Visser 't Hooft and Dr. Blake, pp. 23-39, 71-73.
935. Welcoming address to Patriarch Justinian of Rumania, June 1966, 1 p. typescript in French.
936. Opening address at World Conference of Church and Society, July 1966, in: The Ecumenical Review, Oct. 1966, vol. XVIII no. 4, pp. 417-425.
    For translations see nos. 937, 1000, 1024.
937. German translation in: Evangelische Welt, Jhrg. 20 Nr. 15, 1966, pp. 450-454. Reprinted in no. 950 B.1, pp. 39-47 and in: Appell an die Kirchen der Welt, Dokumente der Weltkonferenz, Stuttgart, Kreuz-Verlag, 1967, pp. 35-42.
    French translation see no. 1000.
    Dutch translation in no. 1024, pp. 40-49.
938. Is de gereformeerde wereld veranderd? Interview met Drs. G. Puchinger, in: Libertas ex Veritate, 12 Aug. 1966 and in: Is de Gereformeerde wereld veranderd? Delft, Meinema, 1966, pp. 281-307.
939. Answers to questionnaire, in: Réalités—20 ans de croissance no. 245, juin 1966.
940. Introduction in: Christians in the technical and social revolutions

of our time by Bishop J. Brooke Mosley. A Foreward Movement Miniature Book 1966, pp. 5-8.

941. Address at Rally, Hongkong, October 30, 1966. Summary 2 p. typescript.

942. Deus pode entrar pela porta de servicio, Portuguese translation of 1965 Christmas message in: Centro ecumenico de informaçao, Rio de Janeiro, no. 18, Dec. 1966 (for the original see no. 896).

943. Questions and answers about the World Council of Churches and Communism, Nov. 1966 (Revised edition became WCC document) 2 p. typescript.

944. Sermon on Lc. 1:53 (Magnificat) held at Westminster Abbey, Dec. 11, 1966, 5 p. typescript.

945. Weihnacht—eine Revolution, in: Die Zeit, Dec. 23, 1966.

1967

946. The tasks of the churches in the new ecumenical situation, in: Outlook for Christianity, Essays presented to Ernest A. Payne, edited by L. G. Champion, London, Lutterworth Press, 1967, pp. 24-36, also in no. 954, pp. 181-198.
For the original see no. 915.

947. Nathan Söderblom, figure de proue du mouvement oecuménique, Conférence given at Strassbourg Ecumenical Centre, March 1966, in: Oecumenica 1967, Gütersloher Verlagshaus Gerd Mohn, pp. 135-148.
German translation see no. 950, B.1, pp. 247-258.
Dutch translation see no. 1024, pp. 186-199.

948. Confessing the Faith in Asia, in: The Ecumenical Review vol. XIX no. 1, jan. 1967, pp. 87-88.

949. Accomodation—True and False. Address at EACC Faith and Order meeting, Hongkong, Oct. 1966, in: Confessing the Faith in Asia Today (II) edited by John Fleming, The South East Asia Journal of Theology Vol. 8 no. 3, Jan. 1967, pp. 5-18.
German translation in no. 950, B.2, pp. 82-97.
French translation see no. 987.
Dutch translation in no. 1024, pp. 155-172.

950. *Die ganze Kirche fur die ganze Welt* und *Oekumenischer Aufbruch, Hauptschriften*, Band I und II, Stuttgart-Berlin, Kreuz-Verlag, 1967, Redaktion: Hans Jürgen Schultz, 313 und 341 pp.
Dutch translation see no. 1024.

951. Bilanz des Ökumenischen Rats der Kirchen. Talk for Westdeutscher Rundfunk, 11 Nov. 1966, In: Neue Grenzen—ökumenisches Christentum morgen, herausgegeben von Klaus von Bismarck und Walter Dirks, Stuttgart-Berlin, Kreuz Verlag und Olten und Freiburg in Breisgau, Walter Verlag, 1967, pp. 190-195.

952. A situaça ecuménica actual, published by Comissao intereclesiastica Portuguesa, March 1967, (for the original see no. 907).

953. *Vrede tussen Christenen* (met Kardinaal A. Bea) (translation from

German by G. J. Borghart) 's Gravenhage, Boekencentrum N.V., 1967, 190 p. (for the original see no. 905).

954. *Peace among Christians* (with A. Cardinal Bea) (translation from German by Judith Moses), New York, Herder and Herder and Association Press, 1967, 236 pages.
For the original see no. 905.

955. Sermon on Revelation 21:1-5a held in French at Russian Orthodox Liturgy, Geneva, Jan. 1967, in: Prédications romandes, no. 192, Nov. 1967.
For translation see no. 956.

956. Russian translation in Journal of the Moscow Patriarchate, 1967, no. 10, pp. 66-67.

957. Luc. 14:1-6 and Ephes. 4:1-6. Kurzpredigte in: „Für den Sonntag" Credo-Schallplatten, Junge Gemeinde 1967.

958. Wohin führt der ökumenische Weg? Address in Aula of University, Bern, Feb. 1967, in no. 950 B.2, pp. 317-326 and in: Johanniter-Orden H.2/1967, pp. 2-3 mit Titel: Der Auftrag Jesu an unsere Zeit ist die Oekumenische Christenheit.
For translation see nos. 959 and 1001.

959. La Mission que Jésus-Christ a impartie à notre temps: Edifier la chrétienté oecuménique (translated from German), in: Johanniter-Orden H.3/1967, pp. 9-10 and reprinted in: Choisir, revue mensuelle, Genève, No. 101, mars 1968, with the titel: Unité, L'avenir du mouvement oecuménique.
Swedish translation see no. 1001.

960. Word of thanks to Geneva authorities for "Bourgeoisie d'honneur" Feb. 1967, 2 p. typescript.

961. *Christians for the future* (Lent talks), London, BBC Publications, 1967, 24 p. and in braille by: The Royal National Institute for the Blind. Also in: The Listener, March 2, 9, 16 and 23, 1967.
Material need as a spiritual concern (talk no. 3) also in: The Ecumenical Review, vol. XIX, no. 2, Apr. 1967, pp. 228-230 and reprinted in: New Testament themes for contemporary man by Rosalie M. Ryan, C. S. J., Englewood Cliffs, N. J., Prentice Hall, Inc., 1969, pp. 123-125.

962. Sermon at Memorial Service for Dr. Leslie E. Cooke, March 1st, 1967, 3 p. stencilled.

963. Geleitwort in: Die trinitarische Basis des Oekumenischen Rates der Kirchen, Dissertation von P. Wolfdieter Theurer C.Ss.R., Bergen-Enkheim, Verl. Gerhard Kaffke, 1967.

964. Méditation sur le lavement des pieds (John 13) at Hopital Cantonal, Geneva, 1967, 6 p. typescript.
German translation see no. 974.

965. The inevitable development toward Pluralism, address at International Political Science Association, Istanbul, May 1967, 4 p. stencilled.

966. Sermon on John 16:7 (French), Taizé, Pentecost 1967, 5 p. typescript.

967. Sermon on 2 Cor. 4:13-18, at funeral of Philippe Maury (in French), Lyons, (and Geneva) June, 1967 2 p. stencilled.
968. Was sollen wir tun? Address at Kirchentag, Hannover, June 1967, in: Deutscher Evangelischer Kirchentag, Hannover 1967—Dokumente, pp. 790-795.
   Dutch translation in no. 1024, pp. 94-100.
969. Sermon on Jesaja 26:12. Kirchentag, Hannover, June 1967, in: Deutscher Evangelischer Kirchentag, Hannover 1967—Dokumente, pp. 799-802.
   Dutch translation in no. 1024, pp. 50-53
970. Vrede-belofte en werkelijkheid, (translated from German), in: Christen-Studenten Raad Lezingencyclus, Wegen naar vrede, Leiden 1967.
971. Sermon on Phil. 2:1-11 (in French), Vandoeuvres, 18 June 1967, 5 p. typescript.
972. The Ethics of Diplomacy as Public Service, address at Clarence Quaker Conference for Diplomats, July 1967, 6 p. typescript.
973. Gedanken zur Friedensmission des Buches, in: Sonderbroschure des Börsenvereins des Deutschen Buchhandels, 1967.
974. Sermon on John 13, preached at Conference on Christian Presence in Higher Education, Basle, September 1967. Partially in French, German and English, 5 p. typescript.
   For the original see no. 964 partially.
975. Significance of the Bible for the Ecumenical Movement, address at UBS Regional Conference for Europe, St. Cergues, Sept. 1967, in: UBS Regional Conference report no. 2, (1967), pp. 35-39.
976. To serve and to reconcile. Address at Conference of European Churches, Pörtschach, Sept. 1967, in: The Covenant Quarterly, 1967, 12 p. stencilled.
   For translations see nos. 977, 978, 988.
977. Dienen und Versöhnen als Aufgabe der Kirchen Europas Heute, in: Evang. Welt Jhrg. 21 Nr. 20, Okt. 1967, pp. 590-594, in: Universitas, 22. Jhrg. H. 1, Dez. 1967, pp. 1273-1279 and in: Die Diakonie Schwester, Jan. 1968, Jhrg. 64 Nr. 1, pp. 3-9.
978. Servir et réconcilier, 12 p. stencilled.
   Dutch translation see no. 988.
979. Introduction of Prof. Hans Küng at University, Geneva, Nov. 1967 (French), 3 p. typescript.
980. Sermon on Matth. 12:30 on occasion of visit of Patriarch Athenagoras, Geneva, Nov. 1967, English translation, (for the original see no. 1037) 3 p. stencilled.
981. Wir kennen unsern Nächsten nicht., Gespräch mit Dr. Visser 't Hooft. Alfred A. Häsler in: Die Tat, 20 dec. 1967. Reprinted in: Leben mit dem Hass, 21 Gespräche, by A. A. Häsler, Reinbek-Hamburg, Rowohlt, 1969, pp. 173-179.

1968

982. *Kristen enhet i sikte?* Augustinus Bea and W. A. Visser 't Hooft
(Translation from German by Eskil Cronlund), Stockholm, AB
Tryckmans, 1968, 132 p.
For the original see no. 905.

983. L'Église contemporaine, 8 p. stencilled.
For the original see no. 1085.

984. Die gegenwärtige Kirche, 11 p. stencilled.
For the original see no. 1085.

985. Kirkja Samtidarinnar, (translated from English into Islandic by
O. O. Jonsson), in: Ordid, 4, Argangur, 2 tölublao, 1967-1968, pp.
16-23 (for the original see no. 1085).

986. De Kerk van heden, in: Heel de Kerk voor heel de Wereld, pp. 173-
185.
For the original see no. 1085.

987. Accomodation: le problème de la juste ou fausse adaptation, in:
L'Evangile, hier et aujourd'hui, Mélanges offerts au Prof. Franz-J.
Leenhardt, Genève, Labor & Fides, 1968, pp. 277-292.
For the original see no. 949.

988. Dienen en verzoenen in: De Open Deur/Onderweg, 16 Feb. 1968.
For the original see no. 976.

989. Elijah's mantle, sermon on John 11, (Reunion—the goal of a
dying or living church), preached at Great St. Mary's, the University Church, Cambridge, May 1965, in: Sermons from Great St.
Mary's, London, Fontana Books, 1968, pp. 211-216.

990. First chapter in: From New Delhi to Uppsala, Geneva, World
Council of Churches, 1968, pp. 7-23.
For translations see nos. 991-992.

991. French translation in: Nouvelle-Delhi Upsal, Geneva, World
Council of Churches, 1968, pp. 5-22.

992. German translation in Von Neu-Delhi nach Uppsala, Geneva,
World Council of Churches, 1968, pp. 7-26.

993. Wir befinden uns in einer Uebergangslage. Interview by Günter
Heidtmann in: Evangelische Kommentare, Jan. 1968, 1. Jhrg. Nr.
1, pp. 3-5.

994. Dutch résumé of no. 993 in: Gereformeerd Weekblad, 16 Febr.
1968, p. 230.

995. Waartoe Christelijk Voortgezet Onderwijs? Openingsaddress at
Christelijk Lyceum Dr. W. A. Visser 't Hooft, Leiden, Oct. 1967,
in: Schoolportret, 1968, pp. 5-7.

996. Politiek behoeft oecumenisch accent. Interview by Henk Bier-
steker, in: Trouw, 27 Jan. 1968, p. 19.

997. Introduction in: Bread and Laughter by Leslie E. Cooke, Geneva,
World Council of Churches 1968, p. 13.

998. Vorwort in: Vielfalt der Kirche in der Vielfalt der Jünger, Zeugen
und Diener by: Patrick V. Dias, Freiburg, Herder, 1968, pp. 7-8.

999. Foreword in: Multiplying the loaves. The Bible in Mission and

Evangelism by G. H. Wolfensberger, London, Fontanabooks, 1968, pp. 11-12.

1000. La responsabilité du chrétien dans un monde en transformation Opening address of Church and Society Conference, Geneva 1966, in: R. Bosc, S. J., La Société internationale et l'Église, tome II, 1958-1968, 1968, pp. 247-256.
For the original see no. 936.

1001. Den ekumeniska rörelsen framtid, in: Katolsk informationstjänst Nr. 7, 6 arg., 16 Apr. 1968, pp. 142-148.
For the original see no. 958.

1002. Liefde tot de naaste in deze eeuw: Ontwikkelingshulp. Discussion with Dr. Visser 't Hooft (by M. de Vries) in: Hervormd Nederland, 17 Feb. 1968, p. 3.

1003. Assistentie wereldwijd, address at press conference "Kom over de brug", Amsterdam, Feb. 1968, 5 p. stencilled.

1004. Die Zeit der mutigen Schritte. Interview with Günther Mack, in: Deutsches Allgemeines Sonntagsblatt Nr. 7, 18 Feb. 1968, p. 14.

1005. History's lessons for to-morrow, address at Conference of USA member churches, Buck Hill Falls, Apr. 1968, 11 p. stencilled.

1006. Arme und reiche Länder—Poor and rich countries—Les pays pauvres et riches, address at Johanniter Orden meeting at Nieder-weisel, June 1968, in: Johanniter-Orden H.3, 1968, pp. 12-15.

1007. Christenen van morgen, address at meeting of Bond van Gerefor-meerde Jeugdverenigingen, Barneveld, May 23, 1968, in: Gerefor-meerd Weekblad, 7 juni 1968, pp. 359-360 and in: Jong Gerefor-meerd no. 499, 31 mei 1968, pp. 1090-1092.

1008. Les tâches de l'Église locale dans le cadre de l'Église universelle, address for "Conseillers de paroisse" etc. of Église Nationale Pro-testante de Genève, 11 mai 1968, in: La Vie Protestante, 28 juin 1968, p. 10.

1009. Sermon on "Sehe ich mache alle Dinge neu", June 9, 1968, Wester-kerk, Amsterdam—Radio Bremen, in: Die Diakonieschwester, Aug./Sept. 1968, 64. Jhrg. no. 8/9, pp. 150-151.

1010. Dutch translation in: Hervormd Nederland, 8 Juli 1968, p. 2.

1011. In memoriam Dr. Franklin Clark Fry. Press release June 7 and talk in memorial service June 10, 1968 (in English), 2 p. typescript.
For translation see no. 1012.

1012. German translation: In Memoriam Dr. Franklin Clark Fry, An-sprache beim Gottesdienst am 10. Juni 1968, in: Oekumenische Rundschau 17. Jhrg. H. 4, pp. 329-330.

1013. On Philippe Maury in: Philippe Maury Memorial Fund for the World Student Christian Federation, June 1968, 1 p. printed.

1014. The Mandate of the ecumenical movement, Address at Fourth Assembly of the WCC, Uppsala, 1968, in: The Uppsala Report 1968, pp. 313-323.
For translations see nos. 1015-1020.

1015. Der Auftrag der ökumenischen Bewegung, in: Bericht aus Upp-sala 68, pp. 329-341.

1016. Le mandat du mouvement oecuménique, in: Rapport d'Upsal, pp. 309-319.

1017. Hungarian translation: Az ökumenikus mozgalom küldetése, in: Lelkpasztor, Okt. 1968, pp. 580-592.
For the original see no. 1014.

1018. Swedish translation in: Kristengemenskap H. 4, 1968, pp. 169-183 (for the original see no. 1014).

1019. Polish translation: Zadanie Ruchu Ekumenicznego, in: Posłannictwo Nr. 10, 1968, pp. 19-25.
For the original see no. 1014.

1020. De opdracht van de oecumenische beweging in: Uppsala 68, Rapporten en enkele andere dokumenten van de vierde vergadering van de Wereldraad van Kerken, Kampen, Kok, n.d., pp. 12-31.
For the original see no. 1014.

1021. Leren leven met de Oecumene, 20 radio-toespraken, Nijkerk, G. F. Callenbach N.V., 1968, 110 p.
French translation of three chapters see no. 1043.

1023. Auf der Höhe der Zeit—Skizzen aus der Geschichte der ökumenischen Bewegung, broadcast Süddeutscher Rundfunk, 1968, 49 p. typescript, translation of eight chapters of no. 1021.
German translation of two more chapters of no. 1021 see no. 1081.

1024. Heel de Kerk voor heel de wereld, Balans van de oecumene, Utrecht, Ambo n.v. & Baarn, Bosch & Keuning n.v., 1968, 494 p.
For original see no. 950.

1025. Visie op Uppsala, radiotalk with C. M. de Vries at the NCRV, Afd. Gesproken woord, July 1968, 4 p. stencilled.

1026. Generation unter der Atombombe, Interview with Anouchka von Heuer and Christian Roux-Petel, in: Der Bund, 6 Okt. 1968, p. 35.
For translation see no. 1027.

1027. Dans un univers clos, la révolte (Translation from German), in: Réforme, 26 oct. 1968, pp. 8-9.

1028. Address in French at meeting of UNIAPAC, Brussels, Oct. 1968, 3 p. typescript.

1029. English translation in: UNIAPAC, Special issue, Nov. 1968, pp. 15-16.

1030. Hervormingsdag: Zin en tegenzin, interview for Dutch radio with A. H. van den Heuvel, 28 Oct. 1968, 6 p. stencilled.

1031. Opening address at Universitair Instituut Vorming Bedrijfsleven (Dr. W. A. Visser 't Hooft Centrum), Rotterdam, 16 Nov. 1968, 4 p. typescript.

1032. Confessing our Lord Jesus Christ as God and Saviour. Interview by Philip Potter, in: International Review of Missions, vol. LVII no. 228, Oct. 1968, pp. 441-447.

1969

1033. Zum Tode Kardinal Beas, radio-address West-deutsche Rundfunk, Nov. 1968, in: Börsenblatt für den Deutschen Buchhandel, 7. Jan. 1969, pp. 17-18.

1034. In Memoriam Karl Barth, Basel 14 Dec. 1968. in: Gedenkfeier im Basler Münster, Heft 100 der Theologischen Studien, Zürich, EVZ-Verlag., pp. 51-53 and in Oekum. Rundschau H.2, Jhrg. 1969, pp. 247-249.
    For translations see nos. 1035 and 1036.

1035. English translation in: South East Asia Journal of Theology, Autumn 1969, pp. 6-7.

1036. Dutch translation: Barth en de Oecumene in: Woord en Dienst, 25 Jan. 1969, p. 19.

1037. Sermon on St. Matthieu 12:30. On occasion of visit of Patriarch Athenagoras, St. Pierre, Geneva, Nov. 1967, in: Prédications romandes janvier-février, 1969.
    English translation see no. 980.

1038. The significance of the Reformed position in an Ecumenical Age, Paper for WARC Consultation, July 1968, in: Bulletin of the Department of Theology of the World Alliance of Reformed Churches, Geneva, Summer 1969, vol. 9 no. 4, pp. 6-9.

1039. Un grand anniversaire, Rembrandt, in: Almanach protestant 1969, pp. 48-51.
    For translations see nos. 1040, 1041.

1040. Un grande anniversario: Rembrandt, in: L'Eco delle Valli Valdesi, 31 ott. 1969, p. 3 and in Voce Evangelica, Ott. 1969.
    For the original see no. 1039.

1041. Rembrandt en de Bijbel, in: Woord en Dienst, 14 June 1969.
    For the original see no. 1039.

1042. De oecumenische beweging (shortened translation of no. 1069), in: Spiegel Historiael, Bussum, Fibula-Van Dishoeck N.V., 1969, Special issue on: Schisma en Oecumene, pp. 309-317.

1043. Visser 't Hooft raconte ... (translation from Dutch of three chapters of no. 1021), in: La Vie Protestante, 11, 18 Apr. and 2 May, 1969.

1044. *Kein anderer Namen, Japanese translation* by Masaru Haibara, Tokyo, Board of Publications, The United Church of Christ in Japan, 1969, 196 p.
    For the original see no. 802.

1045. Easter Message 1969, broadcast in English (German, French, Dutch translations).

1046. Sermon on Mt. 6:33 at Closing service Student Christian Movement Congress on: Response to Crisis, Manchester Cathedral, Apr. 13, 1969, 5 p. typescript.

1047. Facteurs dynamiques dans la situation oecuménique, address at Istituto Storico Olandese, Rome, Apr. 24, 1969, 13 p. typescript.
    For translations see nos. 1048-1052.

1048. Dynamic factors in the ecumenical situation (Translation from no. 1047), in: The Ecumenical Review vol. XXI no. 4, Oct. 1969, pp. 320-331.

1049. Dynamische Faktoren in der ökumenischen Situation (Translation from no. 1047), in: Oekumenische Rundschau, July 1969 (Hanns Lilje zum 70. Geburtstag) pp. 368-379.

1050. Factores dinamicos en el dialogo ecumenica (Translation from no. 1047), in: Unidad cristiana, Oriente Cristiano, Madrid, July 1969, no. XIX, 3, pp. 274-282.

1051. Dinamica e rischi della situaziona ecumenica (Shortened translation from no. 1047), in: L'Ecco delle Valli Valdese, 2 maggio 1969.

1052. Dynamische factoren in de oecumenische situatie (Translation from no. 1047), in: Gereformeerd weekblad, Aug. and Sept. 1969; Woord en Dienst, Jrg. 18 no. 23, 13 Dec. 1969 and in: De Maand, Antwerpen, Nov. 1969, pp. 538-547.

1053. Reflections on WCC action concerning interracial relations, with: A chronological record. Paper for the Consultation on Race Relations, London, May 1969, 5 plus 4 pages stencilled.
    For translation see no. 1054.

1054. Réflexions sur l'action du COE dans le domaine des relations interraciales avec tableau chronologique des activités du COE en matière de relations raciales, 5 plus 4 pages stencilled.

1055. Vorwort in: Armin Boyens, Kirchenkampf und Oekumene 1933 bis 1939, Darstellung und Dokumentation, München, Chr. Kaiser Verlag, 1969.

1056. Foreword in: Patterns of Ministry, Theological education in a changing world, by Steven C. Mackie, London, Collins, 1969.

1057. Vorwort in: George Bell—Alphons Koechlin Briefwechsel 1933-1954, ed. Andreas Lindt, Zürich, EVZ Verlag, 1969.

1058. Service of Remembrance for J. H. Oldham. St. Martin-in-the-Fields, June 3, 1969 in: The Ecumenical Review, July 1969, vol. XXI no. 3, pp. 261-265.

1059. The thirst for life, sermon on John 10:10, Ridderdag, Het Loo, June 1969, in: Verslag van de 64e Ridderdag Johanniterorde in Nederland, pp. 17-21.
    For translations see nos. 1060-1061.

1060. Eletszomjusag—hova vezet? Hungarian translation) and

1061. Lebensdurst—wohin?, published by Hungarian Association of the Johanniter Order, München, 1969, pp. 10-16 and 17-23.

1062. How the revolt against Hitler looked from Geneva, in: Encounter, September 1969, pp. 92-94.

1063. Eenheid in hierarchie van waarheden, Interview by H. Bronkhorst on visit of Pope Paul VI, in: De Tijd, 21 June 1969.

1064. Quel développement? Pour quel homme? Address at Assemblée générale de la Fédération Protestante de France, Grenoble, Nov. 1969, in: Foi et Vie, 68e année no. 4, pp. 26-44.

1065. Message de Noël 1969 for Paroisse de Chêne-Bourg, 1 p. typescript.

1066. Introduction in: Report 1968-1969 of the Commission of the churches on International Aflairs, pp. 5-6.

1067. Interview by F. Klopfenstein on Development, in: Le monde jour et nuit, cahier no. 1 de la Vie Protestante, dec. 1969.
For translation see no. 1068.

1970

1068. Translation from French in: Kirchenbote für den Kanton Zürich, 16 Feb. 1970.
1069. The General Ecumenical Development since 1948, in: The Ecumenical Advance, A History of the Ecumenical Movement vol. II, 1948-1968 ed. by Harold E. Fey, London, S.P.C.K., 1970, pp. 1-26.
For translation see no. 1042.
1070. Foreword in: The Churches and the Nations by O. F. Nolde, Philadelphia, Fortress Press, 1970.
1071. Les trois dimensions d'une société internationale responsable, Lecture at Institut universitaire de hautes études internationales, Oct. 1969, in: Annales d'Etudes internationales, 1970, publiées par l'Association des Anciens de l'Institut Universitaire de Hautes Etudes Internationales, Genève, 1970, pp. 203-213.
1072. Introduction to: The Long Road to Unity by Marc Boegner, London, Collins, 1970.
1073. The ecumenical situation, Gallagher Memorial Lecture, Canada, Jan. 1970, 13 p. typescript.
1074. Has the day of ecumenical structures passed? Gallagher Memorial Lecture, Jan. 1970, 13 p. typescript.
1075. In Memoriam Joseph Hromadka (English), radio talk, January 1970, 3 p. typescript.
1076. Sermon on 1 Peter 5:5. Service of the Alliance of Orders of St. John at Valetta, Malta, Apr. 1970, 2 p. typescript.
1077. Speech at celebration of the 50-year jubilee of Order of St. John, Sweden, May 1970, 3 p. typescript.
1078. De heropening van de Nederlandse Kerk in Jaffna, May 1970, in: Hervormd Nederland, 13 june 1970.
1079. In memory of Henri Johannot, Memorial service at John Mott House, June 1970, 2 p. typescript.
1080. Statement on Paris Basis of the World Alliance of YMCA's, Geneva, in: Paris Basis Study Documents no. 1, 1970, pp. 19-20.
1081. Gelebte, miterlebte Oekumene (Translation from Dutch), in: Evangelische Kommentare, September 1970, p. 510-513.
For the original see no. 1021.
1082. Zum 25. Jahrestag der Stuttgarter Schulderklärung, in: Zeichen der Zeit, Sept. 1970, pp. 323-325 and in: Oekumenische Rundschau, 19. Jhrg. H.4, Okt. 1970, pp. 361-366.
1083. *Auf dem Weg zur Einheit*, (Translation from English of two lectures at the Ecumenical Institute, Oct. 1969) Wetzhausen, Schloss Craheim, Rolf Kühne Verl., 1970, 80 p.

1084. Address at Third Synod of the Evangelical Church in Germany, March 1966 in Berlin Spandau and in Potsdam-Babelsberg, in: Berlin und Potsdam 1966, Bericht über die vierte Tagung der dritten Synode der Evang. Kirche in Deutschland, Hannover, Verlag des Amtsblattes, 1970, pp. 231-233 and 270-273.

1085. The Contemporary Church, address at Centennial of American University, Beirut, Apr. 1967, in: God and Man in Contemporary Christian Thought, Beirut, 1970, pp. 1-11.

For translations see nos. 983-986.

1086. Ecumenical Movement; World Conferences of Christian Youth; World Council of Churches. in: Concise Dictionary of Christian Mission, World Christian Books, London, United Society for Christian Literature, Lutterworth Press, 1970, pp. 180-182; 655-656; 657-660.

INDEX OF SUBJECTS

INDEX OF NAMES